Britain and the Congo Question 1885–1913

IBADAN HISTORY SERIES
General Editor K. O. Dike Ph.D
Published by Northwestern University Press

CHRISTIAN MISSIONS IN NIGERIA 1841–1891
by J. F. A. Ajayi

THE ZULU AFTERMATH
by J. D. Omer-Cooper

Published by Humanities Press

THE MISSIONARY IMPACT ON MODERN NIGERIA
1842–1914
by E. A. Ayandele

THE SOKOTO CALIPHATE
by Murray Last

In preparation (to be published by Humanities Press)
THE INTERNATIONAL BOUNDARIES OF NIGERIA
by J. C. Anene

NIGER DELTA RIVALRY
Itsekiri–Urhobo Relations and European Enterprise 1884–1936
by O. Ikime

THE LAGOS PROTECTORATE
by A. B. Aderibigbe

Ibadan History Series

Britain and the
Congo Question
1885–1913

S. J. S. Cookey

Humanities Press

*First published
in the United States of America 1968
by Humanities Press Inc.
303 Park Avenue South
New York, N.Y. 10010*

Library of Congress Catalog Card No. 67-16973

Printed in Great Britain

Contents

Acknowledgements

We are indebted to the following for permission to reproduce copyright material:

The Baptist Missionary Society for extracts from their papers of 29th November 1888 (Bentley to Baynes) and 14th June 1895 (Stapleton to Baynes); Controller of H.M. Stationery Office for crown-copyright material in respect of letters from Bannister to Foreign Office (FO.10/731) and from Grey to Bryce (FO.367/115), for extracts from 'Congo atrocities: Remarks by Mr. Pickersgill' (FO.10/731) and for an extract from a memorandum by Grey (FO.367/31) and Note given by King Leopold II to Jones; London School of Economics and Political Science for an extract from *The Morel Papers*; proprietors of *The Times* for an extract from an article which appeared in their edition of 15th December 1906.

Introduction to the Ibadan History Series

The 'Ibadan History Series' grew out of the efforts of some members of the Department of History, Ibadan University, Nigeria, to evolve a balanced and scholarly study of the history of African peoples South of the Sahara. In the years before the Second World War, the study of African history was retarded, and to some extent vitiated, by the assumption of many scholars that lack of written records in some areas of Africa meant also the absence of history. Documentary evidence had become so overwhelmingly important for the European scholar that he tended to equate written documents with history, and to take the absence of documents to mean the absence of events worthy of historical study. As a result in the 19th century, when Europe occupied Africa, her scholars did not attempt to understand or to build on the historical traditions in existence there; they sought instead to challenge and to supplant them. The history of European traders, missionaries, explorers, conquerors and rulers constituted, in their view, the sum total of African history.

Fortunately for the historian of today, African historical consciousness remained alive throughout the period of colonial rule: that tradition was too much a part of the African way of life to succumb to the attacks of the European scholar. Even in the heyday of white supremacy some educated Africans of the period were sufficiently dominated by their past to feel impelled to commit to writing the laws, customs, proverbs, sayings and historical traditions of their own communities. Notable among these may be mentioned James Africanus Horton of Sierra Leone, Reindorf and Sarbah of Ghana, Otomba Payne and Samuel Johnson of Nigeria, Apolo Kagwa of Uganda, to name but a few. The published works they left behind have become important

ix

sources of African history today; but they were swimming against the current of their time and made little impression on contemporaries. Historians continued to write as if Africans were not active participants in the great events that shaped their continent.

The decided change towards a new African historiography came with the movement towards independence. African nationalists rejected the European appraisal of their past. They demanded a new orientation and improved educational facilities to effect this re-appraisal. With the establishment of new universities in Africa, it was inevitable that the teaching of history and the training of African historians would receive a new impetus. For obvious reasons the changeover was slow in coming. Even in the new universities the old theories for a time prevailed: besides European history, there were courses only on "European activities in Africa" at the under-graduate level, and at the post-graduate level research was generally on British and French policy towards their African territories.

By the late 1940's, however, African research students were insisting that African history must be the history of Africans, not of Europeans *per se* in Africa; that local records and historical traditions must be used to supplement European metropolitan archives; in short, that Oral Tradition must be accepted as valid material for historical reconstruction. No doubt the validity of non-written sources for historical research had been pointed out before, but it was new for university departments of history to accept it, especially in relation to African Oral Tradition. Even then not everyone was happy about it. Anthropologists replied cautiously that Oral Tradition, even when seemingly factual, was not history and could only be interpreted in terms of its functions in society and within the particular culture. But this did not destroy its validity as material for history; it only argued for a return to the link between history and sociology advocated in the fourteenth century by the famous Tunisian historian, Ibn Khaldun.

Even in studies of European impact on African societies and cultures, where European archival material still remains our major source, this source should be checked and supplemented by Oral Tradition, material artefacts and other sources of history in Africa. The achievement of the present position in the study of African history has been the result of individual and co-operative efforts of many scholars in different parts of the world, but I think it is fair to say that the Universities in Africa, and Ibadan in particular, have played and are playing their part in this pioneering work.

K. ONWUKA DIKE

To John and Matilda

Preface

There are many references in several books to the Congo Reform Movement, which played a significant role in the affairs of the Congo during the decade before the First World War; no published work, however, has examined the origins, aims and activities of that movement in the light of the abundant documents that exist on the subject. This has not been the fault of historians but a result of the inaccessibility of many relevant documents, especially the archives of the Foreign Office at the Public Records Office, London. The opening of the latter to scholars was essential if the relationship between the reform movement and the Foreign Office was to be properly understood. This author is fortunate that his interest in the subject coincided with the period when all the existing documents had become available.

The present work, in studying the Congo Reform Movement, has naturally developed many strands. One of these reviews the system of administration introduced in the Congo by King Leopold II of Belgium from 1885 and its effects on the African inhabitants. Another relates the foregoing to the re-awakening of British humanitarian and commercial interests in the Congo and the influence of both on British Diplomacy as well as on Anglo-Belgian relations during the period. Yet another strand examines the policy of Belgium towards the Congo following annexation in 1908 and why British recognition of that annexation was withheld until 1913. In the process new light has been thrown on the character of the principal participants: E. D. Morel, John Holt, Roger Casement, King Leopold II and Sir Edward Grey.

I owe a great debt of gratitude to many individuals who have helped me at various stages of this work. In particular,

Preface

I am grateful to the librarians and staff of the British Museum, the London School of Economics, Rhodes House, Oxford, the *Ministère des Affaires Africaines*, Brussels, and the Baptist Missionary Society, London, for patiently enduring my many requests. M. Desneux of the *Ministère des Affaires Etrangères*, Brussels, kindly guided me through the official archives in his charge. I seize this opportunity to thank Mr Cecil Holt who gave me access to the carefully preserved papers of his late father, John Holt, and also to Lord Salisbury for his permission to consult the Salisbury Papers.

I have sought and received much advice from many scholars, none of whom must be held responsible for any errors in this book. I specially wish to thank Professor W. N. Medlicott, Stevenson Professor of International History, University of London, who persuaded me to embark on this work and from whom I learnt so much at the London School of Economics. Professor J. Stengers of the *Université Libre de Bruxelles* and Professor R. Oliver of the University of London, placed their knowledge of the subject at my disposal on several occasions and saved me from many pitfalls. I am grateful to both of them. I cannot thank Dr Roger Anstey of Durham University enough for reading through the manuscript and for his valuable comments. Finally, I thank two women without whom this work would not be appearing now: first, Dr Freda Harcourt of Queen Mary College, University of London, whose hospitality, advice and sympathetic ear were readily available throughout the period of my research in England, and second, my wife for her secretarial assistance and devotion.

S. J. S. COOKEY

Dept. of History,
University of Nigeria,
Nsukka.
May 1967

Abbreviations

A.F.	*Aborigines Friend.*
A.P.S.	Aborigines Protection Society.
A.S.	Anti-Slavery and Aborigines Protection Society Papers.
B.D.	*British Documents on the Origins of the War* 1898-1914.
B.M.S.	Baptist Missionary Society.
B.O.	*Bulletin Officiel du Congo.*
C.B.M.	Congo Balolo Mission.
C.O.	Colonial Office.
C.R.A.	Congo Reform Association.
D.D.F.	*Documents Diplomatiques Français* 1871–1914.
Encl.	Enclosure.
F.O.	Foreign Office.
G.P.	*Die Grosse Politik der Europäischen Kabinette* 1871–1914.
H.O.	Home Office.
J.A.H.	*Journal of African History.*
J.H.P.	*John Holt Papers.*
L.Q.V.	*Letters of Queen Victoria.*
M.P.	Morel Papers.
n.d.	no date.
O.O.C.R.A.	*Official Organ of the Congo Reform Association.*
S.P.	Salisbury Papers.

The Congo Free State

I
Introduction

The history of Great Britain in the nineteenth century is punctuated by humanitarian crusades. Thus the crusade to abolish the trade in slaves and the outburst of philhellenism during the first half of the century had been followed by Gladstone's campaign against the Bulgarian atrocities in 1876 and against the Armenian atrocities twenty years later. At the beginning of the present century there was to be another crusade against atrocities in Macedonia. The British campaign for reform in the administration of the Congo between 1885 and 1913, with which this book is concerned,[1] must be seen as part of that humanitarian tradition.[2] This of course does not mean that British motive was entirely altruistic. It was not and could not be so. It is true, however, that British intervention led to the Belgian annexation of the Independent State of the Congo,[3] and to an alleviation of

---

[1] Some attempt has been made to study the subject in A. B. Keith: *The Belgian Congo and the Berlin Act*, Oxford 1919; and in *Cambridge History of British Foreign Policy*, Cambridge 1923, iii, 366–73, 424–29. Both are now outdated.

[2] Cf. J. Stengers: *Belgique et Congo: l'élaboration de la Charte Coloniale*, Brussels 1963, p. 67.

[3] Its official name was *l'Etat indépendant du Congo* which was popularly translated as the Congo Free State. It will be frequently referred to in the present work as the Congo State.

the crushing burden imposed on the Congolese by King Leopold II's concession policy.[1]

The basis of British intervention lay in two international agreements, one bilateral and the other multilateral. The Anglo-Congolese Convention of 16 December 1884 arose out of the peculiar circumstances which gave birth to the Congo State. The flag of the *Association Internationale du Congo* which masked the design of Leopold II for an African empire was already recognized by the United States and by Germany.[2] The British government was pressed to do likewise by British humanitarians and merchants and also by Prince Bismarck,[3] all of whom felt that it would be a fitting substitute for the stillborn Anglo-Portuguese treaty.[4] In recognizing the flag of the Association as that of 'a friendly government', the convention bound the latter to certain undertakings.[5] According to Article I, the Association was not to levy any duties on goods imported by British subjects in the Congo. In Articles II and III the right to enter and establish themselves in the Congo was also reserved to British subjects together with the right to most-favoured-nation treatment. The subsequent articles of the convention laid down carefully the right of British consuls to establish their own courts for the trial of British subjects. Finally, it was agreed that the engagements accepted by the Association should pass on to the new occupant of the territory in the event of its cession.

---

[1] Few serious historians doubt the disastrous consequences of the Leopoldian régime in the Congo. See L. de Lichtervelde: *Léopold II*, Brussels 1926, p. 267; and P. Daye: *Léopold II*, Paris 1934, pp. 339–41. But see also F. Masoin: *Histoire de l'Etat Indépendant du Congo*, Namur 1912, vol. i, which defends and justifies King Leopold's Congo policy.

[2] The United States recognized the flag as that of 'a friendly government', *State Papers*, 1883–1884, lxxv, 377; and Germany as that of 'un Etat ami', ibid., p. 355.

[3] R. T. Anstey: *Britain and the Congo in the 19th Century*, Oxford 1962, pp. 168–85; S. E. Crowe: *The Berlin West Africa Conference*, London 1942, pp. 142 ff.

[4] This is the well-known Anglo-Portuguese treaty of 1884 which would have handed the Congo over to Portugal.

[5] *State Papers*, 1883–1884, lxxv, 30.

Meanwhile the Berlin West Africa Conference was sitting and arrangements as regards the freedom of commerce and navigation as well as the good treatment of the Congo inhabitants were being hammered out.[1] Although the Association had as yet no legal status or representation at the conference, it loomed large over the discussions. It was realized that the authority of the Association in the Congo must be recognized if the decisions at Berlin were to be executed in Africa. The reluctant recognition of the Association by Britain was followed on similar terms by Italy, Austria-Hungary, Holland, Spain, Russia, Norway, Sweden, Denmark and finally Belgium. The recognition of France and Portugal, on the other hand, was accompanied by a territorial settlement, supplemented, in the case of the former, by the right of pre-emption which it had secured by the Franco-Congolese declaration of 23 April 1884.[2] Thus on 23 February 1885 the Association was able to announce to the conference that it had been recognized by all but one of the participating powers.[3] The Association was therefore invited to adhere to the General Act of the Berlin conference.[4]

It is this Act which forms the second link in Anglo-Congolese relations and it is essential to examine here its relevant features in order to appreciate all the aspects of the subsequent controversy, which became known as the Congo question.

Pre-occupation with the establishment of free trade in the Congo ensured it a prominent place in the Act although each power had secured it in its separate convention with the nascent Congo State. Article I laid down that the commerce of all nations should enjoy complete freedom in the conventional basin of the Congo. Article II provided for freedom of navigation on the Congo, while the next Article interdicted

---

[1] The best account of this conference is still in Crowe: op. cit.

[2] R. S. Thomson: *Fondation de l'Etat Indépendant du Congo*, Brussels 1930, pp. 163–9.

[3] The exception was Turkey, which gave its recognition on 26 June 1885. Keith: op. cit., p. 150.

[4] *State Papers*, 1884–1885, lxxvi, 4–20.

differential taxes. Article IV prohibited the imposition of import duties, subject to a review at the end of a twenty-year period, and Article V forbade the granting of commercial monopolies or privileges of any kind. Article VI enjoined all the powers to watch over the welfare of the native populations and to care for the amelioration of their moral condition and material well-being. They were also to suppress slavery and especially the slave trade and to grant special protection to travellers and Christian missionaries as well as maintain freedom of worship. Then Article XVII provided for the setting up of an International Commission for the Congo charged with the execution of the provisions of an Act of Navigation which was contained in the main Act. Finally, Article XII called upon the powers, before taking recourse to arms, to submit points in dispute to mediation or arbitration.

Acceptance by Leopold II of these international obligations in the Congo, however, was an act of opportunism and diplomacy rather than of conviction. As duke of Brabant, Leopold II had been full of imperial ideas for his country. Imaginative, patriotic and far-sighted, his horizons were far wider than those of most of his countrymen.[1] His knowledge of the outer world had been extensive. He had visited Egypt and sailed down the Nile. He had travelled across the Middle East and the Near East. In March 1862 he was at Seville 'going through the archives and calculating the profit which Spain made then and makes now out of her colonies'.[2] About two years later he went to the Far East—Ceylon, India, Burma, Indo-China, China and the Dutch East Indies—from which he returned, it has been said, laden with notes and documents on methods for the exploitation of colonial territories.[3]

---

[1] These qualities, well recognized later by his collaborators and praised by his biographers, are given, perhaps, their best assessment by Colonel Strauch, first Administrator-General of the Congo Department of Interior. See Strauch to Wauters, 1 May 1911, Strauch Papers, AF 1–13. See also Daye: op. cit., pp. 336–8.

[2] De Lichtervelde: op. cit., p. 49, quoted in N. Ascherson: *The King Incorporated,* London 1963, p. 46.

[3] Ascherson: op. cit., p. 47.

He did not share current views on free trade. What apparently fascinated him were the policies of the Dutch East India Company and the profits which the Netherlands had reaped therefrom. He probably saw colonies strictly and unequivocally in mercantilist terms. Once he wrote:

> If Belgium, which already possesses its railways, could add to them some new Java, one might be able to hope for a reduction in the salt duty, the suppression of customs dues, etc., etc., etc., all achieved without the slightest call on our own resources or on our current expenditure . . .[1]

As for the inhabitants of the colonies Leopold II's subsequent attitude seemed to show that he regarded them more as means of production than as human beings. He hoped that civilization might follow in the foot-steps of forced labour; but if it did not he need not worry about it.[2]

Thus the colonial ideas of Leopold II, hazy as they were before he actually acquired a colony, indicate that he was indifferent to those very principles of free trade and humane treatment of the indigenous population which the Berlin Act sought to secure. There is hardly any evidence to show that he subsequently allowed these principles of the Act to dictate his policy in the Congo State. Although he referred to them from time to time in his decrees, their practical application seem to have been ignored largely because of his overriding aim to make the State a financial success.

Meanwhile the king of the Belgians had to find a colony. At first it was the Far East and Central America which attracted his attention. But as sovereign of a weak, neutral and introspective state he could only watch helplessly as the prizes he coveted were won by others. It was not until ten years later, as the Belgian historian, Father Roeykens, has revealed, that we find an indication that the king was turning his attention towards Africa. 'I intend to find out discreetly', he wrote to Auguste Lambermont, secretary-general of his

---

[1] L. le Febve de Vivy: *Documents d'Histoire précoloniale belge*, Brussels 1955, p. 31, quoted in Ascherson: op. cit., p. 47.

[2] Daye: op. cit., p. 341.

5

Ministry for Foreign Affairs, 'whether there may not be anything to be done in Africa'.[1]

Several volumes have since been written on the subsequent evolution of that discreet inquiry: the summoning of the Geographical Conference in 1876; the formation of the philanthropic *Association Internationale Africaine*; the metamorphosis of the Association into a commercial undertaking known as the *Comité d'Etudes du Haut-Congo* which despatched H. M. Stanley, the African explorer, to study the economic possibilities of the Congo; and finally, the emergence of the political organization called the *Association Internationale du Congo*, already mentioned.

The recognition of the latter Association by the powers assembled at Berlin, coupled with its adherence to the General Act of Berlin, enabled the shadowy Congo State of Leopold II to assume a substantial form. In accordance with Article 62 of the Belgian Constitution he sought permission from his parliament to accept the crown of the Congo. Reluctantly and without enthusiasm the permission was granted, but on the distinct understanding that the union between Belgium and the new State should be entirely personal. The king of the Belgians thus also became sovereign of the Congo State and henceforth began to be addressed by the grandiose title of *le Roi-Souverain*.

In Brussels he set up a Congo cabinet of three, consisting of the administrators-general for the departments of foreign affairs, finance and the interior.[2] These were to be known from 1894 as secretaries-general and a higher post of secretary of state was created.[3] At Boma, which became the capital of the Congo State, he appointed another administrator-general, soon changed into governor-general, and under this official all the administrative paraphernalia of a colony were laid out.[4] It was a highly centralized administration with real authority firmly held in Brussels and directly exercised

[1] A. Roeykens: *Les Débuts de l'œuvre africaine de Léopold II*, Brussels 1955, p. 95; quoted in Ascherson: op. cit., p. 84.

[2] *B.O.*, no. 2, February 1885.

[3] *B.O.*, no. 10, October 1894.

[4] F. Cattier: *Droit et Administration de l'Etat Indépendant du Congo*, Brussels 1898, pp. 198 ff.

by the king-sovereign himself unfettered by any parliament or assembly. Absolutism was seldom more complete.

The foremost problem was how to secure revenue to meet the needs of the new State. Colonial experience in tropical Africa had shown that these colonies took a long time to become self-supporting and longer still to pay dividends. Colonial revenue accrued from customs duties on imports and exports; then followed a direct tax on the indigenous population some years later. But while such colonies had been able to rely on subsidies from the imperial government, Leopold II could only look to his privy purse and such loans as he could raise. Furthermore, by interdicting import duties for twenty years, the Berlin Act had robbed the Congo State of a valuable source of income. In any case Leopold II was not a patient man and did not believe in long-term investments. He sought quick returns for his money in order to execute the great public works in Belgium that he was beginning to conceive.[1] And he believed that the key to the fulfilment of this objective lay in those colonial principles which, as we have seen above, he had absorbed.

It has become usual to divide the history of the king-sovereign's economic policy in the Congo into two phases: a first phase dating from 1885 to 1891, when he endeavoured to apply a policy of unrestricted trade, and a second phase after 1891, when he engaged exclusively in the policy of granting monopolies and concessions. Although this division is convenient, it ought to be borne in mind that the policy of the later period was implicit in the former; that the elaboration of the former gave rise to the evils of the latter. The difference between the two periods was one of degree rather than of fundamentals.

The policy of the first period was embodied in several decrees published in the official gazette of the State, known as the *Bulletin Officiel du Congo*. The first and the most important appeared in the form of an ordinance of the administrator-general in the Congo dated 1 July 1885. Article 2 of this ordinance, while stating that no one had the right to

---

[1] F. Cattier: *Etude sur la situation de l'Etat Indépendant du Congo*, Brussels 1906, p. 61.

occupy *terres vacantes* nor to dispossess the Congolese of the land which they occupied, also declared that the *terres vacantes* should be considered as belonging to the State. As some writers have pointed out, there was nothing wrong with this ordinance, which indeed soon came to be adopted by the colonial powers in Equatorial Africa.[1] Such legislation was useful in safe-guarding communal land from being alienated to unscrupulous foreign agents and speculators. In the case of the Congo State, it must be observed, nevertheless, that there was no attempt to define the limits of land occupied by the Congolese or of the vacant lands. However, it seemed at the time that far from the State wishing to attack the rights in land of the Congolese, it was anxious to confirm them. Thus a royal decree of 14 September 1886 made lands occupied by the Congolese subject to their laws and customs and the decree of 30 June 1887 laid down that foreigners wishing to buy land should negotiate direct with the inhabitants, subject of course to final approval by the administrator-general in the Congo.[2]

Similarly, the Congo State seemed content to facilitate the expansion of free trade. A decree of 22 August 1885 asked foreigners occupying lands in the Congo to have them registered at a nominal fee of 25 francs. The decree of 30 June 1887 already mentioned also allowed merchants in the Upper Congo to occupy lands up to 10 hectares without formal authorization from the government and they could own the land if they paid 100 francs as costs for its demarcation.

But even at this time the direction in which the king-sovereign was planning to go could be seen in the arrangements which he concluded with the *Compagnie du Congo pour le commerce et l'industrie*, the Belgian company formed for the purpose of constructing a railway line to circumvent the Yellala Falls.[3] As compensation for surveying the route of

---

[1] Britain accorded the right of exploiting vacant lands to the British Imperial East Africa Company in 1888. France and Germany reserved vacant lands in the French Congo and Tanganyika in 1891 and 1895 respectively.

[2] *B.O.*, no. 9, September 1887.

[3] For the background to the formation of this company see Anstey: op. cit., pp. 186–208.

the railway within eighteen months, the State undertook to concede to the company 150,000 hectares of land. In addition, if the company agreed to construct the line, the State guaranteed to concede to it all lands which the company might desire to obtain within a zone of 200 metres on each side of the track as well as the concession of 1,500 hectares of land for each kilometre of track laid and opened to traffic.[1] Thus the system of granting concessions was foreshadowed. Soon afterwards State trading was also initiated. Officers of the State began to compete with private traders in purchasing ivory and to receive, as Grenfell of the Baptist Missionary Society (B.M.S.) noted, a commission on the quantity of ivory they collected.[2]

Furthermore, the State issued a decree by which the collection of india-rubber, copal gum and other vegetable products in those districts where such collection did not already exist, and especially in the region bounded by Bolobo and River Aruwimi, and in the forests along the banks of the Congo River itself and its affluents, could only be carried on by virtue of special concessions granted by the government. Infraction of the decree was made punishable by fines ranging from 50 to 2,000 francs and the confiscation of the produce.[3]

State trading in ivory and the decree on the collection of forest produce provoked vigorous protests from private traders in the Congo and particularly from the Dutch firm, *Afrikaansche Handelsvereeniging*, which was one of the largest commercial enterprises in the Congo.[4] The British government, following a protest from Hatton and Cookson, the sole British firm in the Congo State, also made inquiries,[5] while the French government threatened to refuse to sign the General Act of the Anti-Slave Trade Conference which

---

[1] *Moniteur Belge*, 4 January 1887; *B.O.*, no. 4, April 1887. The land concession was later exploited by an offshoot of the company, *Compagnie du chemin de fer du Congo, B.O.*, no. 1, January 1890.

[2] H. H. Johnston: *George Grenfell and the Congo*, London 1908, i, 445.

[3] Decree of 17 October 1889. *B.O.*, no. 10, October 1889.

[4] See Vivian to Salisbury, 3 May 1890, FO 84/2024, no. 23, Africa, confidential.

[5] Vivian to Salisbury, 11 July 1890, ibid., no. 39, Africa.

was then sitting in Brussels. Under the pressure of Belgian traders in the Congo, and with the loan which Leopold II was asking as a lever,[1] the Belgian government also intervened with the king-sovereign. He surrendered with a bad grace. In a decree of 9 July 1890, the State relinquished to private traders exclusively the collection of ivory in all the regions above Stanley Falls accessible to steamers and established a tax of two francs on every kilogramme of ivory collected. In addition, a heavy export duty of 200 francs was imposed on every 100 kilogramme of ivory and 50 francs on every 100 kilogramme of rubber.[2] The Congo State, Leopold II blandly explained to Lord Vivian, the British ambassador, could not possibly dispense with the revenue derived from its domain; and if the merchants objected to competition with the government, they must pay compensation in the form of duties.[3] Nevertheless, following further pressure the export duties were reduced.[4]

No sooner had this measure of satisfaction been granted to private traders than Leopold II launched a chartered company in order to extend the influence of the Congo State to Katanga. In March 1891 an agreement was announced between the Congo State and the *Compagnie du Congo pour le commerce et l'industrie*[5] which resulted in the formation of the *Compagnie du Katanga*. In return for the effective occupation of the Upper Congo and an investigation into its agricultural, commercial and mining resources, the company was to receive one-third of the lands of the State in the basin of the Lualaba above Riba-Riba and of the Upper Lomami. On 21 October 1891 the *Compagnie du Katanga* floated a new company, the *Syndicat commercial du Katanga*, in order to exploit its commercial concession; but in May 1892 the activities of the company was brought to an early end when the Arabs in the territory routed the trading expedition

---

[1] Infra, p. 7, note 1.

[2] *B.O.*, no. 7, July 1890.

[3] Vivian to Salisbury, 27 September 1890, FO 84/2204, no. 70, Africa.

[4] Decree of 19 February 1891, *B.O.*, no. 2, February 1891.

[5] F. Masoin: op. cit., ii, 199 ff.

which the company had entrusted to Hodister.[1] It was not until 5 July 1898 that it re-emerged under the name of *Compagnie du Lomami*.

The concession granted to the *Compagnie du Katanga* was found to be too big for it. Furthermore, by 1898 the Congo State had succeeded in crushing internal opposition from the Arabs and was in a position to take a more active part in the exploitation of Katanga. An agreement between the State and the company dated 19 June 1900 resulted in the setting up of a new body known as *Comité Spécial du Katanga* which received the right to direct the exploitation of the land and minerals in Katanga for ninety-nine years. By a royal decree of 6 December 1900 the *Comité* became a civil person and was entrusted with all administrative functions in Katanga, except justice, taxation and postal services.[2]

Long before this time the Congo State had cast aside all subterfuges and clearly embarked on a policy of monopolies and concessions. Leopold II had managed in 1890 to secure from the Anti-Slavery Conference a modification of Article IV of the Berlin Act in order to enable him levy an import duty of ten per cent. But the revenue from such orthodox sources were no longer sufficient for his extravagant schemes. He was impatient not merely to secure the yet undelimitated borders of his vast African empire but also to push them out as far as possible. Thus he was challenging the Portuguese in the South, the British South Africa Company in the South-East, the British and German governments in the East, the French in the North, and the Arabs within the country. Above all, he was fascinated by the Nile, to which he wished to link the Congo, and it has been suggested that he hoped thereby to become a modern pharaoh.[3] Thus, although the exports of the State had more than doubled between 1887 and 1889 and nearly doubled again in

---

[1] Keith: op. cit., pp. 95–6.
[2] Ibid., p. 89.
[3] Cf. J. Stengers: 'La première tentative de reprise du Congo par la Belgique' *Bulletin Société Royale belge de Géographie*, 1949 (extract), p. 71 and A. J. Wauters: *Histoire Politique du Congo Belge*, Brussels 1911, p. 154.

1890,[1] Leopold II was not satisfied. He wanted more startling results.

By a decree dated 29 September 1891, he instructed the district commissioners of the Aruwimi-Uele and the Ubangi to adopt 'urgent measures necessary to keep at the disposal of the State the resources of the domain, especially ivory and rubber'.[2] This decree was put into execution by a series of local circulars. One signed on 15 December 1891 by Baert, district commissioner for Ubangi-Uele, ensured that the Congolese in that area would exploit its produce exclusively for the State with effect from 1 January 1892. The area was extended to cover the Bomu basin in two circulars signed on 14 February 1892 by le Marinel, commandant of the Ubangi-Bomu expedition which had been despatched a few months earlier to protect the rubber-rich region explored by Van Gèle. Another circular dated 8 May 1892 by Lemaire, commissioner of the Equator district, enforced a similar regulation in his area of jurisdiction.

The circulars led to an outburst of protests far greater than those of two years earlier. Under the pressure of Dutch Congo traders, the Dutch government decided to make a formal protest in Brussels against what they believed to be a violation of the Berlin Act. They were persuaded by their astute ambassador in Brussels, Baron Gericke, to let the brunt of the fight be borne by the Belgians themselves.[3] The

---

[1] Table of Exports issued by the Congo State gave the following figures:

Year	Commerce special
	Fr.
1887	1,980,441.45
1888	2,609,300.35
1889	4,297,543.85
1890	8,242,194.43

B.O., no. 4, April 1891.

[2] *Mouvement Géographique*, 24 July 1892.

[3] Monson to Rosebery, 18 October 1892, FO 84/2202, no. 94, Africa, most confidential.

hardest hit was the *Société belge du Haut-Congo* which had rapidly expanded its trading operations during the past few years. Its president was the powerful Belgian financier, Albert Thys, and under him, and with the aid of its secretary, A. J. Wauters, the geographer, the company launched a vigorous campaign against the Congo State.[1] In the Belgian chamber of deputies, the circulars were attacked from all sides as a violation of natural rights as well as of the Berlin Act and an act of ingratitude by the Congo State towards Belgium.[2] The Belgian press took up the protests.[3] Belgians who had collaborated with the king-sovereign in founding the Congo State, like Beernaert, Banning and Lambermont, came out against the circulars and the governor-general of the State, Camille Janssen, resigned.[4] The Belgian government at last intervened again with their royal master and urged him to withdraw the circulars.

At first Leopold II remained adamant. He maintained that he had a perfect right to the produce of the land and could exploit it to the exclusion of private traders. In defence of this position he published the opinion of several experts in international law to whom he had submitted leading questions arising from the principles on which the circulars were based.[5] News of the disaster which overtook the trading expedition launched by the *Syndicat commercial du Katanga* under Hodister in May 1892 arrived at an opportune moment to reinforce the arguments of the Congo government. The disaster, the Congo Secretary of State for Foreign Affairs told the press, showed that it was necessary to close the Upper Congo to private traders until such time as it was safe for them to go there.[6]

Leopold also sought to secure the support of foreign

---

[1] E.g. see Société belge du Haut-Congo to Beernaert, 8 August 1892, E.I.C., 6/19; and Wauters, op. cit., p. 94.

[2] *Annales Parlementaires* (Chambre), 14 May 1892.

[3] E.g. see *La Chronique*, 14 April 1892; *Indépendance Belge*, 9 May 1892 and 20 July 1892.

[4] J. Stengers: *Textes Inédits d'Emile Banning*, Brussels 1955, p. 47; Cattier: *Etude sur la situation*, p. 63.

[5] Encl. in Eetvelde to Beernaert, 17 October 1892, E.I.C. 6/26.

[6] *Journal de Bruxelles*, 29 July 1892.

governments. He consulted the German government which had no traders in the Congo, and apparently received an unofficial assurance of support.[1] The king-sovereign tried to do the same with Britain but the Foreign Office preferred at this stage to ignore his initiative rather than enter into a discussion on the interpretation of the provisions of the Berlin Act.[2]

In the end the king-sovereign modified his position. By a royal decree dated 30 October 1892[3] he permitted private companies to trade in the Upper Congo with the exception of certain areas to the west and north-east of the country and subject to the rights of third parties either in existence or to be conceded in the future. The decree silenced the Belgian protests for it seemed to throw a vast area of the Congo State open to private enterprise. Furthermore, the concessions which the Congo government soon proceeded to hand out to Belgian capitalists diverted their attention from the principle of free trade which they had sought to uphold. The wily monarch, however, had not altered in the least the position which he had occupied from the beginning as regards State ownership of vacant lands. All such lands and their produce still belonged to the State and the State retained the unlimited right of giving them away as concessions.

The decree of 30 October 1892 cleared the way, then, for the creation of what was called the *Domaine Privé* which consisted of those territories where private companies and traders were excluded. These territories the officers and agents of the State began to exploit directly. In the regions outside this *Domaine Privé* the Congo State also began to grant large concessions.[4] In 1892 an Anglo-Belgian India Rubber Company (more commonly known as Abir) presided over by the Englishman, Colonel North, received for thirty years the right to exploit the land in the basins of the Lopori

---

[1] Monson to Rosebery, 21 October 1892, FO 84/2202, no. 95, Africa, most confidential.

[2] Infra, p. 24, note 2.

[3] *B.O.*, no. 10, October 1892.

[4] Details of these concessions are given in Cattier: *Etude sur la situation*, pp. 65–70, 191–99.

and Maringa.[1] Soon afterwards a similar concession was granted to the *Société anversoise du Commerce du Congo* (Anversoise) in the basin of the Mongala. In October 1892 a concession around Lakes Leopold II and Mantumba was granted to 'the Duke of Saxe-Coburg-Gotha'.[2] Subsequently, the area of this concession was extended and by a decree of 8 March 1896 it was constituted under the title of *Domaine de la Couronne*.[3] It was not until 1901, however, that its existence was mentioned for the first time in the *Bulletin Officiel*.

There were several other concessions of which only the most important need be mentioned. The *Comptoir Commercial Congolais* constituted on 26 July 1895 received the basin of the Wamba, an affluent of the Kwango. The *Compagnie des Chemins de fer du Congo supérieur aux Grands Lacs Africaines*, set up on 2 January 1902 for the construction of the railway between Stanley Falls and the upper lakes, was given four million hectares forming a band which extended from the Stanleyville–Ponthierville railway to Lake Albert. Another railway company, *La Société d'Etudes du chemin de fer du Stanley-Pool au Katanga et de l'Itimbiri à Uele et à un point à déterminer sur la frontière franco-congolaise*, formed on 14 March 1903, received ten thousand hectares to be chosen among vacant lands in the basin of the Uele and another ten thousand from the left bank of the Congo below Stanleyville.

Meanwhile, some of the private companies and traders had taken advantage of the provisions of the October decree to establish trading stations in the basin of the Kasai. A fierce rivalry developed among them and several went into liquidation. When in 1901 Leopold II proposed to the fifteen remaining companies the subscription of fifty per cent of the shares of a company which would receive the

---

[1] It now seems that Colonel North was merely a cover for Leopold himself and had no money in the company. See Anstey: op. cit., p. 209, note 4, quoting H. Waltz: *Das Konzessionswesen im Belgischen Congo*, Jena, 1917, i, 40, 54.

[2] Wauters: op. cit., p. 203.

[3] The purpose for which the domain was created is indicated in *Journal de Bruxelles*, 11 January 1908.

concession of the whole Kasai basin the offer was readily accepted. Thus the *Compagnie du Kasai* came into being on 31 December 1901.

By the beginning of the present century, therefore, the entire Congo State, with the exception of a negligible proportion, had been parcelled out into monopolies and concessions. In all of them Leopold II, either through the Congo State or through some minion, had large investments. Article 1 of the Berlin Act had become, to all intents and purposes, a dead letter.

It was almost inevitable that the system of concessions would have the worst possible repercussions on the life of the Congolese. In particular, it had two effects. In the first place, the direct exploitation of a vast area of land by the State led to the imposition of a tax in labour or in kind or both. Secondly, the absence of any competition allowed the State and the monopolist companies to pay only nominal prices or wages to the Congolese for the produce which they were compelled to collect.

The commission of inquiry which Leopold II was obliged to set up in 1904[1] has left a critical description of how the system operated to the advantage of the State and the companies. There was no legislation of any kind regulating the tax which the Congolese had to pay. This meant that the State officials and the company agents were free to levy what taxes they liked, to collect them by whatever means they chose, and to impose any punishment they fancied in case of a default. Furthermore, and this was most important, the officials and agents received inducements in the form of premiums on the quantity of produce which they collected and could be prosecuted only with the consent of the executive. Thus, while their cupidity was inflamed, the impression was given to them that they would be protected by the State. Following the Stokes–Lothaire affair in 1895, the German government extracted from the Congo State a promise to discontinue the premiums.[2] Nevertheless, the premiums were

---

[1] Infra, Chapter V.

[2] J. Willequet: *Le Congo belge et la Weltpolitik*, Brussels 1963, p. 20. For the Stokes-Lothaire affair see infra, pp. 31–4.

surreptitiously replaced the following year by a system of bonuses. Each officer received a bonus at the end of his contract not as of right but according to the wishes of the State. It was understood, however, that only those whose work satisfied the government received these bonuses and that meant those who could collect the expected quotas of produce. Thus the old system continued in practice.

In 1899 the Congo court of appeal ruled that under the existing law (or lack of law) no one could legally force the inhabitants to work.[1] The decision was ignored until 1903 when another decision of the same court restated the view. By that time the protest against the Congo system was reaching enormous proportions and it was essential for the king-sovereign to begin putting his house into some semblance of order. Consequently, a royal decree of 18 November 1903 legalized the labour tax. At the same time a secret circular was sent round to warn the agents that far from attempting to reduce the impositions they must ensure an increasing return in revenue.[2]

A system of exactions such as this required an unusually large army to impose it. In the early years of the State, recruitment took place along the east and west coasts of Africa.[3] This system, however, had obvious difficulties: it was very expensive and the number which could be recruited was limited. By the royal decree of 30 July 1891 the procedure for recruitment by both voluntary enlistment and levies within the Congo State itself was introduced. According to the decree, the local chiefs were to determine those in their villages who should offer military service. In practice, the system operated differently. The chiefs distrusted the new imposition and the people under them were unwilling to be dragged away from their homes to serve in distant places. The recruitment was therefore entrusted to State officials whose activities were stimulated by the payment of premiums depending on the numbers that they were able to recruit. The soldiers thus recruited were quartered on rival tribes

---

[1] Cattier: *Etude sur la situation*, pp. 111 ff.

[2] Ibid.

[3] Infra, p. 25.

and local animosities were relied upon to inspire them to inflict gruesome punishments at the slightest opportunity.

Thus the concession system, apart from infringing the provisions of the Berlin Act on the freedom of trade, also made it necessary, indeed inevitable, for the Congo State to ignore that section of the Act which urged the powers exercising authority in the Congo basin to protect and further the welfare of the inhabitants.

This, then, was the basis of the Congo question which forms the subject of the present study. As more than one writer has pointed out, the Berlin Act made no adequate provision for the enforcement of its principles.[1] The mere expression of vague and pious hopes about freedom of trade and good treatment of the native populations left each power to interpret the Act according to its interests and in the absence of an enforcing machinery, what had been assumed to be the business of everyone, in fact became, as is often the case, the business of none. Even the International Commission for the Navigation of the Congo which was provided for in the Act was forgotten and never set up. In any case, the theory of vacant lands, as has already been pointed out, was soon applied by the powers in Equatorial Africa and, although Leopold II alone carried the point to its logical conclusion, it clearly became inconvenient for the rest to examine it too closely until their own colonial policies had been suitably modified; otherwise a *tu quoque* retort was inescapable and unanswerable.

Nevertheless, the Berlin Act did not entirely fail in its purpose as far as the Congo was concerned.[2] Although it had not prevented the establishment of a monopolist system nor provided an effective machinery for action against its infraction, yet it came to afford an essential weapon, which, taken up by British public opinion, at last compelled diplomatic intervention. It was in the name of the Act, backed by the Anglo-Congolese Convention, that the British government

[1] Keith: op. cit., pp. 284–5; L. Woolf: *Empire and Commerce in Africa*, London 1919, pp. 308–9.
[2] Cf. Crowe: op. cit., p. 3, who seems to have thought that the Act was an unmitigated failure.

goaded Belgium into annexing the Congo and then refused to recognize the annexation until the Congo administration had been suitably reformed.

In the Foreign Office the Congo question was handled by the African Department. Before 1883 affairs relating to Africa were generally managed by a small department designated Slave Trade and Consular. Following the reorganization initiated in 1881 under the Foreign Secretaryship of Granville a department known as Consular and African (East and West) was created. The head of this department was H. P. Anderson, a senior clerk, and under him were C. L. Hill and E. A. W. Clarke. Anderson was promoted assistant under-secretary on 1 January 1894 and continued to be responsible for the department until his death in 1896.

Meanwhile in 1894, a separate Consular Department had been created but both the African and Consular Departments continued to be under Anderson. After his death the supervision of the African Department was entrusted to F. Bertie,[1] while F. H. Villiers[2] took charge of the Consular Department.

The African Department was further split in 1902. A department was created for African Protectorates (East Africa, Uganda, British Central Africa and Somaliland) and an African Department for South-East, West and South-West Africa. Thus there were now three separate departments performing the functions which one had undertaken before 1883, a reflection of the growth of the empire in Africa during the later period. This position, however, was modified in 1906 when the department for African Protectorates disappeared.

As far as the Congo question was concerned, the influence wielded by the African Department in the determination of policy was not considerable after the death of Anderson, for no one of similar stature or experience emerged in the department. His successors Bertie (1896–1903), Villiers

---

[1] Ambassador to France, 1905–18.
[2] Minister in Brussels, 1911–20.

(1903–6), E. Barrington (1906–7), and W. Langley (1907–12) were much more interested in the European implications of British African policy than in African affairs *per se*; consequently, their intervention in the Congo question was sporadic. The same was even more true of the permanent under-secretaries. It was therefore the clerks in the African Department who really dealt with the Congo. One of these was H. Farnall, who was the recognized authority on African questions between 1896 and 1904, but he does not seem to have exercised any decisive influence over policy. Another was E. A. W. Clarke, who served in the department from 1883 to 1909 when he was appointed consul at Zanzibar. His undistinguished career perhaps demonstrates how insignificant was his influence.

Such secondary role as the department played in the Congo question will be indicated later; that they did not do more was probably not entirely their fault. The room for manoeuvre on the subject was limited. Under Salisbury intervention was hardly desired either by the Foreign Secretary or by the Foreign Office. Lansdowne, his successor, followed a similar policy with the general support of the permanent officials and the minister in Brussels until their hands were forced by the House of Commons. When Grey took office in December 1906 pressure from Britain was already being exerted on the Congo government and he openly advocated Belgian annexation of the Congo State.

Both the Foreign Secretary and the African Department were susceptible to pressure from outside and, as we shall see, it was public opinion which on many occasions successfully urged policies on them. Another feature of the Congo question with regard to the Foreign Office was that consular officers in the Congo State often expressed opinions which affected policy. Lastly, the ministers in Brussels, in particular F. Plunkett (1893–1900) and A. Hardinge (1906–11), were experienced diplomatists and their views were generally accepted. Sometimes, especially in the case of C. Phipps[1] and R. Casement,[2] the views of the minister were in conflict

---

[1] Minister in Brussels from 1900 to 1906.
[2] Consul in the Congo State from 1899 to 1904.

with those of the consul and since the consuls were all
independent of the embassy, the African Department was
called upon to arbitrate between them. In such circumstances, the verdict depended on who had the greater
influence in the department or with the Foreign Secretary.
Casement, on the whole, was too formidable for Phipps;
under Grey, Hardinge maintained a more dominant position
in the determination of policy.

But this is to anticipate. Having outlined the nature of
the Congo question it is now time to examine in greater
detail the factors which led to British intervention and the
role of British diplomacy in bringing about the reform of
the Congo administration.

II

Early Evidence on Congo Maladministration

The concession system, it has already been said, made atrocities almost inevitable in the Congo. Reports of them soon began to trickle into Europe through missionaries, travellers and consular agents until by the end of the century the weight of evidence had become overwhelming. In no country was popular reaction as pronounced as in Britain and there it was expected that the government would intervene. In fact, as a result of her vast imperial commitments, Britain's capacity for intervention had become limited, a fact which public opinion did not generally appreciate. Hence, as the Congo agitation mounted, it was largely ignored by the Foreign Office. While willing to protect British subjects and essentially British interests, they refused to intervene on behalf of the Congolese. Their policy during this period was rather to maintain friendly relations with Leopold II as much as possible.

Evidence of this policy could be seen in the decisions taken by the Foreign Office, firstly, as regards the right of extra-territorial jurisdiction reserved to Britain in Article V of the Anglo-Congolese Convention of 1884; and, secondly, on the Congo State decree of 17 October 1889 providing for the granting of concessions.

A royal decree of 28 December 1888 on the subject of succession had empowered the Administrator-General for

Foreign Affairs to administer and liquidate the property of foreigners deceased in the Congo State if no heir or testamentary executor was known on the spot.[1] The decree was clearly irreconcilable with the convention of 1884 in which jurisdiction over the person and property of British subjects was entirely reserved to the British government.[2] Consequently, it was regarded as inoperative as far as British subjects were concerned and the establishment of British consular jurisdiction in the Congo was projected.[3] Fearing that British example would be followed by other powers, the Congo government pleaded that the jurisdiction was unnecessary since they had established a complete system of criminal, civil and commercial justice.[4] So serious did Leopold II consider the danger that on 25 March 1890 he suddenly appeared in London to urge Salisbury to drop the idea of the consular courts.[5] Salisbury readily obliged; while not abandoning the right altogether it was decided to waive it for the meantime.[6] In fact the right was never again to be asserted. This was unfortunate. The exercise of consular jurisdiction by Britain and other powers would have curbed at an early stage what amounted to an autocratic and irresponsible rule by Leopold II in the Congo and might altogether have averted the Congo question.

Similarly, when the royal decree of 17 October 1889 providing for the granting of concessions in the Congo was published, it had been pointed out that its provisions were 'opposed not only to the spirit but to the letter of the Berlin Act'.[7] The Congo government explained vaguely that the measure was necessary for the assertion of the rights of the State over its forests and for their preservation from

---

[1] *B.O.*, no. 12, December 1889.
[2] A. H. Oakes, 24 January 1890, FO 84/2024, memorandum; H. P. Anderson, 5 March 1890, ibid., minute.
[3] Salisbury to Vivian, 4 February 1890, ibid., no. 38, Africa.
[4] Van Eetvelde to Vivian, 21 February 1890, encl. in Vivian to Salisbury, 22 February 1890, ibid., no. 11, Africa.
[5] Vivian to Salisbury, 25 March 1890, S.P. A/49.
[6] Salisbury to Vivian, 23 April 1890, FO 10/730, no. 91, Africa.
[7] E. Hertslet, 26 November 1889, FO 84/1946, memorandum.

23

uncontrolled destruction,[1] and the Foreign Office dropped the matter. Although the decree was eventually withdrawn, the principle was reintroduced, as we have seen, in a series of secret circulars which were attacked by private traders. The company most affected, the *Société belge du Haut Congo*, had as one of its directors an Englishman, Alfred Parminter, and he got the African section of the Manchester Chamber of Commerce to pass a resolution urging the Foreign Office to protest against the violation of the Berlin Act.[2] The help of the Aborigines Protection Society (A.P.S.) was invoked by Manchester because 'the natives will be, and are, seriously debarred from trading in the very products which form their most valued articles of exchange',[3] and a member of the society tabled a question in the House of Commons. Anderson admitted that Leopold II had carried the control of vacant lands 'to an extreme point', but he warned the Minister not to allow the government to be dragged into a discussion on the theory of vacant lands.[4] Consequently, the questioner was merely told that it was 'difficult to define the extent and validity of the doctrine of State domains',[5] and there the matter conveniently rested for several years.

The Anti-Slavery Conference of 1890 affords another example of the sympathetic policy of the Foreign Office towards the Congo government. It was Salisbury who had invited Leopold II to take the initiative in convoking the

---

[1] Van Eetvelde to Vivian, 14 December 1889 (copy), encl. in Vivian to Salisbury, 14 December 1889, FO 84/1946, no. 139, Africa. Anderson sagely observed that 'if universally applied in the Free State, it would be an evasion of the Congo Act, as immense trade regions might be made monopolies; but on the other hand, it would seem *prima facie* fair that the Administering State should be able to grant concessions as to unoccupied territory.' Anderson, 16 December 1889, ibid., minute. Hertslet who had originally raised the issue was contented to note: 'If it's clearly understood that these concessions in no way interfere with trade, or export, or transit duties, I think the explanation may be considered satisfactory.' E. Hertslet, 18 December 1889, ibid., minute.

[2] Charles Roskill to Fox Bourne, 24 January 1893, A.S. Papers, C. 152.

[3] Ibid.

[4] H. P. Anderson, 16 March 1893, FO 10/604, minute.

[5] Hansard, 17 March 1893, 4th ser., x, 380-1.

conference in Brussels.[1] Salisbury had also lent his support
to the king-sovereign when the latter asked the conference
to repeal Article IV of the Berlin Act and make it possible
for him to levy import duties in the Congo basin.[2]

Finally, the friendly attitude of the British government
towards the Congo government could be seen in the extension to Leopold of facilities for recruitment in the British
colonies and protectorates.[3] By the close of 1890 the Congo
government had established a system of regular recruitment
of labour in West Africa. The contract was held by the
African Steamship Company whose agents, stationed at the
ports of Freetown, Accra and Lagos, were responsible for
signing on and transporting the emigrants. This arrangement
contained the seeds of future trouble. While British complaints against the commercial policy of the Congo State
were not insistent, the treatment of British subjects soon
evoked loud and continuous protests.

The first of these protests reached the Foreign Office in
June 1891 when the Colonial Office forwarded a petition
from Reverend James Johnson of Lagos giving details of
the deplorable plight of certain mechanics recruited to work
in the Congo.[4] Transmitted to Brussels, the Congo government readily agreed to institute an inquiry.[5] Nevertheless,
the complaints continued to multiply. In October 1891 the
Colonial Office despatched another petition from Johnson.[6]
Four months later the governor of Sierra Leone sent a

---

[1] Salisbury to Vivian, 17 September 1888, FO 84/1895, no. 15, Africa.
[2] Vivian to Salisbury, 20 August 1889, FO 84/1946, no. 88, Africa,
confidential; Salisbury to Vivian, 30 September 1889, ibid., no. 53,
Africa.
[3] Leopold II to Victoria, 22 December 1889, *L.Q.V.*, 3rd ser., i, 537;
Vivian to Salisbury, 9 January 1890, FO 84/2024, no. 2, Africa; Salisbury to Vivian, 15 May 1890, ibid., no. 140, Africa. For a fuller treatment of this subject see S. J. S. Cookey: 'West African Immigrants in
the Congo, 1885–1896', *Journal of the Historical Society of Nigeria*, vol. 3,
no. 2, December 1965, pp. 261–70.
[4] C.O. to F.O., 26 June 1891, FO 10/730.
[5] Van Eetvelde to Gosselin, 21 July 1891, encl. in Gosselin to Salisbury,
23 July 1891, ibid., no. 56, Africa.
[6] C.O. to F.O., 28 October 1891, ibid.

protest on behalf of his colony[1] and soon came a similar one from Accra.[2] The complaints of the West Africans employed in the Congo were the same: they were treated like beasts of burden; imprisoned without trial or flogged to death when they complained; forced to remain in the country after the expiration of their contracts; impressed into military service when they had contracted to work as labourers or artisans; and so on. It was these complaints that led the Foreign Office to consider more seriously the appointment of a permanent consular officer for the Congo. The effusion of good faith and the promise of speedy action by the Congo government were no longer regarded as sufficient guarantees.

The first consular officer for the Congo had been appointed in 1888 but he had been diverted to Old Calabar to replace consul Hewett, whose failing health made it imperative for him to retire from the Oil Rivers.[3] In February 1892 Edward Bannister who traded in Loanda and had acted as consul there from time to time was appointed vice-consul for the Congo. The following July William Clayton Pickersgill was appointed consul for the Portuguese possessions in West Africa together with a supervisory jurisdiction over the Congo though he was to reside at Loanda.

The instructions of Pickersgill are interesting because of the light they throw on the attitude of the Foreign Office towards what were regarded as the responsibilities of Britain in the Congo.[4] The consul was reminded of the international obligations of the powers exercising sovereign rights or influence within the Congo basin as laid down in chapters I, II, III and IV of the Berlin Act. His attention was then drawn to the question of the treatment of labourers who had emigrated from British West African colonies for service in the Congo and he was told to give them protection and

---

[1] C.O. to F.O., 10 March 1892, ibid.

[2] C.O. to F.O., 25 April 1892, ibid.

[3] George Annesley was appointed consul for the Congo State on 20 March 1888. From 13 December 1889 to 19 April 1891 and again from 30 May to 6 July 1891 he was acting consul at Old Calabar. He retired on 21 February 1892.

[4] F.O. to Pickersgill, 5 September 1892, FO 84/2224, no. 3, Africa, confidential.

assistance. He was warned, however, to be 'careful to avoid any interference with the internal administration of the Free State'.[1] The fact that it was confidently believed in the Foreign Office that the provisions of the Berlin Act could be enforced by a foreign power in another State without interfering in the internal affairs of that State shows how little attention had as yet been paid to the implications of the Act. Furthermore, and significantly, the Foreign Office did not think it was their business how the Congo government treated the Congolese.

It fell to Bannister to carry out these instructions since Pickersgill was too far away from Boma, the seat of the administration. Bannister was quick-tempered and possessed more zeal than tact. These failings were shortly to cost him his job. But Bannister, although historians of the Congo have ignored him, occupies a significant place in the evolution of the country for he was the first of a line of British consular officers whose devotion to what they considered to be their duty in the Congo State, coupled with their inquisitorial approach to it, was to ensure the reform of the Congo administration. Bannister quickly convinced himself that the complaints of the British immigrants were well founded and that they were really being cruelly treated.[2] Acting through

---

[1] Ibid.

[2] The following letter to the Colonial Secretary was characteristic:

'When I first came here the agreements were all made out as between the Congo State and labourers, the term "labourer" being also a euphemism for soldier. I had hundreds of complaints, and am still occupied with grave charges of cruelty practised on these men by officers of the State who stop short at nothing in brutality under the guise of discipline.

'When I complained I laid stress on the fact that the men had contracted to serve as labourers, and the State authorities had no right to submit them to so-called discipline. I stigmatized the whole thing as "fraudulent enlistment". Up to the present I have gained very little for these poor fellows my efforts being met by remarks from the Governor-General . . . to the effect that it was not my business to interfere, I must confine myself to commercial questions, pure and simple. That, however, did not deter me in the least, it simply had the opposite effect.

'One case in point. Some time ago (about June last) 14 Accra men came to me from a place several days' march from here. They had been sent by the commandant of the place to raid a town and seize men to

the local authorities in the West African colonies, he was able to secure a quick result.

The Colonial Office laid down conditions under which further recruitment in the British West African colonies would henceforth be permitted, namely: that the men should only be employed on the work for which they were engaged in the colony; that they should not be required to enter into any new contracts unless such contracts were executed before, and witnessed by, the British consular authority at Boma after careful explanation to the men; and, finally, that the wages of deceased emigrants should be regularly remitted to the colony from which they came.[1] These conditions, which were accepted by the Congo government, were made too late to stop the Accra administration from taking more drastic action. In the autumn of 1894 the governor had banned further recruitment from his colony 'until the government officers of the State responsible for the breaches of contract . . . and for the inhumanities

---

be sent to Boma as recruits. If the men ran away on their approach the women were to be seized and held as hostages until the men turned up. Five women were brought to camp. The Chief came in and released the women and then complained that two of them had been outraged on the road, and that a duck had been stolen. The Accra men were paraded, and then thrown face downward on the ground, one by one, and fifty lashes administered to each. One died a few days afterwards. Of course the commandant said "from fever".

'In the meantime, before the Chief of the town appeared, a brother of his who happened to be away at the time of the raid, appeared at the camp and was seized. On being questioned as to the whereabouts of the Chief he simply said he knew nothing as he had been away. The Commandant ordered his boy to bring a table knife and cut an ear off the native, which was promptly done. This and the flogging . . . so frightened the Accra men that they ran away. They are now serving 12 months' imprisonment each for "having deserted".' Bannister to Colonial Secretary, Accra, 13 October 1894, encl. in C.O. to F.O., 11 February 1895, FO 10/731. Cf. Bannister to Pickersgill, 24 January 1894, encl. in Pickersgill to Rosebery, 16 March 1894, FO 10/730, no. 14, Africa; Bannister to F.O., 17 June 1894, ibid., no. 1, Africa; Bannister to Pickersgill 28 December 1894, encl. in Pickersgill to Kimberley, 21 January 1895, FO 10/731, no. 7, Africa.

[1] Kimberley to Plunkett, 11 February 1895, FO 403/304, no. 18, Africa.

28

practised upon the men had been called to account, and
until the government of the State had taken steps to put an
end, once and all, to the recurrence of anything of the sort
hereafter'.[1] His action was backed by the Secretary of State
for the Colonies,[2] and was adopted by the Sierra Leone
administration.[3]

The Foreign Office, also, no longer remained passive and
the complaints of the immigrants were considered serious
enough to require a consular investigation.[4] Pickersgill was
charged with this investigation because Kimberley, who was
now at the Foreign Office, did not trust Bannister.[5] The
over-zealous vice-consul was in disgrace, having been convicted by a Congolese court of assaulting one of its officials.[6]
Pickersgill was instructed to proceed to Boma and obtain
full details of the complaints together with names and dates
and any corroborative evidence that he could discover so
that a formal protest could be lodged in Brussels.

When Pickersgill arrived at Boma Bannister had left and
the Elmina men who had complained of ill-treatment had
been conveniently repatriated by the Congo authorities.
Pickersgill, therefore, had as evidence only the notes which
Bannister had prepared on the cases. Relying on these, the
Consul reported that he was convinced of the accuracy of
Bannister's charges against the Congo administration. He

---

[1] W. Brandforth Griffith to Marquess of Ripon, 9 January 1895, encl.
in C.O. to F.O., 11 February 1895, F.O. 10/731.

[2] C.O. to F.O., 26 March 1895, ibid.

[3] Ag. Colonial Secretary, Freetown, to C. Barlatt, 12 September 1895,
encl. in C.O. to F.O. 18 December 1895, ibid.

[4] F.O. to Pickersgill, 7 March 1895, ibid., no. 7, Africa.

[5] Kimberley, 13 February 1895, ibid., minute.

[6] On 2 June 1894 Bannister boarded the *Akassa* which was carrying
a number of immigrants from West Africa to the Congo. He demanded
to see a list of them and their terms of engagement and when the Congo
State official refused Bannister snatched away the papers and shoved the
official aside. He was fined 500 francs and ordered to pay costs of the
action. These were subsequently remitted by the Congo government
following a protest by the Foreign Office. But the removal of Bannister
was requested and agreed to. H. P. Anderson, 31 July 1895, FO 10/644,
memorandum.

29

recommended, however, that no further action needed to be taken and that the

> refusal of the Gold Coast Administration to sanction any further contracts for service with the Free State and Lord Ripon's support of the Colonial action, form a practical rebuke which may, perhaps, be left for a time to make the impression which it certainly ought to produce, if the Belgians in Africa are not less civilized than the natives.[1]

Nevertheless, the Pickersgill inquiry led Joseph Chamberlain, the new Colonial Secretary, to proclaim a formal ban on further recruitment from the British West African colonies,[2] an action which was welcomed by the A.P.S.[3]

Van Eetvelde, the Congo Secretary of State, protested to the Foreign Office against the imputation, conveyed by the action of the Colonial Secretary, that the British subjects were barbarously treated,[4] and then took steps to obtain a repeal of the ban on recruitment. On 17 April he handed a note to the British ambassador in which he made a formal request for the withdrawal of the ban and put forward proposals for preventing the reoccurrence of abuses.[5] The British immigrants would present themselves before their consul at Boma and specify the special work for which they had engaged themselves, thereby obviating the complaint of having been employed as soldiers against their will, and similar precautions would also be taken at the port of embarkation. He also promised that the Congo government would again impress on all their agents the necessity of treating the men fairly. This move by Van Eetvelde was promptly followed, no doubt under his inspiration, by that of George Walford, an important British shareholder in the *Compagnie du Congo pour le commerce et l'industrie* and agent in Antwerp of the African Steamship Company, who called on the British ambassador in order to invoke his assistance in

---

[1] Pickersgill to Kimberley, 27 May 1895, FO 10/731.
[2] Hansard, 12 March 1896, 4th ser., xxxviii, 771–2.
[3] *A.F.*, April 1896.
[4] Plunkett to Salisbury, 27 March 1896, FO 10/731, no. 81, Africa.
[5] Plunkett to Salisbury, 18 April 1896, ibid., no. 93, Africa.

removing the ban. Walford urged that there had been much exaggeration in the accusations against the Congo State and he desired the British government to withdraw 'a prohibition which seriously hampered English interests in the Congo, and tended to throw that State more into French hands'.[1] Plunkett, too, was in favour of repealing the ban on the grounds of the injury which the British company might suffer.[2]

In London, F. W. Bond, President of the African Steamship Company, and Francis de Winton, a director of the company and first administrator of the Congo State, called on Anderson to make similar representations but the latter only referred them to the Colonial Office.[3] A few days later, Walford again addressed a letter to Chamberlain putting forward the same arguments as he had used in his interview with Plunkett.[4] The combined pressure from the Congo government and the African Steamship Company led Chamberlain to modify his attitude: prohibition was maintained with regard to recruitment for the services of the Congo State, but was to be allowed in the case of engagements for the Congo Railway Company in which the British businessmen had substantial interests.[5]

The settlement of this question of recruitment suitably in accord with British imperial interests was contemporaneous with and facilitated by the satisfactory settlement of the Stokes affair, which had for some time united Britain and Germany in joint diplomatic intervention at the seat of Congo government in Brussels. Charles Henry Stokes was a British trader of considerable importance in East Africa and had been specially popular among the Germans because he traded through their East African ports. On 2 August

---

[1] Plunkett to Salisbury, 2 May 1896, ibid., no. 103, Africa.

[2] '. . . I have reason to know, from other sources', Plunkett added, 'that the motive of the Congo Government in paying so high a subsidy to them for the mail service, is to secure the continuance of their services as recruiting agents.' Ibid.

[3] H. P. Anderson, 5 May 1896, FO 10/731, memorandum.

[4] Walford to Chamberlain, 16 May 1896, encl. in C.O. to F.O., 20 June 1896, ibid.

[5] C.O. to F.O., 2 June 1896, ibid.

1895 Count Metternich, the German minister in London, sent a brief note to Sanderson, Permanent Under-Secretary of State for Foreign Affairs, informing him that Stokes had been arrested in the Congo in January 1894 on a charge of supplying arms to the Arabs, had been tried by court-martial and executed.[1] This information, which the Congo government had succeeded so far in concealing, caused some stir in the Foreign Office and Plunkett was asked to obtain 'the fullest explanation' from the Congo government. Meanwhile the news of Stokes' fate had leaked to the British press, presumably from German sources, and it gave rise to strong condemnation of the Congo State.[2] Encouraged by this reaction, the German Foreign Minister threw out a hint that 'it was time these high-handed proceedings of the Congo government should be taken *au serieux*'.[3]

Although the Foreign Office was not taken in by the enthusiasm of the German government,[4] it also took a strong view of the incident. The response of the Congo government, which included documents on the trial, was regarded as unsatisfactory. One thing stood out clearly: Commandant Lothaire who had presided over the trial and had ordered the execution had blundered in not allowing Stokes an appeal to the court at Boma. Salisbury declared that 'there was no justification for the summary execution of Mr Stokes' and instructed Plunkett to address a note to the Congo

---

[1] Metternich to Sanderson, 2 August 1895, F.O. 10/652, private.

[2] E.g. *Pall Mall Gazette* declared in a leading article of 19 August 1895 that 'should absolute confirmation of the news arrive, this cold-blooded murder ought to raise a storm of indignation from the whole of Europe'.

[3] Gosselin (Berlin) to Salisbury, 23 August 1895, FO 10/652, no. 101, Africa. See also Gosselin to Salisbury, 30 August 1895, ibid., no. 104, Africa.

[4] According to Gosselin, 'there can be no doubt that the real reason which induces the German government to take up so keenly the case of Mr Stokes is not so much a personal interest in the fate of an unfortunate British subject, who was, it is true, on very good terms with the Colonial authorities in German East Africa, as the belief that Captain Lothaire's act will enable them once and for all to stop the efforts of the Congo government to monopolise the ivory trade from the Lakes Districts to the serious detriment of German East Africa.' Gosselin, 10 September 1895, ibid., minute.

Secretary of State inquiring whether the Congo government had brought Commandant Lothaire to trial, or intended bringing him to trial.[1] At the same time, it was decided to cancel the arrangement of 1890 by which the jurisdiction over British subjects was provisionally conceded to the Congo courts and the Law Officers of the Crown were requested to advise on the terms in which notice should be given to the Congo government of the intention of Britain to assume her right of extra-territoriality.[2]

This decision alarmed Plunkett, the brilliant and experienced diplomatist in Brussels. Appointed in 1893 to succeed Edmund Monson, whom Leopold II had not found 'conciliatory' after a year in Brussels,[3] Francis Plunkett was able until his departure in 1899 to maintain intimate relations with both the Congo and the Belgian governments. He had a way of ferreting out valuable information from the Congo Secretary of State and the Secretary-General of the Belgian Foreign Ministry and sometimes even acted as a go-between for the two Brussels governments.[4] Writing privately to Anderson he said: 'I trust we are not really going to insist on the resumption of extra-territorial jurisdiction in the Congo'; and he warned that it would be 'a grave mistake to insist on a right which would make a bitter enemy of the Congo State, and lead probably to dangerous discussions with France, under her claim to pre-emption'.[5] Three weeks later he again informed Anderson that Van Eetvelde had told him the Congo State was being harassed to death by

---

[1] Salisbury to Plunkett, 9 September 1895, ibid., no. 92, Africa.

[2] F.O. to Law Officers of the Crown, 11 September 1895, FO 403/219. The Law officers advised that they should refer to the terms of the treaty of 16 December 1884, especially to articles V and VI reserving extra-territorial jurisdiction to Britain and inform the Congo government of their decision to exercise it now. Law Officers to F.O., 26 September 1895, ibid.

[3] Rosebery to Queen Victoria, 5 April 1893, *L.Q.V.*, 3rd ser., i, 244.

[4] There was indeed no love lost between the two governments. Lambermont once irately called the Congo secretaries-general, the 'black ministers' of Leopold II. Monson to Rosebery, 13 October 1892, FO 84/2202, no. 90, Africa.

[5] Plunkett to Anderson, 15 September 1895, FO 10/652, private.

'chantage' of all kinds and if these were to continue the position of the king would become intolerable, and the existence of the Congo State might become impossible. Plunkett concluded that it showed 'how hard the Congo State is pressed, and what temptations they have to throw up the sponge and let the whole concern go to smash'.[1]

The frantic appeals by Plunkett had their effect and the idea of establishing consular courts was put aside. The Congo government, on its part, readily came to terms: it promised that Lothaire would be prosecuted; that an indemnity of 150,000 francs would be paid as consideration for the irregularity in the procedure followed at the trial; and that all the property belonging to Stokes would be restored.[2] Lothaire, however, was not brought to trial till the spring of 1896 and then he was acquitted.[3] But after the settlement of November Salisbury was satisfied.[4] The significance of the Stokes' affair is that it was the second time that Salisbury had had an opportunity of exercising the British right to consular jurisdiction and had waived it. In fact, without saying so, the right had by now been completely abandoned.

Meanwhile, although the Congo government had weathered the Anglo-German pressure, their troubles were only starting for it was at this time that complaints against the ill-treatment of the Congolese began to multiply.

---

[1] Plunkett to Anderson, 6 October 1895, ibid., private.

[2] Plunkett to Salisbury, 3 November 1895, ibid., no. 274, Africa. The German government received 100,000 fr. and was promised 1000 marks for each of Stokes' carriers who was not returned.

[3] Lothaire returned to the Congo in August 1897 as an employee of the *Société Commerciale Anversoise*. This company, Plunkett writes, is 'in reality nothing more than the King, who is trading under such a name'. Plunkett to Bertie, 5 September 1897, FO 10/686, private.

[4] See his minute of 18 December 1895, FO 10/654. 'Are we not becoming a trifle too hot in pursuit of Lothaire? To assert Her Majesty's rights, and to secure British subjects for the future, we have rightly insisted that Lothaire should be brought before a competent tribunal. But we have no interests in a severe sentence. Indeed if he were hanged it would be very inconvenient as it would make a sort of blood-feud between us and the Belgians.'

As early as 1888 British humanitarians had attacked the ruthlessness which Stanley, as agent of the Congo State as well as leader of the Emin Pasha Relief Expedition,[1] had shown at Stanley Falls in conniving at the plunder and destruction of African villages and recruiting slaves as carriers. What was perhaps worse in the eyes of his critics, he had appointed Tippu Tib, the notorious Arab slave trader, as Governor of Stanley Pool. The A.P.S. inspired a parliamentary question in the House of Commons,[2] but the Congo government emphatically denied the allegations. Nevertheless, they were confirmed by an officer in the expedition,[3] and the publication of Stanley's record of the expedition[4] strengthened rather than mitigated the case. Consequently, on 4 December 1890, the A.P.S. sponsored a public meeting 'for the purpose of considering recent disclosures as to the alleged ill-treatment of African natives by English and other adventurers in the Congo Free State'.[5] A resolution was adopted calling on the British government to take 'such action as may prevent the occurrence of similar offences in future'.[6] The public, unlike the Foreign Office, were in no doubt as to the right and the obligation of Britain to intervene officially in the Congo State.

At the same time, in the Congo State itself, travellers and missionaries were beginning to notice with increasing uneasiness what they described as the callous and inhuman methods of the administration. One of the earliest to launch an open attack on the situation was George Washington Williams, who has been described as the first negro historian.[7] Williams had seen in the Congo Free State another

---

[1] For details of this expedition see H. M. Stanley: *In Darkest Africa*, London 1890, 2 vols.; R. T. Anstey: *Britain and the Congo in the Nineteenth Century*, Oxford 1962, pp. 214 ff.; F. Masoin: op. cit., ii, 233–4.

[2] Hansard, 19 April 1888, 3rd ser., ccxxix, 1709.

[3] William Bonny.

[4] Stanley: op. cit. See also H. R. Fox Bourne: *The Other Side of the Emin Pasha Relief Expedition*, London 1891.

[5] *A.F.*, April 1891.

[6] Ibid.

[7] P. McStallworth: *The United States and the Congo Question*, 1884–1914, Ph.D., Ohio State University 1954, p. 196. I am indebted to Dr R. Slade for making this thesis available to me.

Early Evidence on Congo Maladministration

Liberia where educated American negroes could be usefully established and his visit to the Congo in February 1890 was a fact-finding mission. He was bitterly disappointed by the economic and administrative principles and practices of the State which he witnessed and he published startling denunciations of the Congo system.[1] His early death in August 1891 coupled with the fact that the king-sovereign took care to discredit him in advance,[2] saved the Congo government from what might have been an embarrassingly formidable opponent.

From 1891 onwards Williams was followed by other critics of the Congo administration. They included missionaries like George Grenfell and W. L. Forfeitt who observed with apprehension the unsatisfactory treatment to which the Congolese were being subjected by the officials of the administration.[3] In June 1895 Walter H. Stapleton reported to Alfred Baynes, secretary of the B.M.S., how State soldiers had looted and destroyed a town, killing two men and two children whose right hands were then cut off.[4] There had been no reason for the raid, he said, except to incite the town against their neighbours from whom the attacking troops had been drawn. Reviewing the position so far he wrote:

> The State has driven away all the people from near our station at Kinchassa. At Lukolela there is left but a mere handful just the work people [sic] and a few of their relatives. This

[1] These are contained in the following:

(a) 'An Open letter to His Serene Majesty Leopold II, King of the Belgians and Sovereign of the Independent State of the Congo', 18 July 1890. Copy in the archive of the American Antiquarian Society, Worcester, Massachusetts.

(b) Williams to Blaine (Secretary of State), 15 September 1890, Department of State, Miscellaneous Letters, September, Part I, 1890.

(c) 'A Report upon the Congo State and Country to the President of the Republic of the United States', 14 October 1890. Copy in the archive of the American Antiquarian Society, Worcester, Massachusetts.

[2] E.g. Vivian to Salisbury, 4 April 1891, FO 84/2118, no. 23, Africa, confidential.

[3] R. Slade: *English-speaking Missions in the Congo Independent State*, 1878–1908, Brussels 1959, pp. 239 ff.

[4] Stapleton to Baynes, 14 June 1895, B.M.S. Papers.

district is miserable compared to its condition six years ago. We have six groups of towns. During the past five years the group above us has been burned out twice; Bondembu below us, three times; Mongala below that, twice; further down still Bokemila, twice; now the towns are cleared out at our very doors. . . . The districts occupied by the American Mission are in like condition. . . . Bwemba is disappearing. Equator station has but a very few people left, Irebo has been devastated and made into a State camp. The missionary of the last station opened by that society on Lake Mantumba has seen a big population driven away before his eyes. If the peoples of the Upper Congo were subject to an administration characterized by the barest elements of justice the prospects of our work would be bright with hope, but I am day by day forced into the conviction that unless some radical change in the government soon comes we are largely wasting our money and strength.[1]

Concluding this remarkable testimony Stapleton berated the home committee and his superiors in the Congo for 'endeavouring at all costs to avoid hurting the susceptibilities of the State'.

By allowing the State authorities to see that we looked for and expected to get favours in the matter of taxation and to be favoured in State administrative regulations, we have sacrificed that independent attitude by which alone we could hope to directly influence their policy. In my judgment the State would not have dared to have committed many of the outrages that disgrace its name in the face of the moral pressure the [Baptist Missionary Society] from an independent stand point could have brought to bear.[2]

If Stapleton had thought that he could change the policy of his home committee he was to be disillusioned. Neither the B.M.S. nor the C.B.M., the most important British missionary organizations in the State, was prepared to indict the administration publicly or to invoke the diplomatic

---

[1] Ibid.
[2] Ibid.

support of the Foreign Office. Both considered at this time that the maintenance of friendly relations with the Congo authorities was of paramount importance in the expansion of their activities.[1] Consequently they restricted themselves to making representations in Brussels which in the end proved futile.

Under these circumstances, the sources from which stories of atrocities committed in the Congo became current in England were not, as might have been expected, from the large number of British missionaries serving in the Congo, but from secular witnesses or from non-British missionaries.

In 1894 Bannister had hinted that the events in the Lower Congo which he saw and heard of were 'insignificant' compared with what was 'perpetrated in the regions of the Upper Congo'.[2] He would probably have investigated further if he had not been overwhelmed by the complaints of British immigrants and, perhaps, deterred by his instruction not to interfere in the internal administration of the State. It is also possible that his premature withdrawal frustrated any such intentions on his part. Soon after his departure, the acting British consul in Loanda, A. Nightingale, forwarded a signed statement from one Matook, an Indian and a former State interpreter in the Upper Congo, in which the Congo authorities were accused of the gravest abuses.[3] Matook himself promised to visit the British embassy in Brussels and furnish more details about 'the Slavery which the officers of the State encourage in the High Congo, and the ill-treatment of the poor natives, burning their villages, seizing their wives and children, taking men by force and making them soldiers . . .' Anderson, who was impressed by the evidence, described it as 'a fearful array of charges' which though 'there may be exaggeration' nevertheless bore 'the stamp of truth'.[4]

Similarly, Henry Kennedy Smythe, an English doctor,

---

[1] Slade: *English-speaking Missions*, pp. 264–5.

[2] Bannister to Colonial Secretary, Accra, 13 October 1894, encl. in C.O. to F.O., 11 February 1895, FO 10/731.

[3] Nightingale to F.O., 26 August 1895, 11 February 1895, ibid., no. 22, Africa.

[4] Anderson, n.d., ibid., minute.

wrote to inform Salisbury that four years ago he had witnessed at Lusambo, on the Kasai, how the administration
encouraged slavery and slave-raiding. He added that 'flogging of both sexes with the lash of dried hippopotamus hide'
was of frequent occurrence, and that a Congo official made
the boast, 'je frappe pour sauter le sang'.[1] The following year
statements of the same sort continued to reach the Foreign
Office. Vice-consul Leonard Arthur, who had been appointed to succeed Bannister, reported:

> I have also ascertained, from a purely private source of
> information, that Captain Francqui was in the habit of sending
> out small parties of troops under a non-commissioned officer
> to the villages and neighbourhoods for the purpose of demand-
> ing ivory and rubber. If these articles were not forthcoming, he
> would dispatch another armed party to attack the natives. On
> the return of the party the non-commissioned officer in charge
> would report that so many natives had been killed. This,
> however, would not satisfy Captain Francqui, who demanded
> proofs in the form of human hands that the number stated had
> been killed, and the armed party would again be sent out for
> this purpose, returning in due course with the right hands of
> the natives who had been killed, and having seized whatever
> ivory and india-rubber that could be found in the village.[2]

Three months later he commented that the West Africans
in the Congo were still being ill-treated,[3] a confirmation of
information already elicited by Anderson during an interview with Captain Salisbury, an English officer who had
recently returned from service with the Congo State.[4]

In addition to the evidence coming directly to the Foreign
Office, there were also the sensational charges of brutality

---

[1] Smythe to Salisbury, 10 September 1895, FO 403/219.
[2] Arthur to Salisbury, 20 July 1896, FO 10/731, no. 26, Africa, confidential.
[3] Arthur to Salisbury, 19 October 1896, FO 403/304.
[4] Anderson, 21 August 1896, FO 10/649, memorandum. The views of
Captain Salisbury were also printed in *United Services Magazine*, June
1896.

against officials of the Congo State which featured prominently in the British press. These charges were laid by three outstanding witnesses. The first was J. B. Murphy, an American missionary from Equatorville, who denounced the Congo State's lust for rubber to Reuters Agency and confirmed the stories of mutilation of Congolese by rubber agents.[1] A similar interview was next given, again to Reuters Agency, by an Englishman, Alfred Parminter, whose record in the service of the Congo State lent great weight to his statements.[2] Parminter alleged that the Congo government had not established any administration beyond the river banks and that 'the country is, as it was in 1884, one dense, swampy forest, absolutely unknown to Europeans'. He pointed out that since 1884 the condition of the natives had considerably deteriorated and he ascribed this to the inexperience of the Belgian officers as well as to the impossibility of checking their actions from the headquarters. On the current question of brutality and mutilation, the following was one of the examples he gave in confirmation of its existence:

> On one occasion, at Bopoto, having dined with lieutenant Blochteur . . . I was smoking with him on the bank. It was late in the evening when suddenly a force of his troops returned from an expedition on which he had sent them in the morning. The sergeant held up triumphantly a number of ears fastened together on a string . . . [The soldiers] were praised for their success, and ordered to return next day and capture the chief.

Finally, there was the evidence of Reverend Sjöblom of the Swedish Baptist Church which was given great prominence in the Swedish, French, Belgian as well as the British press,

---

[1] R. Slade: *King Leopold's Congo*, Oxford 1962, pp. 179–80; *The Times*, 18 November 1895; *Daily Chronicle*, 18 November 1895; etc.

[2] From 1884 to 1886 Parminter worked under Stanley and Francis de Winton on the Lower Congo. Between 1887 and 1893 he was employed by the *Société anonyme belge* as director of the Congo Transport Service and from 1893 to 1895 he was in command of the commercial district of the Upper Congo. *The Standard*, 8 September 1896. Parminter later became a director of the *Société belge du Haut Congo*. Supra, p. 24.

and which confirmed earlier stories of the ill-treatment of the Congolese.[1]

The unanimity of the evidence is impressive and the details offered reflect the authenticity of most of the evidence. But even if there were doubts as to this, the despatches of Plunkett, who had the confidence of Van Eetvelde, tend to dispel them. In October 1895, for example, Plunkett had reported that the Congo Secretary of State admitted that there was some foundation for many of the horrid stories.[2] A year later, he again wrote that Van Eetvelde had made a similar admission to him.[3]

The Congo government was alarmed by the influence which the charges were having on foreign opinion. The press in France and Germany, for example, were reprinting the stories of atrocities and commenting adversely on the Congo State. It was realized that some dramatic and significant action had to be taken to check the chorus of these criticisms. In September 1896, therefore, a decree was promulgated by the Congo government instituting a Commission for the Protection of the Natives and at the same time a State Inspector to ensure the enforcement of government decrees was appointed.[4] The appointment to the commission of six missionaries, three Catholics and three Protestants, separated by hundreds of miles of territory, with scarcely any means of transportation and weighted down by onerous pastoral duties, in order to superintend the activities of State officials scattered over nearly 900,000 square miles, was not a practical measure

---

[1] E.g. *Le Patriote*, 19 September 1896, quotes Sjöblom: 'When the the soldiers of the Free State are sent on an expedition to "punish the rebels" of a village', he says, 'they are ordered to bring back the right hand of each of their victims and in order to prevent putrefaction until the day when they will be shown to the commissioner, these hands are smoked.'

[2] Plunkett to Salisbury, 20 October 1895, FO 10/642, no. 263, Africa, very confidential.

[3] Plunkett to Salisbury, 26 September 1896, FO 403/304, no. 251, Africa, very confidential.

[4] *B.O.*, no. 9, September 1896; Slade: *English-speaking Missions*, pp. 247-9.

of reform.[1] But it satisfied the Foreign Office who were in any case anxious not to intervene.[2] On the other hand, the measure merely whetted the appetite of the A.P.S. for more reform and it now launched its severest attack yet.[3]

While welcoming the appointment of the commission and the State Inspector, the Society expressed the fear that the proposed measures were *'quite inadequate'*.[4] At the same time it despatched letters to the Foreign Office and to Leopold II enclosing a long and detailed memorandum which criticized, on the basis of the decrees promulgated by the State, the administrative and economic principles on which the country was being run.[5] This remarkable document, prepared by H. R. Fox Bourne, the indefatigable secretary of the society, embodies all the arguments subsequently elaborated by Morel and the Congo Reform Association. The last paragraphs vividly summarize the society's gravamen and remedy:

> Through more than ten years the State has been becoming more and more of a trading enterprise, a monopoly in itself and a dispenser of monopolies, instead of an agency for opening up Central Africa to the free trade of the civilized world. Through more than ten years it has been becoming more and more of an oppressor of natives, instead of an organization for protecting their legitimate interests and promoting their welfare.
>
> The time has surely arrived when the Powers that agreed upon what was supposed to be a great and necessary philanthropic work, and sought in the Brussels General Act to improve

---

[1] The composition of the commission was criticized at the time by Grenfell, one of its members. See H. H. Johnston: *George Grenfell and the Congo*, London 1908, ii, 440; Slade: *English-speaking Missions*, ibid.

[2] H. Farnall, n.d., minute on Plunkett to Salisbury, 22 September 1896, FO 10/731.

[3] Cf. Slade, who concludes, however, that 'the mere appointment of the commission seemed sufficient to check criticism of the Congo State in Europe'. Slade: *King Leopold's Congo*, p. 180.

[4] *A.F.*, December 1896.

[5] *A.F.*, December 1896. A.P.S. to Salisbury, 12 December 1896, FO 10/731.

upon their plans in the Berlin General Act, should insist on the terms of the agreement being carried out.[1] The Congo government was sufficiently alarmed by this protest to inquire discreetly at the Foreign Office what reply they proposed making to the society.[2] When they were assured that the Foreign Office would not move in the matter, they, too, sent no reply.

Farnall advised that there was evidence that the Congo government was becoming alive to its responsibilities and that it was too early to dismiss the recently appointed commission as a failure.[3] When the society received this opinion, it came forward with another remarkable declaration, the far-reaching implications of which were not immediately appreciated. Rejecting the optimism of the Foreign Office, the society declared that

> as most of these abuses are the direct and almost inevitable outcome of rules and methods of procedure appointed and sanctioned by successive Decrees of the Sovereign of the Congo State . . . no adequate reform can be looked for until the Decrees now in force have been suitably modified.[4]

The issues raised in the memorandum of 12 December and the subsequent letter to Salisbury were to place the Congo squarely in the realm of international diplomacy early in the twentieth century. It was the first time that the reports of the atrocities committed in the Congo State had been directly linked with the legislation existing in that country and the responsibility of the powers to intervene invoked. The Congo question had thus emerged from a mere proliferation of sensational stories to an academic discussion of colonial principles and the observance of treaty obligations. Its further development is the subject of the next chapters.

---

[1] Ibid.

[2] Ministère des Affaires Etrangères to Whetnall, 21 January 1897, Ier sér., Congo, ii, 553.

[3] Farnall, 12 December 1896, FO 10/731, minute; *A.F.*, December 1896.

[4] A.P.S. to Salisbury, 23 December 1896, FO 10/731; *A.F.*, December 1896.

But at this point the Foreign Office refused to face the issues involved and it was vaguely asserted that the circumstances were not such as to call for interference by the British government.[1]

The appointment of the Commission for the Protection of Natives, therefore, although it had been a shrewd move to stem the rising tide of criticism against the Congo government, especially in Great Britain, had failed to attain that objective. Indeed, following the publication of the A.P.S. memorandum, a fierce press controversy developed. In Belgium all the newspapers, with the exception of the socialist *Le Peuple* and the radical *La Réforme*, rallied to the support of the Congo State and attacked the English critics. In England a heated debate for and against the Congo State was being waged in the opinion columns of *The Times*, principally between Hugh Gilzean Reid and Jules Houdret[2] on the one hand and Fox Bourne and Charles W. Dilke on the other.

In January 1897 it was considered necessary by the Congo government to issue a lengthy memorandum defending its administration and justifying its legislation.[3] This was clearly an indirect response to the action already taken by the A.P.S. The memorandum, which was signed by the Congo Secretary of State, after referring briefly to the growing prosperity of the State, affirmed that the government 'considers it to be one of its first duties to observe faithfully the obligations which it has contracted'. The Congo State, it went on, had put down the slave trade, protected and encouraged missionary enterprise without distinction as to creed, and assured to all flags the free navigation of its waters. It had also not established any kind of monopoly. On the question of what it called *droits de propriété* that had been created in the State, the memorandum quoted the

---

[1] 'Interference', Hill commented, 'would be useless even if it were justifiable, and it would moreover be a dangerous precedent.' C. Hill, 6 January 1897, FO 10/731, minute.

[2] Consul for Belgium in London since 1886 and consul-general for the Congo State since 1891. *B.O.*, February–March 1892.

[3] *B.O.*, no. 1, January 1897; *A.F.*, May 1897.

opinion of some international jurists as well as the colonial legislation of Germany, France and Great Britain to show that the provisions of the Berlin Act had not been contravened. Turning to the practice of taxation in kind and the use of forced labour, it was maintained that the former would disappear with the introduction of money and that the latter was essential for the development of the country. The memorandum ended by describing the administrative and judicial system of the Congo State, which it regarded as adequate, and also the network of road, river and rail communications already constructed.

As a reply to the case brought against it by the A.P.S., the Congo State memorandum, although superficially impressive, was weak indeed. In particular, it failed to refute the charge that the State itself had become a trading concern or that the administrative and economic policy of the government inevitably led to abuses which could not be satisfactorily checked by judicial proceedings. It was therefore not surprising that the A.P.S. was more than ever determined to press forward its case.

Having failed to move the British government to action by direct appeals, the society changed its tactics and attempted to force the hand of the government through parliament. It was planned that on the motion for adjournment, Dilke, one of the parliamentary spokesmen of the society and henceforth an unrelenting critic of the Congo administration, should move that

> It is the duty of the Foreign Office to consult European Powers having possessions in Africa as to whether they will attend a Conference at which measures agreed to at the Berlin Conference of 1884–85 and the Brussels Conference of 1889–90 with questions appertaining thereto, shall be considered with a view to the adoption and enforcement of further measures for securing equitable treatment of the natives of Africa.[1]

---

[1] Hansard, 2 April 1897, 4th ser., xlviii; *A.F.*, May 1897. The plan was foiled because a motion by another member on a different subject had been negatived earlier and according to the rules of the House, a second vote could not be taken.

The motive of Dilke in bringing forward this motion has been generally attributed to his desire to prove that British commercial and philanthropic opinion had been mistaken in opposing the Anglo-Portuguese Congo Treaty, which he had favoured while he was Parliamentary Under-Secretary for Foreign Affairs.[1] This might well have been the case although there is no evidence to show that he had nursed this disappointment for thirteen years or that it was sufficient to keep him in the forefront of the Congo reform movement for the next fifteen years. It might be pointed out, on the other hand, that Dilke was a humanitarian as well as a radical, and it is more likely that his interest in the Congo question was based on principles rather than on pique or wounded pride.[2]

Dilke seized the opportunity to denounce European administration in Africa generally and singled out the Congo State as a classic example. It was not a good speech on tactical grounds and he also erred on the evidence adduced to support the denunciations. It was indeed strange tactics to call on Great Britain to initiate a conference of the powers to consider accusations against the Royal Niger Company and other British protectorates, and it was factually wrong to charge the Congo administration with making gin its chief article of trade or to assert that S. L. Hinde[3] had accused Baron Dhanis, the Belgian commander of the Congo Arab campaign, of having rationed his troops with smoked human hands.[4] Nor did Dilke's subsequent assertion to the London correspondent of a Brussels newspaper[5] that he desired a partition of the Congo among Germany, France and Britain

---

[1] E.g. Slade: *King Leopold's Congo*, p. 181; A. Stenmans: *La reprise du Congo par la Belgique*, Brussels 1949, p. 220; D. C. Bougler: *The Reign of Leopold II*, London 1925, ii, 100.

[2] Cf. Gwynn and Tuckwell: *Life of Sir Charles W. Dilke*, London 1917, ii, 377–9.

[3] Dr Hinde was the author of the book, *The Fall of the Congo Arabs*, London 1897.

[4] For a refutation of statements made by Dilke in this speech see leading article by A. J. Wauters in *Mouvement Géographique*, 18 April 1897. Wauters himself was also a critic of the State.

[5] *Le Soir*, 9 April 1897.

aid the cause for Congo reform. Such a statement by a former member of the British government and prominent leader of the anti-Congo campaign was a useful weapon with which to whip up sympathy against what a Belgian paper dismissed as the rapacity of so-called philanthropists.[1]

Nevertheless, in Belgium as in Britain, the circle of Congo-phobes was widening. It was joined by the socialists and radicals, who found in the agitation a means of attacking the monarchy as well as embarrassing the ruling Catholic party which supported and defended the king. G. Lorand, the radical leader, mounted an attack against the king and his administration in the Congo from the platform of the newspaper, *La Réforme*.[2] In three consecutive issues the *Indépendance Belge*[3] also gave prominent place to reports from its Congo correspondent who was very critical of the excessive severity of Congo State officers. But the most serious and objective criticism of the régime installed in the Congo was made in 1898 by an eminent Belgian expert on Colonial Law, Professor Felicien Cattier.[4]

The culmination of this phase of Belgian hostility towards the Congo came in 1900 when reports of the repression of the Budja revolt was made known. The Budjas of Mongalla, it was alleged, driven to desperation by the incessant demands for rubber and the atrocities committed by the agents of the Anversoise when enough rubber was not forthcoming, had killed four Europeans. An expedition was despatched against them and no fewer than 1,300 were massacred.[5]

Relying on this report, Lorand put in an interpellation in

---

[1] *Belgique Coloniale*, 11 April 1897. Plunkett reported that Van Eetvelde regarded the British attack as 'inspired by the same motives as Dr. Jameson's famous raid'. Plunkett to Salisbury, 11 April, 1897, FO 403/304, no. 55, Africa, confidential.

[2] E.g. *La Réforme*, 21 April 1897.

[3] *Indépendance Belge*, 29 and 30 June, and 1 July 1897. The paper itself remained sceptical of the reports.

[4] Cattier, *Droit et Administration, passim.*

[5] *Petit Bleu*, 3 April, 17 April and 26 April 1900. *Le Patriote*, 12 April, 15 April 1900; *La Réforme*, 13 April 1900. See also Major Pulteney to Salisbury, 10 May 1899, FO 2/217.

the Belgian Chamber but the issue was skilfully evaded by the Belgian government. 'This State', the Foreign Minister declared, 'is for us a foreign State, in whose administration the Belgian government cannot interfere, no more than it can be held responsible for what it decides.'[1] The *Petit Bleu*, on the other hand, declared that the administration of the Congo State, staffed as it was by Belgians, must be of direct concern to all Belgians and it declared that it had opened an impartial inquiry with the purpose of purifying the Congo and aiding the repression of abuses. Its efforts in this direction, however, seem to have ended with the publication of two more pieces of condemnatory evidence from the Congo[2] for it soon became an ardent supporter of the administration.

In England, at the same time, the A.P.S. had placed the Congo in the forefront of its activities and it continued to maintain its demand for a fresh European Conference on Africa.[3] The Society was helped in sustaining interest in the Congo question by further evidence of atrocities which continued to feature in the British press. The most sensational of these came from two Englishmen, E. J. Glave and Lieutenant Frank J. Andrew. Glave had served in various capacities in the Congo since 1883 and had died at Matadi in May 1895. In September 1897, the *Century Magazine* carried long extracts from the diary he had kept from 1884 in which he accused the State of conducting its pacification of the country after the fashion of the Arabs. He also alleged that villagers who refused to furnish rubber were 'attacked, and killed, or taken prisoners'. Andrew served as *chef de station* at Barumba on the Upper Congo. An extract from his evidence which appeared in several London newspapers is revealing and deserves quoting in full:

> The Lower river from the coast to the railway terminus at Leopoldville is quiet and fairly civilised, but once Leopoldville is left a region in which perpetual war reigns is entered. From Leopoldville to the distant shores of Tanganyika the whole

---

[1] *Annales Parlementaires* (Chambre), 19 April 1900.
[2] *Petit Bleu*, 2 May and 11 May 1900.
[3] E.g. *A.F.*, May 1897.

interior is the scene of fighting in some form or another. There is, perhaps, scarcely a single post on the whole of the Congo at which a portion of the garrison is not absent on expeditions against the natives. . . . Personally I saw no actual barbarities, as my station was coffee and not rubber-producing. But that they exist as badly as ever I have no doubt. They are the direct outcome of the rubber and ivory trade. A Lieutenant's pay on the Congo is about £200 per annum, but on a rubber station another £300 can be made on rubber commission. On reaching their posts, officers are told how much rubber is expected from each village. If that amount does not come in . . . war is made against that village, and natives are killed, the black soldiers, in order to justify their statements as to the number dead, afterwards cutting off hands and ears.[1]

But even before these accounts appeared in the press, the Foreign Office had received a report from its representative in the Congo confirming the existence of a cruel system of government in that country. In July 1897, Pickersgill submitted a memorandum commenting on the evidence of Sjöblom and his colleague, Charles Banks. 'At first', Pickersgill wrote, 'I was disposed to doubt the correctness of the statements which he and his companions made . . . but after questioning them closely I came to the conclusion that I was dealing with truthful men, who were speaking of things with which they were well acquainted.' He adduced two reasons for the existence of abuses. In the first place, he claimed that the officials of the State were left free to perpetrate abuses. Next, he asserted that 'the barbarities referred to are but the natural outcome of the system of government'. He went on:

Equatorial Africa and its climate are notoriously brutalising . . . . In such country and such a climate put a rough-grained Belgian army officer unaccustomed to the management of coloured races and untrained to civil government, give him absolute power over the native population, and orders to raise revenue to the utmost of his ability; above him place a military autocrat of a governor, as sternly determined to be obeyed as if he were at the head of a regiment; and,

---

[1] *A.F.*, June 1899; *The Times*, 25 May 1899.

higher still, appoint a resolute Minister, desirous above all things of proving his royal master's enterprise to be commercially sound, and the train is fully laid for exactions enforced by cruelty. The Minister fires the Governor, and the Governor fires the Commissaire, and the whole force of the explosion falls upon wretched aborigines.

Pickersgill concluded that 'the amazing thing about the Congo atrocities is not that they have occurred, but that they have been so impudently denied'.[1] So impressed was the Foreign Office with the Pickersgill report that it seemed for a while that some action would be taken against the Congo government. It was generally agreed that the Congo administration was 'horrible'[2] and Salisbury instructed that the report should be printed for the Cabinet.[3] But although this was done no further action was taken. When Leopold II visited Salisbury in June 1897 he was able to remark that the attitude of the Prime Minister was 'très conciliante'.[4]

Two years later another consular officer in the Congo was to report that accusations against the excessive severity of State and concessionnaire agents were 'substantially correct'.[5] In a subsequent report he referred to the earlier statements of Pickersgill and confirmed the existence of grave abuses.[6]

---

[1] 'Congo Atrocities: Remarks by Mr. Pickersgill', 1 June 1897, FO 10/731, confidential.

[2] See minutes by Hill, 3 June; Bertie, 3 June; Curzon, 7 June 1897, ibid.

[3] Salisbury, n.d., ibid., minute.

[4] Whetnall to Favereau, 5 June 1897, Ier sér., Congo, ii, 594.

[5] Pulteney to Salisbury, 10 May 1899, FO 2/217.

[6] 'The methods employed in the collection of rubber are cruel in the extreme, and are the cause of much bloodshed; an example of what is done was told me up the Ubangi. This officer told me he had instructions to collect rubber in the district between Yakoma and Congo Ute. His method of procedure was to arrive in canoes at a village, the inhabitants of which invariably bolted on their arrival; the soldiers were then landed, and commenced looting, taking all the chickens, grain, etc., out of the houses; after this they attacked the natives until able to seize their women; these women were kept as hostages until the Chief of the district brought in the required number of kilogrammes of rubber.

'The rubber having been brought, the women were sold back to their owners for a couple of goats a-piece, and so he continued from village

It is clear, then, that in the period after 1885 there was abundant evidence on which the British government could have justified an intervention in the Congo if this had been desired. The question naturally arises why it did not intervene now as it was to do later. Already reasons of a general character have been suggested. But there was a special reason, connected with the future of the Upper Nile Valley, why it was not wise to pursue a policy hostile to Leopold II.[1]

British policy in the Southern Sudan after the occupation of Egypt was directed towards the exclusion of any major European power from the headwaters of the Nile. Such a policy seemed to have been achieved in 1890 with the signing of the Anglo-German agreement. Britain, however, reckoned without the ambitions of Leopold II who, as has been mentioned, wanted an access to the Nile. Already he had secured a treaty with Sir William Mackinnon which granted the latter's Imperial British East Africa Company a strip of territory five miles wide between Lakes Tanganyika and Edward. In return, the company had agreed to recognize the sovereign rights of the Congo State over territories lying to the west of the Nile from Lake Albert in the south to Lado in the north. This agreement, to which Salisbury gave an equivocal assent, afforded Leopold II a cover for despatching an expedition towards the Nile Valley.

By the winter of 1892 reports that Congo troops had advanced to the Upper Nile were widespread. The exact position of the expedition was the subject of speculation and the Congo government evaded Foreign Office demands for assurance that the rights of Britain in the Upper Nile would

---

to village until the requisite amount of rubber had been collected.' Memo., encl. in Pulteney to F.O. 15 September 1899, FO 10/731, no. 5, Congo, confidential.

[1] Details of the diplomatic history of the Upper Nile Valley lie outside the scope of the present work. They could be followed in A. J. P. Taylor: 'Prelude to Fashoda: The Question of the Upper Nile, 1894–5', *English Historical Review*, 1950, lxv, 52–80; W. Langer: *The Diplomacy of Imperialism*, New York 1956, pp. 101–41; R. O. Collins: 'The Anglo-Congolese Negotiations, 1900–1906', *Zaire*, 1958, xii, 479–91. G. N. Sanderson: *England, Europe and the Upper Nile, 1882–1899*, Edinburgh 1965, is the latest and best account.

be respected. Meanwhile the French, following the conclusion of the Franco-German Agreement of 4 February 1894
which gave them free access to the Nile, were preparing for
a march on Lado or Fashoda. At the same time it was known
that they were negotiating with Leopold II in order to secure
their route to the Nile Valley. These developments alarmed
the Foreign Office for Britain was as yet not in a position to
defend the strategic Upper Nile. Since the French threat
was more formidable it was considered safer to reach an
understanding with Leopold II as soon as possible. The
result was the well-known Anglo-Congolese agreement dated
12 May 1894, a month later than the actual date in order to
avoid French displeasure, the terms of which were similar to
the earlier agreement between Leopold II and Mackinnon.

For Britain the agreement of 12 May meant first, that a
wedge of Congolese territory was temporarily thrown between
the advancing French expedition and the Nile and second,
that the Cape-to-Cairo route could be completed through the
corridor acquired from the Congo State. Leopold II on his
part considered himself fortunate that he had obtained a fairly
free hand to pursue his Nile schemes. These expectations,
however, were to be frustrated by the joint pressure of France
and Germany. The French were angry that while negotiations were proceeding between them and Leopold II with
regard to the Upper Nile Valley he had entered into an
agreement with Britain on the same subject and thereby
barred their way to the Nile. The Germans, on their part,
resented the fact that Britain had kept them in the dark
about the Anglo-Congolese negotiations and the method by
which they had secured the corridor to the west of their
East African colony. In the end Britain had to renounce the
corridor and France obtained a modification of her boundary
with the Congo State which left open the route to the Nile.

France now renewed her advance to the Nile. So also did
Leopold II. At the same time he tried to maintain friendly
relations with both the English and the French and carefully
fostered the impression that he might take the side of one
power or the other in the race to the Nile. The prospect of
a Franco-Congolese collaboration in the Nile question was

one which the Foreign Office could not ignore for both countries together were better placed strategically for arriving at the Nile before Britain was ready to assert herself there. It became imperative, therefore, that nothing should be done by Britain to drive the Congo State into the arms of France; or, what was worse, to surrender the Congo State to France under her right of pre-emption.

This was clearly the fear of Plunkett for he was convinced that the king-sovereign had no regard for 'the ordinary rules of common honesty'.[1] In 1895 when reports of atrocities were reaching Europe in greater numbers Plunkett was insistent that if Britain took action it might compel the Congo government to hand over its territory to France.[2] Following the Stokes affair he had also warned that 'any attempt on the part of Great Britain to resume her extra-territorial jurisdiction . . . will throw the [Congo State] straight into the arms of France'.[3] Six months later, as the Congolese expedition penetrated farther into the Nile Valley, Plunkett suggested that the king-sovereign was 'preparing there an "effective occupation" which at any suitable moment he hopes to utilize, either with England or with France, as may seem to be most profitable to himself'.[4]

There is evidence that this apprehension of a Franco-Congolese understanding communicated itself to the Foreign Office. Salisbury, explaining why he did not wish to encounter Leopold II on business more than he could help, said it was because if he gave 'too rough a refusal' the king-sovereign might 'rush at once into the arms of the French'.[5] Similarly in September 1896 Salisbury expressed a 'shrewd suspicion' that Leopold II might help the French to get to the Nile[6] and considered it essential, therefore, to conciliate the king-sovereign. Thus strategic considerations regarding

[1] Plunkett to Salisbury, 15 November 1896, S.P., A/49.
[2] Supra, p. 33.
[3] Plunkett to Salisbury, 14 June 1896, FO 10/665, no. 150A, Africa, confidential.
[4] Plunkett to Hill, 31 January 1897, FO 10/685, private.
[5] Salisbury to Arthur Bigge, 5 December 1895, *L.Q.V.*, 3rd ser., ii, 578.
[6] Salisbury to Arthur Bigge, 2 September 1896, *L.Q.V.*, 3rd ser., iii, 72–3.

---

the Nile Valley were a factor of cardinal importance which must have acted as a brake to any move on the part of the Foreign Office to intervene in the Congo question.

By the spring of 1896 the British government had decided to establish its influence on the Upper Nile Valley. As the French had sent an expedition under Captain Marchand towards the same destination the prospect of a clash between Britain and France drew nearer. Meanwhile, Leopold II, tired of the lukewarmness with which his Nile schemes were greeted at Downing Street, now thought that he would gain more if he worked with the French. Consequently, the Marchand expedition was given every facility to travel through the Congo State and Leopold II also despatched an expedition of his own to ensure that his interests were physically represented in the Nile Valley. Misfortune, however, overtook the Congo State expedition, for its African troops mutinied. During the next couple of years the energies of the Congo government were absorbed in putting down the mutiny and therefore it could not exercise any influence on events in the Upper Nile Valley. Here Kitchener, fresh from his victory over the Dervishes, confronted Marchand at Fashoda and the French thought it better to withdraw than to fight.

It might have been expected that with the issue of the Nile thus settled the Foreign Office would have felt its hands free to deal with the Congo question. Indeed, on the eve of Fashoda, Salisbury had instructed that a catalogue should be prepared 'of all the brutalities imputed to the Congo Government',[1] and three years later he was still wanting the catalogue to be kept up to date 'for at any time we might need it'.[2] Events in South Africa culminating in the Anglo-Boer war, however, then supervened to distract attention from Congo affairs.

Nevertheless, a trend had gradually emerged in Anglo-Congo State relations; there was a growing disenchantment

---

[1] Salisbury, n.d., minute on Pickersgill's report 1 June 1897, FO 10/731. See also W. R. Louis: 'Roger Casement and the Congo', *J.A.H.*, vol. v, no. 1, 1964, p. 100.

[2] Salisbury, 30 April 1900, FO 10/754, minute.

with the administration of the Congo. The increasing volume of testimony against the commercial monopoly introduced into the Congo basin, the harrowing details of atrocities committed by officers of the State and the agents of commercial companies, all these were beginning to work in favour of British intervention.

III
Origins of British Intervention

The unique feature of the popular agitation in Britain in the years already considered is that the movement lacked direction and co-ordination. It depended for its manifestation on spontaneous and unsolicited evidence revealed by individuals who happened to have visited the Congo and to have been appalled by what they saw. The A.P.S., it is true, had organized some protest but Congo reform was only one aspect of its world-wide interests and although the Society had arrived at the fundamental issue involved in the Congo question, it had failed to press these home. At the turn of the century the position remained unchanged. Nevertheless, the question was attracting the attention of a wider circle. In particular, its commercial aspects became very prominent. The consequence of the fusion of the commercial and humanitarian forces interested in the Congo was to make the intervention of Britain as inevitable as the movement in Britain for the abolition of the slave trade six decades earlier following the fusion of similar forces.

The commercial aspects of the Congo question assumed great significance, not directly as a result of the policy of the Congo State, but because of the march of events in the neighbouring French Congo.[1] The evident prosperity of the Congo State, organized on the system of concessions,

---

[1] For a fuller discussion of these events see Renée Jeaugeon: 'Les Sociétés d'exploitation au Congo et l'opinion française de 1890 à 1906', *Revue Française d'Histoire d'Outre-Mer*, xlviii, 1961, 353–437; J. Saintoyant:

attracted the attention of students of colonial administration in France. Under the leadership of Eugene Etienne, a former Under-Secretary for Colonies, the French government was urged to emulate the example of the Congo State. The arguments seemed irresistible. The French Congo, far more than any of the French colonies in West Africa, had failed to interest French investors; it was also a great drain on the exchequer. The solution to both problems, it was urged, would be to grant concessions to French businessmen.

In February 1899 the French Minister for Colonies signed forty concessions for exploitation by various French commercial societies. The areas thus conceded included those where the two Liverpool commercial houses of John Holt and Company, and Hatton and Cookson had traded before the advent of the French. Soon the relationship between the French and English companies became strained and one of the French companies took the extreme step of confiscating the trade goods of certain agents of John Holt.[1] The latter brought an action before the tribunal at Libreville but the judgment went in favour of the defendant and this decision was confirmed by the court of appeal in November 1901.

The importance of the Holt case was that it centred on the question of the validity of concessions in the conventional basin of the Congo and on whether these concessions could be reconciled with the provisions of the Berlin Act. Holt contended that these concessions were an infringement of the Act in so far as they constituted monopolies and interdicted freedom of trade guaranteed by Article 1 of the Act. The appeal court at Libreville, in dismissing this contention, argued, however, that the concession company had obtained the right to exploit the agricultural produce of the conceded lands and consequently the produce belonged to it and not to the Congolese who gathered the produce and received

---

L'Affair du Congo 1905, Paris 1960; S. H. Roberts: *The History of French Colonial Policy*, 1870–1925, London 1963, 2nd ed., pp. 347–61; and S. J. S. Cookey: 'The Concession Policy in the French Congo and British Reaction, 1898–1906', *J.A.H.*, vol. VII, 2, 1966, pp. 263–78.

[1] Holt to Salisbury, 22 April 1899, FO 27/3756. A year later the other British firm received the same treatment. Hatton and Cookson to Salisbury, 26 June 1900, ibid.

remuneration for his services. It also pointed out that no commercial relationship could exist between the indigenous African and a third party because it was the company and not the former who owned the produce. On the fundamental principle whether the State had the right to grant the concessions, the Court asserted that such concessions did not contradict any of the clauses of the Berlin Act. These were arguments which the British commercial interests would not accept and the appeal to law having failed, recourse was had to diplomacy.

Diplomacy, however, could really only be effective in such cases if backed up by public opinion. Here, the ground had already been prepared. The A.P.S. had been appealing since 1896 against the concession system in the Congo State which it believed was indissolubly linked with atrocities. This theme was now added to the case of the merchants. Henceforth, humanitarian and commercial opinions were yoked together, pulling against a common foe—monopoly. This identity of interest was convenient for both: on the one hand, the abolition of concessions would remove the basis for the wrongs inflicted on the Africans; on the other hand, it would open the way to the unrestricted expansion of British commerce. Nevertheless, it would be wrong to imagine that the merchants adopted the humanitarian argument as a pose. What is clear is that until the goods of British merchants had been seized in the French Congo, the British chambers of commerce had evinced no significant interest in the campaign of the A.P.S.

The alliance of humanitarianism and free trade in the Congo question was symbolized by the relationship between the two men who came to take the lead in the movement for Congo reform—Edmund Dene Morel and John Holt. In 1890, at the age of twenty-three, Morel had entered the firm of Elder Dempster and Company as a clerk.[1] It was here,

---

[1] There is as yet no good biography of Morel. F. S. Cocks: *E. D. Morel, the man and his work*, London 1920, which is often quoted, is largely the printed version of Morel's autobiography which he incorporated in his unpublished *History of the C.R.A.*, M.P., Box H. As such, it must be read with more discrimination than most authors have shown.

according to his own account, that the affairs of West Africa attracted his attention. Characteristically, by unremitting probing and reading, he mastered the subject as much as, if not more than, anyone of his time. He arrived at two fundamental principles from which he never deviated. In the first place, he recognized that the policy of Free Trade and the Open Door was the only one that could be beneficial to European interests as a whole in West Africa. In the second place, he saw that the rights of the natives, especially their rights in the land and its produce, must be respected by the colonial powers since it was the guarantee of their equitable treatment. In his mind, these two principles achieved a synthesis: there could be no free trade if the Africans were deprived of their rights in the land and the Africans could not be fairly treated if they were not free to buy and sell to the highest bidder.

There was, of course, nothing original in these principles; Fox Bourne, as has been seen, had asserted the same as early as 1896. What was unique in Morel was the way in which he expounded his views. Morel was a fanatic though an honest and sincere one. He was also courageous, tireless and extremely obstinate. It was these qualities which were soon to place him at the head of the Congo movement and to eclipse the earlier initiative of Fox Bourne.

John Holt, unlike Morel, was a trader who had built up a very prosperous business in West Africa. His trade methods distinguished him in the commercial world of Liverpool.

> His intense individuality, his resentment of control, his scorn of assistance, made him repudiate any interference, whether by companies or by the State. He wanted no backing either of politician or of soldier. He had absolute confidence in his own methods of dealing with the African, apart from all government complications. . . . Such a merchant as John Holt, far-sighted, self-reliant, guided by an unfailing instinct for good business, was never lured by the plea of quick profits to the exploitation of the native. He was pledged, if by only his sense of successful commerce, to a system of free labour for the inhabitants of the country.[1]

---

[1] Alice Stopford Green: 'A founder of the Society', *Journal of the African Society*, October 1915, pp. 11–16.

Holt felt a sense of sincere gratitude towards the West African. 'They made me what I am', he often declared. 'Their labours, their muscles, their enterprise, have given me everything I possess. I am bound to try and protect them against outrage and injustice.'[1] It is not surprising, then, that Holt and Morel worked so well together. Their principles and their ideals with regard to the affairs of West Africa ran along the same channel.

The intimate collaboration which developed between them dates, however, from the seizure of Holt's trade goods in the French Congo. Morel, unsolicited by Holt, immediately decided to champion his cause.[2] His contributions in the British press soon won the admiration and gratitude of Holt[3] which increased rather than diminished in the coming years. Meanwhile, for Morel, the question of the French Congo had a wider aspect which transcended the immediate inconvenience suffered by Holt. Since 1898, he had become convinced by what he had read of the Leopoldian régime in the Congo State that this form of exploitation was disastrous for the Africans. He feared that the imitation of a similar policy in the French Congo would have the same evil consequences. He felt that the facts were not sufficiently appreciated by the British public and it was because of this that in 1900 he wrote a series of articles in *The Speaker* entitled 'The Congo Scandal'.[4] It was a skilful and powerful presentation of evidence about the Congo administration known to only a few. The attention of Dilke and Fox Bourne was drawn to the author of the articles and henceforth Morel entered a new phase of his life as a respected member of the humanitarian circle.

Morel was inspired, as he said later, by the idea that 'the

[1] *African Mail*, 2 July 1915.
[2] Morel to Holt, 23 May 1899, J.H.P. 18/1.
[3] 'I congratulate you', Holt wrote, 'on the masterly way in which you have treated the subject. . . . I feel thankful to you that you have given so much thought to affairs African and consider you a distinct gain to the small circle of those to whom all things African are of interest.' Holt to Morel, 18 August 1899, M.P., F. 8.
[4] *The Speaker*, 28 July; 4 August; 25 August; 1 September; 6 October; and 1 December. Cf. Slade: *King Leopold's Congo*, pp. 182–3.

expulsion of British subjects from French Congo may yet serve as the lever whereby the edifices of fraud and greed and cruelty reared by Africa's self-styled "regenerator" may be overthrown'.[1] He approached Holt, who was by now his unreserved admirer and friend, with this idea. While assuring Holt that his case was 'an illustration of great principles',[2] Morel also fired his imagination:

> I don't know whether you are properly aware of it. But upon you at the present moment hang the destinies of many millions of people. It works out like this. The French Government will probably offer you very shortly a Concession in the Congo to close your mouth, or compensation to get you out of the place. It would be perfectly natural and practical for you to accept the latter (the former I know you would not) and if you consulted your own interests merely, you would. If on the other hand you stick to the principle of insisting upon the correct interpretation and application of the Berlin Act, you may be directly instrumental in raising the entire Congo question—the the violation of Leopold in constituting the Domaine Privé and all the evils, including the French Congo business of which that is the immediate basis. To few men in the course of their lives has it been given to be the arbiter of so much. If you take your stand, firm as a rock, upon that vital principle, aided by the Press, another Conference will be brought about, so sure as we are living this day.[3]

At first Holt demurred. 'So far as I am able to discern', he informed Morel, 'my destiny arranged by Providence is to be a distributor of Merchandise'.[4] But Holt was genuinely horrified by the reports of atrocities coming from the Congo[5] and it was relatively easy for Morel to achieve his purpose. It took only one more effort in which he assured Holt:

---

[1] E. D. Morel: *Affairs of West Africa*, London 1903, p. 304.

[2] Morel to Holt, n.d., J. H. P., 18/1.

[3] Morel to Holt, 31 December 1901, ibid.

[4] Holt to Morel, 31 December 1901, M.P., F. 8.

[5] As early as June 1900, for example, he had told Morel 'Alas for the woes of the slaves of the Congo! Accursed be the nation which allows these abominations to go unpunished.' Holt to Morel, 20 June 1900, M.P., F. 8.

It has been given, at certain times, at certain epochs, in certain countries, to the humblest born, the most unknown and obscure individual to bring about great reforms. The finger of God, the hand of fate or whatever you may like to call it has appointed these individuals for the task. History offers many such examples. How much more then the power, how much greater the facility of one who like yourself is known, respected and in many respects, the wielder of considerable influence.[1]

Holt immediately rallied to the call. His answer is worth quoting as much for its historical as for its human interest because here was no selfish calculation for gain, of which the Congo reformers came to be accused, but an elevated sense of purpose. Holt said:

How glorious it is to be young! What abundant enthusiasm thrills you over this Congo affair! It is a noble aspiration! The happiness—nay the very lives of many depends upon its successful attainment. As for me I am not destined to take a place with the immortals—I am not heroic—anyhow I will do my little according to my light.[2]

Morel had cast a specific role for Holt which the latter came to fill admirably well. He himself was as yet a relatively unknown free-lance journalist,[3] with neither influence nor financial resources but with an incisive pen. Holt, on the other hand, had a strong case and the financial resources to fight it. As vice-president of the African Section of the Liverpool Chamber of Commerce, he could also exert considerable influence in commercial and industrial circles as well as in Whitehall. Morel and Holt, therefore, were complementary to each other. The genius of Morel is that he grasped the significance of Holt's case against the French Congo and exploited it in order to achieve the reform of the Congo State administration.

The important position occupied by Holt soon became evident, for his case had readily been taken up by British

---

[1] Morel to Holt, 1 January 1902, J.H.P., 18/1.

[2] Holt to Morel, 1 January 1902, M.P., F. 8.

[3] Morel had resigned from Elder Dempster & Company in December 1900 to devote himself to journalism.

commercial interests under the inspiration of the Liverpool Chamber of Commerce. In October 1901, this Chamber presented a memorial to the Foreign Secretary protesting against the concession policy in the French Congo and asking for British intervention in order to see that the Berlin Act was respected.[1] Within a few weeks identical memorials had been presented by most of the other Chambers of Commerce[2] and soon after, Lansdowne received a delegation at the Foreign Office from ten of them who came to make a similar protest. The arguments put forward by the Chambers of Commerce are interesting because of their close resemblance to those of the A.P.S. They claimed to be interested in the matter not only because the concession policy was detrimental to British commerce but also because that policy endangered the welfare of the Africans. The integration of humanitarianism and free trade already seen in the Morel-Holt relationship had thus been achieved on a wider level. Its popular manifestation will soon be discussed.

Meanwhile, another and equally significant influence exerted by Holt was in the contact which he maintained with Martin Gosselin at the Foreign Office.[3] Gosselin was a close friend of Holt.[4] Consequently, when Holt's case reached the Foreign Office he took more than an official interest in it. Gosselin was also subject to the influence of Fox Bourne. It is clear that these two influences, coupled perhaps with his earlier knowledge of Congo affairs, had led Gosselin gradually to adopt a sympathetic attitude towards those who wanted to reform the Congo administration. This reaction

---

[1] Liverpool Chamber of Commerce to F.O., 1 October 1901, FO 27/3757.

[2] E.g. Birmingham 17 October; Cardiff 17 October; Bury 17 October; Manchester 22 October; Oldham 23 October; Dublin 28 October; ibid.

[3] Gosselin was appointed Under-Secretary on 25 July 1898 and assigned to the department of Western Europe. He was transferred in 1900 to head the West and South-West African department. Gosselin's contact with Congo affairs dated from 1885 when he was appointed secretary of the legation in Brussels and acted as chargé d'affaires on various occasions between 1886 and 1892. He was one of the secretaries to the Slave Trade Conference at Brussels and was also delegated to discuss and fix the duties to be imposed on imports in the Congo basin.

[4] For Gosselin's correspondence with John Holt see J.H.P. 13/3.

was understood for his transfer to Lisbon in 1902 was lamented by both Holt and Fox Bourne as a distinct loss to the cause.[1]

What is more important with regard to Gosselin was his responsibility for the appointment of Roger Casement as the first British consul for the Congo,[2] an appointment which was to have such fateful consequences for the Congo State. Gosselin was aware that before his appointment Casement's views were decidedly hostile towards the Congo administration. In April 1900 Casement forwarded to Gosselin from Cape Town a private letter he had received from a missionary serving in the Congo and another from an official of the Congo government in which were accounts of the cruel treatment to which the Congolese were being subjected. Casement had then suggested that when British pre-occupation in South Africa was over it might be found possible to 'join Germany or any other interested power in putting an end to the veritable reign of terror which exists in the Congo'.[3] Four months after this letter was written Casement was appointed to the Congo State.[4] The influences to which Gosselin has been shown to be subject lead to the tentative[5] conclusion that sending Casement to the Congo might not have been a mere routine official transaction, but a well-considered move to focus the attention of the Foreign Office on the seamy sides of the Congo question.

Despite the fact that much has been written on Casement,[6] the role which he played in the movement for the reform of the administration of the Congo, probably his greatest title

---

[1] Holt to Morel, 7 June 1902, M.P., F. 8; Fox Bourne to Holt, 5 June 1902, J.H.P., 12/4.

[2] F.O. to Casement, 20 August 1900, FO 10/739.

[3] Casement to Gosselin, 30 April 1900, FO 403/304, private.

[4] F.O. to Casement, 20 August 1900, FO 10/739.

[5] 'Tentative' because I have been unable to trace the record in which the decision was taken. It is possible of course that no such record exists.

[6] They range from those who passionately believe him to be a virtuous man, like A. Noyes: *The Accusing Ghost; or Justice for Casement*, London 1957, to those who uncompromisingly regard him as a villain, like R. MacColl: *Roger Casement; A New Judgment*, London 1956. The nearest to a balanced judgement is Singleton-Gates and Girodias: *The Black Diaries*, New York 1959.

to fame, has never been fully appreciated. The reasons for this are obvious. In the first place, because of his official position as member of the consular service his activities as a private individual had to be behind the scenes and the record of these activities could only be known from the correspondence of those with whom he worked. Unfortunately, this source has hitherto not been carefully examined. In the second place, the tragedy surrounding Casement's execution for treason in 1916 has distracted attention from an objective study of his role as a humanitarian. Thus Casement has come to be remembered in England as a traitor and as the author of the famous (or infamous) *Black Diaries*.[1] A study of documents now available reveals, however, that the idea of the Congo Reform Association (C.R.A.) which was formed in England early in 1904, originated from Casement and not from Morel as has been generally supposed; that he participated actively in its work; and that he contributed regularly to its coffers. If then the C.R.A. is accorded a place in modern imperial history as an organ which helped to rouse the conscience of the powers against the ruthless exploitation of the colonial races,[2] the praise should go in great measure to Roger Casement.

Casement was born of an Irish parentage on 1 September 1864. His first employment was, like Morel's, in the shipping line of Elder Dempster and Company. It was here that his love of Africa and of travel developed. In 1884 Casement left the shipping company and entered the service of the *Association Internationale du Congo* and two years later he joined the Sanford Exploring Expedition which was absorbed into the *Société anonyme belge pour le commerce du Haut-Congo* in 1888. He soon resigned and worked for a few months with the Congo Railway which he abandoned in 1889 and returned home. Before then, however, he served as a 'lay-helper' to the B.M.S. on their station at Wathen from December 1888 to March 1889.[3]

---

[1] See bibliography, p. 320.

[2] *Cambridge History of British Empire*, iii, 675.

[3] This is an aspect of Casement's life which is not generally known. See Appendix I.

'Coming home in 1889', Casement later told Morel,[1] 'I found myself still a very young man with all the love of Africa upon me, but no wish to continue in what was clearly becoming a Belgian enterprise.' In spite of this he returned to the Congo the following year and organized the transport service on the Lower Congo for the *Société anonyme belge pour la commerce du Haut-Congo*, his energy earning him the commendation of the company as an 'agent exceptionnel'.[2] The subsequent offer of a Colonial Office appointment on the Niger Coast in 1891 enabled Casement to continue his career in Africa. In 1895 he was appointed consul at Lorenço Marques and in 1898 he was transferred to Loanda. It was here that he resumed his earlier contact with the Congo for his territorial jurisdiction embraced the Congo State. His relations with the Congo colonial authorities were not happy, and it is possible that he bore a grudge against the Congo government for the ruined career of Edward Bannister,[3] who was married to his aunt.[4] From December 1898 to March 1899 he was on the Lower Congo extracting the salaries of British subjects employed by the Congo State and securing their repatriation and the punishment of those Congo officials who had been accused of their maltreatment.[5] His vigorous action won the approval of the governor of the Gold Coast.[6] Meanwhile, following the report of an official inquiry,[7] it had been decided to establish a full consulate for the Congo

---

[1] Casement to Morel, 27 June 1904, M.P., F. 8.

[2] *Biographie Coloniale Belge*, Brussels 1948, i, 220; Casement to Lansdowne, 9 October 1905, FO 10/815, private.

[3] Supra, pp. 27 ff.

[4] See Appendix I.

[5] Casement to Salisbury, 31 March 1899, FO 10/815, no. 12, Africa; Casement to Salisbury, 25 April 1899, ibid., no. 14, Africa.

[6] Hodgson to Chamberlain, 9 October 1899, encl. in C.O. to F.O. 22 November 1899; F.O. to Casement, 22 December 1899, FO 10/731, no. 12, Africa.

[7] This inquiry, conducted by W. P. Pulteney, F.O. to Pulteney, 3 January 1899, FO 10/726, reported that the British consular post should be established at Kinchassa (Stanley Pool) because of its climatic attractions and accessibility to the Upper Congo. Pulteney to Gosselin, 29 August 1899, ibid., private. Hence it was here that Casement came to reside.

State. As has been indicated, it was Casement who was appointed to the post.

Before his departure for the Congo, Casement was interviewed twice in Brussels by Leopold II.[1] At the first interview, a veiled clash of ideals between the king-sovereign and the consul is discernible.[2] With regard to the treatment of the Congolese and forced labour, the king had asserted that his sole desire was to improve the condition of the Africans, that it was a process which would inevitably take time, and that the Congolese must be taught the value of work. Casement, however, interposed his own views that the best means of achieving this objective was to introduce a Hut Tax, that is, to levy a direct tax instead of a tax in labour. Casement also threw out a hint that the task of ensuring good government of such a large territory as the Congo might be too great for the king, but the latter brushed this aside. At the second interview, the following day, the question of freedom of trade was discussed.[3] Leopold II claimed that there was complete freedom of trade in the Congo except that his government had reserved, under the name of *Domaine Privé*, certain districts of the country from which a revenue for the administration was obtained without recourse to direct taxation. Casement was sceptical and warned that as public opinion, which was such a power factor in England, was interested in free trade only such a policy would be unwise.

If the king-sovereign had thought of converting the new consul, as he no doubt intended, the effort was wasted. For Casement, the interview changed none of his views about the administration of the Congo State; indeed, his own

---

[1] These were arranged by the new British ambassador at the suggestion of the Congo government, probably in order to win Casement's sympathy for the Congo State.

[2] 'Memorandum of Conversation with the King-Sovereign of the Congo State', 10 October 1900, encl. 1 in Casement to Salisbury, 14 October 1900, FO 2/336, confidential.

[3] 'Memorandum of Conversation with the King-Sovereign of the Congo State', 11 October 1900; encl. 2 in Casement to Salisbury, 14 October 1900, ibid., confidential.

investigations on the spot seemed only to confirm them. On the question of monopoly, he soon noted:

> With the exception of a few scattered and relatively insignificant properties acquired by individuals (either missionaries or traders) by private arrangement with the native owners prior to the establishment of the International Association of the Congo as the Congo Independent State, and which properties that Government was called upon to recognize and to register at its inception, the entire area of the Congo State . . . has become, by a stroke of the pen, the sole property of the governing body of the State, or it should in truth be said, the private property of one individual—the King of the Belgians as Sovereign of that State.
>
> That this vast sole ownership is in the interests either of the 'work of civilisation' contemplated by that international goodwill which gave this Government its existence; or of those would-be European immigrants, whether as missionaries, land settlers, or traders it was designed to assist, I do not for a moment believe.[1]

He provided a full report on the case of certain employees of the Anversoise who had been condemned for atrocities by the Boma Court of Appeal.[2] This company, he pointed out, was, 'sweeping away all subterfuge aside, as much a part of the Congo State machinery of Government for India-Rubber as any branch of the Executive' and he concluded by emphasizing that the 'crimes of the S.C.A. . . . do not stand alone as isolated horrors'.

The truth was that Casement, soon after his first observations at Kinchassa, had lost complete confidence in either the honesty or the good faith of the king-sovereign. Even when Leopold II renewed the appointment of the Commission for the Protection of Natives, Casement immediately dispelled any illusion which the Foreign Office might have

---

[1] Casement to Lansdowne, 7 May 1901, FO 2/491, no. 3, Africa, confidential.

[2] Casement to Lansdowne, 28 June 1901, ibid., no. 21, Africa, confidential.

wished to entertain as to its beneficial effects.[1] His solution for the Congo question was the immediate annexation of the Congo State by Belgium.[2]

The idea of Belgian annexation of the Congo was in the air. Its antecedents date back to a will of 2 August 1889, by which Leopold II had made Belgium heir to his African empire. In a letter dated three days afterwards, he had announced his readiness to hand the Congo State over to Belgium before his death if there should be a demand for this. Nothing, however, was farther from his thought at this time as the will and the letter were ingenious preliminaries for securing financial assistance from the Belgian exchequer.[3] On 3 July 1890, a convention was signed between Belgium and the Congo State by which the king-sovereign was given an interest-free loan of 25 million francs: 5 million francs to be paid at once and 2 million francs every year for the next ten years. The king, on the other hand, undertook to contract no other loan without the consent of the Belgian government. Six months after the expiration of the ten years, Belgium was to have the option either of annexing the Congo State or of obtaining the repayment of the loan after a further period of ten years, interest at the rate of 3.5 per cent being paid in the meantime.

In the autumn of 1894, Leopold II surprised his cabinet with the news that two years earlier he had in fact concluded an agreement with a Belgian banker, Brown de Tiège, by which, on the security of 16 million hectares of Congo

---

[1] 'It is perhaps well to point out that this Commission, as thus constituted, cannot exercise any united control whatsoever.' Casement to Lansdowne, 26 July 1901, ibid., no. 32, Africa.

[2] 'The only hope for the Congo, should it continue to be governed by the Belgians, is that it should be subject to an European authority responsible to public opinion, and not to the unquestioned rule of an autocrat, whose chief pre-occupation is that this autocracy should be profitable.' Casement to Lansdowne, 28 June 1901, FO 403/305, no. 21, Africa, confidential.

[3] Stenmans: op. cit., pp. 114–15 and 126; Stengers: *Belgique et Congo*, pp. 32–3. It is believed that both the will and the letter were actually signed on the eve of the debate on the loan and deliberately back-dated. See Ascherson: op. cit., p. 187.

territory, he had obtained a loan of 5 million francs.[1] As the loan was due for repayment in 1895 and the king-sovereign professed to have no money to meet it, it seemed as if the future Belgian Colony would lose the 16 million hectares. It was a clear breach of the 1890 convention and the government decided on immediate annexation of the Congo State. That project failed, however, partly because of a protracted negotiation with France on her right of pre-emption which enabled opposition against annexation to harden; but mainly because of the hostility of the king-sovereign to the project.[2] In the end a *modus vivendi* was reached. By a law of 29 June 1895 the Belgian government lent the Congo State the sum of 6,850,000 francs to meet her obligations, the condition of repayment being the same as those of the original 25 million francs. This arrangement satisfied those Belgians who were apprehensive of the repercussions of a colonial policy on the neutrality of their country. It also satisfied Leopold II whose original scheme had been to obtain additional funds by every means in order to fulfil his Nile dreams.

The Convention of 1890 expired on 18 February 1901 and, as has already been said, the question of annexation of the Congo emerged on the Belgian political plane.[3] The majority of Belgians were not ready to accept a colonial policy. Public opinion still feared the international complications into which the country might be plunged. Belgian merchants and industrialists were content with the *status quo* which ensured enormous dividends from Congo shares at the Bourse. King Leopold himself was as unwilling as ever to hand over the colony. In March 1901 the government of

---

[1] It was later revealed that 'the greater portion, if not all of this money was advanced to the Congo State by the King himself'. Plunkett to Kimberley, 2 June 1895, FO 10/641, very confidential. This information was given to Plunkett by Van Eetvelde; see Plunkett to Anderson, 2 June 1895, ibid., private and confidential.

[2] Cf. J. Stengers: 'La première tentative de reprise du Congo par la Belgique', *Bulletin Société Royale belge de Géographie*, 1949 (extract). He suggests that Leopold II was favourable to annexation until the middle of March 1895 when he suddenly changed his mind.

[3] For the Belgian discussion on annexation in 1901 I have followed Stenmans: op. cit.

de Smet de Naeyer which was completely dominated by
Leopold II introduced a bill in the Chamber deferring
annexation and waiving, for the present, the repayment of
the sums lent in 1890 and 1895 as well as the interest on these
loans. The bill caused a division in the ranks of the ruling
Catholic party as Beernaert promptly introduced another
bill for the immediate annexation of the Congo State. The
deadlock was resolved by the direct intervention of the
king-sovereign himself. In a letter to Woeste, leader of the
extreme Right, which the latter read to the Chamber,
Leopold II made it clear that he was opposed to annexation
and that he would refuse to co-operate if it was voted.
Beernaert tamely withdrew his bill and the government bill
was passed. Thus the decision whether or not Belgium
should annex the Congo was deferred indefinitely.

The failure of annexation alienated everyone in Britain
interested in the Congo question. It was not Casement alone
who had pinned great hopes on the success of the project.
The A.P.S. had clearly welcomed the prospect of annexation
and in a memorial to every member of the Belgian parliament it had hoped that precautions would be taken to secure
the humane and equitable treatment of the Congolese.[1]
'That the change would, in every respect, be beneficial,
there are no grounds for doubting', had also been Morel's
view at this time.[2] When annexation was abandoned there
was a consensus of opinion in favour of British intervention.
For the first time, *The Times* left the fence on which it had
long been sitting and came down on the side of the reformers.[3] The A.P.S. also reverted to its earlier role of

---

[1] *A.F.*, July 1901. This memorial had been inspired by Lorand.
Lorand to Fox Bourne, ? April, and 6 April 1901, A.S., G.261.

[2] *The Speaker*, 24 March 1900.

[3] 'Miscellaneous adventurers, including a slight element of criminals
and desperadoes, landing in countries as wild as the Congo, have in the
past, without aid from any State, sometimes done as good work as this
State which was to be a pattern to people who had acted in their wars
against savagery and their colonization in rough fashion. Not joining in
indiscriminate complaints as to the policy of the Congo State or shutting
our eyes to much good work carried out in the true spirit of the principles

pressing the Foreign Office to initiate an international conference on the Congo.[1]

By this time, however, British public opinion no longer stood alone in opposition to the Congo régime, for the attention of the Germans had once more focussed on events in the Congo. Since the execution of Stokes, German public opinion had become alienated from the enterprise of Leopold II, and the decreasing trade of German East Africa was ascribed to the unscrupulous determination of the king-sovereign to divert the trade of Central Africa to Congo ports. The German agitation of 1902, however, was a direct consequence of the circumstances surrounding the death in the Congo of an Austrian trader, Gustave-Marie Rabinek, who had recently entered into a partnership with a German trader, Ludwig Deuss, for exploiting the commercial resources of Katanga.[2] It was believed in Germany that Rabinek had been murdered and in England Morel spread the rumour that the victim had in fact been arrested on board a British ship and in the British territorial waters of Lake Mweru. The German press, supported by the German Colonial Society and the Chambers of Commerce, denounced the Congo régime and called for a revision of the Berlin Act.[3]

Both in Germany and in Britain, then, the desire for an international conference on the Congo question had become current. But neither the Wilhelmstrasse nor the Foreign Office was willing to take the initiative. Lansdowne, who had succeeded Salisbury as Foreign Secretary since November 1900, was definitely opposed to Britain taking such

---

enunciated at Berlin, we may say that it has by no means fulfilled expectations.

'It would be unfortunate if the decision [to postpone annexation] retarded even for a day a thorough examination of the administration of the State in the light of the practice of countries with larger colonial experience than Belgium.' *The Times*, 29 July 1901. This was a *volte face*. Six years earlier the same paper had cautioned Belgium against annexation. *The Times*, 18 March 1895.

[1] A.P.S. to Lansdowne, 2 August 1901, FO 403/305.

[2] The Rabinek Affair has been treated in greater detail in *Biographie Coloniale Belge*, iv, 729–33. See also Willequet, op. cit., pp. 51 ff.

[3] E.g. see *Kölnische Zeitung*, 24 May 1902.

initiative[1] although he was eager to know the attitude of Germany.[2] It was clear that the German government itself would not raise the Congo question. It touched the interests of France whose policy in the French Congo would have to be discussed in any conference on the Congo and Germany had decided to avoid any conflict with French interests on the West Coast of Africa.[3] Meanwhile, the A.P.S. had resolved to bring the Congo question into full focus before public opinion and thereby to force the hand of the Foreign Office.[4] This was the object of a public meeting held at the Mansion House on 15 May 1902 under the auspices of the Society. The Liverpool and London Chambers of Commerce were officially represented while Manchester pledged its full support. Even the German Colonial Society sent a delegate. In spite of the intervention of two representatives of the Congo State, the meeting unanimously adopted two resolutions, one calling on all the powers signatory to the Berlin and Brussels Acts to co-operate in procuring the reform of the Congo administration, and the other urging the British government to take the initiative in inviting the powers to fulfil the obligations which they had assumed in the Congo.[5]

The Mansion House meeting was a remarkable demonstration of the unanimity of all sections of British public opinion on the Congo question. In particular, it brought into the open the identity of interests between the humanitarians and the commercial world. Finally, it rallied together the British press to the side of the reformers. For example, *West Africa*, the organ of Liverpool commerce, declared that

---

[1] Lansdowne, 16 April 1902, FO 10/773, minute.

[2] Lansdowne to Lascelles (Berlin), 16 April 1902, ibid., no. 64, Africa.

[3] H. Farnall, 9 June 1902, FO 27/3759, Memorandum; Lansdowne to Monson (Paris), 4 June 1902, ibid., no. 125, Africa, confidential.

[4] That this was the only logical course is shown by the following minute by Farnall: 'The state of things in the Congo has not yet really moved public opinion either in this country or on the continent. . . . Neither this country nor any other is likely to take active steps in the matter unless more or less forced to do so by public opinion.' Farnall, 3 April 1902, FO 10/773.

[5] *West Africa*, 17 May 1902.

'the great meeting at the Mansion House should serve as a trumpet call to the Signatory Powers of the Berlin and Brussels Acts to remember their responsibilities and look to the future.'[1] The *Morning Post* urged the British and German governments to secure the co-operation of France in order to constitute a tribunal of inquiry into the Congo maladministration;[2] and the *Manchester Guardian* saw 'no valid ground for refusing to support the demand that inquiry should be held'.[3] The *Daily News*, the organ of British non-conformity, had already proclaimed that it was the duty of Britain, with its past history and with its great stake in Africa, to take the first steps for a concerted action.[4] Public interest was sustained by a renewed controversy in *The Times* and the *Morning Post* between Morel and a certain Houdret,[5] which was joined from time to time by partisans on both sides. In June the Congo government, no longer content to pass on information to its consul-general, entered directly into the controversy by issuing a communiqué in which it proclaimed that 'the reproach levelled at the Congo State of having violated the Berlin Act disappears before the evidence of facts'.[6]

The attitude of Lansdowne, however, did not change. He was acutely conscious of the hostility shown by German public opinion in the Anglo-Boer War, of the failure of the negotiations for an agreement between Britain and Germany in March 1901[7] and of the differences which had arisen in the Chinese and Moroccan policies of the two countries.[8]

---

[1] Ibid.

[2] *Morning Post*, 16 May 1902.

[3] *Manchester Guardian*, 16 May 1902.

[4] *Daily News*, 29 March 1902.

[5] The letters published under the name of Houdret were actually written by the Congo Foreign Ministry in Brussels, see Whetnall to Favereau, 4 June 1902, Ier sér, Congo, iv, 895, confidential.

[6] Phipps to Lansdowne, 12 June 1902, FO 403/327, no. 37, Africa.

[7] J. A. S. Grenville: 'Lansdowne's abortive project of 12 March 1901 for secret agreement with Germany', *Bulletin of the Institute of Historical Research*, 1954, xxvii, 201–13.

[8] G. W. Monger: *The End of Isolation; British Foreign Policy 1900–1907*, London 1963, p. 43.

He regarded the idea of inviting German collaboration on the Congo question as objectionable.[1] Meanwhile, one man was gradually undermining the complacency of the Foreign Office. This was none other than Casement who kept in close touch with opinion on Congo reform in England. Simultaneously with the meeting at Mansion House, he had urged on Gosselin that 'the Congo Government should be forced to surrender to the use of legitimate commerce and competitors, its illegally acquired market of the Domaine Privé.'[2] He had also suggested the course of action that should be taken: if an international conference failed, the Maritime Commission provided for in the Berlin Act should be set up and Britain should exercise consular jurisdiction over its subjects in the Congo State. These startling suggestions reveal the extremity to which Casement had by now been driven by his dislike of King Leopold's rule. No one by this time, not even Fox Bourne or Morel, had proposed such a far-reaching procedure against the Congo State.

In order to justify British action, Casement continued to discredit the state of affairs in the Congo. No epithet was too strong for him to employ against the Congo administration. He described the vesting of all land in the State as 'a deliberate act of theft', and the Congo State itself as a 'benevolent conception designed primarily for the moral and material welfare of the natives whom today it exploits, in its own sordid interests, by an extensive machinery of oppression and exaction'.[3] He dismissed the reduction by fifty per cent of the direct and personal taxes on religious, scientific and charitable institutions established in the Congo as 'a somewhat cynical method of lightening the burden of taxes' since those who made up the difference were the already over-taxed Congolese.[4] He paid particular attention to the question of Congo monopoly in several despatches in order to

---

[1] Lansdowne to Buchanan (Berlin) 23 June 1902, FO 403/327, no. 103, Africa. Fox Bourne to Holt, 5 June 1902, J.H.P., 12/4.

[2] Casement to Gosselin, 16 May 1902, FO 10/773, private.

[3] Casement to Lansdowne, 10 July 1902, FO 2/626, no. 9, Africa, confidential.

[4] Casement to Lansdowne, 10 August 1902, ibid., no. 21, Africa.

show how the government had virtually excluded free trade. He drew a striking contrast between the promises of Stanley in 1885 to the Manchester Chamber of Commerce concerning the increase of British commerce in the Congo and the present condition, in which British trade had considerably fallen in volume.[1] As regards the administration of the Congo State itself, Casement portrayed it as bad beyond belief and its officers as almost entirely without honour or humanity.[2] The claim of the Congo administration that it had suppressed the slave trade was met with the retort:

> It has not suppressed the Slave Trade, it has merely substituted itself for the Arab who formerly exacted service from the native.
>
> Instead of selling him it only requires him to serve it under compulsion, and to give it, for the sole benefit of far distant European speculators and financiers, whatever his soil is capable of producing.[3]

The magisterial pose, the tone of righteous indignation, assumed by Casement was infectious; it still is to anyone now reading his despatches. E. A. W. Clarke of the African Department was moved to lament that but for other external considerations, 'it would certainly seem as if the times were ripe for combining a general assault on the administration of the Congo.'[4] Lansdowne himself regarded the Congo story as 'terrible'[5] and later admitted that 'Mr Casement's

---

[1] 'According to Mr. Stanley, one firm alone imported into the Lower Congo in 1879 English cotton goods worth £138,000. He averred that by backing up the A.I.C., Manchester might create a trade "in the course of time in cottons alone, in the basin, amounting in value to about £26,000,000 annually."

'In 1901 the official figures in the Bulletin Officiel show that imports of English cotton goods amounted to only £54,000 while Belgium, whose trade in cotton with the Congo did not exist in 1879 sent £179,000 worth in 1901.' Memorandum on Congo Imports, encl. in Casement to Lansdowne, 10 August 1902, ibid.

[2] Casement to Lansdowne, 18 July 1902, FO 10/773, no. 10, Africa, confidential.

[3] Casement, 15 February 1903, FO 403/338, memorandum.

[4] Clarke, 2 September 1902, FO 10/773, minute.

[5] Lansdowne, 12 September 1902, ibid., minute.

indignation is natural and justified.'[1] The question now was really no longer whether atrocities had been committed: there was a consensus of opinion at the Foreign Office that this had been established beyond disproof. It was the action which Britain could take to satisfy the national conscience that had to be decided. The summoning of an international conference which was advocated by the reformers was regarded as outside the realm of practical politics. As Lansdowne pointed out to Dilke, such a conference might reopen the whole question of the partition of Africa which 'would not be desirable in our own interest'.[2] The evidence afforded by Casement that British subjects in the Congo were still being maltreated provided a clue. The idea of establishing consular courts was once more considered.[3] However, Farnall, who was regarded as the expert on such questions, poured cold water on it[4] and once again this suggestion was dropped.

The British minister in Brussels, now Constantine Phipps, alone remained sceptical about the truth of Casement's reports. A conceited and conservative man with limited imagination, he was charmed by Brussels and could not bring himself to believe that the genial Belgians among whom he moved could be responsible for the atrocities revealed by Casement. The influence which Casement's despatches were beginning to exercise in the Foreign Office nettled him and he resented the seemingly endless representations which he was obliged to make to the Belgian and Congo governments.[5]

---

[1] Lansdowne, n.d., FO 2/764, minute.

[2] Lansdowne to Dilke, 13 March 1902, Dilke Papers, British Museum, Add. MS. 43917, quoted in Louis: op. cit., pp. 100–1.

[3] F.O. to C.O., 24 September 1902, FO 10/773.

[4] 'The Congo might say: "Very well, we request you to resume it: we shall not arrest any British evil-doer except with the express sanction of the British Consular authority and if British criminals go unpunished, the blame will be yours." The British natives are scattered all over the vast country and we could not exercise our jurisdiction without a very large increase in our consular staff.' Farnall, 18 April 1903, FO 10/803, minute.

[5] Complaining later to Grey, Phipps wrote: 'In fact, I was a sort of Balaam sent to curse and not permitted to bless in any respect.' Phipps to Grey, 19 January 1906, FO 800/41, Grey Papers.

Officially, he posed as an impartial observer in the conflict between Casement and the reformers on the one side and the Congo government on the other;[1] privately, he expressed his sympathy for the latter. 'He [Casement] is no doubt a most experienced African', Phipps informed Campbell, the Assistant Under-Secretary, 'but he curses that State as persistently as Balaam blessed in former days. I should be sorry to become the apologist of King Leopold or his régime but surely there must in that country be some progress, some organization.'[2] In fact Phipps, who, not unnaturally considered the reformers as humbugs, had joined the large band of those who could not resist the charm of Leopold II. His faith in the benevolent intentions of the Congo government was to remain unshaken. Gradually, he even came to develop towards Casement a personal animosity which the latter readily reciprocated.

Meanwhile whether the Foreign Office was willing to take action against the Congo government no longer really mattered. The decision was soon imposed on it by Parliament. The Mansion House meeting had been a demonstration of strength. Fox Bourne called at the Foreign Office afterwards to feel what impact it had made. After a long interview with Gosselin he came away with the view that Lansdowne would need pressing.[3] As has been mentioned, the reformers had

---

[1] 'When reading at Brussels the Decrees under which the administration of the Congo State is conducted, under which the relations of the natives with the local authorities and inspectors and the contract system is arranged, it is impossible not to be struck with the fact that no African country can be more wisely governed and that no broader humanitarian principles could possibly be enforced. When on the contrary, a perusal is made of Consul Casement's despatches (since that official, possessed so eminently of African experience, has been actually resident in the Congo State) it is impossible not to arrive at the conclusion that in practice no country is administered in so odious a manner.' Phipps to Lansdowne, 20 September 1902, FO 10/773, no. 71, Africa.

[2] Phipps to Campbell, 27 September 1902, ibid., private. A year later he told Lansdowne: 'I am rather afraid that our Consul on the spot is somewhat disposed to "curse" right and left and *never* to bless.' Phipps to Lansdowne, 26 September 1903, FO 800/116, Lansdowne Papers.

[3] Fox Bourne to Morel, 7 June 1902, M.P., F. 8.

launched a sustained press campaign against the Congo administration.[1] This was followed at the beginning of 1903 by the publication of no fewer than three books all exposing the system of monopoly established by the Congo State and details of the stories of atrocities which had been reported to arise from that system.[2] The remedy they proposed was the joint intervention of the powers. This salvo was succeeded in March by the support of the Associated Chambers of Commerce of Great Britain. At its annual general meeting, it adopted a resolution moved by John Holt that,

> in view of the principles and practice introduced into the administration of the affairs of the Congo Free State being in direct opposition to the Articles of the Act of Berlin, 1885, and to the interests of traders in general, the British Government should be requested, in conjunction with the other Great Powers who signed the Berlin Act, to consider how far fresh action and reform are necessary.[3]

The following month the third annual session of the Baptist Union assembly adopted a motion approving the resolution of the B.M.S. to secure the support of all societies which had missionaries in the Congo State for an appeal to the Belgian government to institute an immediate and exhaustive inquiry into the charges of cruel treatment of the Congolese.[4] It was also agreed that a joint deputation by missionary and philanthropic organizations should wait on the British government in order to request it to secure the enforcement of the terms and provisions of the Berlin Act. A few weeks later, the A.P.S. held a public meeting in London which was addressed

---

[1] According to *Petit Bleu*, 23 January 1903, 'Il y a décidément un campagne systématique en Angleterre contre l'Etat du Congo.'

[2] E. D. Morel: *Affairs of West Africa*, London 1903; H. R. Fox Bourne: *Civilization in Congoland*, London 1903; G. Burrows: *The Curse of Central Africa*, London 1903. Burrows was later prosecuted and convicted for libel.

[3] *Liverpool Daily Post*, 4 March 1903; Associated Chambers of Commerce to Lansdowne, 31 March 1903, FO 10/803.

[4] 'Memorandum on Treatment of Natives in the Congo Free State', ? April 1903, B.M.S. Papers.

by Reverend W. Morrison of the American Presbyterian
Mission on the atrocities being committed in the Congo.
The meeting later adopted Dilke's motion appealing to the
British government to use its influence with the other signa-
tory powers towards securing humane and equitable treat-
ment for the Congolese.[1]

A similar campaign had also been set in motion in the
House of Commons. On 2 March Dilke asked whether the
government had taken, or proposed to take, steps to secure
the co-operation of the powers in order to intervene in the
Congo question.[2] A few days later both Channing and
Mansfield, under the inspiration of Fox Bourne, pressed
similar questions on Cranbourne, the Under-Secretary for
Foreign Affairs.[3] Then on 1 May Herbert Samuel,[4] a member of the A.P.S., gave notice of a motion which he intended
to table on the Congo.[5] Within the same week both Dilke
and Bayley, another member of the Society, raised the Congo
question in the House.[6] These were clearly tactics aimed at
keeping alive the interest of parliament and the public in the
Congo.

The systematic assault was viewed with great apprehension
in Brussels where attempts were made to counteract its
effects. Leopold II tried frantically to enlist the sympathy of
his people by an unprecedented disbursement of his Congo
fortune. Phipps noted:

---

[1] A.P.S. to Lansdowne, 5 May 1903, FO 403/338.

[2] Hansard, 2 March 1903, 4th ser., cxviii, 1107.

[3] Hansard, 11 March 1903, 4th ser., cxix, 381.

[4] Later Viscount Samuel, died 4 February 1963 at 93. *The Times*,
6 February 1963.

[5] The grounds were carefully prepared for this motion. Morel wrote:
'At Sir Charles Dilke's request, I have drafted out today some tentative
resolutions for the debate of the 20th May. . . . I do hope you will write
to McArthur and Col. Sadler etc., to take part in the debate. Let us do
all we can to do away with the idea that the thing is a party question;
nothing will impress the Government more than if some of their own
supporters below the gangway, take the matter up.' Morel to Holt,
24 April 1903, J.H.P., 18/1.

[6] Hansard, 4 May 1903, 4th ser., cxxi, 1196; Hansard, 7 May 1903,
4th ser., cxxiii, 23.

The liberal expenditure of Congolese funds at the present moment undoubtedly contributes to enhance the popularity of the enterprise. His Majesty is expending an enormous sum on the improvement of the Brussels Palace, whilst £16,000 is being devoted to that of Laeken. House property and land is being acquired in all directions both at Ostend and in the Capital; £600 have again been assigned to summer fêtes at Ostend . . .[1]

Both in London and in Brussels, as in the other major European capitals, the king-sovereign disposed an extensive propaganda machine. In the former, the officers of the Tanganyika Concessions, a British company with substantial interests in Katanga, were encouraged to write glowing accounts of the Congo to the press. A powerful weapon exploited by the royal campaign in Brussels was the recent fate of the Boers. 'We say', the semi-official *Tribune Congolaise* reaffirmed, 'that the accusations were in part inspired by motives which could hardly be admitted.'[2] *Le Matin* was less reticent: after recalling the scheme of Cecil Rhodes for the Cape to Cairo railway and telegraph link-up, it concluded that 'that is why England would want to reopen the question of the existence of the State'.[3]

For the Belgians, indeed, the cause of the Congo State had become a national cause—the cause of the patriot. The Congophobia in England was seen as a deeply laid plot by the British government to seize the Congo. Only the Socialists dared to focus attention on the crux of the agitation, namely, the king-sovereign's system of exploitation in the Congo.[4] Even the Belgian government was infected by this attitude. Although they had avowed in the Chamber that in relation to them the Congo State was a foreign State, yet the diplomatic machinery of Belgium was now completely placed

---

[1] Phipps to Lansdowne, 27 January 1903, FO 403/338, no. 12, Africa.
[2] *Tribune Congolaise*, 29 January 1903.
[3] *Le Matin*, 5 March 1903.
[4] In a review of Fox Bourne's *Civilisation in Congoland*, for example, Vandervelde, the Socialist leader, declared that 'the system nonetheless exists; the abuses that it engenders are undeniable'. *Le Peuple*, 4 February 1903.

at their service,[1] as well as the columns of the *Journal de Bruxelles*, official organ of the Belgian government. It is possible that the attitude of the government might have been modified if it had properly understood the reform movement in England. Unfortunately, it did not have in London representatives of high calibre. Grenier, an easy-going aristocrat, generally ignored the anti-Congo campaign. Count Lalaing who succeeded him dismissed the reform movement as the agitation of a few greedy and disappointed merchants and industrialists.[2] In fact, nothing could be farther from the truth. Although, there was evidently close collaboration between the humanitarians and the merchants, the initiative never left the hands of the former. Furthermore, as has been shown, the Congo question had humanitarian and commercial aspects which were closely linked. To recognize one and ignore the other was to misunderstand the whole question. These aspects were once more to be emphasized in the famous Commons debate of 20 May,[3] which came as a climax to the energetic campaign mounted by the reformers since the beginning of the year.

The debate was opened by Samuel, who reviewed the evidence from the Congo State with regard to atrocities and concluded that the administration had fallen far below the expectations of civilized government. At the end of his speech, he moved that,

> the Government of the Congo Free State having at its inception guaranteed to the Powers that its native subjects should be governed with humanity, and that no trading monopoly or privilege should be permitted within its dominions, and both these guarantees having been constantly violated, this House requests His Majesty's Government to confer with other Powers, signatories of the Berlin General Act by virtue of which the Congo Free State exists, in order that measures may be adopted to abate the evils prevalent in that State.[4]

[1] Arendt (Director of Political Affairs in the Ministry for Foreign Affairs), 13 February 1903, Ier sér., Congo, iv, 972, memorandum.
[2] Lalaing to Favereau, 24 October 1903, Ier sér., v, Congo, 1334.
[3] Hansard, 20 May 1903, 4th ser., cxxii, 1289–32.
[4] Ibid.

Dilke then discussed in some detail the commercial principles on which the Congo administration was based and the injury which British enterprise had suffered therefrom. The question of Britain's legal right to intervene was examined by John Gorst, member for the University of Cambridge, and he assured the House that the right was indisputable. Finally, Emmott summarized the humanitarian, commercial and legal arguments of the previous speakers. The government was in an embarrassing position. They did not wish to defend an administration which they knew was bad, but on the other hand they had no desire to join in the chorus of condemnation. They had also played into the hands of the reformers by publishing that morning papers on the Rabinek Affair, in which the British Commissioner for Central Africa confirmed that the Austrian had in fact been arrested on board a British vessel lying at anchor in British territorial waters.[1] As Lansdowne informed Phipps

> The feeling in the House was so strong and widespread in support of the resolution and in condemnation of acts complained of that Lord Cranbourne found it difficult to obtain any consideration for what he had to say in mitigation of the attack on the Congo administration. Any attempt to obtain withdrawal or rejection of the resolution would undoubtedly have resulted in the defeat of the Government.[2]

On the eve of the debate Lansdowne had sought to obtain from the king-sovereign an assurance that he would appoint an impartial commission to investigate allegations against the Congo State[3] but Leopold II was away from Brussels and Phipps had been unable to see him before the debate. The best that the prime minister found it possible to do was to secure the deletion of the clause 'and both these guarantees

---

[1] 'Report from H.M.'s Commissioner for British Central Africa respecting the Anglo-Congolese frontier in the neighbourhood of Lake Mweru and the circumstances attending the arrest of the late M. Rabinek', *Accounts and Papers,* 1903 (Cd. 1536), xiv, 631.

[2] Lansdowne to Phipps, 21 May 1903, FO 10/803, tel. no. 3, Africa.

[3] Lansdowne to Phipps, 14 May 1903, ibid., tel. no. 1, Africa.

having been constantly violated', which, however, did not change the meaning of the resolution.[1]

The unanimous adoption of the Samuel resolution, although it was not realized at the time, was a turning point in the history of the Congo. It set in motion a chain of actions and reactions which inevitably forced Leopold II to surrender his African empire. Meanwhile, having also undertaken to champion the cause of Congo reform, the Foreign Office had either to produce or to secure the production of official evidence to justify its demand for reform. The British government had indeed been forced into a position from which retreat was unthinkable until the Congo atrocities had been disproved or abolished and the Congo system justified or reformed.

In Belgium, the press and the public did not hide their resentment at the turn events had taken at Westminster. The *Indépendance Belge*, which had become vigorously Anglophobe since the Boer War, condemned the rapacity of the reformers who it thought were jealous of the prosperity of the Congo State.[2] The *Petit Bleu*, recently subsidized by the Congo government, sneered at the pretence of the British government that its hands were forced.[3] The unanimity of Belgian support for the royal enterprise in Africa was demonstrated when Emile Vandervelde interpellated the government on the Congo question. The Liberal Opposition promptly rallied to the support of the Catholic majority in voting against the Socialists because they considered the moment as one demanding a national front.[4] Soon

---

[1] See Dilke's explanation: 'Balfour, though he took out some of the words, did so admitting that we could carry the motion against him if we liked. We had an overwhelming majority. I advised that we take his proposal, as it makes the Government more inclined to go forward with the Powers, and I was more inclined to do this as he had not noticed that the motion still assumes the proof to be complete; because in the last words it describes the evils in a manner which could not be adopted if a mere attitude of impartial enquiry was intended.' Dilke to Holt, 23 May 1903, J.H.P. 13/2.

[2] *Indépendance Belge*, 23 May 1903.

[3] *Petit Bleu*, 22 May 1903.

[4] *Annales Parlementaires*, (Chambre) 1 July 1903.

afterwards the *Fédération des Sociétés industrielles, commerciales, scientifiques et patriotiques pour la défense de nos intérêts à l'étranger* was launched in Brussels.[1] Its purpose was said to be to determine the best means of defending the work of the king in Africa against hostile criticism abroad, and to draw up a programme of the methods to be adopted.[2] The result was the regular appearance, in French, English and German of a propaganda leaflet called *La Vérité sur le Congo*, in which was published every scrap of evidence that could be found to emphasize the humanitarian character of the Belgian enterprise in Africa. This leaflet was widely distributed in Europe and America by agents of the Congo State as well as by the Belgian legations.[3]

It was however in the period after the issue of the first British Note[4] to the powers that the role of Belgian diplomacy becomes most significant. The Note was the initiative taken by the Foreign Office as a result of the adoption of the Samuel resolution. It was an appeal to the powers to join Britain in seeking a solution to the Congo question, namely, to ameliorate the condition of the Congolese and to re-examine the principle of freedom of commerce by referring the interpretation of this section of the Berlin Act to the Hague Tribunal. The Note elicited no response from any of the powers. There were three main reasons for this.

First, the Note was conceived in general terms and seemed to be uncertain as to the grounds on which it was based.

[1] Soon to be known as *Fédération pour la défense des intérêts belge à l'étranger*.

[2] *L'Etoile Belge*, 30 July 1903. One of the vice-presidents of the Association was Baron Wahis, a former governor-general of the Congo State.

[3] Other publications widely distributed by Belgian representatives were Descamp's *L'Afrique Nouvelle*, Brusselles 1903 (translated into English and German), and M. Boillot Robert's *Léopold II et le Congo—Nos fils au continent noir*. Robert, the Belgian consul at Neuchâtel, Switzerland, was paid a bonus of 1,500 fr. for this effort by the Belgian Ministry for Foreign Affairs. See Arendt, 26 November 1903, Ier sér., Congo, v, 1361, minute.

[4] 'Despatch to certain of H.M. Representatives abroad in regard to Alleged Cases of Ill-treatment of Natives and to the existence of Trade Monopolies in the Independent State of the Congo, 8 August 1903.' *Accounts and Papers*, 1904 (Cd. 1809), lxvii, 517.

The Congo government was able to point out with telling effect that

> The English note proceeds above all by hypotheses and assumptions: 'It was alleged . . . It is reported . . . It is also reported . . .' and it goes as far as saying that 'His Majesty's Government do not know precisely to what extent these accusations may be true.' This demonstrates that, in the eyes of the British Government itself, the accusations in question are neither established nor proved. And, indeed, the violence, the passion and the improbability of a number of these accusations makes them suspect to impartial minds.[1]

It is curious that the Foreign Office did not make use of the abundant evidence in its possession, or some of it, to illustrate its case. Their publication would probably have aroused considerable support. We are fortunate because Farnall who drafted the Note has left an answer to the puzzle. 'We must not make the circular too strong', he said, 'or we shall be blamed by the House of Commons, to whom the circular is in one sense as much addressed as it is to the Powers, for not having made a representation long ago.'[2] In the event, the reformers rejoiced that they had been able to get the Foreign Office to act at all, but the international action which was desired failed to materialize. The step taken by the Foreign Office is defensible only when it is realized that the Note was meant to be the forerunner of the evidence which Casement was now expected to furnish.[3]

Given the fact that the Note offered no satisfactory basis for concerted action, the ground was made relatively easy for Belgian diplomacy to erase whatever impressions it might have had. In Berlin, St Petersburg and Washington, the most likely capitals from which support for the British position might have come, Belgium, as it happened, deployed

---

[1] *Accounts and Papers*, 1904 (Cd. 1933), lxii, 357. The Congo reply was virtually written by Leopold II and, according to Phipps, he was proud of it. Phipps to Lansdowne, 26 September 1903, FO 800/116, Lansdowne Papers.

[2] Farnall, 5 June 1903, FO 10/805, minute.

[3] Infra, Cap. IV.

her ablest diplomatic representatives. In Berlin, Jules
Greindl, who wielded enormous influence within diplomatic
circles, was able to keep the Belgian government informed
of every move and mood of the German government with
regard to the Congo question.[1] It was evident, however, that
since German interests were not directly involved the Wilhelmstrasse would not act in concert with Britain.[2] In St
Petersburg, Raymond Leghait was fervently devoted to the
cause of the king-sovereign. Like Greindl, he also exercised
great influence at the Russian court and his close relations
with Count Larmsdorff helped to secure Russian abstention
from interference in Congo affairs.[3]

While in Berlin and St Petersburg the defence of the
Congo State was directed by the Belgian Ministry for
Foreign Affairs,[4] in Washington it was the king-sovereign

---

[1] Greindl to Favereau, 29 May 1903, Ier sér., Congo, iv, 1076; Greindl
to Favereau, 27 June 1903, Ier sér., Congo, iv, 1147; see also Willequet:
op. cit., pp. 15 ff.

[2] Ibid.

[3] Leghait to Favereau, 4 June 1903, Ier sér., Congo, iv, 1049; Leghait
to Favereau, 9 August 1903, Ier sér., Congo, v, 1197; Leghait to
Favereau, 26 August 1903, Ier sér., Congo, v, 1231; Leghait to Favereau,
17 September 1903, Ier sér., Congo, v, 1268; Leghait to Favereau,
22 December 1903, Ier sér., Congo, v, 1421.

[4] E.g., Favereau to Leghait, 25 July 1903, Ier sér., Congo, v, 1177:
'We know the great influence which the Minister of Finance exercises
on the course of affairs in Russia. It cannot be doubted that to achieve
the result which we are seeking, his support would be particularly useful
and effective.

'Therefore I desire that you seize an early opportunity to see M. Witte.
During the interview you will bring the conversation round to the affairs
of the Congo and to the move proposed by England.

'It might be opportune to remind M. Witte that on several matters,
especially Persia and the Far East, we have had occasion to show, as far
as our international position allows, the value which we attach to
pleasing the Russian Government.

'In the Empire itself, through great effort and applying capital which
amounts to several hundreds of millions, our nationals have created
numerous and important industries. If, on one side, the interests of
Belgian investors in most of these enterprises do not suffer to a large
extent from the crisis they are passing through, there can be no doubt,
on the other side, that as Russia draws considerable advantages for its

himself who, as we shall later see, organized the campaign for the neutralization of the Note. The result was the same: complete silence from the powers. There was no hope, of course, that France would support the British position. As has been pointed out, the principle of concessions had been adopted in the French Congo and so long as it was maintained, France could not really act otherwise in the Congo question than by defending the position of the Congo State. It is not surprising, therefore, that the Belgian ambassador could report that 'the French press, with a rare unanimity, declares itself in favour of the Congolese administration against its detractors';[1] or that the move of 'the British Government does not seem to have made much impression on the Department of Foreign Affairs'.[2] Indeed, M. Cogordan, the French Director of Political Affairs at the Quai d'Orsay, cynically remarked that 'the complaints formulated against the Congo could be applied to all countries possessing colonies, especially to Great Britain; France would not escape either.'[3] Without a lead from the great powers, the lesser ones showed a total lack of interest.[4]

Finally, it must be pointed out that Phipps also made a considerable contribution towards the failure of the British Note. He had always remained sceptical of the accusations brought against the Congo administration. He did not trust Casement and his reports. He even requested the Italian minister in Brussels to put him in direct communication with Italian officers of the Congo State passing through Brussels who, he believed, could furnish him with impartial and useful

---

economic prosperity from these concerns she will in the future drawn even more.

'These considerations, brought out with the necessary discretion, cannot fail to make an impression on a mind as sharp as that of M. Witte.'

[1] Baron D'Anethan (Paris) to Favereau, 19 May 1903, Ier sér., Congo, v. 1214.

[2] Anethan to Favereau, 20 August 1903, Ier sér., Congo, v, 1218.

[3] Ibid.

[4] E.g. see Comte de Grelle Rogier (The Hague) to Favereau, 26 July 1903, Ier sér., Congo, v, 1181, confidential; Borchgrave (Vienna) to Favereau, 9 September 1903, Ier sér., Congo, v, 1249.

information.[1] Phipps seemed to have felt that it was his duty to frustrate the initiative taken by the Foreign Office. Thus he virtually let it be known in diplomatic circles that a reply need not be sent to the Note. To the Italian Minister in Brussels he said that 'the note of 8 August had been prepared rather reluctantly and in order to please certain groups in the House of Commons.'[2] After a visit to London in October, he revealed to the German Minister in Brussels, Count Wallwitz, that no one had replied to the Note and that the whole episode would soon blow over.[3] In London itself he had told Lalaing that '*l'esprit de lucre* of Liverpool, as it is disappointed because it does not draw some of the profit which the Congo trade produces (because it had neglected to invest capital at the opportune moment), is the main source of the attacks against the king's work.'[4]

By the autumn of 1903, the British move in despatching the Note had been effectively checkmated in all the European capitals as well as in the United States. An attempt by the A.P.S. in September 1903 to draw world attention to the Congo question met the same fate. At the International Parliamentary Union meeting in Vienna permission to introduce a motion on the Congo favoured by the Society was refused following the intervention of Sam Wiener, Belgian senator and counsellor to Leopold II.[5] The king-sovereign had reason, therefore, to instruct that all Belgian diplomats be thanked for the zeal they had shown.[6] The Congo question thus remained essentially a British affair, a private quarrel between Britain and the Congo State. In Britain, however, interest did not wane. The entire press regardless of political complexion was united in support of

---

[1] L. Ranieri: *Les relations entre l'Etat indépendant du Congo et l'Italie*, Brussels 1959, p. 149.

[2] Ibid.

[3] Willequet: op. cit., p. 83.

[4] Lalaing to Favereau, 8 July 1903, Ier sér., Congo, v, 1160. This was probably the source of Lalaing's views on the reform movement in England.

[5] Stenmans: op. cit., pp. 278–9.

[6] Minute (unsigned), 26 November 1903, Ier sér., Congo, v, 1372.

the British initiative.[1] The Belgian reply, effective as it evidently was, only evoked scorn and resentment. For the *Standard*,[2] the reply was 'the very reverse of candid or conclusive' while the *Daily Telegraph*[3] called it 'an insolent reply'. *The Times*,[4] after weighing the evidence judiciously, described the reply as 'a very unsatisfactory rejoinder' and 'a poor apology'. Meanwhile the final verdict was reserved, for it was known that at that very moment the Foreign Office had instructed its representative in the Congo State to undertake an inquiry into the administration of the territory.

---

[1] 'All these papers are hostile to the King's work. Even though they belong to different political parties, they are unanimous in supporting the initiative taken by Lord Lansdowne.' Lalaing to Favereau, 24 October 1903, Ier sér., Congo, v, 1334.

[2] *Standard*, 24 October 1903.

[3] *Daily Telegraph*, 7 December 1903.

[4] *The Times*, 24 October 1903.

IV

The Casement Inquiry and its Aftermath

As early as July 1902 Casement, at his own request, had been granted permission to tour the Upper Congo. Ostensibly, his object then was to investigate the condition of any British subjects that might be living in that region and to obtain redress for such complaints as might come to his notice.[1] In fact it is fair to surmise from his despatches before July that he harboured a plan to expose, in an unmistakable manner, the defects of the Congo administration. This initiative, however, was checked by ill-health and it was not until his return from leave in April 1903 that he took up the plan again. By the time he reached Stanley Pool in June 1903 events at Westminster enabled him to abandon the investigation of the plight of British subjects and concentrate entirely on an inquiry into the operation of the Congo administration in the interior. The result of this mission was far-reaching. It generated a popular movement in Britain for Congo reform, made it certain that the Foreign Office would not drop the Congo question and compelled Leopold II to send out his own commission of inquiry. But for the Casement inquiry, there might have been no Congo question after 1904.

The assignment of this inquiry to Casement suggests the mood of the Foreign Office at the time. The views of the consul were known for none of his despatches suggested that

---

[1] Casement to Lansdowne, 21 July 1902, FO 10/773, no. 12, Africa.

he was keeping an open mind on the Congo question. What was urgently required was an indictment to save the face of the Foreign Office from the confident and almost jeering retort of the Note from the Congo government. Casement was expected to produce such an indictment. No other result was considered possible and, in the circumstance, no better man was available.

Casement received the instruction by telegram on 4 June;[1] the following day he was off on his journey. He remained on the Upper Congo for the next two and a half months, during which he kept a full diary of his day to day, and sometimes even of his hour to hour activities, and it is from this diary that one catches glimpses of the content of his subsequent report. This diary cannot be read without also seeing what Casement really was, a wildly passionate man tortured by his own emotional conflicts and enraged by the suffering of the people around him. At times these feelings erupt into incoherent poetic language, as when at Lukolela he wrote, 'Poor frail, self-seeking vexed mortality dust to dust—ashes to ashes—where then are the kindly heart the pitiless thought together vanished.'[2] At other times his indignation just flared up unrestrained as was the case at Bongandanga, in the concession of the Abir. Here, after observing that the people who brought in the rubber were 'all guarded like convicts' he remarked that 'To call this "*trade*" is the height of lying.'[3] The following day at this same place he saw sixteen men, women and children tied up together and on this he wrote: 'Infamous! The men were put in the prison, the children let go at my intervention. Infamous! Infamous Shameful system!' When it was clear from his lengthy despatches that he had obtained enough evidence to strengthen the British case the tour was cut short.[4]

On returning to England to prepare his report Casement

---

[1] Entry for 4 June 1903, HO 161/2. This is the diary for 1903.
[2] Entry for 27 July 1903, HO 161/2.
[3] Entry for 29 August 1903, ibid.
[4] Villiers, 3 November 1903, FO 10/806, minute; F.O. to Casement, 3 November 1903, ibid., tel. no. 9, Africa.

was not altogether satisfied that the Foreign Office was paying as much attention to the Congo question as he thought the subject deserved. After his first call at the Foreign Office he indignantly noted that they were 'a gang of stupidities in many ways'.[1] This rather reflects Casement's impatience because for some days at least he attracted more attention in the Foreign Office than was usually accorded to consuls. Percy who had now replaced Cranbourne as Parliamentary Under-Secretary first received him.[2] The following day he was invited to the home of Lansdowne and after the interview, according to Casement, Lansdowne remarked: 'Proof of the most painfully convincing kind Mr Casement.'[3] Casement's spirits revived, but it was only for a fortnight, during which the first draft of the report was completed. Its reception by Villiers, who was now in charge of the African Department, did not satisfy Casement, for he described him as 'an abject piffler'[4] and noted that Farnall 'seemed very desponding'.[5] By 22 December, however, Farnall was unreservedly praising the report[6] and a week later Villiers gave his blessing as follows:

> The report seems to be very well prepared and to be free from all trace of exaggeration. Taken together, report and appendices form a strong indictment and are sufficient to prove the extent to which maladministration has prevailed. The decrees and regulations of the Government are in most cases good enough. The rapacity at headquarters has made their observance impossible.[7]

One might be puzzled by the lukewarmness of the Foreign Office officials before 28 December and their sudden

---

[1] Entry for 1 December 1903, HO 161/2.
[2] Casement wrote: 'Note from Farnall Lord Percy wished to see me. Went [and] saw him [and] had a long talk. Think I gave him some eye openers.' Entry for 2 December 1903, ibid.
[3] Entry for 3 December 1903, ibid.
[4] Entry for 16 December 1903, ibid.
[5] Entry for 18 December 1903, ibid.
[6] 'His report is terse, full of matter and written in dispassionate style.' Farnall, 22 December 1903, FO 10/807, minute.
[7] Villiers, 28 December 1903, ibid., minute.

93

enthusiasm after that date until the activities of Leopold II at this time are examined. Even before Casement's return from the Congo it had become known in Brussels that his report would be hostile to the Congo government.[1] The king-sovereign therefore sought to exercise some pressure on the Foreign Office in order to secure the non-publication of the report or to minimize whatever impact its publication might have. One of the actions he took was to issue a Royal Decree dated 18 November 1903[2] which reorganized the direct and personal taxes enforced in the State, including the Congolese *prestations*. While before the decree these *prestations* were in no way defined and were arbitrarily imposed on each village by the local official, Article 2 of the new decree now stated that 'These *prestations* consist of work to be carried out for the State. This work should be paid; it should not exceed a total duration of forty effective hours per month.' By Article 28, the district commissioners were to decide, under the supervision of a royal high commissioner, what labour was to be performed by each Congolese and Article 31 permitted the commissioners to indicate the amount of produce to be furnished by the Congolese in lieu of the forty hours of monthly labour. Finally, punishments ranging from imprisonments of two months to one year or fines of 100 fr. to 2000 fr. were to be imposed on officials who did not conform to the terms of the decree.

The agent for the execution of his other plan was Alfred L. Jones, shipping magnate, chairman of the African section of the Liverpool Chamber of Commerce and consul of the Congo State in Liverpool. The fact that his shipping line, Elder Dempster and Company, possessed the profitable monopoly of the Congo–Antwerp traffic[3] had made him

---

[1] E.g. see Phipps to Lansdowne, 20 November 1903, ibid., private. On 7 December the *Morning Post* had commented:

'Secrecy is naturally maintained regarding his report but Reuter's Agency is informed it will show that horrible outrages are still being perpetrated under the rubber régime and that slavery and barbarism in the most revolting forms exist today.'

[2] *B.O.*, no. 10, October 1903.

[3] The Elder Dempster and Company ran this monopoly under the name *Compagnie belge Maritime du Congo*.

one of the foremost defenders of the Congo State régime
from the very inception of the agitation in England. His
great influence in Liverpool had checked much of the
enthusiasm that would otherwise have been roused by the
Congo question. He was soon to spend considerable sums
of money in sending private investigators to the Congo to
write favourable reports on the Congo State. The contract
for this shipping monopoly, however, was due to expire at
the end of 1904. On 11 November, *L'Etoile Belge*, the inspired
organ of the Congo State, announced that negotiations were
in progress for the creation of a Belgo-German line between
Antwerp and the Congo which would replace the existing
English line whose contract would not be renewed.[1]

This threat to British shipping interest brought Jones to
seek help from the Foreign Office. He informed Villiers[2] that
he was in great fear of the Elder Dempster and Company
losing the West African trade altogether. The Germans, he
pointed out, were negotiating to obtain his contract with the
Congo government and in spite of the fact that the trade
had been created and developed by British enterprise the
Congo government would probably transfer the contract
to the Germans in consequence of the attitude of the British
government with regard to the administration of the Congo.
The Congo trade was not in itself of first class importance,
Jones continued, but whoever held it had an advantage
against which rivals could not contend. The powerful
Hamburg–America line were beginning to take an interest
in West Africa and if the Germans succeeded in their attempt
which was being supported by the German government,
with the approval of the emperor, they would sweep the
board and drive out all British trade. Jones wished to know
whether the Foreign Office could give a hint through the

---

[1] *L'Etoile Belge*, 11 November 1903. The announcement was repeated
in *Mouvement Géographique*, 13 December 1903. See also Willequet:
op. cit., p. 97, n. 2, which reveals that the king never seriously contemplated the alteration of the Anglo-Belgian shipping arrangement.
Nevertheless, the threat to do so was a useful lever in his diplomatic
manoeuvres.
[2] Villiers, 10 December 1903, FO 10/805, memorandum.

British minister in Brussels that 'any action causing detriment to British trade would not "make it any better over here for the Congo government" '. He also asked whether the British government would 'be satisfied and let the atrocities question drop' if King Leopold wrote 'a very diplomatic letter' acknowledging the faults of the past and promising complete reform in the future. As an alternative to this, Jones wanted to know 'whether it would be useful for the king to write the "nice" note after the publication of the Casement reports'.[1]

It is at first sight not clear whether Jones was acting with the connivance of Leopold II or whether he was genuinely alarmed by the obvious threat to his shipping line and was making a spontaneous bid to obtain a counter with which to stave off the loss. If it were the latter, it would be very difficult to understand his first question about getting Leopold II to write 'a very diplomatic letter' except on the basis that he was committing the king-sovereign in a rash and far-reaching way. But even if he was acting spontaneously his second call on a similar mission a few days later was, as we shall soon see, as the messenger of Leopold II. It might be noted, however, that whatever the origin of the Jones mission the prospect of the loss to British shipping of the profitable Antwerp–Congo route was a factor which the Foreign Office could not ignore; nor could the interests of a prominent Liverpool Unionist like Jones be lightly disregarded. On the other hand, the Foreign Office had permitted Casement to meet Morel and both had discussed the extent of Congo maladministration which he had seen.[2] There was no doubt also that there would be a great public clamour for the publication of the report. In these circumstances, while the various conflicting interests jostled one another, it was inevitable that Farnall and Villiers would be hesitant about the fate of the report.

Meanwhile, Jones had called again to see Villiers.[3] This time, his arrival was heralded by a private letter from

---

[1] Ibid.
[2] E. D. Morel: *History of the C.R.A.*, M.P., Box H.
[3] Villiers, 21 December 1903, FO 10/807, memorandum.

Hertslet,[1] now British consul-general in Antwerp, in which
the alarm was repeated that the Germans were eagerly
negotiating to secure the British shipping contract and that
the king-sovereign was so irritated with Britain that he might
yield to the Germans. The consul-general revealed that
Jones was bringing a proposal from Leopold II which should
be favourably considered. Jones, who had evidently seen
Hertslet in Antwerp, duly produced the draft of a letter
given to him in Brussels by the king-sovereign.[2] The latter
was prepared to address such a letter to the Foreign Secretary
if there was an assurance of its acceptance. The king-
sovereign, it would appear, had realized the futility of
obtaining the suppression of the report. He had also become
confident that he would be able to discredit Casement's
charges against the Congo State.[3] In the draft letter, therefore, he requested to be furnished with consular reports on
the Congo to which reference had been made during the
May debate so that the allegations they contained might
be investigated by him. At the same time he wanted a copy
of the Casement report to enable a reply to be prepared
for simultaneous publication.

Percy, who took a great interest in the Congo question,
was inclined to be sympathetic towards the request for an
advance copy of the Casement Report. There were, he
wrote,[4] three courses of action which might be taken on the
report: its publication at an early date and despatch to
the powers with an invitation to give an immediate reply to the
Note; withholding the report until a copy had been given

---

[1] Hertslet to Sanderson (Permanent Under-Secretary for Foreign
Affairs), 18 December 1903, ibid., private.

[2] This letter (Appendix II) shows that there is no basis for the assertion of Casement, adopted by Slade, that Leopold II offered to institute
a commission of inquiry at this stage in exchange for the suppression of
the Casement report. See Slade: *English-speaking Missions*, pp. 287–8.

[3] The one case of mutilation investigated by Casement had been
proved to have been caused not by a Congo official but by a wild boar.
This was the case of the Epondo boy, a minor case, which the Congo
government later sought to emphasize in order to show that the Casement report was unreliable. The Foreign Office, however, refused to
be drawn into a controversy over this side issue.

[4] Percy, n.d., FO 10/807, minute.

to Leopold II on the condition that it must be published before parliament met; and finally, suppression of the report for the moment on the condition that the Congo government appointed an international commission of inquiry immediately to which a copy of the Casement report would be given to help in the subsequent investigations. Percy favoured the last course. According to him, the first suggestion might impress the powers but they might also order their own inquiries and Leopold would 'issue new regulations on paper —the House will be pleased, and no practical result obtained'. On the second suggestion, he doubted whether it would satisfy the king-sovereign, 'or help Sir A[lfred] Jones', while the Belgians would be given an opportunity of diminishing whatever influence the report could have carried. Farnall, however, was opposed to Percy's views. Influenced by Casement with whom he had been in constant consultation on the final revision of the report, he strongly objected to withholding its publication. 'If the report is published' he pleaded, 'we shall at least be uncompromised and can at any time take what further action may be possible on behalf of the natives.'[1] Villiers was swayed by this argument and so also was Lansdowne soon afterwards.[2]

The decision to publish was a severe blow to the king-sovereign. The failure of his plan was probably due to the incapacity of Jones to serve his ends as well as the inability of Leopold II himself to gauge the temper of the Foreign Office. The modification in the original demand for non-publication as a guarantee for the renewal of the shipping contract helped to stiffen the attitude of the Foreign Office. The shipping contract, it was realized, was in no serious danger and the royal bluff could conveniently be called. In the end, he even failed to attain the limited objective of a simultaneous publication of the report with his reply.[3]

---

[1] Farnall, 28 December 1903, ibid., minute.

[2] Villiers to Percy, 21 January 1904, ibid., private.

[3] It was decided that the king-sovereign ('such a dodger', as the Permanent Under-Secretary for Foreign Affairs called him) should receive the copy of the Casement Report simultaneously with the other Powers. Villiers, 30 January 1904, ibid., minute.

A decision in favour of publication had hardly been taken when Casement introduced a new element into the discussion. Asked for his comment on how the report should be treated, he suggested not merely that the report should be published but that, if after publication the powers did not join Britain in collective action, British consular courts should be established in the Congo. 'Such a Court', he said, 'would present a striking contrast to the natives, undermine Congo State prestige and induce reforms as compensation for withdrawal by Britain of the Court.'[1] It was a suggestion characteristic of Casement: simple, direct and extreme. Farnall again supported Casement.[2] Percy, however, was more cautious, for he did not wish the king-sovereign to be driven too far. The 'moral effects' of consular jurisdiction, according to him, would be insignificant and its 'practical results' would not be helpful since there might be no British subjects in those Congo regions 'where the system of administration was being disrupted'.[3] Lansdowne himself also maintained a cautious attitude and ordered that the threat to exercise consular jurisdiction should merely be 'held in reserve'.[4]

On 11 February the Casement Report was presented to Parliament.[5] The White Paper opened with a brief but damaging extract of a despatch which Cromer had written at the beginning of 1903 on his observations during a visit to Kiro, Lado and Gondokoro. 'I had heard so many and such contradictory accounts of the Belgian Administration', he said, 'that I was very desirous of ascertaining some concise and definite evidence on this subject.' He had noted that the territories under the Congo administration were deserted except for Belgian officers and their retinue. He gave a striking reason for this: 'The Belgians are disliked. The people

---

[1] Casement, 2 January 1904, ibid., memorandum.
[2] Farnall, 5 January 1904, ibid., memorandum.
[3] Percy, ? January 1904, ibid., minute.
[4] Lansdowne, ? January 1904, ibid., minute.
[5] 'Correspondence and Report from His Majesty's Consul at Boma respecting the Administration of the Independent State of the Congo', *Accounts and Papers*, 1904 (Cd. 1933), lxii, 357. For an unedited copy of the report see Casement to Lansdowne, 11 December 1903, FO 10/806.

fly from them, and it is no wonder they should do so, for I am informed that the soldiers are allowed full liberty to plunder, and that payments are rarely made for supplies.' Cromer concluded that the government, so far as he could judge, was conducted almost exclusively on commercial principles.

The Casement Report which followed went into far greater detail. Together with appendices, it takes up fifty-six pages of closely printed foolscap and was devoted to a cold and systematic exposition of Leopoldian wickedness.

According to this document, the area visited by Casement was 'one of the most central in the Congo State' and he was able to contrast the prevailing conditions with what he had seen during a visit in 1887, that is, before the imposition of colonial rule. In less than two paragraphs he admitted the beneficial effects of 'energetic European intervention' in the Congo and 'the great energy displayed by Belgian officials'. The visible results were that 'admirably built and admirably kept stations greet the traveller at many points'; 'a fleet of river steamers' afforded regular means of communication 'to some of the most inaccessible parts of Central Africa'; and a railway which circumvented the cataract region of the Lower Congo linked the ocean ports with Stanley Pool.

The report then proceeded to expose the plight of the Congolese. One of the major recurring themes in the report is what Casement describes as the 'great reduction observable everywhere in native life'. He laments: 'Communities I had formerly known as large and flourishing centres of population are today entirely gone, or now exist in such diminished numbers as to be no longer recognizable.' Thus the Bateke middlemen, who formerly numbered about 5,000 on the southern shore of Stanley Pool, had migrated to the French colony in the north. At Chumbiri, where the population numbered 4,000 to 5,000 in August 1887, most of the villages were entirely deserted and the remainder contained no more than 500 people. Bolobo, at the inception of colonial rule, 'numbered fully 40,000 people, chiefly of the Bobangi tribe' and 'used to be one of the most important native settlements along the south bank of the Upper Congo' but in 1903 could only boast of 7,000 to 8,000 persons. Casement afforded similar statistics for the other towns of the Upper Congo. Lukolela had declined from 5,000 in 1887 to 'less than 600'; Irebu which numbered 3,000 'had entirely disappeared'; and the population of the towns around Lake Mantumba had diminished by 60 or 70 per cent.

The report noted that one of the causes for the diminishing population was sleeping-sickness, an 'incurable' disease which had spread from its 'home, or birth-place' in the cataract region eastwards across Africa. But Casement also hastened to point out that the principal causes lay elsewhere. One was the services demanded from the Congolese by the government or Concession Companies and the methods employed in exacting them. These impositions forced some of the inhabitants to emigrate; others resisted and had to face military expeditions which took a heavy toll in lives and property; the remainder soon grew too weak from their exertions to replenish the population or to resist disease. In return for their labours, the inhabitants hardly received any remuneration or benefits which could serve as an incentive.

Casement illustrated these factors in great detail. At a government station like Leopoldville (now renamed Kinshasa) the surrounding villages were forced to provide each week food for the European staff and their Congolese employees. The report commented that this was not a 'welcome task to the native suppliers who complain that their numbers are yearly decreasing, while the demands upon them remain fixed, or tend even to increase.' At Chumbiri, higher up the river, the villagers were compelled to clear the roads along the telegraph line, cut wood for the government steamers and supply food to the government station. The State official was thus 'forced to exercise continuous pressure on the local population. . . . Armed expeditions have been necessary. . . .' The report stated that the 'people have not easily accommodated themselves to the altered condition of life brought about by European Government in their midst.' During one such expedition sixteen people were killed, ten were detained until their friends exchanged them for sixteen goats, and a number of houses were either burnt or pillaged. A similar state of affairs prevailed at Bolobo. According to the Report:

> Complaints as to the manner of exacting service are much more frequent than complaints as to the fact of service being required. If the local official has to go on a sudden journey men are summoned on the instant to paddle his canoe, and a refusal entails imprisonment or a beating. If the Government plantation or the kitchen garden require weeding, a soldier will be sent to call in the women from some of the neighbouring towns. To the official this is a necessary public duty which he cannot but impose, but to the women suddenly forced to leave their household tasks and to tramp off, hoe in hand, baby on back, with possibly a hungry and angry husband at home, the task is not a welcome one.

Farther up the river, in the region where india-rubber was tapped, the exactions on the population were evidently worse for refugees had to flee from there to Chumbiri. These people, who used to inhabit the *Domaine de la Couronne*, declared that

> they had endured such ill-treatment at the hands of the Government officials and the Government soldiers in their own country that life had become intolerable, that nothing had remained for them at home but to be killed for failure to bring in a certain amount of rubber or to die from starvation or exposure in their attempts to satisfy the demands made upon them.

As one of the appendices to the report, Casement included the statement of one of the refugees (obviously a literal translation) describing the kind of life rubber-collecting meant:

> It used to take ten days to get the twenty baskets of rubber— we were always in the forest to find the rubber vines, to go without food, and our women had to give up cultivating the fields and gardens. Then we starved. Wild beasts—the leopards killed some of us while we were working away in the forest and others got lost or died from exposure and starvation and we begged the white men to leave us alone, saying we could

get no more rubber, but the white men and their soldiers said: 'Go. You are only beasts yourselves, you are only nyama (meat).' We tried, always going further into the forest, and when we failed and our rubber was short, the soldiers came to our towns and killed us. Many were shot, some had their ears cut off; others were tied up with ropes round their necks and bodies and taken away.

Also attached was a letter written by one Rev. Whitehead of the B.M.S. station at Lukolela to the Governor-General of the Congo State dated 28 July 1903 which seemed to corroborate the evidence of the refugees:

The pressure under which they live at present is crushing them; the food which they sadly need themselves very often must, under penalty, be carried to the State post, also grass, cane string, baskets for the 'caoutchouc' (the last three items do not appear to be paid for); the 'caoutchouc' must be brought in from the inland districts; their Chiefs are being weakened in their prestige and physique through imprisonment, which is often cruel, and thus weakened in their authority over their own people, they are put into chains for the shortage of manioc bread and 'caoutchouc'.

Casement himself summarized his own impressions as follows:

A careful investigation of the conditions of native life around the lake [Mantumba] confirmed the truth of the statements made to me both by M. Wauters, the local American missionary, and many natives, that the great decrease in population, the dirty and ill-kept towns, and the complete absence of goats, sheep, or fowls—once very plentiful in this country— were to be attributed above all else to the continued effort made during many years to compel the natives to work india-rubber. Large bodies of native troops had formerly been quartered in the district, and the punitive measures undertaken to this end had endured for a considerable period. During the course of these operations there had been much loss of life, accompanied, I fear, by a somewhat general mutilation of the dead, as proof that the soldiers had done their duty.

So far the illustrations had been drawn from areas directly administered and exploited by the government. After passing through yet another government station named Coquilhat-ville where the surrounding native population endured the same conditions as in the other places lower down the river, Casement arrived at a branch of the Congo River known as the Lulongo River. This river, the principal tributaries of which were called the Lopori and Maringa Rivers, flows through one of the 'most productive rubber districts of the Congo State' and was being exploited under a concession granted to the Abir Company. The company imported large quantities of 'cap-guns, which are chiefly used in arming the sentinels—termed "forest guards"—who, in considerable numbers, are quartered on the native villages throughout the Concession to see that the picked men of each town bring in, with regularity, the fixed quantity of pure rubber required of them every fortnight'. Casement remarked that prior to a government enactment in 1900 the Concession companies had exercised unlimited power to levy war on the local inhabitants in the interest of their commercial operations. That right had been regulated later by requiring all fire-arms to be licensed but there had been cases of evasion. The result was that the companies could terrorize the surrounding villages and inflict whatever punishment they deemed necessary. Casement recorded that those who failed to bring in the expected quota of rubber were detained in the *maison des otages* where they were subjected to flogging resulting sometimes in the death of the victims. In some cases, women were detained until redeemed by their husbands with the correct quota of rubber or foodstuffs. In other cases, the sentries exacted a more terrible punishment by maiming either dead or living victims. One case which later became virtually a *cause célèbre* was that of a fifteen-year-old youth, called Epondo, who informed Casement that a sentry of the La Lulanga Company had cut off his hand. On this issue of mutilation there was apparently no difference between the practice in the areas controlled by the government or the Concession companies, for in the case of the former Casement had earlier commented:

104

Of acts of persistent mutilation by Government soldiers of
this nature I had many statements made to me, some of them
specially, others in general way. Of the fact of this mutilation
and the causes inducing it there can be no shadow of doubt.
It was not a native custom prior to the coming of the white
man; it was not the outcome of the primitive instinct of savages
in their fights between village and village; it was the deliberate
act of the soldiers of a European administration, and these men
themselves never made any concealment that in committing
these acts they were but obeying the positive orders of their
superiors.

Throughout the report Casement emphasizes that the
material advantage derived by the Congolese from European
rule was minimal or even non-existent. Rather, the country
and its people were exploited solely for the benefit of Belgian
commercial interests which were making enormous profits
from their small outlay. At government stations in the Lower
Congo the villagers were paid in barter goods like cheap
cotton cloths; higher up the river they received brass rods,
which were the recognized local currency. The length of
these rods varied from one district to another, but in general
it had decreased from a length of 18 inches to not more than
7 or 8 inches. 'The nominal value', according to Casement, 'of one of these rods is ½d., twenty of them being
reckoned to the franc; but the intrinsic value, or actual cost
of a rod to any importer of the brass wire direct from
Europe, would come to less than a ¼d.' The Concession
companies also used brass rods as well as barter goods,
consisting of cotton cloths, Sheffield cutlery, matchets,
beads and salt, as currency. Neither the brass rods nor the
barter goods bore any relation to the real market value of
the services rendered by the villagers or the produce (mainly
rubber and gum-copal) which they were under compulsion
to collect, and that fact accounted for the prosperity of the
Congo State.

Finally, Casement drew attention to a Circular of the
Governor-General dated 29 March 1901 and addressed to all
local officials, which had deplored the diminution in the output

of rubber and urged greater vigour in its collection. He commented:

> The instructions this Circular conveys would be excellent if coming from the head of a trading house to his subordinates, but addressed, as they are, by a Governor-General to the principal officers of his administration, they reveal a somewhat limited conception of public duty. Instead of their energies being directed to the government of their districts, the officers therein addressed could not but feel themselves bound to consider the profitable exploitation of india-rubber as one of the principal functions of Government. . . . The praiseworthy official would be he whose district yielded the best and biggest supply of that commodity; and, succeeding in this, the means whereby he brought about the enhanced value of that yield would not, it may be believed, be too closely scrutinized.

In the memorandum[1] accompanying the report, the Foreign Office felt itself justified in calling upon the powers to reply to its circular of the previous August. It was urged that the evidence now furnished made international action against the Congo State necessary and justifiable.

The publication of the report and the second British Note to the powers did not afford any satisfaction to Casement.[2]

---

[1] *Accounts and Papers*, 1904 (Cd. 1933), lxii, 357.

[2] After submitting the report Casement had requested the suppression of the names of all State officials and agents of the concession companies in the published version. (Casement to Farnall, 4 January 1904, FO 10/807, private.) The Foreign Office, however, went a step further. Not only were those names suppressed but the names of the Congolese witnesses, towns and villages as well as the dates—all constituting evidence which might help in the identification of Casement's witnesses —were eliminated from the report when it was published. Casement complained bitterly about this, particularly when the Congo government asked for details, and even threatened to resign from the consular service. (Casement to Farnall, 20 February 1904, FO 10/808, private.) It was characteristic of Casement that though the omissions eventually had little effect on the outcome of the report he became disillusioned with the Foreign Office and felt a sense of betrayal against the government. As months passed and he waited in vain for his next consular appointment, his attention began to turn to Irish affairs. He began to study

In the meantime, he had set in motion what he conceived to be a more effective scheme in his private campaign against Congo misrule.

Since August 1903 Casement had been in regular correspondence with Morel through a mutual friend, Herbert Ward, the traveller and sculptor. It was about this time that Morel was beginning to dominate the agitation in England against the Congo State. As early as February he had founded the *West African Mail* with the financial backing of John Holt and some Liverpool friends to afford him his own platform for lashing out against the Leopoldian system. Many leading papers like the *Morning Post, The Times, Pall Mall Gazette* and *Daily News* also opened their columns to him. It was this year also that he published under the patronage of John Holt *The British Case in the French Congo*, which closed with an attack on Leopold II. This publication had been followed by a less oblique assault in the shape of a pamphlet entitled *The Congo Slave Trade*.[1] Again with Holt's financial help this pamphlet was distributed gratis to members of both Houses of Parliament and to the press. Most of these writings had found their way into the hands of Casement in the Congo and he heartily approved of them. It was not surprising that

---

Irish history and the tragedy of the English domination of his native land. When at last in November 1904 he was posted to Lisbon a crisis in his life had been reached. Lisbon offered him no attractions and after only a month there he applied, ostensibly on health reasons, to be placed on the non-active list. Once more he returned to Ireland and to his study of Irish history and politics. Only his diminishing income drove him to seek employment again with the consular service, but he had to wait until August 1906, when he was appointed to São Paulo in South America. Neither a knighthood in 1905 nor a tribute in the House of Lords by Fitzmaurice the following year was enough to wipe out his conviction of having been the victim of a betrayal; but now he could add another count of having been left in the wilderness for so long. Nevertheless, he was to conduct another famous inquiry at Putumayo, South America, in 1910. That was his last act in the service of the British government. At the outbreak of war in 1914 he placed his loyalty to the Irish cause above his allegiance to the English Crown and in 1916 he was executed for treason.

[1] This booklet provoked a retort from King Leopold's publicist in England, Demetrius C. Boulger, who wrote a pamphlet entitled *The Congo State is not a Slave State*.

on his return to England he should seek to meet the author of these works.[1]

They met for the first time in Ward's London home ten days after Casement's return from the Congo. It is clear that both men were immediately attracted to each other and that the foundation of a life-long friendship was there and then laid. 'The man is honest as day', Casement noted in his diary[2] and Morel's reaction was much the same.[3] 'I hope you will soon meet Casement', he told John Holt, 'He is a man in 10,000.'[4] Casement at this meeting revealed the nature of his report and Morel's confidence in the bold stand he had taken on the Congo question was fortified. Caution, however, was maintained. Nothing appeared in the *West African Mail* to anticipate the report, Morel contenting himself with the publication of lurid stories furnished by missionaries of the mutilation and the depopulation of the Congo under Leopold's régime.

It was not until a month later that Casement brought forward a plan which he hoped would consolidate the Congo reform campaign and generate fresh enthusiasm. This was no less than to 'found now and at once a Congo Reform Committee'.[5] He explained at length the need for the formation of such an organization:

> It seems quite clear to me that if those of us who feel strongly—whose hearts are moved as well as their heads by this terrible wrong-doing on the Congo—wish to bring home to the public the reality of that wrong-doing on the Congo, we must unite in an organised association having one clear sole aim—namely to enlighten systematically and continuously public opinion in this country, and abroad, upon the actual condition of the Congo people under the system of pillage and continuous extortion imposed on them by armed and ruthless force.

---

[1] E. D. Morel: *History of the C.R.A.*, M.P., Box H.
[2] Entry for 10 December 1903, HO 161/2.
[3] Morel: op. cit.
[4] Morel to Holt, 24 January 1904, J.H.P. 18/2.
[5] Casement to Morel, 25 January 1904, M.P., F.8.

Sporadic meetings and occasional lectures—articles in the press from time to time are not sufficient. They do good, of course, but they are not systematic. The defenders of the monstrous régime we are each individually attacking in our separate paths are all banded together in one powerful and wealthy league with a Sovereign State for execution and a King for Chairman.

They are systematic—and only systematized effort can get the better of them.

They can organize and maintain a vast agitation with an entire people misled for cheering supporters. We, at present, appeal only separately and at occasional gatherings or privately or by the columns of such few papers as are open to the voice of misery from the Congo.

We want an entire people, too, behind us, moved by the same impulses of pity. I am confident that once any decent man or woman here in this country learns and appreciates the ghastly truth of the wrong done to the Congo man and woman—aye, and to the poor, hunted child!—they will not desert them.

We shall grow in strength and numbers day by day until there go up from all the length and breadth of England one overwhelming Nay to the continuance of a system which is a disgrace to our race and colour.[1]

At the same time that Casement put these ideas to Morel he also made them known to Grattan Guinness of the Regions Beyond Missionary Union (parent organization of the C.B.M.) and W. T. Stead, editor of the *Review of Reviews*.[2] It was only from Morel, however, that he received an immediate response.

---

[1] Ibid.

[2] Casement must have put these ideas to Morel, Guinness and Stead a little earlier than 25 January when he formally elaborated them in the letter already quoted. The date is unknown but Morel received his on 23 January. Morel to Holt, 24 January 1904, J.H.P. 18/2. Casement also put the scheme to Fox Bourne. See Casement to Fox Bourne, 25 January 1904, A.S., G. 261. This was certainly after he had discussed it with Morel and he might have unwittingly alienated Fox Bourne at this stage by suggesting that the association should be run with Morel as secretary. For Fox Bourne's reactions see below.

Morel plunged himself at once into working out the scheme in Liverpool. He had at his disposal the sum of £100 which Casement had enclosed in his letter of 25 January to help with the initial expenses for founding the organization. On one man he could unquestionably rely for support and that man was of course John Holt. The moment was propitious for two reasons. Firstly, a change had taken place in the policy of the C.B.M. Disillusioned by the persistent refusal of the Congo government to grant them sites for their work, encouraged by the apparent determination of the British government to enforce their rights in the Congo, and suddenly awakened to the fact that the cry for Congo reform could open men's pockets for the mission, Grattan Guinness had thrown his whole energy into the reform campaign. At that very time he was storming the country with public meetings and illustrated lectures on Congo atrocities. Consequently, it was easy to bring him into the new organization; and with him, the powerful influence of his mission. The second reason for the time being propitious was that the publication of Casement's report had aroused unprecedented interest in the Congo question since all the leading newspapers gave prominence to it.[1] The report seems to have been taken as an excellent opportunity to avenge the scathing attacks of the Belgian press during the Boer War. The Belgian consul in Liverpool was alarmed and reported that 'the attacks of the English press against the Independent State of the Congo take a more and more aggressive and disturbing turn.'[2] Its immediate result was to influence many people to identify themselves with the cause of Congo reform. Thus the enthusiasm of Casement and Morel, the timely conversion of Grattan Guinness and the impact of the

---

[1] For example, under the headline 'Land of Desolation and Woe', the *Daily Telegraph*, 18 February 1904, said 'If every country were like the Congo Free State, this would, indeed, be a world of "massacre, murder, and wrong"'. Other headlines read: 'Stories of Fiendish Belgian Rule', *St. James Gazette*, 15 February 1904; 'A policy of Extermination', *Daily News*, 15 February 1904; 'Wholesale Murder and Mutilation', *Daily Mail*, 15 February 1904, etc.

[2] Edouard Sève to Favereau, 15 February 1904, Ier sér., Congo, vi, 1470.

Casement report were factors which prepared the ground for the emergence of a unified Congo reform movement.

But there were initial obstacles to be surmounted. Curiously enough, they were presented by some of the friends of the Congo. Fox Bourne and his associates in the A.P.S. refused to join the proposed Congo reform movement. Fox Bourne had for long been disappointed by the reticence and caution of the British missionaries working in the Congo.[1] When it seemed that Grattan Guinness, whom he had found 'a slippery customer',[2] had at last come forward to champion Congo reform, he remained suspicious and even hostile.[3] But underlying personal antagonisms was the more fundamental question whether a firmly established body like the A.P.S., for so long a pioneer in the Congo reform movement, should subordinate itself to a new organization such as Morel and Casement envisaged. Fox Bourne did not think so. His society would be incurring the risk, in the event of differences of opinion arising as to policy or methods, of an open rupture which would prove injurious to the common cause. In any case, the new association could only lead to a division of force and a consequent waste of energy.[4] Morel's plea that his association, formed for a specific purpose, stood a better chance of rallying more support than the A.P.S. with its catholic interests, was of no avail.[5] Casement was for a moment discouraged in the face of Fox Bourne's determination and was willing to drop or postpone the formation of the new body. Morel, however, once his mind had been made up, was obstinate in his persistence. Casement's enthusiasm accordingly revived. In fact the danger of friction did not materialize and cordial relations between the A.P.S. and the Congo Reform Association (C.R.A.) were complete. Indeed, three months later, the committee of the A.P.S. sent

---

[1] Fox Bourne to Morel, 24 November 1903, M.P., F.8.

[2] Fox Bourne to Casement, 29 November 1903, ibid.

[3] Fox Bourne to Casement, 4 March 1904, encl. in Fox Bourne to Morel, 4 March 1904, ibid.

[4] Ibid. See also Dilke to Casement, 12 February 1904, A.S., G. 261 (copy).

[5] Fox Bourne to Morel, 10 March 1904, M.P., F.8.

Dilke, Francis W. Fox and Fox Bourne to represent it on the executive committee of the C.R.A.[1]

Before this rapprochement was made by the two organizations, Morel and Casement had been able to make the C.R.A. a reality. Membership was relatively easy to obtain. The cause was virtually non-controversial and humanitarianism was fashionable. When its existence was announced in March by Morel at the Liverpool Philharmonic Hall, the C.R.A. had on its manifesto the names of eight peers, four bishops, eleven members of parliament and a representative group of merchants, clergy and scholars. At the head of the executive committee was Earl Beauchamp and Morel became the honorary secretary. The aim of the C.R.A., as stated in its manifesto, was 'to secure for the natives inhabiting the Congo State territories the just and humane treatment which was guaranteed to them under the Berlin and Brussels Act.'

The C.R.A. provided a counterpoise to the *Fédération pour la défense des intérêts belges à l'étranger*. Its significance was not lost on Belgian representatives in England. Sève warned that the names of its adherents showed the power of the Association,[2] and Lalaing, apparently for the first time became alive to the danger of the British Congo reform movement.[3] Leopold II, however, was not unduly perturbed. Although his wish to receive a copy of the Casement Report in advance had not been met, his recent visits to Paris, Vienna and Berlin had reassured him that there was nothing to fear from those capitals. President Loubet had reaffirmed to him, in spite of the approaching signature of the Anglo-French entente, that 'the interests of France and the Congo State were identical in this question'.[4] For the Austro-Hungarian government the question was essentially still a private quarrel between Britain and the Congo State in

---

[1] Fox Bourne to Morel, 3 June 1904, ibid.

[2] Sève to Favereau, 26 March 1904, Ier sér., Congo, vi, 154.

[3] 'I consider this movement' Lalaing wrote, 'as a new and serious proof of the very active propaganda which is going on against the system adopted by the State.'

[4] Leghait to Favereau, 13 February 1904, Ier sér., Congo, vi, 1463.

which they need not be involved.[1] As for Berlin, shrewd observers noticed that the king-sovereign's sojourn at the Wilhelmstrasse had stiffened his attitude with regard to Congo affairs.[2]

In Belgium itself, King Leopold's position was as strong as ever for, as Phipps remarked, 'whatever may be the short-comings from a humanitarian point of view of the Congo scheme . . . that scheme has been adopted by the Belgian nation in its entirety'.[3] A staunch Anglophile like Van Eetvelde was alienated, though temporarily, by the action of the British government in this question.[4] In the circum-stance, it would have seemed wiser to ignore the Casement Report, and reform, if such had been intended, should have been initiated. Nevertheless, encouraged no doubt by the strength of Belgian public opinion, which he controlled,[5] assured that no power was prepared to intervene in the Congo question, perhaps confident that he could play at the same game and beat his English critics thus compelling the British government to give up the issue, the king-sovereign decided to answer Casement's charges. It was an imprudent move and against the advice of the knowledgeable Van Eetvelde, who was aware that isolated intervention in the

---

[1] Plunkett to Lansdowne, 27 February 1904, FO 403/351, no. 4, Africa.

[2] Phipps to Lansdowne, 5 February 1904, FO 10/807, no. 7, Africa, confidential; *La Dépêche Coloniale*, 2 February 1904; see also Willequet: op. cit., pp. 93 ff.

[3] Phipps to Lansdowne, 18 February 1904, FO 403/351, no. 13, Africa, confidential.

[4] Phipps to Lansdowne, 5 February 1904, FO 10/807, no. 7, Africa, confidential.

[5] Phipps, who had some insight into Belgian political life, wrote: 'There is practically no public opinion in Belgium. Though nominally enjoying a constitutional régime, the country is guided by a dexterous triumvirate composed of King Leopold, Count de Smet de Naeyer [Prime Minister] and M. Woeste. The latter in his capacity as President of the Catholic Associations of the Country, juggles with the electorate, and, granted a free hand by the King, rules the Parliament. He can make or mar Ministries, and they hold office at his will. . . . Unless that triumvirate . . . be broken up, it is very unlikely . . . that any genuine public opinion can find expression.' Phipps to Lansdowne, 25 September 1904, FO 403/351, no. 93, Africa, confidential.

Congo by the British government was impossible and therefore counselled that 'a contemptuous silence should be maintained'.[1] The fault with King Leopold was that he could never resist a game in diplomacy particularly when it seemed that he had an ace.

Soon after the publication of the Casement Report *L'Etoile Belge* carried an inspired communication in which it was requested that judgement should be reserved until the Congo State published its reply.[2] The reply duly appeared a month later in what was called 'Preliminary remarks suggested by Mr. Casement's Report'.[3] After regretting that the British government, in spite of repeated requests, had failed to make available to the Congo government the previous consular reports which it claimed to have, the Note turned to dismantling the Casement Report. The depopulation, it observed, was due to sleeping-sickness, and not 'to the exercise on the native population of a too exacting and oppressive' tax system. The evidence of Monsignor Van Ronslé, Vicar Apostolic of the Belgian Congo, and of Rev. W. H. Bentley of the B.M.S. were quoted. The existence of forced labour was acknowledged. But this, it was bluntly stated, was 'legitimate'. Turning to the question of atrocities the Note blamed the British consul for relying for his evidence on the untruthful Congolese who had misled him and on some biased protestant missionaries. The case of the boy Epondo whose mutilation was investigated by Casement and reinvestigated by the Congo government was shown as a concrete example of this. The boy's hand had been bitten off by a wild boar and not shot off by the gun of a sentry. 'It is only natural to conclude', the Note commented here, 'that if the rest of the evidence in the consul's report is of the same value as that furnished to him in this particular case it cannot possibly be regarded as conclusive.'[4]

Embedded in this long document, however, were two short passages which were to have far-reaching consequences

[1] Phipps to Lansdowne, 23 February 1904, FO 10/808, no. 16, Africa.
[2] *L'Etoile Belge*, 16 February 1904.
[3] *Accounts and Papers*, 1904 (Cd. 2097), lxxi, 445.
[4] Ibid.

for the Congo, consequences that could not have been contemplated by Leopold II at the time. The first of these statements declared that Casement's 'proofs are insufficient basis for a deliberate judgement, and that the particulars in question require to be carefully and impartially tested'. The second stated:

> Now, however, that the Consul has drawn attention to these few cases—whether cases of cruelty or not, and they are all that, as a matter of fact, he has inquired into personally and even so without being able to prove sufficiently their real cause—the authorities will of course look into the matter and cause inquiries to be made.

These two statements gave the Foreign Office the idea that an inquiry was contemplated by Leopold II and that the inquiry would be impartial. It was the insistence by the Foreign Office on this interpretation of Leopold's intentions that gave birth to the famous Congo commission of inquiry. King Leopold was to realize, when it was too late, that he had over-played his hand.

The inquiry which the king-sovereign intended to institute was in fact different. Soon after the publication of the Congo Notes, the Foreign Office was informed of the appointment of an Italian Inspector of State who was to inquire into the administration of the State, investigate how its laws were being executed, 'make the truth known at Brussels' and institute judicial proceedings against defaulting officials.[1] In order to facilitate this inquiry, the Congo government expressed a desire to be placed in possession of the full text of the Casement Report.[2] This was no doubt the full extent to which Leopold II intended that his inquiry go. The appointment of an Italian, instead of a Belgian, was meant to be a guarantee of impartiality.

The Foreign Office welcomed 'the announcement that a searching and impartial inquiry will be made' and asked the Congo government to give an assurance that adequate

---

[1] Villiers, 16 March 1904, FO 10/808, memorandum.
[2] Phipps to Lansdowne, 23 March 1904, ibid., no. 25, Africa.

measures would be taken to protect those Europeans and Congolese who had given evidence before Casement.[1] The king-sovereign, however, was determined not to give way so easily. In his reply, he asserted that his government would not interfere with 'such legal measures as persons who might find themselves wrongfully accused might consider it necessary to take'.[2] This reply raised apprehensions in the Foreign Office for it became obvious that the intentions of the Congo government were questionable. Consequently, the dramatic step was taken of defining the kind of inquiry that would be acceptable to the British government. It was suggested that 'a Special Commission should be appointed, composed of members of well-established reputation, and in part, at least of persons unconnected with the Congo State, to whom the fullest powers should be intrusted both as regards the collection of evidence and the measures for the protection of witnesses.'[3] The British government promised to give the full text of the Casement report to a commission constituted on such basis.

The tables were thus turned on the king-sovereign. The British suggestion was eminently reasonable. It was a challenge to the good faith of the Congo government that could not be lightly evaded without compromising the international good-will which Leopold II so anxiously sought to retain.

What worried the king-sovereign most, however, was whether public opinion in England would not compel Lansdowne to take stronger action if the suggested commission was not accepted. Since the publication of the Casement Report and the formation of the C.R.A. there were clear signs of an increasing awareness in that country of the ramifications of the Congo question. The records of the Foreign Office reveal petitions and resolutions pouring in from all parts of the country in condemnation of the Congo régime. The handful of Congo supporters who tried to defend the Congo State merely goaded the reformers into further

---

[1] *Accounts and Papers*, 1904 (Cd. 2097), lxii, 445.

[2] Ibid.

[3] Ibid.

exertions.[1] The national press continued to support the reformers even when Captain Guy Burrows was condemned for libel for the publication of *The Curse of Central Africa*. As the *Pall Mall Gazette* declared, 'The verdict given—an absolutely right and just verdict—does not in any way exculpate the Belgian administration of the Congo; it does not and cannot do that.'[2] Soon after, the sensational and gruesome details of the Caudron judgement wiped off even the insignificant gain which the Burrows trial had made.[3]

It was evident, indeed, that the Congo reformers viewed with growing impatience the tortuous diplomacy of Lansdowne.[4] On 5 April Fox Bourne had urged the government to take a definite step towards obtaining the co-operation of the United States.[5] About a month later he and Casement composed a second petition hoping that the government would continue its efforts to secure the combined action of the powers and that Britain would take an independent line by asserting her rights to consular jurisdiction.[6] Humanitarian influence on the Congo question remained strong and as a result of these representations the Foreign Office kept the State Department informed of the correspondence with the Congo government in spite of the fact that the United States had not ratified the Berlin Act and her intervention

---

[1] People like Jones and the other Congo consuls in Britain made no impression on the public mind in spite of their vigorous campaigns.

[2] *Pall Mall Gazette*, 28 March 1903. See also *The Times*, 28 March 1903; and *Morning Post*, 31 March 1903.

[3] Caudron, a Belgian agent of the Anversoise, was charged with (*a*) the illegal detention of six prisoners; (*b*) the shooting of a woman; (*c*) the killing of a native chief in prison after destroying his village and massacring the inhabitants in cold blood; (*d*) a campaign with sixty State soldiers which resulted in the murder of several Congolese and the destruction of their villages; etc., etc. He was sentenced to twenty years penal servitude which was later reduced to fifteen years. Consul Nightingale to Lansdowne, 7 April 1904, FO 10/809, no. 18, Africa, confidential. On this Lansdowne minuted: 'The finding of the Court is a terrible indictment of the whole régime.' Lansdowne, 15 May 1904, ibid.

[4] Fox Bourne to Morel, 7 April 1904, M.P., F.8.

[5] A.P.S. to F.O., 5 April 1904, FO 403/351.

[6] A.P.S. to F.O., 14 May 1904, FO 10/809. See also Fox Bourne to Morel, 9 May 1904, M.P., F.8.

was most doubtful. In addition, the question of extra-territoriality was once more resurrected and Consul Nightingale asked to furnish a report.[1]

The reformers were of course not informed of the action which the Foreign Office was taking to meet their demands and so continued the pressure. They arranged for questions on the Congo to be asked in parliament and organized public demonstrations at which resolutions were passed condemning the administration of the Congo State. The climax was reached on 9 June when Dilke, inspired by Casement,[2] raised a second debate on the Congo question.[3] A barrage of invective was unleashed against the Congo government in this debate and radical proposals for action against the Congo State were put forward. The keynote was sounded in Dilke's speech, when he blamed Lansdowne for putting the clock back by asking the Congo government in the 'weak despatch' of 19 April to institute 'a searching and impartial inquiry'. Enough, he said, had been disclosed and the House should force the British government 'to take stronger measures than mere words'.[4] Subsequent speakers, including Emmott, Gorst, Samuel and Fitzmaurice, explained what that meant: collaboration with the United States, an International Conference, the assumption of consular jurisdiction, establishment of the International River Commission provided for in the Berlin Act and an appeal to the Hague Tribunal. It was in this debate that Grey, as Liberal spokesman on foreign affairs, stated the line which he was to pursue from 1906 onward, for he gave the first intimation that his cardinal policy towards the Congo State was to secure its annexation by Belgium.[5]

Percy was barely able to contain the onslaught by pointing out the essential weakness of the British position, namely, that no other power had responded to the British initiatives.

---

[1] Villiers, 27 May 1904, FO 10/809, minute; Lansdowne to Nightingale, 30 May 1904, ibid., no. 8, Africa.

[2] Dilke to Casement, 5 May 1904, A.S., G. 261 (copy).

[3] Hansard, 9 June 1904, 4th ser., cxxxv, 1236–1290.

[4] Hansard, ibid., 1261.

[5] Hansard, ibid., 1289.

It was impossible, however, for the Congo government to take much consolation from Percy's defence. Subtly, he had committed them before parliament to an inquiry the scope of which they had certainly not contemplated. Commenting on the debate, Lalaing warned in a long and significant despatch:

> Lord Percy has been able to persuade the members of the [House of] Commons that the Government was, in the main, convinced of the nobility of their cause; and then to formulate, all things considered, a programme with which the House was satisfied. It is a question of a storm, which, expected for a long time, has at last burst. But the parliamentary atmosphere remains charged with electricity, and other tempests are to be feared. The enemies of the Congo are not disarming and announce new meetings.

> All danger could be averted for a while at least, if the British Government announced that the composition of the commission of inquiry is such that the English public could be sure that the impartiality which it is demanding would prevail, but a telegram from Brussels published last night makes it foreseeable that this inquiry will be refused. This would obviously give rise to a new attack which the government would find difficult to withstand . . . .

> If the inquiry is refused I think that the parliamentary agitation will begin again more strongly, with a view to forcing the British Government to ask for extra-territorial jurisdiction for its subjects in the Congo since the cabinet has declared to the House that the existing treaties give it the right to demand it.[1]

It was the debate of 9 June more than anything else, therefore, which finally compelled Leopold II to institute the commission of inquiry two months later. Although his position in Europe was still very strong, thanks to his extraordinary propaganda campaign,[2] the last thing he

---

[1] Lalaing to Favereau, 10 June 1904, Ier sér., Congo, vi, 1640.

[2] About this Phipps wrote: 'Many of my colleagues consider it to be unquestionable that considerable sums of money are being spent on the Belgian and foreign press in defence of the Congo State, and it is a matter of notoriety that the saloons and sleeping cars throughout Europe

wanted was the establishment of British consular courts in the Congo. But even this strong position must have seemed to him uncertain and precarious. The recent conclusion of the Anglo-French entente must have minimized in his eyes the Franco-Congo solidarity on the Congo question.[1] Furthermore, owing to Morel's visit[2] to the United States and the unprecedented campaign of the American missionary societies, there had emerged, for the first time, a demand for an 'international scrutiny' of the Congo in one of the leading New York papers.[3] Even in Brussels a modification of attitude towards the support which Belgian diplomacy could accord to the Congo had taken place. 'In effect', Arendt warned, 'the maintenance of our good relations with England is a national interest of paramount importance which the Government can not allow to be compromised without incurring the gravest responsibility towards the *Chambres* and in the country.'[4] It was imperative, therefore, that Belgium should no longer be openly identified with the Congo State. Finally, although the king-sovereign may not have been aware of it, the advisers to whom he cared to listen were secretly hostile to the authoritarian role which his position in the Congo enabled him to play in Belgian politics, and sought to undermine it. Thus, for example, Van Eetvelde had on more than one occasion recently suggested to Phipps that the British government should exercise pressure on the king-sovereign so that he might surrender the Congo State to Belgium.[5]

---

at this travelling season are full of pamphlets amended periodically and entitled "La Vérité sur le Congo", with which it is sought to influence the opinions of the travelling public with regard to the Royal enterprise during the idle hours of a railway journey.' Phipps to Lansdowne, 29 June 1904, FO 10/810, no. 78, Africa.

[1] By June Lansdowne was pressing the French government to submit to arbitration at the Hague the interpretation of the commercial clause of the Berlin Act which would compel the Congo government to give way on this point. Lansdowne to Monson, 6 June 1904, FO 403/351, no. 99, Africa; Lansdowne to Cambon, 17 June 1904, ibid.

[2] Infra, p. 171.

[3] *New York Tribune*, 15 June 1904.

[4] Arendt, 13 June 1904, Ier sér., Congo, vi, 1650, memorandum.

[5] Phipps to Lansdowne, 15 May 1904, FO 10/809, no. 49, Africa, confidential.

On what date, then, did Leopold II decide to institute the commission of inquiry? In the absence of the records of the Congo State, it is impossible to fix a precise date. Nevertheless, there is reason to believe that the decision was taken between 11 June and 4 July. On the earlier date Favereau had expressed doubts as to its possibility;[1] but on the latter date Phipps reported that the Foreign Minister had found the Congo government 'fully alive to the fact that an inquiry . . . was imperative'.[2] Thereafter, the questions left to be resolved were the composition of the inquiry and the extent of its powers. The man who played the leading role in finding a satisfactory solution to the first was Phipps; for the latter, it was, curious as it may seem, Professor Felicien Cattier and his Congo reform friends.

Phipps had always sought to convince the Foreign Office that it was futile to expect a change in the Congo system through British intervention. He was forced to modify his stand after Dilke's personal attack on him during the June debate[3] and to concentrate his energy on securing a commission of inquiry that would be acceptable in England. Here, the relationship he had built up with Belgian official circles proved useful. He was aware that Leopold II would never accept an international inquiry in the real sense: that is, an inquiry nominated by the powers. The suggestion he placed before Van Eetvelde, therefore, was for the appointment by the Congo government of a commission whose members, like those of the Congo Court of Appeal and of the then defunct Commission for the Protection of the Natives, would consist of men of different nationalities.[4]

As regards the powers of the commission, it is generally known that the first report on the appointment of the

---

[1] Phipps to Lansdowne, 11 June 1904, FO 10/810, no. 68, Africa.
[2] Phipps to Lansdowne, 4 July 1904, ibid., no. 80, Africa.
[3] Hansard, 9 June 1904, 4th ser., cxxxv, 1237.
[4] Phipps to Lansdowne, 11 July 1904, FO 10/810, no. 69, Africa. Cf. Phipps to Lansdowne, 4 July 1904, ibid., no. 80, Africa, in which his suggestion of Baron Nisco, the Italian Congo judge, was promptly accepted.

commission appeared in the *Mouvement Géographique*.[1] It has, however, remained a mystery up to now how and why the announcement came to appear first in this journal which was so critical of the Congo administration. On 24 July the *Mouvement Géographique* informed its readers that the Congo government had decided to institute an inquiry by means of a commission comprising the Belgian judge, Emile Janssens, the Italian judge, Baron Nisco, and 'a third magistrate of Swiss or Norwegian origin'. The report further stated that seven conditions would govern the conduct of the commission, namely, that it would be public and *contradictoire*; that foreign governments and philanthropic associations would be at liberty to demand the hearing of a witness and witnesses could be subjected to cross-examination; that the commission would have access to all administrative or judicial documents as well as copies of letters to and from Congo stations; that the inquiry would apply to the present as well as to the past; that it would apply especially to the condition of the Congolese in the rubber districts; and finally, that the reports of the proceedings of the commission would be published as soon as possible.

This is the report which has puzzled Congo historians for so long. It was inconceivable that King Leopold ever contemplated a commission of such far-reaching powers. The mystery is solved, however, by a letter in the private papers of Morel, addressed by Fox Bourne to him two days after the announcement in the *Mouvement Géographique*, an extract of which reads:

> I may tell you in strict confidence, that the announcement in the *Mouvement Géographique* is mainly a 'balloon'. It is apparently the fact that Janssens (a weak, amiable tool of King Leopold), and Nisco (a more accomplished tool), with another figurehead, are to institute a bogus enquiry in September. . . . But the seven 'conditions' following this announcement are merely put forward as a guess or feeler—or rather as a shrewd device for reducing the proposal to an absurdity. I have just come from the actual author of the

[1] Wauters, op. cit., p. 230; Stenmans, op. cit., p. 287.

'conditions' who has run across from Brussels to warn me and others as to the purport of his *ruse*. His and his friends' intention (serviceable or not) is to put a stop to the bogus enquiry and to force King Leopold to admit that it will satisfy none of the requirements of the reformers.[1]

The emissary from Brussels in fact was Professor Cattier, as Fox Bourne subsequently revealed,[2] and his collaborators undoubtedly included A. J. Wauters, editor of the journal. This episode was the first indication that a small but determined and influential group of Congo reformers were emerging in Belgium bent on securing the annexation of the Congo State in the not too distant future.

Meanwhile, Cattier had obtained Fox Bourne's co-operation and the latter, intentionally assuming the genuineness of the announcement, began to press the Foreign Office to ensure that King Leopold fulfilled the seven conditions.[3] In this way, it was hoped that the king would drop the idea of the inquiry entirely and his administration in the Congo would stand condemned.

Leopold II was obviously baffled by this manoeuvre. It would probably never be known what conditions he might have imposed on the commission. Certainly they could not have been as extensive as those of Cattier. However, to scotch further speculations the decree instituting the commission was soon published.[4] It was a short decree affirming that the inquiry was to examine impartially the allegations that in certain parts of the Congo State the inhabitants had been subjected to acts of cruelty. The decree revealed that the announcement in the *Mouvement Géographique* had correctly given the names of two members of the commission and that the nationality of the third, Dr Edm. de Schumacher, of the Canton of Lucerne, was almost correct. The decree went on to state that the commissioners were invested with the powers of judicial officers; that they should insure that witnesses gave evidence in absolute freedom; and that

---

[1] Fox Bourne to Morel, 26 July 1904, M.P., F. 8.
[2] Fox Bourne to Morel, 17 August 1904, ibid.
[3] A.P.S. to F.O., 26 July 1963, FO 10/810.
[4] B.O. no. 7, July 1904; *Accounts and Papers*, 1905 (Cd. 2333), lvi, 437.

they had the power to demand the production of all administrative and judicial documents connected with the subject
of the inquiry.

Although these directives fell short of the seven conditions
there is little doubt that their content was determined by the
latter. The pressure of the Foreign Office, goaded on by
the reformers, was to enlarge them even further. In Brussels,
the *Mouvement Géographique* dismissed the commission as a
replica of the well-known but ineffective Commission for the
Protection of the Natives.[1] Fox Bourne took the hint. He
demanded that the British government should insist on the
reformers being given an opportunity for cross-examining
witnesses and for adducing evidence before the commission
in support of the charges they had made against the Congo
State. He also urged that the British government itself
should be represented on the proposed inquiry both by the
consul at Boma and by 'at least one competent agent familiar
with the laws of the Congo State as well as with international
law'.[2] Lansdowne's comments on the proposed inquiry,
although influenced by the A.P.S., were, however, less
ambitious. Firstly, he urged that the sittings of the commission should be held in public and that any persons,
including missionaries of all denominations and nationalities,
should be permitted to give evidence if they so desired.[3]
Secondly, he expressed the view that sufficient time should
be given to the commission for their investigation and that
adequate protection be given to witnesses.[4] Finally, he
discreetly inquired from Lalaing whether he could announce
that no objections would be raised to the presence at the
sitting of the commission 'of any person who might be
deputed for the purpose of watching those proceedings'.[5]

The Congo government was willing to placate the Foreign
Office but was unwilling to appear to be truckling to the

---

[1] *Mouvement Géographique*, 7 August 1904.
[2] A.P.S. to F.O., 8 August 1904, FO 10/811.
[3] Lansdowne to Phipps, 10 August 1904, ibid., no. 100, Africa.
[4] Ibid.
[5] Lansdowne to Phipps, 10 August 1904, FO 10/811, no. 102, Africa;
same to same, 19 August 1904, ibid., no. 104, Africa.

reformers. Since the demands of the Foreign Office were identifiable with those which had appeared in the *Mouvement Géographique* and supported by Fox Bourne, they met with only limited success in Brussels. The main suggestions, that the commission should sit in public and that observers should be present at the proceedings, were declined.[1] On the question of the length of time the commission would be given, Phipps was assured that it would not be unduly hurried.

The reformers were determined to press home their point. Fox Bourne tackled Villiers but discovered from him that the Foreign Office was willing to support the commission. 'I did all I could to point out its fundamental worthlessness and mischievousness', he informed Morel, 'but, I fear, in vain.' He complained that the Foreign Office was more 'weak-kneed' than he thought, 'and not unwilling to have an excuse for sneaking out of such comparative boldness as we last year forced it to assume'.[2] Two days later, in co-operation probably with Cattier, whose professional acquaintance with Congo administration was useful, he fired off a memorandum to Villiers criticizing, almost clause by clause, the decree constituting the commission.[3] He pointed out that the commission was invested with no more than *'les pourvoirs attribuées par le roi aux officers du ministère public'* which, as defined in article 18 of the decree of 27 April 1888, were under the control of the *directeur de la justice*, and limited to investigations, *en matière pénale*, of *infractions* of the laws of the Congo State. The commission had not been given the authority to demand the production of evidence nor to cross-examine witnesses. It also had no power to initiate the production of witnesses useful for eliciting the truth; nor could it extend its inquiries to affairs outside such territories as may be designated by the Congo Secretary of State on whom devolves, by Article 6 of the decree, the sole responsibility for carrying out its provisions. He noted that the

---

[1] Phipps to Lansdowne, 12 August 1904, ibid., no. 97, Africa, and Phipps to Lansdowne, 19 August 1904, ibid., no. 100, Africa.

[2] Fox Bourne to Morel, 18 August 1904, M.P., F. 8.

[3] A.P.S. to F.O., 20 August 1904, FO 10/811.

commission was only authorized to make suggestions and the Congo government was under no obligation to act upon them nor to publish its findings. He argued that it was not possible for a searching inquiry to be made in two or three months as the Congo government was intending; but, on the other hand, there was a danger that the inquiry would be indefinitely prolonged. Finally, the memorandum stated that no provision had been made for the participation in the inquiry of the British consul at Boma 'or some other suitable custodian of the interests of Consul Casement whose inquiry, it may be assumed, was the subject of the present inquiry'.[1]

Phipps was instructed to raise these various points with the Congo government. Instead, however, he approached his friend and nominee on the commission, Baron Nisco. Together they hammered out an answer for Fox Bourne. The powers of the commission, Phipps reported,[2] were not in this case under the control of the *directeur de la justice* and it could therefore inquire into any *infractions* whether or not they were brought before them. As for the commission, it was its desire to be furnished with evidence of abuses from any reliable witness. Furthermore, as the commissioners were experienced jurists they did not require the guidance of a lawyer. Phipps did not believe that the Congo government would assume the obligation of acting on the suggestions of the commission since this would raise it to a legislative and an executive committee. He indicated that the inquiry was expected to last for six months. With regard to the composition of the commission no fundamental change was possible and Casement could not be legally represented as his name was not mentioned in the decree constituting the commission.

It was a wearisome negotiation and both the Foreign Office and the Congo government were obviously seeking means of escape without exposing themselves to the criticisms of their supporters. Leopold II was unwilling to give way on the main issues of public sitting and the presence of a

---

[1] Ibid.
[2] Phipps to Lansdowne, 3 September 1904, FO 10/811, no. 106, Africa.

British observer. However, he placed the final decision on both questions on the members of the commission. In the letter which he wrote to them and published on the eve of their departure for the Congo the commissioners were urged to devote themselves to discover the whole truth and for this purpose, they had 'perfect freedom of action, independence, and right of initiative'.[1] *The Times* welcomed the instructions as 'liberal and ample' although they demanded 'a great deal of moral courage' from the members of the commission.[2] Nevertheless, the Foreign Office had failed to secure its two main demands of public sitting and representation, and resolved, as Lord Percy put it, to be 'nasty'.[3] Thus Phipps was instructed to inform the Congo government that since it persisted in refusing these demands they should not 'feel surprised or aggrieved if the result should be to destroy in advance all the moral authority which might otherwise attach to the commission in the eyes of independent observers'.[4] Having made this reservation the commission was given the full text of the Casement Report together with the names of persons and places omitted in the published version. Fox Bourne was informed that it would be fair to suspend judgement until the commission had been observed in action.[5] In effect, the commission had received the blessing of the Foreign Office, which, however, had left a loophole so that it might escape blame should the inquiry fail to fulfil public expectations.

As for the reformers, Fox Bourne had persuaded Morel to issue fresh protests to the Foreign Office simultaneously with him. Unfortunately their criticisms, based as they were on the decree of 23 July, appeared at the same time as the instructions of 14 September. In the circumstance, the protests were coldly received and Fox Bourne was forced to beat a hasty retreat. He next fought a farcical rear-guard

---

[1] *Accounts and Papers*, 1905 (Cd. 2333), lvi, 437.
[2] *The Times*, 20 September 1904.
[3] Percy, n.d., minute on Phipps to Lansdowne, 6 September 1904, FO 10/811, no. 109, Africa.
[4] Lansdowne to Phipps, 28 September 1904, ibid., no. 129, Africa.
[5] F.O. to A.P.S., 1 October 1904, FO 10/812.

action which ended in his total discomfiture. On 20 September, he wrote to *The Times* revealing that the secretary of the commission, Henri Grêgoire, was a brother of King Leopold's private secretary. A letter in the same newspaper by Carl Hermann, secretary of the *Fédération pour la défense des intérêts belges à l'étranger* showed this to be false. A few days later Fox Bourne admitted his error but asserted at the same time that he had discovered a new link: the secretary of the commission was the son of King Leopold's private attorney.[1] This time it was Phipps who, writing to the Foreign Office, pointed out that Grêgoire's father was *procureur du Roi*, or public prosecutor, at the small town of Huy, and had no possible direct connexion with King Leopold.[2] The Foreign Office mischievously passed on the information to Fox Bourne and he was forced to confess his 'blunder' to *The Times*.[3] While still maintaining his lack of confidence in the commission, he henceforth kept a sullen silence.

Morel's embarrassment in the Benedetti affair was even greater as we shall soon see. While Fox Bourne had maintained a direct pressure on the Foreign Office, Morel was content to keep public opinion informed on the Congo question and to build up popular support. His literary output excelled that of the previous year. Apart from the publication of a monthly supplement on the Congo with his *West African Mail*, he waged a fierce battle in the press with all defenders of the Congo régime. Between January and July 1904 he published six pamphlets exposing the evils of the Congo system.[4] Then in October, while he was in America, his greatest literary effort up to now appeared.

---

[1] *The Times*, 3 October 1904.

[2] Phipps to Lansdowne, 20 October 1904, FO 10/812, no. 137, Africa.

[3] *The Times*, 3 November 1904.

[4] He began the year with the publication, under the auspices of the International Union, of the leaflet *The New African Slavery, or King Leopold's Rule in Africa*, in which he brought together fresh evidence of atrocities supplied by the missionaries, Weeks and Scrivener. Then followed *La Question Congolaise* where he appealed to the French to support Britain in her fight against the Congo régime. In March, he republished some of his earlier articles in a booklet called *The Congo Horrors*.

Entitled *King Leopold's Rule in Africa*, the book set out to attack the administration of the Congo State from a revealing angle which he proclaimed as follows in the preface:

The wrong done to the Congo peoples originates from the substitution of commerce which is based upon the recognition by Europe of native ownership in land and in the produce of the land (which the native alone can gather), with the consequent onus upon the European to PURCHASE that produce which modern industrialism requires, by a system based upon the right of a European State to expropriate the Native of tropical Africa from his land and from the produce of the land (which produce constitutes in tropical Africa the element of commerce), with the consequent elimination of the onus upon the European to PURCHASE produce which has ceased to belong to the gatherer of it.

On this basis he examined the trade statistics of the European possessions on the West Coast of Africa. The result was remarkable. Only in the Congo State did exports exceed imports. The published trade figures of the Congo State showed that between 1899 and 1902 the value of exports consisting mainly of rubber was over £7 million while the value of imports was only about £3.5 million. If the figures of 1903 were added, he went on, it would mean that the Congo State exported about £9.5 million and imported less than £4.5 million. Morel calculated that by the standards of other West African colonies the Congo State should have imported goods valued at £11.5 million. Furthermore, he noted that of the £4.5 million goods imported, over £3 million were goods not intended for the Congolese. Thus he came to the startling result that, for the export of goods worth £9.5 million, the Congolese got in return goods scarcely worth a million. 'It proves conclusively', Morel concluded, 'that the vast india-rubber out-put of the Congo territories

On the eve of the June debate appeared *The Scandal of the Congo* pleading for the establishment of British consular courts. The following month he issued two further pamphlets: *The Treatment of Women and Children in the Congo State, 1895 to 1904—Appeal to the Women of the British Empire, and of the United States*; and *The Commercial Aspect of the Congo Question*, a reprint of his article in the *Journal of the African Society*.

129

is not a voluntary production, but that it is a production FORCED UPON the natives.' It proved that the system itself was 'at fault'.[1]

The argument was very striking and the book was favourably reviewed in the British press as well as in Germany and the United States. In reality, there was nothing new in the book. At one time or another the various arguments and statements in it had appeared in the press either under the name of Morel himself or his friends. Their collection and collation in one book, however, was evidence of toil, tenacity and perseverance. These were the qualities which his closest friends and admirers recognized in him and from the autumn of 1904, indeed, Casement began to address him as 'My dear Bull-dog'.

But the year was to close in gloom. On 1 December, the *Indépendance Belge* carried a sensational headline, *Comment les Anglais Combatent le Congo*. Beneath was the story of how Morel, through one Shanu, a Lagosian trader who lived at Boma, had induced an Italian employee of the Congo government to abandon his post in the Congo in order to participate in the reform campaign. It was stated that the Italian, Benedetti, suspicious of the genuineness of Morel's humanitarian motives, played into the hands of Morel and John Holt with a view to exposing the aims of the C.R.A. The British consul at Boma was alleged to have given him £10 as travelling expenses.[2]

The Benedetti affair was blown up by the Belgian press to the great embarrassment of the reformers. The real story, which has never been told, may be briefly summarized. Benedetti, an Italian employed as *commissaire de police* at Boma, approached the British acting consul, Nightingale, in February 1904 with an offer to give damaging information against his employers if a substantial offer was made to him by the British government.[3] Nightingale was promptly

---

[1] E. D. Morel: *King Leopold's Rule in Africa*, London 1904, pp. 46 ff. Cf. Slade: *English-Speaking Missions*, pp. 259–60.

[2] *Indépendance Belge*, 1 December 1904.

[3] Nightingale to Lansdowne, 10 February 1904, FO 10/807, no. 7, Africa.

instructed not to entertain the offer. Nightingale reported some months later that Shanu, who was also a correspondent of Morel, had informed him that Benedetti was going to Liverpool in order to expose the administration of the Congo State.[1] In return Benedetti's passage was to be paid by Morel together with a sum of two thousand francs as compensation for throwing up his appointment. Shanu claimed to have been shown by Benedetti several documents incriminating the Congo administration.

Benedetti duly left Boma for England; but, curiously enough, his passage had been paid by the Congo State. In Liverpool, anyway, Morel negotiated a contract with Benedetti on the basis already reported by Nightingale and undertook to publish the evidence in a series of articles to be vetted by him. Benedetti then left England and turned up next in Brussels. The result was the publication in the *Indépendance Belge* on 1 December. The explanation is simple. Benedetti had seen in the Congo agitation a quick way of making some easy money and had sold himself to the highest bidder. The episode showed him up as a shady character, which he was; it also undoubtedly harmed the cause for Congo reform in the minds of some people, since the Foreign Office did not reveal its side of the story.[2]

The departure of the commission of inquiry for the Congo coupled with the Benedetti affair abated the enthusiasm for Congo reform in England. As Casement bitterly discovered in December, interest in the Congo question was 'practically dead'.[3] It was, as will be seen in the next chapter, only the calm before the storm. Already a great step forward had been taken. The Casement Report, the formation of the C.R.A. and, above all, the setting up of the commission of inquiry were achievements which no one could have predicted a few years earlier.

---

[1] Nightingale to Villiers, 17 October 1904, FO 10/812, private.
[2] Benedetti later apologized to Morel for his action, see *Morning Post*, 12 May 1905, which reprints Benedetti's letter.
[3] Casement to Morel, 14 December 1904, M.P., F. 8.

V

The Congo Commission of Inquiry and the Royal Manifesto

For a long time the evidence of maladministration coming out of the Congo had been challenged by protagonists of the State and its truth had been doubted. The Casement Report had convinced most Englishmen but outside England many were still sceptical. Those who had not forgotten the Anglo-Boer War were even suspicious that the British government harboured a deeply laid plot in the Congo and that the agitation was artificially fostered in order to prepare the ground for snatching the country from Leopold II. The commission of inquiry set up by the king-sovereign himself was expected to uncover the truth once and for all. Consequently, the proceedings of the commission were watched with great interest.

Meanwhile, in the relative calm over the Congo question following the departure of the commissioners, the significance of the instructions issued to them was overlooked by the Foreign Office. It was not until the end of October when the next Congo White Book was being prepared that Percy observed that they had failed to take advantage of the right conferred on the commissioners to declare their sittings public.[1] As that might raise adverse comment in the Commons, he urged that Nightingale should renew to the commissioners the wish of the British government to be

---

[1] Percy, 30 October 1904, FO 10/812, minute.

represented at the hearings. A telegram was accordingly despatched to Nightingale. On 11 December the consul reported that the commissioners had proclaimed their sittings public[1] and he was instructed to attend as many as he could.[2] At the same time consul Mackie in Lisbon was deputed to proceed to the Congo as the official British observer at the commission.[3] The instructions to Nightingale arrived too late to enable him to attend the sittings which took place in the Lower Congo,[4] while Mackie arrived when the commissioners were far in the interior and before he could reach them they were on their return journey to Boma.[5] Thus the British observer was after all not able to witness the commission at work in the Upper Congo.

It was subsequently stated by both Nightingale and Mackie that a deliberate attempt had been made to keep out the British observer from the sittings of the commission.[6] According to Mackie the commission opened its sittings at Boma on 6 October but it was not until 27 October, when they were at Leopoldville and thus on the verge of disappearing into the hinterland where their movements could not easily be traced, that they proclaimed their sittings public. Even then, the consul went on, with the views of the British government on the question of its representation so well known, no attempt was made to convey the decision of the commission to the British consul at Boma. Again, the commissioners had lulled the British government into complacency by the information which Baron Nisco had given to Phipps that the inquiry in the Congo would last six months[7] while in fact they had stayed for less than three.

There is an obvious temptation to accept the view of the

---

[1] Nightingale to Lansdowne, 11 December 1904, ibid., tel.

[2] F.O. to Nightingale, 15 December 1904, ibid., tel. no. 7, Africa.

[3] Mackie to F.O., 16 December 1904, FO 10/813, tel.

[4] Nightingale to Lansdowne, 23 December 1904, ibid., tel.

[5] Mackie to Villiers, 20 February 1905, ibid., private.

[6] Nightingale to Lansdowne, 6 March 1905, ibid., no. 16, Africa, confidential.

[7] Phipps to Lansdowne, 5 November 1904, FO 10/812, no. 140, Africa.

consuls especially as the Congo Secretary for Foreign Affairs had warned earlier that from the discussions between him and the members of the commission prior to their departure he did not think that a British observer would be admitted to the inquiry. Nevertheless, as has been noted, the Foreign Office had itself to blame for failing to settle the question of British representation at the inquiry until as late as October. There is also the fact that the commissioners did not at any time exclude the presence of any observers at their sittings. On the contrary, the testimony of the missionaries, some of whom had been the bitterest critics of the Congo administration and sceptical as to the good faith of a commission nominated by it, was unanimous in avowing the sincerity of the commissioners. Indeed, far from criticizing the commission at work the missionaries were unreserved in their commendation and Nightingale himself once acknowledged that he heard of nothing but 'praise and satisfaction expressed at the impartial and patient way' the members of the commission had conducted the inquiry.[1]

It should also be remembered that Leopold II had always wished to demonstrate that the Congo State was acting in the fullness of its sovereignty and not submitting to outside pressure. It is obvious that this had been impressed on the commissioners before their departure and had consequently influenced their attitude towards the British representatives in the Congo. It is possible that in order to preserve the idea of Congo sovereignty the commissioners had refrained from taking the initiative in inviting Nightingale to attend their sittings. Certainly when Mackie had subsequently sought to read the depositions taken on the Upper Congo the commissioners had declined on the grounds that it would impair the sovereignty of the State.[2]

The missionaries, on the other hand, were not as remiss as the Foreign Office in the attention which they paid to the commission. The evidence of those among them who had

[1] Nightingale to Lansdowne, 27 January 1905, FO 10/813, no. 7, Africa. See also Harris to Nightingale, 15 December 1904, encl. in Nightingale to Lansdowne, 27 January 1905, ibid.
[2] Mackie to Villiers, 20 February 1905, ibid., private.

publicly criticized the administration of the Congo had been attacked as biased and mischievous. Therefore, they saw in the commission an excellent opportunity for vindicating themselves before world opinion and had taken steps to collect evidence and witnesses for the commission. In addition, during the sittings of the commission they were careful to take down minutes of the proceedings. These minutes became very important. Since the *procès-verbaux* of the commission were never published,[1] it is from these missionary reports that we now know how the commission reached its conclusions and on what evidence these were based. It is clear also from the reports sent by Mackie that the influence which the evidence of these missionaries exercised on the minds of the commissioners was very great, at least, while the latter were still in the Congo. Janssens, the president of the commission, admitted that 'many additional and horrid details of the atrocities committed' had been revealed. 'In fact', Mackie wrote, 'he [Janssens] courteously and frankly admitted that the evidence collected agrees in all essential details with Mr Casement's reports on the subject.'[2]

The star witness of the inquiry was undoubtedly John Harris of the Congo Balolo Mission at Baringa, which was within the Abir concession. An ambitious and persuasive man, Harris was subsequently to become secretary of the Anti-Slavery and Aborigines Protection Society and a member of parliament. His path to this future was prepared by the dynamism which he showed in the Congo reform campaign and it was the commission of inquiry which gave him the first opportunity of appearing in the limelight.

Possessing a flair for the dramatic, Harris had drawn up a long indictment against the Abir company and carefully selected his witnesses. At one of the sittings of the commission a youth startled everyone when he suddenly pointed at the director of the company, M. Longtain, and said 'Vous êtes l'homme. Comment osez-vous nous tuer ainsi pour le

---

[1] The Belgian government still continues to suppress the evidence. In spite of repeated requests by the present writer to see the documents permission was refused.

[2] Mackie to Villiers, 20 February 1905, FO 10/813, private.

caoutchouc? Nos mères, nos pères, nos frères sont tous "fini" (tués) par vous. Oui vous! Ecoutez, grands hommes d'Europe, voilà l'homme qui nous tués'.[1] At another sitting, a chief led forward by Harris introduced twenty witnesses and threw down 110 twigs before the commission—each twig, the chief claimed, represented a life taken from his village by the agents of the Abir. At last, it was reported, the president of the commission had asked Harris how long he intended to continue calling witnesses. Harris replied: 'Until the commission and M. Longtain recognize that the reports we had sent to Europe are true.' The result was that the commission and Longtain had then accepted as a true and general statement 'that hundreds of people have been killed in this district alone for rubber and that I [Harris] could prove it by multitude of witnesses'.[2]

This story by Harris is now difficult to corroborate. Nevertheless, its appearance in *Le Temps* and several other British, French and Belgian newspapers acted at the time as an invigorating tonic to the reform campaign. Credibility was lent to the story by the news that Longtain himself had fled from the Congo in order to escape arrest and that Costermans, the vice-governor-general, had committed suicide as a result of the censure passed on him by the commission.[3] The climax to this sensational news was reached with the announcement that Van Calcken, a Belgian employee of the Abir, had been convicted for having ordered his sentries to kill a number of Congolese who had failed to bring in rubber and for having tied up and arbitrarily detained as hostages several Congolese women.[4]

While the report of the commission was anxiously awaited, the C.R.A. took advantage of the anger and disgust evoked by these reports to revive their agitation which had been flagging since the departure of the commission. At the same

---

[1] *Le Temps*, 16 February 1905. See also *Daily News*, 17 February 1905; *Le Peuple*, 17 February 1905; *Le Matin*, 18 February 1905.

[2] *Daily News*, 25 February 1905; Harris to Nightingale, 15 December 1904, encl. in Nightingale to Lansdowne, F.O. 10/813, no. 7, Africa.

[3] *Daily Telegraph*, 23 March 1905.

[4] Hansard, 20 February 1905, 4th ser., xcli, 597.

time they adopted two resolutions, the first calling on the British government to appoint vice-consuls at Leopoldville, Coquilhatville and Stanley Falls and to invest them with powers of extra-territorial jurisdiction, and the second urging the powers signatory to the Berlin Act 'to put an end to the Congolese rubber régime'.[1] This renewed effort on the part of the reformers was immediately fruitful, for Percy announced in the Commons on 7 March that the government had decided to appoint two vice-consuls to reside at Leopoldville and Stanleyville.[2]

Having got the Foreign Office moving, the reformers turned their attention towards consolidating public opinion in favour of Congo reform. The initiative was taken by Casement during a visit to London in May. He got the Irish peer, Lord Norbury, and his sister Lady Margaret Jenkinson as well as Gilmour of the *Morning Post* to help him organize a mass public meeting which would be addressed by Morel. John Holt, as usual, was ready with the necessary finance. But Casement's big catch was Harry Johnston. The latter had been one of those whose favourable opinions on the administration of the Congo State were often quoted by the propagandists of Leopold II.[3] In fact, since the report of Casement was published, Johnston had changed his views and declared himself convinced of the existence of mal-administration in the Congo State, but his name and his earlier views were still cited against the reformers. His association with the proposed meeting was therefore regarded by Casement as a master-stroke.

Johnston, however, did not prove to be a mere tool in Casement's hands. While agreeing to preside over the

---

[1] C.R.A. to Lansdowne, 20 February 1905, FO 10/813; *Daily News*, 18 February 1905.

[2] Hansard, 7 March 1905, 4th ser., cxlii, 570–1. The Congo State was now divided into three consular areas. The consul at Boma was assigned to the Lower Congo and had also to supervise the two vice-consuls on the Upper Congo. Armstrong exercised jurisdiction over the Lualaba-Kasai, Equator, and Bangala districts; and Michell, the Aruwimi and Katanga districts.

[3] For these opinions of Johnston, see *Daily Chronicle*, 1 December 1903.

meeting he insisted on the reformers reviving the idea of Belgian annexation of the Congo as a solution to the Congo question.[1] This was duly proposed by Dilke during the meeting which took place at the Holborn Town Hall on 7 June. But Johnston was not allowed to have his way entirely. In moving the resolution Dilke added the other solution usually favoured by the reformers, namely, a conference of the powers to devise a scheme for the good government of the Congo State.[2]

The Holborn meeting was followed, the next month, by the publication of the evidence which the missionaries had presented before the commission of inquiry. Morel was enabled to do this by the financial backing which the movement received at this time from the wealthy Birmingham cocoa merchant, William Cadbury. Cadbury, who was a Quaker, took great interest in humanitarian causes. Almost single-handed, he was contending at this time against the system of indentured labour employed in the exploitation of Portuguese Angola. It was not surprising therefore that he should identify himself with the campaign for Congo reform. His accession was a great gain for the C.R.A.[3] It not only brought the *Daily News* owned by the Cadbury family under the influence of Morel, it also enlarged the financial resources of the C.R.A. and helped to generate more enthusiasm among non-conformist circles for the reform movement. In April Cadbury donated £100 to the C.R.A. and at the same time got the Society of Friends to set up a special Congo sub-committee.[4] In June he subscribed £1,000 to Morel,[5] this was split up into two parts. First, Morel received, as editor of the *West African Mail*, £50

---

[1] Casement to Morel, 26 May 1905, M.P., F. 8. Cf. R. Oliver: *Sir Harry Johnston and the Scramble for Africa*, London 1959, pp. 347–8.

[2] *Morning Post*, 8 June 1905.

[3] It was an even greater gain for Morel himself. Cadbury became so impressed with the work of Morel that after the dissolution of the C.R.A. he continued to support Morel financially until the latter won a seat in Parliament in 1922.

[4] Cadbury to Morel, 7 April 1905, M.P., F. 8.

[5] Morel to Cadbury, ? June 1905, ibid. (copy).

every quarter for the next two years and this enabled him to maintain the *West African Mail*, which had never really been able to pay its way. The second part of the offer, which amounted to £600, was credited to the C.R.A. itself.[1]

In parliament the reformers kept interest in the Congo alive by periodic questions. Between February and August no less than sixteen questions were asked on various aspects of the administration of the Congo. They formed a prelude to yet another debate which was provoked on 3 August by Dilke and vigorously supported by Emmott and Fitzmaurice. The debate was inconclusive, for it was only intended as a pressure to force Leopold II to publish the report of the commission. Nevertheless, Percy was given the opportunity to state the attitude of the Unionist government. Referring to Johnston's suggestion that a solution to the Congo question lay in Belgian annexation, he declared that it would not be proper for the government to express an opinion either in favour or against such annexation. He hoped, however, that the founders of the Congo State, by which he meant King Leopold, would consider that solution as an alternative when the report of the commission was published.[2]

King Leopold, on his side, was not allowing the reformers to have their way entirely in the fight to influence public opinion in Britain. He sought to win over Catholic support for the Congo by trying to demonstrate that the Congo question was essentially a religious one.[3] An attempt was made to portray the C.R.A. campaign as a protestant organization hostile to the Catholic government of the Congo. At first there was a plan to send an English Catholic mission to the Congo but this failed. On the eve of the Congo debate of 9 June 1904, the Catholic members of parliament

---

[1] Cadbury to Morel, 5 July 1905, ibid. It was with this money that Morel produced a two-penny pamphlet in English and French containing a compilation of the missionary testimony before the commission.

[2] Hansard, 3 August 1905, 4th ser., cli, 145.

[3] R. Slade: 'King Leopold II and the Attitude of English and American Catholics towards the Anti-Congolese campaign', *Zaire*, 1957, ix, p. 598.

were well primed with material for the defence of the Congo State. Again this failed. With the exception of an Irish member who briefly deprecated the Protestant attacks on Catholic Belgium,[1] none of the Catholic members of parliament said a word on behalf of King Leopold in that debate. Outside parliament, however, the *Catholic Herald* was a persistent advocate for the king-sovereign and for some time *The Tablet*, official organ of English Catholicism, made some unsuccessful efforts to rouse catholic opinion. Finally, a desperate effort to compromise the English Catholics was made by the zealous editor of the *Catholic Herald* when he presented a laudatory memorial to King Leopold on behalf, it was claimed, of 'a large number of English Catholics'.[2] In fact, only some Irish Catholics had signed the memorial; in England, the Catholics continued to be indifferent to the wooing from Brussels. The reason for the failure of the attempt to secure British Catholic support is easy to understand. The reformers had been studiously careful to avoid any statement or argument that might lead to a religious controversy.

By the end of the summer of 1905 Leopold II must have realized the futility of attempting to build up in England a body of opinion favourable to his rule in the Congo. No rival body to the C.R.A. emerged. On the other hand, in the face of mounting hostility from across the channel, he had also in his hands the report of his own commission, whose condemnatory tone[3] would not fail to aggravate the agitation. He therefore embarked on a new strategy. The religious argument had failed; the critics might be tempted into acquiescence by economic incentives.[4] The first step was to settle the nature of the bribe and here King Leopold played a clever game. The most notorious of the concession companies was the Abir. Casement's report had focussed attention on its unscrupulous dealings with the Congolese

---

[1] See speech by John Campbell, member for South Armagh. Hansard, 9 June 1904, 4th ser., cxxxv, 1324.

[2] *Indépendance Belge*, 2 March 1905.

[3] Infra, pp. 140–3.

[4] Slade: *English-Speaking Missionaries*, pp. 294 ff.

and more recently the commission of inquiry had thrown an even more lurid light on the company. From Count Lalaing in London he had also learnt that everyone, even those most favourable to the Congo régime, realized that much of the odium which the Congo State had incurred arose from reports emanating from the Abir concession.[1] It was this concession that King Leopold now decided to use as the instrument of his next attempt to silence his English critics.

At the beginning of September Jones once again called on Villiers[2] and revealed that Leopold II had the intention of offering the Abir concession to a company which he (Jones) would form. The administration of the concession under this new company would be entirely in the hands of Englishmen and the Congo government would lend armed force to it if this was required. In return for the concession Jones would pay a certain annual sum to the Congo government and also pay a share of the profits to the Abir shareholders until the latter had been sufficiently compensated for the withdrawal of their concession. The scheme, Jones pointed out, would certainly benefit the Congolese as well as Britain and he would proceed with it if the Foreign Office gave a formal approval.

The implications of this manoeuvre were immediately obvious to Villiers as well as to Lansdowne. On the one hand, the scheme offered some chance of a change for the better in a portion of the Congo State and a substantial share in the prosperity of the country for British enterprise. There was therefore a great temptation to give the scheme an official blessing. On the other hand, it was seen that if it became known that a British company was taking over the much-criticized Abir, the impact of the eagerly anticipated report of the inquiry would be minimized. There was yet another aspect of the scheme which made Lansdowne very cautious. If a British syndicate took over the concession with the approval of the Foreign Office new responsibilities

---

[1] Lalaing to Favereau, 19 June 1905, Ier sér., Congo, vi, 1798.
[2] Villiers, 8 September 1905, FO 403/364, memorandum.

would be incurred by the British government. It might not be possible for the syndicate to transform the administration by a stroke of the pen. Many of the present local agents would have to be retained and unless these changed their outlooks and methods very rapidly, there would still be complaints of cruelty and exactions for which the British government would be held accountable. 'Observe, moreover', Lansdowne concluded, 'that, although the administration is to be entirely in the hands of Englishmen, the State is to lend armed force if required. An arrangement of this kind might lead to all sorts of complications.'[1] Under these circumstances Jones was given the vague information that the British government, while welcoming the scheme, declined to assume 'any responsibilities in excess of those which belong to them in respect of all British enterprise in foreign countries'.[2] At the same time the hint was given that Jones should await the publication of the report of the commission of inquiry before proceeding with the scheme.

Jones was dismayed by the reserved attitude of the Foreign Office. He had hoped to obtain the support of the Foreign Office in order to buttress his position *vis-à-vis* King Leopold himself as well as the Congo reformers, from whom he expected attacks once the details of the scheme were known. Since the Foreign Office would not commit itself to support him, he sought a way of disentangling himself from the scheme without offending the king-sovereign. On 7 October, he let the Foreign Office know that the British syndicate in fact had to work the Abir concession on the same system as that hitherto followed by the company which it was going to replace. In other words, the collection of rubber was to be by forced labour. Jones pleaded that he was unwilling to work the scheme on such terms but he could not tell King Leopold that as it might cost him the lucrative Antwerp–Congo mail contract. What he wished the Foreign Office to do was to declare that they would not view with favour the

---

[1] Lansdowne, 10 September 1905, ibid., minute.
[2] F.O. to Jones, 15 September 1905, ibid.

taking over of the concession by a British syndicate if forced labour was to be used.[1]

Before the Foreign Office could reach a decision, however, Jones changed his mind about abandoning the scheme. The reason is difficult to trace. Perhaps, Jones could not bring himself to throw away a project so potentially lucrative as that proposed by Leopold II. It is also possible that Jones was persuaded not to drop the project owing to the prospect of obtaining the support of the Congo reformers. The latter was part of the grand strategy of King Leopold whereby he hoped to soften the impact of the report of the commission. The move was launched in several directions. There was an approach made by Thomas Barclay of Paris, an attorney and friend of King Leopold, to the C.R.A. through Francis W. Fox, a member of its executive committee. The latter was informed that the reformers should draft a statement showing how they wished the Congo State to be administered and how they expected that revenue sufficient to meet the expenditure could be obtained. Their views would be conveyed to the king who would try and see how the proposals could be met. This overture was repulsed by Morel, who considered it 'extraordinarily impudent and inherently absurd'.[2] A similar approach made by Gilzean Reid to Fox Bourne was no less uncompromisingly rejected.[3]

While Barclay was working on the C.R.A. and Gilzean Reid on the A.P.S., Jones himself sought to draw the C.B.M. into supporting his Abir project. Since Grattan Guinness embarked on his reform campaign, this mission had been foremost in exposing the maladministration of the Congo State. But more important still, this mission was the only one operating in the Abir concession. The role of one of its missionaries, Harris, during the sitting of the commission has already been indicated. With the return of Harris and his wife to England in August, many public meetings had been stirred into indignation by their eye-witness accounts

---

[1] F. A. Campbell, 7 October 1905, FO 10/815, memorandum.
[2] Morel to Fox, 18 October 1905 (copy), encl. in Morel to Cadbury, 20 October 1905, M.P., F. 8 (copy).
[3] Morel to Guinness, 31 October 1905, ibid. (copy).

of atrocities committed in the Congo. Jones felt, undoubtedly, that the support of this mission was essential for any project respecting the change of management in the Abir concession. However, he mishandled the negotiation. The mission was told that the Foreign Office was already in favour of the new Abir arrangement and wanted them also to support it. Morel was consulted by the mission and he promptly forwarded a protest to Lansdowne. The Foreign Office, of course, denied the statement and Morel gleefully published it in the press together with the provisions of the scheme. Grattan Guinness, on the other hand, had been inclined to reach an accommodation with Jones, but neither Holt, Morel nor Fox Bourne would for a moment consider it. Thus isolated, he informed Jones that the C.B.M. 'being essentially a spiritual movement cannot in any case associate itself with a commercial company'. [1]

In the meantime, King Leopold had been anxiously waiting for the reaction in England to the Abir scheme and the result of the approaches made to the missionary and humanitarian societies. The publication by Morel of the intrigues of Jones signalled the failure of the projects and it became unnecessary to delay further the publication of the report of the inquiry. But, still determined to minimize its impact, the king-sovereign took other measures towards this end. In the first place, the report of the inquiry appeared with a decree setting up another commission. This commission, generally known as the 'Commission for Reforms', consisted of fourteen members and was instructed to study the recommendations of the commission of inquiry and to draft the laws necessary for their enforcement. Sound as this measure appeared to be, it could not, and did not, escape attention as a means of deferring reform while at the same time trying to satisfy public opinion. [2] Similarly, the measure paralysed for the meantime such strong diplomatic action as foreign governments, especially the British government, would have liked to take in view of the contents of the report. The second commission, by giving the impression that the

---

[1] Guinness to Jones, n.d., J.H.P., 13/4 (copy).
[2] *Le Patriote*, 28 November 1905.

king-sovereign was ready to consider reforms, rendered it difficult if not impossible on grounds of general policy for any government to intervene at this time.

Having thus hamstrung official action, Leopold II also took special care to weaken the effect of the report in the popular mind. Thus, as has already been said, the *procès-verbaux* of the commission were not published with the report. As critics of the Congo administration then pointed out, the non-publication of the *procès-verbaux* removed much of the sting in the report. This conclusion has also been re-echoed by modern historians. Shorn of concrete cases of cruelty, over-taxation, or maladministration, the influence of the report on the general public fell far short of that of Casement.

In England, King Leopold took extra care to influence public opinion. Not content with the measures already described, he inspired the formation of an ephemeral organization known as the 'West African Missionary Association'.[1] This organization was then given a truncated English version of the report which it distributed to the British press as the 'complete and accurate resumé'. Comparison between that English version and the official French version which appeared later revealed a variation in several vital details. This led to a general inquiry as to the nature of the West African Missionary Association. It was learnt that this organization was known neither in Protestant nor in Catholic circles; that its office was the same as that of the solicitor who had circulated the document; and finally, that its committee consisted exclusively of Irish Catholics who confessed that they did not even know the aims of the Association. It is safe to conclude that the Association was hastily constituted for the sole purpose of issuing the misleading version of the report of the commission. It was never heard of again.

The official report of the commission of inquiry itself was a long document covering 150 pages of the *Bulletin Officiel*.[2] It

---

[1] Slade: *English-Speaking Missions*, pp. 296–7.
[2] *B.O.*, nos. 9–10, September and October 1905.

began by paying a formal tribute to the great progress which the Congo State had made since it was founded and then the commissioners passed on to an examination, under eight headings, of the various criticisms to which the administration had been subjected. The first dealt with the fundamental issue of the system of land tenure and freedom of trade. Here the commissioners categorically admitted that the State had the right to appropriate unoccupied land. They hastened to point out, however, that the welfare of the Congolese depended on the interpretation of the word 'unoccupied'. In the Congo State, according to the report, the word had been rigidly applied and the result was that the Congolese were confined to the land on which their dwellings stood and to their immediate environs. Even there they had no unrestricted enjoyment of their rights, for they were prohibited from disposing of the produce of the soil except to the State or to the concession companies. In addition, local authorities as well as the agents of the companies had also been enabled, by an extremely narrow interpretation of the right to unoccupied land, to prohibit the removal of villages from one place to another and even to prevent the Congolese from leaving their villages. The commissioners therefore recommended that the villagers be offered a liberal allowance of land, after proper delimitation; and that they should be given the right to the free disposal of the produce of that land. On the parallel issue of freedom of trade the commissioners admitted that as matters stood it was impossible for the Congolese to trade freely because they were deprived of all the facilities for commercial transactions. They recommended that the modification in the land system should be accompanied by a gradual supersession of the system of barter by the use of money.

Turning next to the question of taxation the commissioners admitted that, in the absence of a money economy, tax in labour was the sole means of raising revenue. They noted, however, that grave abuses had arisen from the methods employed by the Congo government. Prior to November 1903, they said, State agents had arbitrarily fixed the labour tax without regard to the resources of the inhabitants. These agents had been encouraged in this practice by the bonus they received from the State on their exactions. The commissioners observed that it was not until 18 November 1903 that the labour tax had been formally legalized by decree and the rate fixed at forty hours per month. No fault could be found with the decree if in fact the taxes were always paid by so many hours work per month, but the commissioners pointed out that in the vast majority of cases the tax in produce demanded bore no relation to the forty hours per month stipulated by law. The result was that the burden of taxes, already excessive before the decree, still remained oppressive. Their reduction had indeed been rendered impossible by the circular of the governor-general dated 29 February 1904, whereby State agents had been warned that the application of the decree of 18 November ought to bring in ever-increasing revenue to the treasury. The commissioners concluded this section with a thinly veiled rebuke. All government officials, they said, should be encouraged to realize that their first duty was to look after the welfare of the people under their charge and the government itself should reserve its favours, not for agents who brought in the largest revenue, but for those agents who showed tact and moderation in their dealings with the inhabitants.

From the subject of taxation, the report went on to consider the use of military expeditions in the Congo State. These expeditions had often been used illegally to collect taxes by the commercial companies and the administration had connived at this practice. During these expeditions, it was stated, many outrages had been committed against the local people and the Abir, Lomami and Kasai companies had been the most guilty. The commissioners agreed that no mutilation had taken place during the expeditions but they recommended that the use of military expeditions should be restricted solely to the quelling of uprisings.

Closely connected with the subject of military expeditions was the role of the commercial companies in the Congo. The commissioners maintained that the State had the right to grant concessions. They disclosed, however, that the

State had, at first tacitly, and by the decree of 18 November, formally, empowered these companies to levy taxes in labour or produce and to enforce payment. This practice, the commissioners reported, had been subject to grave abuses especially as the State had failed to keep the companies under proper surveillance. The ideal solution would be for the State to resume the sovereignty which it had delegated to the companies and to throw the country open to free trade. The practical step which they regarded as immediately possible, however, was for the existing companies to be maintained as well as the wide powers which they exercised, on condition that the limits of the concessions were not extended and the government supervised the way in which the companies exercised their powers.

The rest of the report was taken up with a consideration of the depopulation of the country, the guardianship of children, the recruitment of soldiers and labourers, and the administration of justice. Compared with the foregoing, these were minor subjects and could be briefly summarized. The commissioners believed that the country had suffered from depopulation; but although they blamed the administration they ascribed the main cause to sleeping-sickness. They seriously criticized the colonies of children established by the State and by the Catholic missions. The methods by which these children were obtained amounted, they said, to a system of slave-raiding and it was recommended that only destitute children should be placed under State guardianship. The commissioners regarded military service as a civilizing agency and therefore suggested that recruitment into the *force publique* should continue. They considered, however, that contracts for labourers should be properly signed and that the maximum period of service should be reduced from seven to three years. Finally, they regarded the administration of justice as satisfactory, but pointed out the danger of the *procureur d'état* being subject to the administration.

The report was generally recognized as a severe blow to King Leopold. The Chairman of the commission was ostracized by the court and the king-sovereign during his lifetime refused recommendations for awarding Belgian honours to the members of the commission.[1] Nevertheless, the press on both sides of the Channel maintained that their views on the Congo question had been vindicated. It is difficult, however, to escape from the verdict of *The Times'* leading article that if one read between the lines of many of the recommendations, it was impossible to doubt that serious cruelties and abuses had been shown to exist, and that the document as a whole constituted a grave indictment against the administration of the State.[2]

The publication of the report accentuated the reform agitation which had been gathering momentum. In several cities and towns, mass meetings were held to adopt the C.R.A. resolution which declared:

> That this meeting condemns the system of personal rule established by the Sovereign of the Congo State, and expresses its conviction that this system—which is based upon an un- restricted claim over the produce of the soil and the labour of the people has led to the revival, under new and worse forms, of the African Slave Trade; that this meeting calls upon His Majesty's Government to convoke an assembly of the Christian Powers, either in the form of a special International Conference or under the Regulations of the Hague Tribunal, in order to devise and put in force a scheme for the good government of the Congo territories; that this meeting urges upon His Majesty's Government the necessity of an immediate assump- tion of its extra-territorial rights in the Congo State, to insure adequate protection to British subjects in that State.[3]

By the end of the year over sixty of these resolutions had been sent to the Foreign Office. Even the B.M.S., which

---

[1] This information was revealed later by Grêgoire, secretary of the commission, to Harris at a meeting of the League of Nations. Harris to Morel, 10 September 1923, M.P., F. 8. See also Wuliger, op. cit., pp. 105–6.

[2] *The Times*, 6 November 1905.

[3] Morel to F.O., 10 October 1905, FO 10/815.

officially had remained aloof and hostile to the reform campaign, soon took action. For long its leading representative in the Congo, George Grenfell, and its secretary in England, A. H. Baynes, had been convinced of the essentially humanitarian aims of Leopold II and had also feared that an open attack on the Congo government would hinder the extension of the mission's Congo work.[1] But in view of the testimony afforded by the commission of inquiry the society was obliged to throw aside its cautious attitude and 'to earnestly and respectfully appeal to His Majesty's Government to take such action . . . as may bring to a speedy termination the present régime of oppression, coercion, and cruelty which now exists in so many parts of the Congo State'.[2]

The report of the commission was published when the cabinet of Balfour was tottering towards its fall. It was therefore impossible for Lansdowne to pay any serious attention to the Congo question. On 4 December Balfour at last resigned and, in the government which was then formed by Campbell-Bannerman, Grey came to the Foreign Office. The change was received with much satisfaction by the Congo reformers, for Grey had condemned the Congo administration in no uncertain terms during the debate of the previous year. Fitzmaurice, who became his Under-Secretary, was known to be hostile towards the Congo régime and, besides, there were well-known sympathizers for Congo reform in the government: John Morley and John Burns, Secretary for India and President of the Local Government Board respectively, were in the cabinet; Beauchamp, President of the C.R.A. (now resigned), Aberdeen, Emmott, and Samuel occupied lesser posts. There was thus apparently every justification for anticipating, as Count Lalaing did, that the 'Gouvernement Liberal . . . ne sera pas bien disposé pour l'Etat du Congo'.[3] In fact, there was not, as one might have expected, a radical change of

[1] Slade: *English-Speaking Missions*, pp. 263–4.
[2] B.M.S. to Lansdowne, 18 October 1905, FO 10/815.
[3] Lalaing to Favereau, 15 December 1905, Ier sér., Congo, viii, 1844.

policy on the Congo question. The policy of Lansdowne had been to handle it with patience and firmness. As we shall see, Grey made no departure from this. The difference between the two in this matter was that, while Lansdowne had sought no definite solution to the Congo question, Grey soon focussed his attention on securing the annexation of the Congo State by Belgium.

The first action taken by Grey was to remove Phipps from Brussels and to substitute Arthur Hardinge. Phipps had become notorious as a Congophile. The previous year, as we have seen, Dilke had attacked him in the Commons for a despatch he had written on the Congo. In September 1905 several newspapers in Brussels and London reported that when Alfred Rollitt, member of parliament, President of the Associated Chambers of Commerce and Knight Commander of the Order of Leopold, had rashly said during a speech in Liège that the reports of atrocities were 'a calumny' the applause had been led by Phipps.[1] This was denied by Phipps but Morel, under the stimulus of Holt, had launched a relentless attack on Phipps in the press. Morel was supported by several newspapers and by December the position of Phipps in Brussels could fairly be said to have become untenable. The change of government merely provided a convenient opportunity for removing him.

With the report of the commission before him the reformers would then have liked Grey to establish British consular courts and invite the signatories of the Berlin Act to a conference on the Congo question.[2] It is clear, however, that Grey was in no position to pursue a dynamic policy in the Congo following the report of the inquiry, since Europe was preoccupied with the Moroccan crisis which had begun in March 1905 and did not subside for nearly a year. Thus it is not surprising that the task which Grey imposed on Hardinge before he left to assume his post in Brussels was to

---

[1] *Petit Bleu*, 5 September 1905; *Daily Chronicle*, 9 September 1905; *Daily News*, 11 September 1905.
[2] C.R.A. to Grey, 18 December 1905, FO 10/815; same to same, 16 Jan. 1906, FO 367/31.

discover the probable attitude of Belgium in the event of a Franco-German War.[1] It was the Moroccan crisis rather than the Congo question which dominated the attention of the British government at this time. Accused by Dilke of inaction on the Congo question, Fitzmaurice placed the issue squarely before him:

> As you know I am not a believer in the King [Leopold] 'at all, at all,' but one has to observe the forms of diplomacy. It is perhaps not unfortunate that this pause coincides with a moment when it is not our interest to be having a row with Belgium also, if perchance we were having a row with Germany.[2]

The Foreign Office did not, however, remain entirely quiescent. A despatch based on the report of the commission was sent to Brussels expressing disappointment at the non-publication of the *procès-verbaux* of the commission and urging the Congo government to publish this.[3] Turning to the report itself, it was claimed to have confirmed Casement's indictment and to have put beyond dispute the existence of abuses which called for administrative reform. While refraining from giving details of its views on the reforms needed in the Congo until the commission for reforms had reported, the despatch indicated that the British government did not favour a labour tax for the advancement of commercial operations in which the Congolese had no interest and from which they could derive no benefit. A system which compelled the personal service of the citizen for such a purpose, the despatch emphasized, must remain open to the imputation of constituting a form of servitude differing in essence but little from actual slavery.[4]

The despatch did not satisfy the reformers and they continued to be very active. Indeed, Lalaing believed that in the general election of January Congo reform served to

---

[1] A. Hardinge: *A Diplomatist in Europe*, London 1927, p. 187.

[2] Fitzmaurice to Dilke, 16 February 1906, quoted in Gwynn and Tuckwell, op. cit., ii, 382.

[3] Grey to Hardinge, 9 January 1906, FO 367/31, no. 2, Africa.

[4] Ibid.

defeat at least one Conservative.[1] Certainly the Liberal land-slide and the election of fifty-three Labour members enlarged the parliamentary ranks of the Congo reform movement. In February, a Congo parliamentary committee was set up under the chairmanship of J. Ramsay Macdonald and the result of this was to subject Grey to increasing parliamentary pressure.[2] Outside parliament, Morel had taken over from the ageing Fox Bourne the strategy of memorializing the Foreign Office. The one solution he sought to secure was the establishment of British consular jurisdiction in the Congo. Once these courts were set up, he told Fitzmaurice, a crisis would be precipitated which might lead to the summoning of an international conference.[3] It seems that he had cast Grey in the role of William II and Boma was to be a second Tangier. Morel also goaded the missionaries to put pressure on Grey. On 2 February the B.M.S. asked Grey to receive a delegation. Two weeks later they repeated the request enclosing this time an appeal signed by fifty-one missionaries serving in the Congo which 'testified that the acts of oppression complained of are still practised'. In the face of this agitation, Grey urged Hardinge to inquire about the delay in releasing the report of the commission for reforms.[4]

While Grey's action made little impression on the Congo government, the reform agitation in Brussels itself was taking a dramatic turn. Since the nature of the Congo commission's report was known the Belgian reformers had been preparing to extend the role they had played in determining its terms of reference by launching a vigorous onslaught against the Congo régime. They had begun to

---

[1] Lalaing to Van der Elst, 5 February 1906, Ier sér., Congo, vii, 1862, private. Lalaing cited the example of the Tory, Thomas Brook-Hitching, who had spoken favourably of the Congo at a banquet in Brussels.

[2] E.g. from the assembling of the new parliament in mid-February to the end of April 1906, thirteen questions were asked on the Congo question. On 13 March a parliamentary delegation waited on Grey. Grey to Hardinge, 27 March 1906, FO 367/31, no. 36, Africa.

[3] Morel to Fitzmaurice, 25 February 1906, ibid.

[4] Grey to Hardinge, 26 February 1906, ibid., no. 25, Africa.

prepare the ground as from October 1905 when the socialist organ *Le Peuple* printed a series of violent tirades against what it described as 'le régime d'extorsion, de brigandage et de meurtres, conséquences de la politique du roi au Congo'.[1] When the report appeared the unfavourable impression which it made on serious-minded Belgians was then exploited by the reformers. The lead was taken by A. J. Wauters who reminded his readers that the grave indictment made against the State by the commission was a justification of the criticisms he had levied as early as 1891. The *Ligue des Droits de l'homme* met on 29 November under the influence of the socialists and adopted a resolution urging all links uniting Belgium and the Congo State to be broken. Even the Catholics who had formed the backbone of King Leopold's defence turned against him. In view of the censure levied against them by the commission for conniving at certain aspects of Congo maladministration, the Superiors of the Catholic Missions protested against their being made scape-goats and revealed, rather belatedly, that they had reported cases of cruelty against the Congolese to the government. This was the beginning of uneasy relations between the Catholic missions and the Congo government.[2] The organ of the Young Right, *Le Patriote*, which had the widest circulation in Belgium, also adopted a distinctly anti-Congo policy.[3] It was soon joined by the *XXᵉ Siècle*, an influential conservative paper, and the ultramontane *Le Bien Public de Gand*. The height of the Catholic reaction arising from the commission was reached with the publication of *La Question Congolaise* by Father Vermeersch, a Jesuit and Professor of Law and of Political Science at Louvain University. This book severely criticized the Congo

---

[1] *Le Peuple*, 10 October 1905. See also 4 October, 11 October, 19 October, 20 October, 21 October, 22 October, 23 October, 24 October and 25 October. The series delighted Morel and he boasted to Cadbury: ' "Le Peuple" is practically my organ . . . and takes up my arguments and statements editorially as though its own, with gratifying enthusiasm.' Morel to Cadbury, 16 October 1905, M.P., F. 8.

[2] Phipps to Lansdowne, 20 November 1905, FO 10/815, no. 110, Africa.

[3] E.g. *Le Patriote*, 23 November 1905 and 2 December 1905.

system and called for a radical reform of the Congo administration.

However, the man whose work played the leading role in Belgium to bring down King Leopold's empire was Felicien Cattier. At the beginning of 1906 he published his *Etude sur la situation de l'Etat Indépendant du Congo*. Basing its arguments on the report of the commission, Hardinge said, the book criticized the current administrative system of the Congo in severe but measured terms.[1] Cattier took the various headings under which the Congo commission had issued its report seriatim and demonstrated, often in contradistinction to the conciliatory attitude of the commissioners, that the Congolese had been robbed of their land and enslaved in their own country.What made the book still more outstanding was the remedy Cattier prescribed. For him, the only possible and logical solution was the immediate annexation of the Congo by Belgium. He gave three reasons for this. In the first place, he pointed out that despotic government was bad in itself and that the despotic government of King Leopold had been particularly bad. Secondly, he argued that any adequate reform of the Congo administration would entail considerable expense and the necessary money could only be found by Belgian intervention. Finally, an entirely new staff of officials in the Congo was imperative and these, he said, could only be supplied when the Congo State had become a Belgian colony.

Cattier then went on to make some sensational revelations. King Leopold, he wrote, had profited from the *Domaine de la Couronne* alone to the sum of £3 million since 1896. Of this sum he had spent at least £731,581 on property speculation in Brussels and Ostend alone. The King had also spent considerable sums in influencing the press to support the Congo administration. Cattier calculated that since the foundation of the State the Budgets had shown only a total deficit of £1,080,000. There need therefore have

---

[1] Hardinge to Grey, 10 February 1906, FO 367/31, no. 20, Africa. This book still remains the best commentary on King Leopold's régime in the Congo.

been no deficit at all. The Congo State, he concluded, had borrowed a total of £5,200,000 to meet its deficit of £1,080,000. What, he asked, had happened to the extra £4,120,000 borrowed?

The extensive publicity which Cattier's book received ensured it a wide hearing. The startling spectacle which was revealed of the king-sovereign battening on Congo millions made a special impact in Belgian parliamentary circles and, as a curtain-raiser to the famous interpellation of Vandervelde and the subsequent five days' debate on the Congo,[1] could not have been bettered. This debate, which was the sixth interpellation on the Congo by the socialist leader, began on 20 February and continued from 27 February to 2 March. Its significance, however, lay in the fact that he abandoned his former demand for a complete break between Belgium and the Congo and his attacks on the 'capitalist' régime of the Congo. His views and his arguments now mirrored those of Cattier and the immediate result was that the Liberal Party decided to align itself with the socialists. At the same time the section of the Young Right which was led by Beernaert was prepared to make common cause with the socialists and liberals. In the face of this threatened coalition, it became possible to pass the moderate motion of Beernaert calling for immediate examination of the bill of 7 August 1901 which would enable Belgium to possess and administer a colony.

The outcome of this debate was very important. The assumption that annexation was now desirable constituted an indirect reflection on the personal administration of Leopold II. A decided moral victory, it was generally recognized, had been won for the cause of Congo reform.[2] It must be pointed out, however, that the debate did not envisage the prospect of immediate annexation during the life-time of King Leopold. The motion merely ensured that

---

[1] E. D. Morel: *Verbatim Report of The Five Days' Congo Debate in the Belgian House of Representatives*, Liverpool 1906.

[2] Hardinge to Grey, 2 March 1906, FO 403/372, no. 32, Africa.

Belgium would be in a position to become a colonial power at the appropriate time.[1] As we shall see, the idea of immediate annexation had yet to be forced on the Belgian government and on the king-sovereign.

The failure of the Belgian Chamber to vote immediate annexation was a disappointment for Cattier. He became convinced that pressure from the outside was necessary and to bring about this he communicated with Fox Bourne and the Foreign Office. His object, Cattier told Grey's private secretary, was to urge the British government to take an early opportunity of publicly declaring their support for Belgian annexation of the Congo State.[2] In a memorandum which he handed to Barrington, he reiterated his firm conviction that no reforms which the present administration of the Congo State would introduce could remove the abuses committed in that colony and that 'l'annexation du Congo à la Belgique est l'unique remède radical aux maux dont souffre le Congo'.[3]

A similar suggestion had been made by Van Eetvelde to Lansdowne the previous year but had been turned down for fear that such a recommendation might be resented by the Belgian government.[4] Grey, on the other hand, was prepared

---

[1] Reporting the debate Hardinge said:

'I asked Van Eetvelde whether the Resolution in favour of annexation would be fraught with any immediate effect. He said that the chief difficulties in the way of early annexation were (1) the King's own objections, and (2) the unwillingness of the Ministry, in view of these objections, to grapple with so thorny a problem. He had spoken to M. Woeste (leader of the ultra-conservative and ultra-clerical section of the present majority in the Belgian Parliament). M. Woeste was personally favourable to annexation but was afraid that if the Congo were taken over by Belgium, the King would continue to interfere, directly and actively in its Government, and that the Crown would thus be dragged into Belgian Party questions . . . [and] the prestige of the Sovereign imperilled. The Ministers and chiefs of both the leading parties (socialists excluded) were all unwilling to place themselves in antagonism to the King. . . .'
Hardinge to Grey, 23 March 1906, FO 367/31, no. 39, Africa.

[2] E. Barrington, 27 March 1906, ibid., memorandum.

[3] F. Cattier, 27 March 1906, ibid., memorandum.

[4] Lansdowne to Phipps, 10 July 1905, FO 2/938, no. 63, Africa, confidential.

to consider the move favourably. The weight of public opinion in England was on the side of the establishment of consular jurisdiction, a demand which had been strengthened by the prosecution of Reverend Stannard of the C.B.M. for criminal libel.[1] A declaration in favour of Belgian annexation was a positive, forward-looking policy which afforded less chance of friction with Belgium and would relieve the British government of the need for further intervention. In any case, Grey himself had always envisaged annexation as the only solution to the Congo question.[2] Consequently, when Cattier brought forward the suggestion Grey agreed to seize a favourable opportunity in the Commons to make the required declaration. Two weeks later, J. Ramsay Macdonald asked whether the Foreign Secretary would be able to give assurances to the Belgian people that the British government would welcome the transfer of the administration of the Congo to the Belgian nation. Grey readily replied that Belgium, with the right to look upon the Congo as a prospective colony, was the proper country to assert responsibility there.[3] Grey's declaration in favour of Belgian annexation, which attracted considerable attention, was far-reaching. It indicated that Britain had no territorial ambition in the Congo; but more important, according to Arendt, 'The question of annexation, raised indirectly but very clearly during the debate in our *Chambre*, is thus placed on an international level.'[4] The Belgian government, he

---

[1] Slade: *English-Speaking Missions*, pp. 317–19.

Reverend Edgar Stannard, who had been one of the most persistent critics of the Congo administration, was prosecuted for criminal libel because of a letter published under his name by Morel. He was condemned at first to a fine totalling 1,395 francs. On appeal the conviction was quashed, no doubt because of an apprehension that the case might be used as an excuse for establishing British consular jurisdiction.

The Stannard case was said to have been unique in British consular history because it was the first time that a consular officer acted as a defence counsel for a British subject on trial in a foreign court. Brant (F.O. Librarian), 31 May 1906, FO 367/3, memorandum.

[2] See Hansard, 9 June 1904, 4th ser., cxxv, 1288.

[3] Hansard, 11 April 1906, 4th ser., clv, 1372, 1378.

[4] Arendt, 17 April 1906, Ier sér., Congo, vii, 1910, memorandum.

warned, could ignore Grey's attempt to exert moral pressure on them but this pressure would inevitably increase and cause some embarrassment in the future. In other words, it was time that the Belgian government took the question of annexation more seriously and thus avoided international complication.

Meanwhile, in Belgium itself, the forthcoming May elections diverted attention from the Congo question though it was clear that the future of the question would depend on the outcome of these elections. The liberals had committed themselves during the Congo debate of February to a policy of annexation which they might initiate if they won. With this possibility in mind, Leopold II shrewdly let it be known that he had decided to lead the movement in favour of annexation.[1] The result of the elections, however, retained the Catholic party in power and he suitably adjusted his position. A few weeks after the elections he issued the long-awaited reform decrees prepared by the commission for reforms. Together with the decrees was published his message enunciating the administrative policy he had hitherto pursued and in a supplementary declaration he laid down the conditions attaching to the eventual union of the Congo State with Belgium.[2] It was these two documents which, more than anything else, brought about the annexation of the Congo by Belgium during King Leopold's lifetime. But before their implications, let us first examine the reform decrees.

These decrees, which were twenty-four in number, were supposed to carry out all the recommendations of the commission of inquiry. There was to be a fresh delimitation of land by which the Congolese would be allotted an area triple the size already under their cultivation. The governor-general would fix taxes proportional to the resources of the

---

[1] Hardinge to Grey, 27 April 1906, FO 367/32, no. 48, Africa, confidential. By appearing to favour annexation the king-sovereign hoped that in the event of a liberal victory he would obtain satisfactory compensation for giving up the Congo.

[2] *B.O.*, no. 6, June 1906.

various regions and to the degree of development of the inhabitants. The tax would not be less than six francs nor more than twenty-four francs per annum and was to be paid either in produce or in labour. The use of armed soldiers and sentinels for the collection of taxes was forbidden and military operations were to be undertaken only in the event of a revolt. The use of money would be introduced and a million francs would be struck for this purpose. The age beyond which children could not be held under State tutelage was reduced from twenty-five to twenty-one and professional schools were to be established at Boma, Leopoldville and Stanleyville for children between twelve and twenty. In future no less than three State inspectors would supervise the execution of the decrees and protect the inhabitants. Finally, the *Domaine Privé* was constituted into a national *domaine* to be administered by a council.

The proposed reforms, made an advance on the recommendations of the commission of inquiry in two respects. In the first place, the concession companies were altogether deprived of the powers of levying and collecting taxes; and, secondly, the tax was given values in money. On the other hand, the decrees fell short of the recommendations in several ways. The suggestion of the earlier commission for an experiment in the exploitation of the country by free labour was ignored. Again the decrees laid down the maximum term of service for conscripts on works of public utility at five years while the commission had recommended three years. On the introduction of a coinage system, the commission had recommended the payment in money for work done, for produce collected, and for wages of hired labourers; the decrees stated that payment should continue in barter-goods. Finally, the recommendation that the judiciary should be made independent of the administration was rejected. Because of these serious short-comings G. H. S. Pearson of the African Department remarked that the opportunities for ill-treating the Congolese were slightly lessened although the chances that the opportunities still left would be made the most of were as great as ever. He concluded:

Some more admirable laws have been added to the already excellent scheme of legislation, one or two ways of breaking the laws have been closed, but the result is practically nil.[1]

This judgement, as will later be shown, was prophetic.

Nevertheless, it was not so much the reform decrees which evoked the subsequent bitter controversy on the Congo question as the documents that accompanied them. The first was in the form of a letter, soon to be known as the 'royal manifesto', addressed by the king-sovereign to the secretaries-general of the Congo State. In reality it was a defiance hurled to Belgian and foreign reformers alike. The passage which attracted most attention was the one where Leopold II declared:

My rights over the Congo cannot be shared; they are the fruit of my labours and my expenditure. You must give them the fullest publicity. . . . It behoves me to proclaim these rights to the world. . . .[2]

Although the letter went on to assure public opinion of the concern of the Congo government for the welfare of the Congolese every paragraph demonstrated that the king-sovereign felt he could act in the Congo as he pleased. For him, no one had the right to question or to criticize his rule in the Congo, much more to compel him to surrender his sovereignty. He would fulfil the provisions of the Berlin and Brussels Acts but no power should intervene to see that he actually did so.

Grey was compelled, in answer to a parliamentary question, to retort that Britain had a right to see that the Congo State observed its treaty obligations—a right which could not be altered by unilateral declarations on the part of the sovereign of the Congo State.[3] This did not satisfy the reformers. They urged him to refuse altogether to consider the reform decrees and to adopt immediately some

---

[1] Pearson, 15 June 1906, FO 367/32, memorandum.
[2] *Accounts and Papers*, 1907 (Cd. 3450), lvii, 799 (translation); *B.O.*, no. 6, June 1906.
[3] Hansard, 14 June 1906, 4th ser., clviii, 1136.

'resolute action . . . with a view to terminating the exercise of this system, and its nefarious consequences'.[1] Grey remained unmoved. Although he was sceptical about the honest intentions of the king-sovereign, he was still willing to see first the spirit in which the new decrees would be applied.[2] Consequently, the consular officers were instructed to observe carefully and report how the local authorities interpreted these decrees, and the steps taken to effect them.

The attitude of sitting and waiting, it has been said, did not appeal to the reformers in Britain. Their next step was to try by parliamentary pressure, to force the government into taking a more positive action. On 3 July Lord Reay provoked the first Lords' debate on the Congo question, and two days later Sir Gilbert Parker did the same in the House of Commons. The manoeuvre succeeded to some extent in spite of the intervention of the Irish nationalist, John McKean, who had been well briefed for the defence of the Congo government.[3] Grey was obliged to declare that if all or any of the powers would join with Britain in pressing for a change, he would gladly welcome such collaboration. Meanwhile, he continued, he agreed that the moment had come when the British government must consider what independent action to take. He would examine further the possibility of setting up the International River Commission provided for by the Berlin Act and might submit the question of free trade as well as the prohibition of monopolies to arbitration at the Hague Tribunal. Referring to the British right of consular jurisdiction he pointed out that if they

---

[1] C.R.A. to Grey, 17 June 1906, FO 403/373.

[2] Grey, n.d., minute on Nightingale to Grey, 14 May 1906, FO 367/32, no. 31, Africa. Barrington was more categorical: 'The new decrees must be given a trial. We are not going to govern the Congo ourselves. . . .' Barrington, n.d., minute, ibid.

[3] The initiative for this intervention was taken by McKean, see Lalaing to Favereau, 10 April 1906, Ier sér., Congo, vii, 1906. The fact that the main body of the Irish Party maintained a benevolent neutrality was largely due to the campaign among them by Casement. He could, however, not influence McKean, who was a Catholic zealot and ' "sees" [*sic*] red at anything affecting his church as he thinks'. Casement to Morel, 29 May 1906, M.P., F. 8.

'establish extra-territorial jurisdiction it will discourage the interest which is now being shown in Belgium' for annexation. But Grey did not leave the matter there. He would wait, he assured the House, but he would not wait for ever. He would only 'like to wait and see what the autumn may bring forth'.[1]

Grey's speech was very tactful. He had said enough to reassure the Belgians as well as the reformers. But he had also said enough to put Leopold II in his place. The report of the commission for reforms had been published, Grey had declared, not with a credible public statement that the government of the Congo had realized the full extent of the mischief it had committed, not with anything that would give full assurance that the conscience of the government of the Congo State had been so touched that matters would be improved in the future, but with a pronouncement of rights in which the sovereign had spoken less as a governor, and more as if he were the owner of private property. Grey had then added that 'Even property has its duties as well as its rights; and every Sovereign of every State, though he has his rights has also his obligations.'[2] This attack brought a protest from the pen of King Leopold himself. But Grey dealt him the *coup de grace* with a finesse which increased the king's humiliation. His reply, a little lecture to the king in diplomatic good manners, stated merely that it was unusual and undesirable for the Foreign Secretary in the British government to discuss the issues raised in the letter by direct correspondence with the sovereign of the Congo State.[3]

The C.R.A. was heartened by the stand which Grey had now taken. A general expectation prevailed that the autumn would witness the crisis in the Congo question. Consequently, efforts were redoubled and the agitation intensified. Morel and Harris rushed the North and Midlands with lecture tours. Early in the autumn Morel published his best-seller

---

[1] Hansard, 5 July 1906, 4th ser., clx, 322–4. See also Barrington to Hardinge, 11 July 1906, FO 367/32, private.

[2] Hansard, 5 July 1906, 4th ser., clx, 319.

[3] Grey to King Leopold, 30 July 1906, FO 403/374.

entitled *Red Rubber*.[1] On the impact which the book had Johnston wrote: 'You have made a great hit with your book, greater perhaps than you realize. I have heard it discussed in rather high political circles.'[2] In *Red Rubber* Morel had compressed into one volume the polemics of his earlier writings together with the scholarly exposition of the Congo question contained in Cattier's recent book. It concluded with a passionate appeal both to self-interest and to all that was best in the English nation to staunch the red rubber flowing from the Congo and he recommended that consular jurisdiction and a man-of-war at the mouth of the Congo was all that was required. *Red Rubber* was typical of Morelian extremism. It must be remembered, however, that he did not share the prevalent optimism that Belgium would annex and that he was looking to a future, not to an immediate, action which might provide a solution. 'If the forthcoming Belgian debate is unsatisfactory, as it is almost certain to be,' he told Harris, 'then the Government must act.'[3]

Meanwhile, although the policy of the British government was to encourage Belgian annexation, Grey was alive to the fact that public opinion might yet compel him to intervene if Belgium did not and in the spirit of the Anglo-French entente he warned Paul Cambon, the French ambassador in London, of this danger.[4] At the same time, the Belgian government itself was left in no doubt as to the seriousness of the position. Thus, speaking at the Guildhall on the occasion of the sixty-fifth birthday of King Edward, Lord Ripon, Liberal leader in the Lords, emphasized that the government of Belgium had the primary duty of reforming the Congo administration. If she undertook this task the British government would do nothing to disturb her right or position in the Congo; but if she did not then Britain would be obliged to intervene.[5] The hint went home. Lalaing wrote to warn that

[1] It ran into six editions.
[2] Harry Johnston to Morel, 27 December 1906, M.P., F. 8.
[3] Morel to Harris, ? October 1906, M.P., F. 8 (copy).
[4] Grey, n.d., minute, on Hardinge to Grey, 20 October 1906, FO 367/33, no. 99, Africa, very confidential.
[5] *The Times*, 9 November 1906.

The Congo question once more reaches an acute crisis here. Developments which will take place in the Belgian parliament before long [are] being awaited. The subsequent attitude of the London Government towards the Congo will depend on what happens in our country.[1]

A few days later Grey met, by prearrangement with Morel, a deputation representing both sides of the House of Commons, the Church of England, the Church of Scotland, the non-conformist churches, the humanitarian organizations interested in the Congo question and the chambers of commerce. Grey reaffirmed his earlier statements, an admixture of encouragement and warning, that Belgium should take the question of Congo reform in hand.[2] Commenting on this deputation *The Times*, more moderate than the other British newspapers, remarked that when both sides of the Houses of Parliament and great cities like Glasgow and Newcastle, Liverpool and Manchester could unite on the same issue with the Church of England, the Free Churches and the philanthropic societies, it was a sign that the British people were pretty much of one mind.[3] Therefore Belgium must decide to annex or . . .

The deputation, however, had more than this import. Since 1884, Britain had adamantly refused to recognize the French right of pre-emption over the Congo State but in his speech to the deputation Grey had admitted this right for the first time.[4] The reason was simple. The Liberal Government did not favour a policy of colonial expansion and there was therefore no need to hinder such ambitions as France might have in the Congo basin. On the other hand, Grey undoubtedly hoped that having whetted French appetite with the prospect of aggrandizement they would be eager to

---

[1] Lalaing to Favereau, 10 November 1906, I⁰ʳ sér., Congo, vii, 1983.
[2] *The Times*, 21 November 1906.
[3] Ibid.
[4] Ibid. See also Paul Cambon to M. Pichon, 22 November 1906, *D.D.F.*, 2nd ser., x, no. 302.

second his diplomatic initiative to secure an international conference on Congo reform. He was to be disappointed.[1]

Meanwhile, since the Congo debate of February and March in the Belgian Chamber the opinion of most Belgian politicians had consolidated in favour of the annexation of the Congo. Although the motion adopted by the Chamber envisaged the annexation to take place after the death of Leopold II there was still a vocal minority who advocated immediate annexation. It was these people that the king-sovereign had in mind when he said in the royal manifesto:

> The adversaries of the Congo press for immediate annexation. These persons hope without doubt that a change in the present régime will cause the wreck of the work now in progress and will enable them to obtain some rich booty from the wreckage.
>
> If you are questioned as to my intentions, you should answer that I consider myself morally bound to inform the country when without prejudice I consider that the moment is propitious for examining the question of annexation. I have nothing to say at present.[2]

It was the plainest warning of the intention of the king-sovereign to retain his hold on the Congo and he hoped by this to defeat annexation now as he had done in 1901.

But the king-sovereign did not stop there. The royal manifesto categorically declared that the royal will of August 1889 no longer formed the basis of the right of Belgium to annex and he went on to lay down conditions which the country must undertake to fulfil if and when

---

[1] That Grey was foiled in this was probably due to the vigilance of the French ambassador. He had immediately warned the Quai d'Orsay of the danger which France would incur for the French Congo if an international conference was convened on the basis defined by Grey: France herself might find her colonial policy in the French Congo the subject of international discussion around the conference table. Paul Cambon to Pichon, 9 December 1906, *D.D.F.*, 2nd ser., x, no. 349. Nevertheless, it was clear, as Leghait the Belgian ambassador in Paris soon discovered, that Leopold II could no longer rely on the benevolent neutrality of France. Infra, p. 180.

[2] *Accounts and Papers*, 1907 (Cd. 3450), lvii, 799; *B.O.*, no. 6, June 1906.

annexation took place. These conditions formed the other document accompanying the reform decrees. In this Leopold II maintained that Belgium must undertake to respect all the engagements of the Congo State with respect to third parties as well as all the Acts by means of which he had established the *Domaine de la Couronne* (henceforth known as *Fondation de la Couronne*) and the *Domaine National.* In particular, the revenues from these institutions were not to be diminished without granting them compensation equivalent to the loss of revenue involved.[1] By emphasizing these onerous obligations Leopold II hoped no doubt to dampen the enthusiasm to assume immediate responsibility for the Congo State.

However successful these tactics must have been for the moment, they eventually proved to have been a blunder on the part of the king-sovereign.[2] They soon diverted attention from the merits or demerits of the reform proposals,[3] and focussed it on the personal policy of the king himself. Once the true implications of the royal manifesto had been digested, once it became clear that the issue was not one between the King of the Belgians and foreign critics, many Belgians realized that they had to choose between the claims of the king and the claims of the country; between absolutism and constitutionalism. The position of the conservative majority became invidious. Devoted as they were to the monarchy and to its defence, to uphold the terms of the

---

[1] Ibid.

[2] Wauters, op. cit., p. 281; Daye, op. cit., p. 500.

[3] The exceptions were Cattier and Vermeersch. On the publication of the decrees Cattier wrote: 'The reform decrees sanctioned by the Sovereign-King, far from giving satisfaction to the reform party, may be considered as a challenge to the civilized world. . . . The only logical solution which can furnish sufficient guarantees to the civilized world is the annexation of the Congo State by Belgium and in conditions which are at the same time compatible with her dignity and with the rights and interests of the Powers.' *The Times,* 19 June 1906.
These sentiments were re-echoed by Vermeersch in a pamphlet entitled *Les Destinées du Congo Belge* circulated on the eve of the Vandervelde interpellation which is discussed in the next chapter.

royal manifesto laid them open to the charge of betraying the interests of the nation.

The choice did not remain long in doubt. Ardent supporters of the Crown though most Belgians were, yet they desired that the king should be a constitutional ruler and inevitably they were led to the conclusion that Leopold II must hand over the Congo State to them.

It did not take the king-sovereign long to discover his folly. The repeated declaration of the Foreign Office that it wished Belgium to annex crushed the hope that Belgian opinion would rally behind him against what had been represented as British jealousy towards Congo prosperity and a desire to deprive Belgium of her heritage. Consequently, he attempted to introduce a new consideration by focussing attention on the implications of annexation for the neutrality of Belgium. He pointed out[1] that even if annexation took place Britain would still complain of Congo misgovernment and that would not stop until she got what she had long desired, namely, a slice of Congo territory which would enable her to complete the Cape to Cairo scheme. Belgian annexation was bound to compromise Anglo-Belgian amity which was so essential to the security of Belgium. On the other hand, so long as the union between Belgium and the Congo State was only in the person of the king-sovereign British attacks would fall only on the king-sovereign himself. He could, with less danger to Belgium than a Belgian government, support the blows which British avarice in Africa would continuously launch.

This ingenuous argument was no more successful than the royal manifesto in view of the insistent affirmations of the British government in favour of Belgian annexation. In addition, Fox Bourne, after consultations with Cattier, addressed a letter on behalf of the A.P.S. to all the Belgian deputies supporting the idea of immediate annexation by Belgium. These actions were sufficient to belie any imputation of malice by Britain towards Belgium. In any case, it was evident that the issue whether Belgium had the right to

---

[1] Hardinge to Grey, 20 October 1906, FO 367/33, no. 99, Africa, very confidential.

annex and under what conditions had been too clearly posed in the royal manifesto to be obscured by conjuring up the ogre of British imperialism. Those Belgians who desired immediate annexation saw this quite clearly and successfully exploited it to attain their objective.

Thus the Congo commission of inquiry and the royal manifesto which arose from it formed a dividing line in the Congo question. Before these events, Belgian annexation was contemplated as an event which would take place in some remote future—probably after the death of Leopold II. After them, Belgian annexation emerged as a problem calling for immediate solution. For Britain, however, new considerations emerged. The question began to be asked whether annexation by Belgium was an end in itself or merely a means to an end. While the permanent officials of the Foreign Office tended to accept the former, Morel and his followers were inclined to the later. Grey hovered between the two ideas. As will be seen in the next two chapters, it was the intervention of the United States which was to give a fresh impetus and direction to British policy.

VI

International Reactions on the Eve of Annexation

For the third time within a decade Belgium was faced with the decision whether to become an imperial power. On the two previous occasions the decision had been shelved, owing partly to the resistance of Leopold II and partly to the fear, natural to a small and introspective people, that responsibility might involve them in undesirable international complications. Now the first factor was still present. Leopold II was more than ever opposed to relinquishing the extremely profitable concern which the Congo had become. On the other hand, the Belgians found themselves in the unenviable position that foreign intervention was unavoidable unless she became an imperial power.

One event which brought home to the Belgians the danger that non-annexation might not guarantee them against international complications was the announcement that the United States would co-operate with Britain.[1] Appearing as this information did under the name of Maurice Low, who was a known confidant of President Roosevelt, it assumed the greatest significance.[2] For a long

---

[1] *Morning Post*, 3 November 1906.

[2] Moncheur, the Belgian minister in the United States, had been very apprehensive of the considerable influence wielded by Low in Washington. He had suggested that Low's benevolence towards the Congo State might be purchased by an award of the Belgian *Croix de Chevalier*

period Britain had stood alone in pressing for reforms in the Congo and it was realized that she must tread softly as long as no other power teamed up with her. The news that the United States government was ready to attend any international conference summoned to discuss the affairs of the Congo State was therefore as unwelcome in Brussels as it was welcome in London.

The intervention of the United States was the result of a reform campaign dating back to 1890. We have already seen that the first protest against the Congo system of administration had been made by Williams, an American negro.[1] He was followed six years later by Rev. W. M. Morrison of the American Baptist Missionary Union working in the Congo and subsequently, individual American missionaries had appealed without much success to their home churches to champion the cause of Congo reform. It was not until March 1904 that a delegation of American Missions called on both the president and Hay, the secretary of state, to induce the government to intervene in the Congo question.[2] Although the president promised to give the matter his careful attention, the government in fact did nothing. Some three weeks later Senator Morgan, under the inspiration of Dr Thomas Barbour who was the current chairman of the Board of American Foreign Missions, presented a Memorial to Congress on behalf of the American Congo missionaries.[3] This memorial was referred to the Committee on Foreign Relations which was then asked to report whether the situation in the Congo Free State called for interference on the part of the United States. Whether the committee ever reported is obscure. But again the American government took no further action.

In September 1904 Morel received an invitation from

---

de l'Ordre du Léopold, Moncheur to Favereau, 2 November 1905, Ier sér., Congo, viii, 1823, confidential; but although the honour was duly conferred it did not seem to have had the desired effect.

[1] Supra, pp. 35–6.

[2] Durand (Washington) to Lansdowne, 26 March 1904, FO 10/808, no. 5, Africa.

[3] Durand to Lansdowne, 21 April 1904, FO 10/809, no. 9, Africa.

Dr Barbour and his friends to visit America and address the International Peace Congress at Boston on the Congo question. The C.R.A. seized the opportunity to prepare a memorandum on the Congo question which Morel duly presented to the president. This visit by Morel resulted in the organization of an American C.R.A.[1] Thus a reform movement was firmly established in America.

Leopold II was alarmed by these activities and took steps to influence the Americans in his favour. By October 1904 he had secretly established what became known as the American Congo Lobby. The direction of this propaganda machine was entrusted to Baron Moncheur, the Belgian Minister in Washington and an enthusiastic collaborator of the king-sovereign.[2] Under him worked Colonel Henry Kowalsky, a San Francisco lawyer reputed as an expert in electoral campaigns; Henry Wellington Wack, a publicity agent; Professor A. Nerincex, a Swiss working at the George Washington University; and James Whiteley, Belgian consul-general in Baltimore.[3] It was largely due to the activities of this lobby, together with its off-shoot, the Belgian Protective Association of America, that American intervention was deferred for so long.[4]

Nevertheless, the American government was also confronted with a more fundamental problem as regards intervention. They had to discover answers to two fundamental questions: firstly, whether intervention in the Congo question could be reconciled with the traditional American policy of non-intervention in the affairs of Europe; and secondly, on what legal basis intervention, even if that was agreed upon, could be based? The reformers naturally sought to allay fears as to the first by pointing out that the

---

[1] Moncheur to Arendt, 14 October 1904, Ier sér., Congo, vi, 1725, private.

[2] The first president was G. Stanley Hall, one of the most widely known educators of the country. The vice-presidents included such eminent names as Samuel L. Clemens (Mark Twain), Booker T. Washington and Henry van Dyke.

[3] *New York American*, 9 December 1906; 10 December 1906.

[4] *Pittsburg Sun*, 11 December 1906.

United States had attended the Berlin and Brussels conferences and were therefore obliged to maintain the principles which had animated them. As regards the second question which was founded on the fact that the United States did not ratify the Berlin Act the reformers argued that the Brussels conference was practically a continuation of the Berlin one. In so far as the Act arising from the Brussels conference was ratified by the government they concluded that the United States had assumed an obligation to intervene.[1]

As the defenders of the Congo administration demonstrated these arguments were tenuous.[2] Nevertheless, the American reformers persisted in their campaign. Reverend John Harris and his wife were sponsored on a whistle-stop tour of the United States during which they addressed over 200 public meetings in several cities. But in spite of all these the Secretary of State, Elihu Root, issued his famous letter to Senator Denby.[3] The American government, according to Root, did not sign the Berlin Act often quoted by the reformers as the basis for international action and in any case it was 'questionable' whether the provisions of the Act afforded its signatories the right of intervention in the domestic affairs of the Congo State. The Congo government absolutely denied such rights. He emphasized that the information which the American government obtained on the Congo administration came at second hand, probably through biased sources, since the United States had no official representative in the Congo who could supply impartial information. His experience was that the Congo government was always ready to afford redress to any complaints that American interests brought to their notice. He wished that some way could be found by which the whole of Central Africa would be fairly administered by the

---

[1] *New York Times*, 1 October 1904.

[2] 'Memorial presented to Senate on behalf of Belgian Protective Association of America', encl. in Durand to Lansdowne, 2 February 1905, FO 10/813, no. 2, Africa.

[3] Root to Denby, 20 February 1906, FO 367/31 (copy). See also Stenmans, op. cit., p. 328.

colonial powers and quickly added that if the United States had to administer a region five times as great and populous as the Philippines she might also have found good government impossible and would have been criticized.[1] Such an excellent defence of the Congo government, Leopold II might have been proud of. It is not surprising that his government had Root's letter printed and widely distributed.

The triumph was short-lived. While Congophiles were hawking Root's views round the European capitals, American opinion was undergoing a steady and rapid change in favour of some form of intervention. Harris reported from Washington:

> Telegrams, petitions, private letters are rolling in here by the thousands. We have been to the Senate House and find that the Senators are all informing themselves upon the subject owing to the enormous pressure. The same applies to Congress. The Foreign Committee members have informed Senators that these charges against the Congo State administration are proved and that something must be done. Mr. Root is wavering in his attitude. The President is safe and with a little more pressure will take some action.[2]

The persistent pressure exerted by the American reformers soon led the State Department to appoint a consul-general to the Congo[3] and through this channel it was hoped that the United States would be able to obtain independent and reliable information about Congo affairs.

By the autumn of 1906, then, Leopold II was faced with the threat of annexation by Belgium under the pressure of Great Britain. As will soon be seen,[4] he could neither rely on the support of France and Germany nor on the abstention of the United States. It was the first time that the king-sovereign had found himself in such a predicament. His

---

[1] Ibid.

[2] Harris to Morel, 14 February 1906, encl. in Morel to Fitzmaurice, 25 February 1906, FO 367/31.

[3] Wyndham (chargé d'affaires, Brussels) to Grey, 20 September 1906, FO 367/33, no. 86, Africa.

[4] Infra, p. 180.

reaction to it was an attempt to influence the various governments by sharing his Congo booty with some of their businessmen. At the same time, he took measures to secure his profits should annexation eventually take place. The mind of the king-sovereign always seemed to work like that of a skilful diplomatist and an unscrupulous merchant rolled into one.

The *Bulletin Officiel* of November announced the formation of four great monopoly companies for the exploitation of the Congo. The first company was the *Union Minière du Haut Katanga*. Its capital was subscribed on a fifty-fifty basis between the British Company, Tanganyika Concessions Limited, and the Belgian commercial octopus *Société Générale du Belgique*. The object of the company was the development of the mineral wealth, chiefly copper, of the Katanga district for a period of thirty years, renewable until 1990. The second, *Compagnie du chemin de fer du Bas-Congo au Katanga*, was formed by Belgian and French capital. It was to construct a railway line between Katanga and the Lower Congo and another joining the former with the Portuguese line from Benguela. It was also given exclusive mining rights over a vast district for eighty-nine years. The third, American Congo Company, which was formed by a syndicate of American millionaires represented by Thomas Ryan and the Guggenheims, was granted for sixty years an area of approximately one million hectares near the mouth of river Kasai together with smaller portions elsewhere for shorter terms. Finally, the *Société Internationale Forestière et Minière du Congo*, whose capital was shared out between American business interests and the Congo State government, was granted rights of mineral exploitation and forest cultivation in large areas situated at the centre of the Congo. Leopold II also sought to attract German capital but the negotiations fell through owing to German distrust in the king.[1]

How far American big business would have been successful in preventing the intervention of the American government in the Congo question cannot now be ascertained. As the *New York American* later revealed, Secretary Root had

---

[1] Willequet, op. cit., pp. 182 ff.

previously acted as an attorney for Ryan and the assistant secretary, Robert Bacon, had been a former partner of J. P. Morgan who was a known agent of Leopold II.[1] It seems more likely, however, that the American financiers merely wanted to capitalize on the difficult position in which Leopold II found himself.[2] Nevertheless, the arrangements came too late really to influence the action of the United States.[3] Under these circumstances, we must view the scandal arising from the subsequent exposure of King Leopold's American Congo lobby as an important but secondary factor which contributed to the intervention of the American government.

On 9 December the *New York American* revealed the existence in Washington of a lobby paid by King Leopold in order to influence Congress[4] and when the very next day Senator Lodge tabled a resolution pledging the support of the senate to any action the president might take it was naturally assumed to have been a result of this exposure of the lobby.[5]

---

[1] For a discussion on Root's complicity, see MacStallworth, op. cit., pp. 288 ff.

[2] Hardinge to Grey, 6 December 1906, FO 403/374, no. 143, Africa, confidential.

[3] The announcement that President Roosevelt was ready to intervene appeared only a few days after the signing of the concession.

[4] Moncheur reported the source of the scandal as follows:

'As you are aware, it had pleased the King to appoint Colonel Kowalsky of California as his attorney in the United States. This individual had, as a special mission, to defend the Congo against the attacks of its opponents in this country. After a year this assignment came to an end, the inquiries made about Kowalsky having proved that he was only a Jew of ill-repute.

'The man felt a deep resentment at this and found a means of reconciling his vengeance with his interests by selling to the *New York American*, the worst organ of the "yellow press", the confidential documents which he had received from Brussels as well as copies of letters which he had written to the King.'

Moncheur to Favereau, 11 December 1906, Ier sér., Congo, vii, 2021.

[5] The only outcome of these revelations was the dismissal of a clerk of the Senate Committee on Foreign Relations who actually appeared to have received bribes from the Congo lobby. *The Times*, 14 December 1906.

The scandal had immediate repercussions in Washington and Brussels apart from the shock it gave to public opinion elsewhere. At the beginning of December, as we have seen, the views of President Roosevelt had been made known through Maurice Low. He now felt it safe enough to inform the British government directly that he would welcome information as to 'the course and scope of action' which Britain might contemplate taking and to offer his co-operation.[1] In Brussels King Leopold II realized that there was no alternative than to yield to the solution of Belgian annexation.[2]

This decision by the king-sovereign on annexation was of comparatively little significance. The temper of the Belgian Chamber by this time had become such that the postponement of the consideration of a project for annexation was impossible. The debate which opened on 28 November and took up three parliamentary weeks was based on an interpellation by the Liberal leader, Paul Hymans, on the situation created for Belgium, as regards the eventual annexation

---

[1] Full text of the statement read: 'The President, moved by the deep interest shown by all classes of the American people in the amelioration of conditions in the Congo State, has observed with deep appreciation the steps which His Majesty's Government are considering towards that humanitarian end. The American Government would be glad to have such information as to the course and scope of action as Great Britain may contemplate under the provisions of the General Act of the Congo, having in view the information which His Majesty's Government may have acquired concerning the conditions in Central Africa, it being the desire of the President to contribute by such action and attitude as may be properly within his function towards the realization of whatever reforms may be counselled by the sentiments of humanity and by the experience developed by the past and present workings of the Administration in the Congo. The President's interest in watching the trend toward reform is coupled with the earnest desire to see the full performance of the obligations of Articles II and V of the General Slave Trade Act of Brussels of July 2, 1890, to which the United States is a party, in all that affects involuntary servitude of the natives.' Memorandum communicated by Carter (United States chargé d'affaires), 11 December 1906. See also Grey, 11 December 1906, FO 367/31, memorandum.

[2] J. Stengers, 'Quand Léopold II s'est-il rallié à l'annexion du Congo par la Belgique?', *Bulletin de l'Institut Royal Colonial Belge*, (1952) xxiii, 3.

of the Congo, by the letter of the king-sovereign of 3 June and the accompanying testamentary act.[1]

Before Hymans actually spoke, the prime minister, de Smet de Naeyer, read a long declaration on the policy of his government as regards the Congo. After tracing the background of Belgium's right to annexation he expressed the support of his government for annexation but pointed out that two preliminary measures were necessary. In the first place, a law defining the régime to be introduced after annexation must be adopted. Next, a convention of transfer would have to be signed with the Congo State. On the issue of the royal manifesto which had been the subject of so much controversy he declared that sovereign states had the right to take special precautions to safeguard crown lands and on these grounds the king-sovereign's arrangements relative to the *Domaine de la Couronne* were justified. He then praised the achievements of the Congo State and hoped that the recent reform decrees would remedy the abuses which had crept into the administration.

By speaking first and by making only a passing reference to the royal manifesto the prime minister had hoped to avoid a discussion on its constitutional implications. Hymans, however, concentrated his speech on this issue. He pointed out that the premier's statement had not removed the apprehensions which had arisen from the royal manifesto. Quoting salient passages he asserted that Belgium could never accept a sovereignty which was mutilated and incomplete, as it would undoubtedly be if the manifesto went unchallenged. Referring to the Congo-Belgian Convention of 1890 he observed that by the law of 1901 Belgium reserved the right of annexation without restrictions or conditions.

The two speeches set the pattern for the subsequent ones. The Congophiles tried to assure the House that the king-sovereign in maintaining his sovereignty was only safeguarding it for Belgium; the arrogant tone of the manifesto was meant for foreign consumption; and the conditions

---

[1] *Annales Parlementaires* (Chambre), 28 November 1906; *The Times*, 29 November 1906.

contained in the testamentary act attached to it were nothing more than paternal advice from the king. But the attempt to divert attention from the constitutional issue did not succeed.

The climax was reached on the last day of the debate when Hymans posed three pertinent questions to the government and demanded a plain answer to each of them.[1] First, were the expressions of the royal will contained in the letter of 3 June mere desires on the part of the king or was their acceptance to be regarded as a condition for the cession of the Congo State to Belgium? Secondly, was annexation to be effected by a unilateral act of the Belgian parliament or by a bilateral convention between Belgium and the Congo State; in other words, would the Belgian parliament be free to deal as it pleased with the future administration of the Congo or would its freedom in this respect be fettered by obligations contracted towards the king? Thirdly, would the government undertake to obtain from the Congo State, for the use of the Chamber, the complete information requisite for drawing up a new Colonial Law with full knowledge of all the elements and conditions with which it would have to deal? A fourth question was added by Beernaert: how soon would the government bring in a bill for annexing the Congo State? To such direct questions obviously supported by a majority in the Chamber there must be categorical answers. The prime minister replied that the expressions of the royal will, as contained in the June letter, were 'solemn recommendations'; that the new law establishing the future government of the Congo would be the work of the Belgian legislature alone; that the government would assist the legislature in procuring from the Congo government the full information required by it; and finally, that they would lose no time in bringing about annexation.[2]

The answers of the prime minister reflected the predicament of Leopold II. By 13 December he had reached a crisis, and a decision.[3] In Belgium, there was the grim

[1] See also Wauters, op. cit., pp. 318–9.
[2] Hardinge to Grey, 15 December 1906, FO 367/33, no. 154, Africa.
[3] Cf. Stengers: *Belgique et Congo*, pp. 80–82.

prospect that the government might be defeated in the Chamber if it continued to support his stand on the Congo question. Abroad, the firm determination of Grey, under the pressure of the reformers, threatened Anglo-Belgian relations. As for France, she had settled her long-standing dispute with England over the compensation of British firms trading in her Congo colony and was modifying her concession policy in the light of criticisms levelled against it by the de Brazza commission.[1] Leghait discovered, after a recent visit to the Quai d'Orsay, that the support of France could no longer be counted upon.[2] Germany, on her part, had never been a warm admirer of the Congo State and consequently was not dependable.[3] Since the beginning of 1905 the Italian government, under the pressure of its opposition, had stopped recruitment of Italian officers for service in the Congo State[4] and no support could be expected from that quarter. Finally, the president of the United States had, as has been noted, declared the willingness of his government to co-operate with Britain. Under these circumstances, only one course of action seemed open to the king and this he took by capitulating to the Chamber of Deputies.

Thus Leopold II had to retreat completely from the position he had taken up in the letter of 3 June. In the meantime, the answers prepared the way for the adoption of a resolution which was to hasten annexation.[5] It was a

---

[1] Cookey: 'The Concession Policy in French Congo', pp. 276–7.

[2] Leghait reported that Pichon 'on account of the present state of Anglo-French relations, is naturally very reserved in expressing his opinion, and it is evident from his attitude that the Paris Cabinet would find itself in a very delicate situation with respect to that of London, if events gave rise to any kind of intervention on its part.'
Leghait to Favereau, 4 December 1906, Ier sér., Congo, vii, 2010.

[3] Greindl to Favereau, 7 December 1906, ibid., 2015.

[4] Ranieri, op. cit., p. 201.

[5] 'The Chamber, bearing in mind the order voted at the sitting of March 2, 1906, and rendering homage to the greatness of the work of the Congo and to the patriotic designs of the founder; being convinced that the civilizing ideals which presided over the foundation of the Free State should still occupy the first place in the country's pre-occupations; considering that Belgium is called by the King's will of August 2, 1889, to assume the full sovereignty of the Free State and that she also possesses

resolution welcomed by all sections of the Belgian press. Although it did not definitely commit Belgium to annexation, everyone but the socialists accepted the fact that it was only a matter of time before the Congo became a Belgian colony. While during the Congo debate of February and March only a few had contemplated annexation during the lifetime of Leopold II, now the majority were reconciled to immediate annexation.

The prospect of Belgian annexation had a different reception in England. This was of course the solution which at one time or another the reformers had advocated and it might have been expected that the campaign would relax. But this did not happen. The long delay which had preceded the decision to consider annexation; the fact that most of the Belgian ruling classes had connived at or condoned the administrative practices of the Congo State; frequent statements by prominent Belgians implying that Belgium would not be bound by the provisions of the Berlin Act;

the right to annex the Congo in virtue of the King's letter of August 5, 1889, and the new law of August 10, 1901, which upholds the principle laid down in the Convention of July 3, 1890, and that it is to the interest of the country to pronounce on the question of annexation during the King's lifetime; taking note of the replies of the government according to which the declarations contained in the letter of June 3 do not constitute conditions, but "solemn recommendations", while "the convention of cession will have no other object than to effect the transference and define the measures for its accomplishment, and the Belgian Legislature will regulate the régime of its colonial possessions in unrestricted liberty"; being further of opinion that the central committee charged to examine the draft law of August 7, 1901, on the régime of the colonial possessions should endeavour to adapt this régime to the conditions and needs of the Free State, and to this end should be furnished with all information necessary for the elaboration of the law; taking note of the Government's declaration that "it is ready to give its assistance in order to furnish the central committee with all documents necessary for the elaboration of the law on colonial possessions"; desiring without prejudice (sans préjuger sur le fond) that the question of the annexation of the Congo should be brought before the chamber in the shortest possible time in accordance with the intention expressed by the Government; records its desire that the central committee should hasten its labours and lay its report at an early date.' *The Times*, 15 December 1906.

all these factors raised the question in the minds of Morel and his friends as to whether Belgian annexation was a sufficient guarantee for the fulfilment of their objectives. Their answer was in the negative. They decided therefore on Britain declaring immediately that Belgian annexation was acceptable only if Belgium gave 'guarantees of a binding character' that the principles of the Berlin Act would be applied in the Congo.[1] It was this search for guarantees that deferred the settlement of the Congo question for so long.

Towards the end of December Morel approached Grey and explained the apprehensions of the reformers. His impression afterwards was that Grey, although 'exceptionally nice' and 'much franker than Fitzmaurice', still did not understand the Congo question.[2] Morel therefore forwarded a few days later a lengthy memorandum in which he proclaimed his firm belief that Belgium would not abandon the fundamental policy of the Congo government. Such a change in policy was impossible because of the great vested interests involved. The king-sovereign, his favourites, and some members of the government and parliament benefited financially from the Congo system. For them to abandon the policy would lead to a fall in the output of rubber and necessitate a Belgian subsidy which would prove extremely unpopular with the electorate. He recommended that Grey should make a clear declaration that the British government would not rest content with annexation by Belgium if that solution set aside the principles of the Berlin Act and the rights secured to Britain by the Anglo-Congolese Convention of 1884. Grey should thus take the initiative and thereby 'do for future generations of African peoples a work of emancipation which it has fallen to the lot of no man to perform since the days of Wilberforce'.[3]

But even before Morel wrote there had begun a vigorous exchange of views in the Foreign Office about the next steps to be taken by Britain in securing reform. On 13

[1] Morel to Holt, 18 December 1906, J.H.P., 18/3.
[2] Morel to Holt, 25 December 1906, ibid.
[3] Morel to Grey, 28 December 1906, FO 367/68.

December, Clarke prepared a memorandum outlining possible modes of dealing with the Congo State on the basis that the time for remonstrance was at an end and that the moment was approaching for decisive action.[1] There were, he said, four courses open. Britain could assume civil and criminal jurisdiction over British subjects in the Congo; establish an International Commission for the Navigation of the Congo which was provided for under Article XIX of the Berlin Act; summon an international conference; or refer the Congo system to arbitration. He considered the assumption of consular jurisdiction often proposed by the reformers as so hedged about with difficulties as to render it practically impossible to establish. The only ground on which the right could be exercised would be to assert that as long as the State continued to trade and the judiciary was not independent of the executive there was no guarantee that justice could be effectively dispensed. But stated so vaguely the Congo State would certainly press for some proof for that assertion and Britain could not adduce any. There was another and more fundamental difficulty. Article XII of the Berlin Act laid down that in the case of a serious disagreement originating on any subject concerning the territories lying within the Congo basin between any of the signatory powers, these powers were bound, before appealing to arms, to have recourse to the mediation of either one or more of the friendly powers. The chances of Britain obtaining a favourable verdict from such mediation, Clarke concluded, was 'very remote', and even if this was not so, the consular courts would not be a very long step forward. Similarly, Clarke dismissed the question of calling into being the International River Commission. It would not be possible, he pointed out, to obtain the co-operation of five powers requisite for establishing it. With regard to submitting the Congo question to arbitration, Clarke suggested that this should only be a last resort. The course of action which he favoured was the summoning of an international conference. He suggested that the most

---

[1] Clarke, 13 December 1906, ibid., memorandum.

influential powers should be approached privately prior to the launching of a general circular and Britain should hold out the bait that she would not object to 'cutting the Congo up' if all other solutions failed.[1]

The memorandum by Clarke raised a consideration which had hitherto been ignored by the champions of consular jurisdiction, that is, whether the Congo State could avert it by appealing to Article XII of the Berlin Act. Grey ordered the matter to be submitted to the Law Officers and they confirmed the view taken by Clarke.[2] In the dismay which followed this verdict C. J. B. Hurst, the legal assistant, suggested a means of escape. If, he said, the Congo State pressed the government to submit their right to establish consular courts to arbitration, they could in their turn demand that the legality of the concession system be at the same time referred to arbitration. He expected that such a proposal would be unwelcome to King Leopold.[3] The difficulty was thus surmounted and the exercise of the right to consular jurisdiction was established as a means of exerting pressure on the Congo State.

It ought to be noted that on the question of convoking an international conference both Morel and Clarke were agreed. They differed, however, as to the timing of such a conference. For Morel, the present was the best for a conference for it would ensure that Belgium did not perpetuate the Leopoldian system of monopoly and oppression. Clarke, on the other hand, wished the conference to be convoked after Belgium had annexed. This attitude conformed more closely to the traditional policy laid down by Grey which was that nothing should be done by the British government to frighten off Belgium from annexation. Thus, since an international conference might have this result, it was not to be convoked until the Belgians had actually annexed the Congo State.

The issue whether a conference of the powers should be

---

[1] Ibid.

[2] Law Officers to F.O., 4 February 1907, FO 403/387.

[3] Hurst, 21 February 1907, FO 367/68, minute.

held if the Congo became a Belgian colony was not a new one in the Foreign Office. When it seemed in 1895 that Belgium would exercise her right of annexation under the will of Leopold II, it had been discussed whether the incorporation of the Congo State as Belgian territory raised the question as to how far a State, itself neutralized, could acquire fresh territory, and, if so, to what extent, if any, such fresh acquisition was affected by the guarantee originally given to that State. The discussions which then took place among the permanent officials had remained inconclusive since Belgium did not annex. But the view of Anderson as to the need for an international conference was generally accepted: annexation would give the guaranteeing powers an opportunity for attaching conditions to their recognition of the neutrality.[1]

In January 1907 the subject was raised again by Paul Cambon in London. With an eye to the exercise of France's pre-emptive rights rather than to an international conference, he asked Grey whether Belgium as a neutral state had the right to annex so large a territory as the Congo without the consent of her guarantors. The question had juridical as well as political aspects. In 1895 the former had not been examined. Now the legal experts made the position quite clear. Neither the Act of 1839 nor the Berlin Act afforded Britain any substantial grounds for arguing that the annexation of the Congo required their consent, which they would not give without a conference; and neither Act affected the interests of the powers so materially that a conference ought to be held.[2] The legal cobwebs, as often happens in diplomacy when other interests are at stake, were brushed aside. Fitzmaurice explained that the issues of law and policy were quite distinct in the matter[3] and Grey assured Cambon that Belgian annexation would necessarily give rise to an exchange of views.[4]

---

[1] Anderson, 2 March 1895, FO 10/649, memorandum.
[2] Hurst, 2 February 1907, FO 367/68, minute; W. E. Davidson, 4 February 1907, ibid., minute.
[3] Fitzmaurice, 6 February 1907, ibid., minute.
[4] Grey to Bertie, 18 January 1907, ibid., no. 9, Africa.

But looking away for a moment from the Foreign Office, it is interesting to contemplate how favourable the international atmosphere was for a conference. We know that after the Congo debate a circular from the German Foreign Ministry was sent to the ambassadors in Brussels, London and Vienna affirming that Germany would participate in an international conference if invited.[1] Indeed, Wallwitz, the German ambassador in Brussels, put out feelers to ascertain from the British representative whether Britain was going to propose one.[2] In Italy, it was almost taken for granted that the British government would initiate a conference which she would attend.[3] The United States had also indicated its willingness to support the British government in whatever action they proposed to adopt. It could safely be assumed that since the interests of the other powers would not have been adversely affected their support might be forthcoming.

The power whose support seemed doubtful was France, one of the most formidable obstacles to international action on the Congo question. The French attitude, as has been said, arose from the fact that she had adopted the Leopoldian system in her part of the Congo. It was true that she had at last settled the claims of the British companies expelled by the French concession companies; nevertheless, she had not renounced the principles behind the system. If France supported the convocation of an international conference there was always the chance that a hostile power, especially Germany, might embarrass her by raising the question of concessions in the French Congo. The British merchants might also reopen their case by attacking the French Congo. Worse still, the treatment of the inhabitants of the French Congo, recognized even in France to be atrocious, might form the subject of awkward discussions.[4] Grey was willing

---

[1] Willequet, op. cit., p. 189.

[2] Hardinge to Grey, 21 December 1906, FO 403/374, no. 162, Africa.

[3] Hardinge to Grey, 25 March 1907, FO 367/68, no. 51, Africa, confidential.

[4] These arguments were developed in M. Pichon (Minister for Foreign Affairs) to M. Milliès-Lacroix (Colonies), 21 December 1906, *D.D.F.*, 2nd ser.' no. 373.

to respect as much as possible French feelings in the matter for the maintenance of the entente was his cardinal policy.[1] Hence he might have been unwilling to take any action which would have precipitated a conference.

This leads to another consideration which might have governed the thinking in the Foreign Office. The Algeçiras conference, it must be remembered, had not resulted in any substantial lessening of international tension as far as the Foreign Office was concerned. On the contrary, German action in Morocco, but more especially the recently announced naval programme, had rather intensified fear and suspicion mingled with resentment in the British official mind against Germany.[2] For the first time in the Congo question, considerations of European strategy in the event of war began to play a prominent role. Thus, for example, the British ambassador in Brussels suggested that Germany wanted to perpetuate friction between England and Belgium over the Congo 'in order to enable her to be regarded as the protector of Belgian interests'.[3] A few days later Eyre Crowe was to prepare his famous memorandum on British relations with France and Germany.[4] Thus, fundamentally, it was the dictates of European strategy rather than any consideration for Belgian susceptibilities which governed Grey's policy. A partition of the Congo between France and Germany might have been sanctioned by Grey if the opportunity had occurred.[5] With the European atmosphere

---

[1] Monger, op. cit., p. 280.

[2] On the anti-German attitude of the Foreign Office, see Monger, op. cit., pp. 99–103.

[3] Hardinge to Grey, 21 December 1906, FO 403/374, no. 162, Africa. Earlier A. Hardinge had told Grey 'Most of my official life has been spent among Orientals . . . but my experience is that for downright brazen cynicism, untruthfulness and deception the modern Prussian diplomatist surpasses any Russian, Turk or Persian . . .' Hardinge to Grey, 5 October 1906, FO 800/41, Grey Papers.

[4] E. A. Crowe, 'Memorandum on the Present State of British Relations with France and Germany', 1 January 1907, Secret, B.D., iii, Appendix A.

[5] Grey, in fact, did suggest to Cambon that 'if France did not desire that right [of pre-emption] in its entirety, it might be very easy for her to make a satisfactory deal with Germany, and she would certainly not

so uncertain, Grey decided to sterilize the Congo question by avoiding international action. It was what he later called a policy of 'benevolent expectancy'.

With Britain thus holding the diplomatic ring, Leopold II soon recovered the composure he had lost as a result of the tension which had built up during the closing stages of the Congo debate. In order to obtain annexation on his own terms he embarked on a game of hide and seek with the Chamber. He was aided by two factors. In the first place, following the resolution of the Chamber, a parliamentary committee (*section centrale*) consisting of seventeen members had been set up to examine the Colonial Law. The opponents and supporters of the king-sovereign were more or less evenly balanced in the commission and the chairman, Franz Schollaert, who exercised a casting vote, tended for some time to side with the latter.[1] Secondly, the cabinet of de Smet de Naeyer, because it wished to retain its majority in the Chamber and also to support King Leopold's Congo policy, had become discredited in the eyes of both. The prime minister was thus forced to hold a precarious position which threatened every moment to topple him and in this circumstance, it was easy for the monarch, by withholding vital information from the commission and by cajoling the cabinet, to exasperate everyone.

At the same time, Leopold II tried to repair the damage done to his international position by attempting to win over the United States again. He had long gained the sympathy and admiration of H. L. Wilson, the American ambassador in Brussels. Soon after the decision of the State Department to support whatever action Britain or any other power might propose as solution to the Congo question, Wilson was prompted to send a despatch deprecating American intervention on the basis that it was contrary to the Monroe

---

find that we should be in any way difficult to deal with.' Grey to Bertie, 19 April 1907, FO 403/387.

[1] See also Stengers: *Belgique et Congo*, pp. 95–110. Schollaert's attitude was to change in favour of the opponents of Leopold II. Hardinge to Grey, 7 November 1907, FO 123/460, no. 164, Africa, quoted in Stengers: *Belgique et Congo*, p. 152.

doctrine. He was duly rewarded by Leopold II with a signed portrait of himself.[1] Wilson's objection, however, was brushed aside by Root in a long telegram which repeated the determination of the American government to ensure that the Congo administration was reformed by Belgian annexation or, failing that, by some form of international action.[2] Leopold II was more successful with Senator Lodge's Congo resolution. Moncheur, in spite of the discomfort he had suffered as a result of the Congo lobby scandal, still wielded considerable influence in American senate circles. Through his intervention the Lodge resolution was neutralized into an innocuous affirmation that the senate would support the president in any steps he might adopt for ameliorating the condition of the inhabitants of the 'Congo Basin', provided such steps were not inconsistent with the traditional American foreign policy of non-interference in European politics.[3] This resolution did not alter the determination of President Roosevelt to intervene. However, it did strengthen for the meantime King Leopold's position vis-à-vis the Belgian annexationists, for he could point out that American policy was directed not merely towards the Congo State but to all the powers having possessions in the Congo basin.[4]

The crux of the discussions on the Colonial Bill centred around the powers which the crown would exercise over the

---

[1] Hardinge to Grey, 24 January 1907, FO 367/68; Favereau to Moncheur, 8 February 1907, Iᵉʳ sér., Congo, viii, 2080.

[2] Root to Wilson, 15 January 1907, Iᵉʳ sér., Congo, vii, 2045 (copy).

[3] Howard to Grey, 19 February 1907, FO 403/387, no. 32, Africa, confidential; *New York Evening Post*, 19 February 1907; R. L. Buell: *The Native Problem in Africa*, New York 1928, ii, 441.
The original Lodge resolution had specified the Congo State by name instead of merging it into the general term 'Congo Basin' which included the possessions of France, Germany and Britain. Again while the Lodge resolution had originally declared in favour of an international inquiry, the one now adopted restricted the president to such steps as would be consistent with American policy of non-interference.

[4] Hardinge to Grey, 22 February 1907, FO 367/68, no. 31, Africa, confidential.

new colony.[1] In the original Bill submitted by the cabinet the authority of King Leopold in the Belgian colony would have remained almost intact. Under the pressure of their opponents the government began to give way on the question of a substantial reduction in the powers of the king. This alienated King Leopold. Complete rupture between the king and the cabinet was reached when the latter agreed to provide the parliamentary committee with full information on the entire financial situation of the Congo State in accordance with the resolution of 14 December. The king was said to have had a fit,[2] but he recovered sufficiently to forbid the information being given. After the Easter recess de Smet de Naeyer, exhausted by the recalcitrance of the king, unable any longer to command a majority in his own party, and altogether discredited in the country, tendered the resignation of his cabinet. It took three weeks for a new government to be formed and meanwhile the Congo question entered into a state of suspended animation.[3] It was revived by the announcement of the new prime minister, Jules de Trooz, that his government would soon bring forward a measure for the annexation of the Congo.[4]

The decision of the new government to deal with annexation immediately reflected Belgian apprehension of the possibility of foreign intervention if annexation continued to be postponed. There was evidence, it appeared in Brussels, that public opinion might compel the British government at last to act. In reviewing the position Arendt warned in the cold analytical style which usually marked his memoranda:

---

[1] This is fully discussed in Stengers: *Belgique et Congo*, pp. 116 ff.

[2] Hardinge to Grey, 22 March 1907, ibid., no. 44, Africa, confidential.

[3] Nevertheless, in order to strengthen his position in future negotiations Leopold II went over to France to induce the French government, as Paul Cambon revealed to Charles Hardinge, to declare that they would exercise their right of pre-emption. M. Pichon however declined. No doubt the King thought that such a declaration would give him a lever for extracting more concessions from his government. Grey to Bertie, 10 May 1907, FO 403/387, no. 22, Africa, confidential.

[4] Hardinge to Grey, 7 May 1907, ibid., tel. no. 3, Africa.

In Belgium it [the anti-Congolese campaign] is often represented as being the work of a group of Liverpool merchants acting with profit as a goal and aiming at conquest. This evaluation does not correspond to the reality of things. Whatever origin one may wish to attribute to it, the Congolese movement has spread to the whole of the upper class; it has echoes and followers in the whole country.[1]

Continuing, Arendt pointed out that the British parliament had rarely shown such unanimity as it was doing over the Congo question. Belgium was isolated for France would support England now that the latter had recognized her right of pre-emption. Even if she did not, Belgium might have to buy her support at an impossible price. The United States would certainly support England and so would Italy. Austria and Russia were indifferent and Germany, although her attitude was inscrutable, might act with Britain if only to bridge the political gap between London and Berlin. 'Will the Belgian Government', he concluded, 'be able to confront, under the circumstances in which a conflict may occur, a power which has such a great hold on Belgium?'[2]

The announcement of the new ministry came also as a great relief for Grey. More than ever he was being pressed by the Congo reformers to intervene. An enthusiastic annual general meeting of the National Council of Evangelical Free Churches passed a resolution in favour of intervention and pressed Grey to receive a deputation.[3] On the third anniversary of the founding of the C.R.A., which was marked by an impressive demonstration in Liverpool, Morel secured the passing of two resolutions calling for intervention.[4] A few days later the Convocation of Canterbury made its voice heard in the same sense.[5] In these circumstances, some permanent officials of the Foreign

---

[1] Arendt, 11 April 1907, Ier sér., Congo, viii, 2161, memorandum.
[2] Ibid.
[3] Evangelical Free Churches to Grey, 21 March 1907, FO 367/68.
[4] C.R.A. to Grey, 25 April 1907, ibid.
[5] Archbishop of Canterbury to Grey, 31 May 1907, ibid.

Office were indeed urging that at least a warning of British intervention should be given.[1]

The Belgian declaration, however, did not lead to any relaxation of the pressure from the reformers. Morel explained the reason.[2] They had no confidence in the ability of the new government to take a sufficiently radical action. The prime minister and Liebraert were members of the old cabinet and consequently were committed to the policy of the king and three other members had connections with the Congo government. He dismissed the Ministers of Foreign Affairs and of War as nominees of King Leopold and the rest of the cabinet as bound to be influenced by the king. 'This Government', Morel affirmed, 'cannot be said to represent the Belgian people on the Congo question.'[3] He therefore urged that Grey, in order to avoid any misunderstanding with the Belgian government should clearly emphasize the following principles in parliament: first, that Belgian annexation could only be countenanced if the existing system in the Congo was totally reversed; secondly, that the power of the king must be limited to what it was in Belgium, namely, constitutional; thirdly, that the Congo should be flung open to legitimate commerce; fourthly, that the basic claim to land, produce of the soil and to the labour of the Congolese must be repudiated; and fifthly, that unless the annexation provided for the foregoing demands and Belgian decision to annex was not prolonged beyond a specified date, the British government would appeal to the powers and if there was no response, would assume consular jurisdiction.[4]

Grey did not receive Morel's letter until after his speech in the Commons. On the other hand, he had in his possession a despatch from Hardinge which advocated a different policy. The ambassador had arrived at the same conclusion as Morel (but independently) that the terms of annexation which would be introduced by the new Belgian government

---

[1] Clarke, 3 May 1907, ibid., minute; Barrington, n.d., ibid., minute.
[2] Morel to Grey, 10 May 1907, ibid., private.
[3] Ibid.
[4] Ibid.

would fall short of the demands of the C.R.A. He recommended, however, that public pronouncements which
Leopold II could represent as foreign dictation or pressure
should be avoided. Britain should adopt 'an attitude of
reserve' until de Trooz had outlined his scheme; then he,
Hardinge, should be instructed to inform the Belgian
Foreign Ministry in a language 'of the most friendly and
confidential character possible' that Britain had the right
to discuss the terms of annexation.[1] In his speech in the
debate which the Congo reformers provoked on 15 May,
Grey steered a course all his own. He wished Belgium to
annex because it was the only straight-forward solution and
because she would reverse the policy of the Congo State.
He had no wish to interfere while the actual terms of
annexation were under discussion. Nevertheless, the patience
of the British government was not inexhaustible, Grey
warned, and he would either invoke or support international
action if Belgium delayed too long to annex under satisfactory conditions.[2]

Grey's attitude exasperated the more radical reformers.
'What prevents him from acting?' Holt asked, 'What crass
timidity or weakness stops him? I feel disgusted with this
government already, Liberal though I would like always to
be.'[3] It was mooted in the executive committee of the C.R.A.
that Grey should be by-passed and a direct approach made
to Campbell-Bannerman. Morel, however, would not hear
of that. Such a step, he explained to Holt, would lead to the
alienation of Grey and consequently to a splitting of the
unanimity in parliament over the Congo question. 'The
opposition trusts Grey', he said, 'and hates C[ampbell]
B[annerman]. If they saw the C.R.A. abandoning Grey in
despair and going to C.B., they would oppose the C.R.A.'[4]
Morel claimed to be in Grey's confidence and so able to
appreciate some of the external and internal difficulties
which others who were not behind the scenes did not. He

[1] Hardinge to Grey, 10 May 1907, ibid., no. 59, Africa, confidential.
[2] Hansard, 15 May 1907, 4th ser., clxxiv, 1011–1016.
[3] Holt to Morel, 27 May, 1907, M.P., F. 8.
[4] Morel to Holt, 5 June 1907, J.H.P., 18/4.

assured Holt that all these international questions hung together:

> For the first time in our history an Anglo-Russian Treaty is being negotiated and will probably be signed this month.[1] It will be an unpopular Treaty with a number of people . . . and it is not to be wondered at that there should be a certain shrinking in G.'s [Grey's] mind to fling into the melting pot another great international question immediately afterwards. There are other things too. The strained relations between Germany and France, and France's right of preference is a difficulty.[2]

Morel having fanned the flame of radicalism over the Congo question was evidently finding it difficult to control.

Meanwhile King Leopold had not relaxed his obstructionist policy in the negotiations. His new government had proposed to expedite annexation by dealing with the Colonial Bill and the terms of annexation simultaneously rather than defer the latter until the Bill had been passed. Early in June the Congo State Secretaries issued a long eulogy of the Congo administration in place of the detailed information on the affairs of the State which the parliamentary commission had been demanding since February. The Belgian liberal and independent press were unanimous in denouncing the report as a mere piece of special pleading. It threw no fresh light on the affairs of the Congo and the plan to use the revenue from the Crown domain to expand Belgian commerce and navy inflamed people like Cattier.[3] Relief was felt only when the prime minister declared that the Congo government had accepted his proposal for the appointment of plenipotentiaries to negotiate the terms of annexation.[4] Some progress, at last, was being made.

The British reformers, however, did not think so. Soon after parliament returned from the Whitsun recess, another Congo debate was provoked both in the Lords and in the Commons. As in the Commons, opinion in the Lords was unanimous on the issue. Lord Clifford of Cudleigh, the

---

[1] The Anglo-Russian Treaty was signed 31 August 1907.
[2] Morel to Holt, 5 June 1907, J.H.P., 18/4.
[3] Wyndham to Grey, 15 June 1907, FO 367/69, no. 82, Africa.
[4] *Annales Parlementaires* (Chambre), 10 July 1907.

Catholic peer, was as enthusiastic as the Archbishop of Canterbury in favour of British intervention. The mood of the speakers was reflected in the attitude of the Earl of Mayo who revived the C.R.A. plea for an international conference, or failing that, an increase of consuls invested with powers of consular jurisdiction. But he also went on to propose the placing of a gun-boat on the Upper Congo. 'Diplomacy and dispatches', he said, 'have had their day, and if the Government choose to act the moment has now come.'[1] While condemning the Congo government Fitz-maurice counselled patience and was backed by Lansdowne on the opposition front-bench.

In the Commons a similar demonstration of impatience was made by the reformers. For the second time an Irish Catholic intervened on behalf of Leopold II but this time the reformers had another Irish Catholic ready to dissociate the block from any support for the Congo State. Grey refused immediate action: he would still leave the Belgians free to act without threats or interference.

The pressure of public opinion in Britain no doubt had some effect in Brussels. It helped in speeding up the preparations necessary for annexation. On 20 September, the Belgian government communicated to the parliamentary committee an amended draft Colonial Bill. The legislative and executive power was vested in the crown but a minister of colonies was to be responsible for his actions. The minister would be assisted by a colonial council consisting of members to be appointed by the crown and, once appointed, could only be removed by a petition of the cabinet. The annual budget was to be passed by the executive and not by parliament. Every year a report would be laid before parliament giving full information on the political, economic and financial situation of the colony and parliament would thus have the opportunity of discussing the actions of the colonial minister. Finally, loans would not be contracted and concessions of the State domains would not be granted except with the approval of the cabinet.[2]

---

[1] Hansard, 29 July 1907, 4th ser., clxxix, 424.
[2] Cf. Stengers: *Belgique et Congo*, pp. 142–3.

The amended Colonial Bill represented a considerable advance on the Bill prepared by the government of de Smet de Naeyer. Arthur Hardinge confessed that under any monarch other than King Leopold the measure might have been regarded as 'entirely satisfactory'.[1] But the British reformers refused to concede that compliment. They agreed with *The Times* that 'the most cursory glance' at the Bill was enough to reveal that it did not afford 'the flimsiest guarantee' of any improvement in the methods by which the Congo was governed.[2] When, soon after, Leopold II issued a decree removing the *Fondation de la Couronne* from Belgian control in the event of annexation, all the fears of the reformers were reinforced. The C.R.A. forwarded to Grey two resolutions which summarized their position.[3] The first declared as 'internationally invalid and contrary to the Treaties made binding upon the Congo State and its successors' the recent decree affecting the *Fondation de la Couronne*. The second pointed out that the Colonial Bill did not make any provision for the reversal of the existing system of government nor for the restoration to the Congolese of the economic rights and human liberties guaranteed to them by the Berlin Act; on the contrary, it ensured the perpetuation 'in all essential particulars of the present autocratic régime'. Therefore, they called upon the government to inform the Belgians that the terms were not acceptable to Britain.[4] This was only a public declaration of what Morel had been steadily urging on Grey privately. He even issued a slightly veiled threat that 'the country will be bitterly disappointed if the month of November should pass without a statement' from the British government.[5]

It was not meant to be an empty threat. At the end of October Morel began to show the wide support which he commanded in the country. The Liverpool Chamber of

---

[1] Hardinge to Grey, 27 September 1907, FO 403/388, no. 131, Africa, confidential.

[2] *The Times*, 27 September 1907.

[3] C.R.A. to Grey, 10 October 1907; Anti-Slavery Society to Grey, 15 October 1907, FO 367/70.

[4] Ibid.

[5] Morel to Grey, 18 October 1907, ibid.

Commerce sent in a resolution urging British intervention immediately.[1] This example was as usual soon followed by all the other chambers of commerce. On 7 November the leading newspapers carried an 'Appeal to the Nation'[2] which was signed by the Archbishop of Canterbury, a representative group of members of both Houses of Parliament, Lord Mayors, bishops, scholars and some other well-known people. The 'Appeal' traced the steps which the reform campaign in Britain had taken from the beginning up to the recent publication of the draft Bill. It described the confidence of the British government in the Belgian rulers as misplaced and demanded the summoning of an international conference as the only means of guaranteeing a just administration for the Congo. If an international conference was not feasible the 'Appeal' expressed the hope that the British people would 'approve and support such independent action as the Government may find it practicable to take'.[3]

The Foreign Secretary still remained adamant. The terms of the new Colonial Bill had been examined in the Foreign Office and judged to be unsatisfactory. It was agreed, however, that nothing should be done until the Bill had passed through the Belgian legislature where it could be amended. Only if the terms of annexation were then not such as would bring about a change in the administrative principles of the Congo State would Britain intervene.[4]

---

[1] Liverpool Chamber of Commerce to Grey, 30 October 1907, ibid.

[2] E.g. *The Times*, 7 November 1907.

[3] Ibid.

[4] Hardinge to Grey, 27 September 1907, no. 131, Africa, confidential; V. Wellesley, n.d., FO 367/69, memorandum. Grey told the Archbishop:

'In a few weeks, Belgium will have decided whether she takes over the Congo State, and if so upon what terms.

'I am anxious that those terms should be as satisfactory as possible, and am convinced that pronouncements from me or any foreign Government at this time would be construed in Belgium as interference which would be resented there, and which would weaken the hands of the Congo reform party in Belgium.

'I cannot, therefore, without in my opinion spoiling the chance of reform, respond to any pressure which is put upon me at this moment.' Grey to Archbishop of Canterbury, 24 October 1907, FO 367/70.

It was this old stand which Campbell-Bannerman restated in his speech at Guildhall on 9 November. 'The position', Lalaing rightly summarized, 'is as follows: in spite of the entreaties of our enemies, English interference under certain eventualities is not abandoned, but postponed. The future attitude of the Cabinet will depend on the decisions which will be taken in Brussels.'[1]

Having decided to act when the terms of annexation were known, the Foreign Office discussion on what form this action should take was resumed. Arthur Hardinge outlined the most comprehensive plan.[2] Recognition of annexation was to be made subject to conditions: when Belgium had decided to annex, the signatory powers should declare that they could not recognize the annexation unless Belgium undertook to reverse the Leopoldian system. If the other powers declined to co-operate, Britain could take unilateral action by refusing to recognize the transfer of the Congo to Belgium and should this not bring about the desired change Britain would be in a position to act more forcibly.[3] The African Department did not agree. They regarded the policy of non-recognition as absurd because it could only harm British interests. They still maintained that an international conference afforded the best means of dealing with the situation and recalled the provisions of Article XII of the Berlin Act which obliged Britain to refer disputed issues to arbitration. The most important difference between the two proposals, however, lay in the fact that while the department's approach depended for its effectiveness on the sympathy of the powers, that of Hardinge afforded opportunity for independent action by Britain. It was this element in the latter which impressed Grey. Although he remained uncertain as to how the arbitration clause was to be dealt with, he adopted Hardinge's views on Britain's right to lay conditions on her recognition of the annexation.

---

[1] Lalaing to Davignon, 11 November 1907, I⁰ʳ sér., Congo, viii, 2305.
[2] Hardinge to Grey, 11 November 1907, FO 403/388, no. 170, Africa.
[3] Ibid.

A policy which could permit Britain to take unilateral action had become advantageous because Grey was really beginning to understand for the first time that France would never co-operate with Britain on this issue. In the course of a discussion with the French ambassador on 18 January Grey had proposed that the signatory powers to the Berlin Act should decide what was necessary to satisfy the conditions of that Act and then demand an assurance from Belgium that she was in a position to effect the necessary changes. He had received no official reply from the French. On 23 October Grey again sounded the French ambassador in order to ascertain the views of France. Cambon reverted to the question of Belgian neutrality. If Belgium, he said, proposed to take responsibility over a great colony which would oblige her to embark on a colonial enterprise, it would raise a question for the powers who had guaranteed her neutrality.[1] According to him, France was in favour of a conference but the basis of the conference would have to be different from that proposed by Grey. Cambon's view on the need for a conference on Belgian neutrality subsequent to Belgium's decision was duly confirmed by the French government.[2] It was soon evident that France would not support Britain even on this question.

The reason lay in the negotiations on the pre-emptive rights of France over the Congo State proceeding at the time between France and Belgium. In 1895, when there had been a prospect of Belgium annexing the Congo, a Franco-Belgian convention had been signed which made the French right of pre-emption applicable should Belgium ever wish to relinquish the Congo. This convention was not ratified because annexation fell through. Now that there was another prospect of Belgian annexation, the Belgian government had asked for French ratification. In a circular to London, Brussels and Berlin, the French Minister for Foreign Affairs claimed that 'the ratification of the convention of 1895

---

[1] Grey to Bertie, 24 October 1907, FO 403/388, no. 53, Africa. When Grey again met Cambon four days later the ambassador repeated this view. Grey to Bertie, 28 October 1907, ibid., no. 54, Africa.

[2] Grey to Bertie, 16 November 1907, ibid., no. 58, Africa.

or the signing of an identical arrangement would imply, on the part of the Government of the Republic, the final recognition of the right of Belgium eventually to substitute itself for the independent State.'[1] France would make the conclusion of the agreement consequent on the satisfactory delimitation of the frontier between the French Congo and the Congo State and the reduction of the tariff on French goods transported by the Congo State railway. If the foregoing claims were settled, France would recognize Belgian annexation without making further conditions and would certainly not take part in any conference or consultations over Congo administration or Belgian neutrality.

This was a contradiction of the undertaking already given to Grey. Paul Cambon, who like Grey attached the greatest importance to the entente, grasped at once the implications of the Franco-Belgian negotiations. He warned the Quai d'Orsay that 'we could not negotiate on this basis with the Brussels Cabinet without failing in the obligations which we have undertaken towards the British Government.'[2] Already France was negotiating with Germany for an economic agreement in Morocco behind Britain's back and there was some apprehension about Grey's reaction if he learnt of this.[3] He suggested that Grey should be informed of the negotiations immediately and that an agreement with Belgium should not be reached without Grey's approval. He pointed out that Grey was relying on the promises of co-operation which the French government had given and would be exposed to the energetic and perhaps fatal attack of his opponents should he be disappointed. It was in the great interest of France, Cambon concluded, that Grey should retain the direction of the foreign affairs of the United Kingdom. Cambon had his way and in so doing

---

[1] Pichon to French ambassadors in London, Brussels and Berlin, 19 November 1907, *D.D.F.*, 2nd ser., xi, no. 202.

[2] P. Cambon to M. Pichon, 22 November 1907, *D.D.F.*, 2 ser., xi, no. 205.

[3] The negotiations failed at this time. H. M. H. Sobhy: *The Moroccan Question (April 1906–February 1909)*, Ph.D. Thesis, London University 1962, pp. 360–83.

was able to win Grey's sympathy without sacrificing the French position. Thus Grey learnt that the Franco-Belgian convention bound France to recognize the annexation of the Congo by Belgium without making conditions about it.[1] Informed by Grey that an international conference would be the best means of ensuring the execution of the Berlin Act, Paul Cambon categorically stated that his government would never support such a conference. Grey then reminded him that he had previously accepted the need to examine annexation on the basis of its effect on Belgian neutrality and the ambassador vaguely accepted that there was still time to discuss the subject.

What, then, was the position of the French government at this time? It is stated clearly in a memorandum of the Quai d'Orsay.[2] France would maintain her determination not to give the powers, and especially Germany, the opportunity, which might arise in an international conference, of interfering in her administration of the French Congo. If Belgium annexed, however, Grey would propose a conference so that the powers which had guaranteed Belgian neutrality could examine whether a neutralized state could annex a large territory which, through adjoining the possessions of other powers, might jeopardize her neutrality in the event of an armed conflict with them.

> We would no longer have to fear, under these conditions, an open and ill-intentioned international inquiry into the administration of the French Congo, and we could legitimately hope that from the study of the problem of international law thus raised would result consequences as fruitful for our possessions in West Africa as for our political position in Europe.[3]

---

[1] Grey to Bertie, 27 November 1907, FO 403/388, no. 61, Africa; Paul Cambon to Pichon, 28 November 1907, *D.D.F.*, 2nd ser., xi, no. 209.

[2] M. Berthelot, 'Projet de reglement de la question du Congo Belge', 5 December 1907, *D.D.F.*, ibid., no. 217.

[3] Ibid.

France, it was then urged, had nothing to gain by taking any initiative in the Congo question since such initiative would probably drive Belgium into the arms of Germany. On the other hand, Britain, acting with the support of the United States, and perhaps Germany, was likely to provoke a conference. The powers would be bound to come to some arrangement with France whose right of pre-emption made her the 'maîtresse de la situation et de la solution'. In that event France

> could at will follow either a general settlement of her position in West Africa, in which would be included the question of Nigeria and the Cameroons, such as to constitute a compact and unified group of territories, or the acquisition of the mouth of the Congo alone and of the rubber regions which, although half-exhausted, nevertheless constitute an important complement to the French Congo. We would continue to pursue towards the Belgians a *politique de dupes*; such a lesson would perhaps cure our neighbours of their German sympathies.
>
> Finally, and it is perhaps not the least important of the expectations which can arise from the theory of a common settlement of the Belgian Congo question among the three guaranteeing Powers, a *rapprochement* on this point would no doubt considerably modify the hostile attitude of Germany in Morocco.[1]

Grey, then, was confronted with a French *non possumus*. For a moment he contemplated forcing the hand of France by approaching Germany and the others and if he succeeded to tell the French that 'Germany will go so far, we hope you will do so too'.[2] But this seemed to have been a passing thought immediately provoked by the French attitude. Indeed the German emperor himself had tried to raise the Congo question with Grey during a recent visit to England. Although he had made no specific proposal, nevertheless he had sought to convey to Grey his detestation of King

---

[1] Ibid.

[2] Langley, n.d., minute on Grey to Bertie, 27 November 1907, FO 403/388, no. 61, Africa.

Leopold's character. Grey, however, ignored the opening. He vaguely intimated his awareness that 'other countries' besides Britain were interested in Congo affairs and was waiting to see whether, and on what terms, Belgium would annex before approaching 'other powers' on the subject.[1] Grey, it is clear, would have approached Germany only as the very last resort. By January, when a French source, with the idea of gaining Belgian sympathy, spread the rumour that Germany had recently made overtures to Britain and France for a tripartite partition of the Congo,[2] it became certain that German co-operation would be impossible to secure.

Thus the prospects of an international conference were very bleak indeed and Grey had to consider what isolated action he could take in order to satisfy British public opinion. Hence it was that the plan outlined by Hardinge attracted him. But although he envisaged Britain acting alone he also wished to avoid it. A cautious man by nature, he dreaded stirring up some hornet's nest which might further complicate international relations. Above all, he did not want the Liberal party to get involved in a second Egyptian question by unilateral action in the Congo. It was because of this that he welcomed American co-operation.

While these factors were being weighed a new stage towards Belgian annexation had been reached on 5 December with the publication of the Treaty of Cession signed since 28 November between the Congo State and Belgium.[3] The Treaty was preceded by an *exposé des motifs* putting forward the views of the Belgian government on annexation. After tracing the history of the annexation since 1889, as well as the events which led to the setting up of the Congo commission of inquiry, the *exposé* made a brief reference to the

---

[1] Grey, 12 November 1907, FO 403/388, memorandum.

[2] Hardinge to Grey, 9 January 1908, FO 403/399, no. 6, Africa, confidential.

[3] It has been pointed out that the treaty was in fact drawn up by the government of de Smet de Naeyer as early as January and had been inherited by the new government. The role of the eight plenipotentiaries was merely to rubber-stamp this treaty. Stengers: *Belgique et Congo*, p. 158.

accusations brought against the Congo administration and then settled to a long and rambling eulogy on the achievements of the Congo State. From there it went on to recapitulate the controversy that had been raging in Belgium during the past two years over the Congo question. With regard to the all-important subject of the administrative principles which Belgium would pursue in the Congo after the annexation, a vague impression was given that the idea of a *régie* or state monopoly of the produce of the soil would be abandoned in the *Domaine Privé* but not in the *Domaine de la Couronne*.

The *exposé* did not outline any programme of reforms such as that advocated by the Congophobes. Indeed, by emphasizing that Belgium would not be called upon to vote a grant-in-aid, the impression was given that the Leopoldian system would be perpetuated. The lofty humanitarian professions with which the *exposé* closed did nothing to obscure this serious issue. An equally significant point was the arrangements concerning the *Fondation de la Couronne*. The *exposé* failed to indicate whether the government would satisfy the demand of the reformers to transfer the proceeds of the *Fondation* from mainly Belgian to Congolese projects. On the contrary, it did appear that Leopold II would retain control of the revenues of the *Fondation* until his death.

The treaty itself only seemed to confirm the fears of the reformers. The main provision of its four Articles was to transfer the Congo to Belgium with all its assets and liabilities together with an obligation to maintain all the rights of third parties. It explicitly bound Belgium to perpetuate the *Fondation de la Couronne* for certain purposes enumerated in a series of voluminous schedules to the treaty such as grants to members of the royal family and the creation, completion and maintenance of naval and other schools, museums and ornamental public works in Belgium.

These documents immediately set off a crescendo of protests both in Belgium[1] and in the United Kingdom.

---

[1] The best analysis of Belgian reaction to the Treaty of Cession is in Stengers: *Belgique et Congo*, pp. 159–65.

Attention was concentrated on the *Fondation de la Couronne*. Cattier in *La Gazette* and Emile Vandervelde in *Le Peuple* pointed out that the old régime in the Congo ought to disappear completely and this would mean a fall in revenue. In order to balance the budget the revenue from the *Fondation* was necessary. Furthermore, if there was no change of system in the Congo international complications would follow. In these circumstances, they concluded, the provisions of the treaty relating to the *Fondation* must be revised.[1] These powerful arguments were taken up by others. *Le Patriote* devoted to the treaty three leading articles on 9, 11 and 15 December concluding with a strong appeal to the Catholic majority that 'Nos droits—les abandonner, ce serait, pour la Droite, un suicide.' On 16 December, *XX*e *Siècle* called the foundation, 'la terrible, l'epouvantable Fondation de la Couronne'. The Liberals held a crucial meeting on 18 December and decided to oppose the treaty because it limited the full sovereignty of Belgium in the colony.[2] A few days later *La Dernière-Heure* published a cartoon ridiculing the Belgian Cabinet by depicting them to be kneeling in prayer before a huge mound of skulls with the caption: 'Au pied du tas d'ossements et de ruines, tous se proternaient en adoration . . .'[3] The stock of the Belgian monarchy had fallen very low indeed in Belgium during the winter of 1907–8.

In Britain the press comments also concentrated on urging the Belgians to reject the arrangements concerning the *Fondation de la Couronne*.[4] Morel was bitterly disappointed with Grey's inaction. He told Lorand that if the British government had not failed to adopt his suggestion for a clear and precise statement relative to the conditions of Belgian annexation which they would regard as a *sine qua non*, the monstrous propositions contained in the treaty would not have been

---

[1] *La Gazette*, 7 December and 13 December 1907; *Le Peuple*, 7 December 1907.

[2] *Le Matin*, 19 December 1907.

[3] *La Dernière-Heure*, 26 December 1907.

[4] E.g. see *The Times*, 13 December 1907, and *Morning Post*, 13 December 1907.

made.[1] In the Foreign Office, also, there was considerable dismay at the treaty. Immediate reaction was delayed by Arthur Hardinge who held out the hope that Belgian public opinion would yet compel the government to offer explanations on the treaty of a nature to modify early impressions and, indeed, have the effect of entirely altering its character.[2]

The State Department, however, was itching to do something to satisfy the great pressure which the Congo reformers there had mounted. It was already weary of waiting for Grey's invitation for action promised since the beginning of the year. Consequently, on 19 November the American ambassador, Whitelaw Reid, told Grey that the American government was dissatisfied with the terms of the Colonial Bill being discussed by the Belgian parliamentary committee and wished to know Grey's views before they reacted.[3] It was Arthur Hardinge who quickly grasped the significance of the interest which the American government was showing. He then initiated a modification in the attitude of the Foreign Office by modifying his own views. His new proposal was no longer that British intervention should be deferred until the Belgians had decided for annexation, but that 'a private hint' might be given by both the British and American governments 'at a fairly early date' that they would insist on compliance with the Berlin Act.[4] This change of attitude was supported by his cousin, Charles Hardinge, the Permanent Under-Secretary. Immediate action with the United States, he said, would show the Belgian government that Britain was not the only power which had serious views on the future administration of the Congo; it would so far compromise the American government as to ensure their co-operation in the future; and it might bring about advantageous modifications in the Colonial Bill.[5]

Having agreed to act with America, the question was to

---

[1] Morel to Lorand, 15 December 1907, encl. in Morel to Fitzmaurice, 15 December 1907, FO 367/70.

[2] Hardinge to Grey, 6 December 1907, ibid., no. 184, Africa.

[3] Grey to Bryce, 19 November 1907, ibid., no. 8, Africa.

[4] A. Hardinge to Grey, 26 November 1907, ibid., no. 176, confidential.

[5] C. Hardinge, n.d., ibid., minute.

determine when this action should take place; that is, to define Hardinge's meaning of 'a fairly early date'. Here the decisive factor was an apprehension in the Foreign Office of the reaction of public opinion if it should be known that the United States had seized the initiative from Britain.[1] On 5 December Hardinge was instructed to concert immediately with his American colleague in order to give the hint. Wilson, however, had to wait for a fortnight before he received the necessary authority to act[2] and by this time opposition to the annexation proposals of the Belgian government had hardened in Brussels. As it was evident that the Belgians themselves would save Britain and the United States from an unnecessary intervention, Hardinge and Wilson agreed that, for the moment, their joint representations would be premature. Events proved them right. On 28 December, Hardinge reported that the chances of the Bill passing in its original form were slight.[3] Eleven members of the Catholic majority led by Beernaert had resolved to vote with the opposition and thus place the government in a minority. On 31 December, the prime minister, worn out, it was said, by the intransigence of the king-sovereign, collapsed and died.

The death of de Trooz made necessary the formation of a new ministry under Schollaert. Meanwhile the terms of annexation remained in the balance and with them future British policy. While the rest of the powers remained aloof, the State Department on the other hand had definitely taken its stand on the side of Britain. Having come late to the attack, it was impatient to deliver a blow and justify itself before its American critics. Together with British public opinion it had in fact become an activating agent on the Foreign Office.

---

[1] The American C.R.A. was aware of the action taken by their government and was keeping the parent organization in Britain informed. Thus Rev. John Harris intimated to Fitzmaurice that they would kick up a great row if the Foreign Office lagged behind. Harris to Fitzmaurice, 20 December 1907, encl. in Harris to Holt, 20 December 1907, J.H.P. 18/4.

[2] Hardinge to Grey, 19 December 1907, FO 367/70, no. 195, Africa.

[3] Hardinge to Grey, 28 December 1907, ibid., no. 201, Africa.

VII
The Belgian Solution

During the winter of 1907 the Congo question entered an acute diplomatic phase. Previously the quarrel had been one between Britain and the inconsequential Congo State; now it was between Britain and the friendly state of Belgium. In the past the reform campaign had been waged by the Foreign Office alone; now the State Department had actively joined forces with it. Although the underlying policy of the British government did not change and Belgian annexation of the Congo continued to be encouraged as the best solution for the Congo question, nevertheless there had emerged a new consideration that Belgian annexation would be acceptable only if it really ensured thorough reform in the Congo— that before she annexed, Belgium must guarantee that she would effect the necessary reforms afterwards. From this position it was a short step to pressing not merely for guarantees but for an announcement of the actual reforms Belgium would introduce. The step was easily taken. Thus the Belgian solution became no satisfactory solution after all and the approval of the annexation by Britain and the United States was withheld.

Towards the end of December, as has already been said, Arthur Hardinge was hoping that the opposition of the Liberals and the revolt within the ranks of the Catholic party would be sufficient to secure a modification in the terms of annexation. In that case there would be no need to express the disappointment of the Foreign Office on the terms of the annexation and probably thus incur the resentment of the Belgian government. In any case the formation of a new ministry under Schollaert afforded an excuse for deferring action.

These reasons for delay were not appreciated in Washington where the State Department was still under strong pressure from several humanitarian and missionary bodies. It had been hoped that a report from the American consul-general on the conditions in the Congo might make out a case for deferring intervention; instead the report which was received in December might have been written by Casement himself. It contained all the usual sweeping indictments of the Congo administration and no redeeming features: there was not a 'shadow of doubt' that the provisions of the Berlin Act with regard to the treatment of the Congolese were being 'openly violated'; the system tended to 'brutalize rather than civilize'; the government was 'but one tremendous commercial organization'; and so on.[1] It was the first direct report on conditions in the Congo which the American government had received and it had a galvanizing effect on the State Department.

On 10 January Wilson showed Hardinge a telegram which he had just received from Secretary Root instructing him to make immediate representations to the Belgian government.[2] Hardinge managed to persuade him to defer taking any steps for a few days when it was expected that the new Belgian cabinet would declare its Congo policy. He impressed on Grey that the opportunity for co-operation with the United States should not be allowed to pass. Grey had also been warned of the State Department's intention and he telegraphed Hardinge to make joint representations with his American colleague.[3] Consequently on 23 January Hardinge and Wilson met M. Julien Davignon, the new

[1] Report of consul-general Smith to Assistant Secretary of State, Washington, December 1907, FO 367/115 (copy).
[2] Hardinge to Grey, 10 January 1908, ibid., no. 7, Africa, confidential.
[3] Grey to Hardinge, 20 January 1908, FO 367/115, tel. no. 3, Africa.

Belgian Minister for Foreign Affairs, for what was to be the first of three such encounters.

It was made known to Davignon that both the British and the American governments favoured Belgian annexation. However, they considered it their duty to leave no doubt in the mind of the Belgian government as to the 'vital importance' which the two governments attached to the observance in 'the spirit as well as in the letter' of the treaty obligations incurred by the Congo State as regards 'freedom of trade, rights of missionaries, and humane treatment of natives'. If Belgium annexed, the two governments were resolved to insist on the fulfilment of those obligations.[1] Davignon seemed appreciative but non-committal. The new Belgian government already knew that the terms of annexation negotiated by their predecessors stood little chance of passing through parliament and consequently they were engaged at that very moment in extracting more concessions from Leopold II.

Meanwhile, unaware that any representations had been made by the Foreign Office to the Belgian government, the C.R.A. plunged into a more extreme programme. On 21 January its executive committee met under Lord Monkswell and adopted a series of resolutions formulated by Morel. The British government was called upon to name 'an early date' before which Belgium should produce a scheme of annexation which would be based on full democratic control of the finances and administration of the Congo and afford 'ample and positive guarantees' that the practices of the Congo State would be reversed. If Belgium failed to produce such a scheme by the given date, the British government should appeal to the powers for joint action with a view to ensuring just government and the freedom of trade in the Congo. If that appeal failed, they urged the British government 'alone or with such of the Powers as may agree' to denounce the Congo State as a 'barbarous' government whose existing status they could no longer recognize; inform the Congo State, the Belgian government and the powers

---

[1] Hardinge to Grey, 23 January 1908, ibid., no. 23, Africa, confidential. Cf. Wauters, op. cit., p. 348.

that any interference with the treaty rights of British subjects on the Congo would be regarded as an unfriendly act; place gun-boats on the Lower and Upper Congo; increase the number of British consuls in the Congo State and invest them with powers of consular jurisdiction; withdraw exequaturs from representatives of the Congo State in England; prohibit the Belgian steamers employed by the Congo State from entering, coaling, taking or landing passengers and mails in English ports or in the ports of the British West African colonies; close the Nile route to supplies for the Congo State; notify the Congo government, the Belgian government and the powers that any serious disturbance in the Congo State involving the security of the contiguous British possessions would be suppressed by British intervention.[1]

In order to ensure the widest publicity for this formidable programme, it was agreed that copies should be sent to the State Department and the American C.R.A.; the prime minister and the Foreign Secretary; and lastly, the various branches of the C.R.A. in Britain with a view to their communicating them to local members of parliament. It was also planned that the Archbishop of Canterbury, Lords Monkswell and Clifford, the Earls of Mayo and Lonsdale, and the Bishops of London, Southwark, Hereford, Bristol, Liverpool and St Asaph should promote another debate in the House of Lords soon. The same thing was to be done in the House of Commons by the chairman and secretary of the parliamentary committee of the C.R.A. The Anglican and Free Church leaders in London also decided to carry on, under the auspices of the C.R.A., a vigorous campaign throughout the metropolis.[2]

The prospect of a parliamentary campaign conducted against the government not only by the opposition but by a vocal minority in the Liberal party produced immediate results. The Foreign Office decided on the appointment of a third vice-consul for the Congo in order to show the

---

[1] C.R.A. to Grey, 24 January 1908, ibid.
[2] *Daily Graphic*, 22 January 1908.

reformers that something was being done.[1] In addition, the Congo for the first time featured in the speech from the throne[2] much to the gratification, though not to the satisfaction, of Morel and his friends.

The agitation in England, the Anglo-American démarche and the speech from the throne made a considerable impact in Brussels. The need was to find the means of satisfying opposition to the Treaty of Cession. As the attack on it had centred on the *Fondation de la Couronne* it was evident that the dissolution of that body would be acclaimed as a victory by the reformers. On 1 February Leopold II informed his cabinet that he was willing to abandon the *Fondation*.[3] It was eventually agreed that in return Belgium should assume certain liabilities incurred by the *Fondation*, including allowances to some members of the royal family. Two special funds were created. The first, totalling 45 million francs, was to be voted from Congo funds and expended on public works in Belgium. From this sum the government undertook not to spend more than 31 million francs without further reference to the Belgian parliament. The second fund, amounting to 50 million francs, was to be paid to the crown from the Congo budget in fifteen annuities as a mark of gratitude. These were to form the main provisions of the Additional Act to the Treaty of Cession published a few weeks later.

Since the king's concession was not immediately publicized the English reformers proceeded with their agitation. In accordance with the programme which they had already outlined a debate in the House of Lords was fixed for 24 February and for two days later in the House of Commons.

---

[1] F.O. to Treasury, 24 January 1908; Treasury to F.O., 27 January 1908, FO 367/75.

[2] King Edward VII declared: 'My Government are fully aware of the great anxiety felt with regard to the treatment of the native population in the Congo State. Their sole desire is to see the government of that State humanely administered in accordance with the spirit of the Berlin Act, and I trust that the negotiations now proceeding between the Sovereign of the Congo State and the Belgian Government will secure this.' Hansard, 29 January 1908, 4th ser., clxxxviii, 3.

[3] Stengers: *Belgique et Congo*, p. 170.

They were preceded by a mammoth public meeting at Queen's Hall, London, which was presided over by the Lord Mayor.

Opening the debate in the Lords, the Earl of Mayo renewed the C.R.A. demand for the appointment of more consuls in the Congo State and urged the government to declare openly that they would not accept annexation on the present terms and that they would insist on the rights of the Congolese to the soil and its produce being respected. Lord Cromer and the Archbishop of Canterbury lent their great authority to Mayo. The demands of the reformers, however, had in part been anticipated by the government. Fitzmaurice was able to point out that in fact a third vice-consul had already been appointed and a steam launch provided for the consul at Boma in order to increase his mobility. He assured the House that the government 'could not regard as satisfactory any arrangement which did not vindicate or secure the vindication of both treaty obligation and the claims of humanity'.[1]

In the Commons, the reformers resorted to a new line of attack. They thought that only timidity and uncertainty of opinion in the country hindered Grey from more positive action. Thus they sought to strengthen his hand by tabling a motion which asked the government

to do all in its power to secure that a fundamental alteration of the system shall be effected by any transfer of control of the State from the present Sovereign to any other authority; and, failing such transfer within a considerable time, assures the government of its hearty support in the measures it may be necessary to take, either alone or in conjunction with the other signatories of the Berlin Act, in order to ensure the effective carrying out of its provisions.[2]

It was a measure of the support still enjoyed by the cause for Congo reform that this motion was passed without a division. Grey confessed that no external question for at

[1] Hansard, 24 February 1908, 4th ser., clxxxiv, 1297.
[2] Hansard, 26 February, 1908, 4th ser., clxxxiv, 1839–40.

least thirty years had moved the country so strongly and so vehemently.[1]

That Grey himself, a humane man, was moved by the Congo question, there could be no doubt. His sympathy was based not on mere sentiment but on the concrete evidence which the consular officers in the Congo State furnished. It would be remembered that in June 1906 Leopold II had issued a series of decrees aimed at introducing reforms. In fact the decrees proved to have been illusory for they were considerably modified by the circulars and orders subsequently issued by the local officials in the Congo, obviously with the connivance of the central government. From Stanleyville, vice-consul George Michell reported that the money values attached to the tax in produce or labour was arbitrary and deceptive. He gave examples to show that the tax imposed on the men and women was 'not only a hardship but an unmitigated evil'. As regards the extension of the land occupied by the Congolese he pointed out that each inhabitant had first to prove that he had been in permanent occupation of his land since 1 July 1885—an impossible task for an illiterate people. Moreover, even if such proof was forthcoming, the land could still be seized for non-payment of tax.[2] Vice-consul Beak, stationed in Katanga, was more sweeping about conditions there. He complained that the time of the Congo staff was 'wholly occupied in pursuits of a commercial character and mainly in the collection of revenue'. The tax imposed was 'wholly disproportionate' to the means of the inhabitants and in return they got very little. He concluded:

> There is no pretence at administration, not even the preservation of peace and the maintenance of law and order, let alone the prevention of disease, the advancement of education, the construction of public works, and the improvement of communication.[3]

---

[1] Ibid., p. 1870.

[2] Michell to Nightingale, 23 March 1907, encl. in Consul-General Cromie to Grey, 18 April 1907. *Accounts and Papers*, 1908 (Cd. 3880), lxxi, 1.

[3] Beak to Nightingale, 8 May 1907, encl. in Consul-General Cromie

A similar conclusion was reached by vice-consul Armstrong who toured the Lake Leopold II district. On the administration, he reported:

> I saw nothing which led me to view the occupation of this country in the light of an Administration. The undertakings of the Government are solely commercial, with a sufficient administrative power to insure the safety of its personnel and the success of its enterprise . . .[1]

His most striking revelation, however, was that instead of the forty hours per month tax which the recent decrees claimed to have introduced, each Congolese averaged 'not less than twenty days per month'. The duration of this tax was demonstrated in an experiment performed by the American consul-general at Yambata, a district which the Congo government was directly exploiting.[2] The only improvement noted in the territories investigated was 'a cessation of the worst form of atrocities'.[3] Summing up the position the British consul at Boma reported that the 'system which gave rise to these abuses still continued unchanged, and so long as it is unaltered the condition of the natives must remain one of veiled slavery.'[4]

It was one thing for Grey to be moved by the existence of such abuses and another for him to propose adequate remedies. While encouraging Belgian annexation on satisfactory terms as the proper solution, he was indeed sufficiently roused to entertain the idea of isolated action by Britain. In his speech during the House of Commons debate he warned that while in Macedonia his hands were tied by the need to act in concert with other powers, he did not consider them to be tied in the Congo question.[5]

---

to Grey, 2 September 1907, *Accounts and Papers*, ibid. See also Beak to F.O., 6 September 1907, *Accounts and Papers*, ibid.

[1] Armstrong to Grey, 17 December 1907, *Accounts and Papers*, ibid.

[2] 'Experiment made by American Consul-General', encl. 2, in Thesiger to Grey, 31 December 1907, *Accounts and Papers*, ibid.

[3] Thesiger to Grey, 31 December 1907, *Accounts and Papers*, ibid.

[4] Ibid.

[5] Hansard, 26 February 1908, 4th ser., clxxxiv, 1877.

Writing two days later to Arthur Hardinge, Grey outlined the steps he proposed to take.[1] With regard to the commercial aspects of the question he would inform the Belgians that if they finally accepted annexation, the matter would have to be referred to arbitration. In addition, the Belgians would have to give an assurance that they were going to carry out effective reforms in the Congo administration. But if by May, when the session of the Belgian parliament closed, annexation had not been resolved he gave the following indication of his line of action:

> In this case, I propose to act on the assumption that we shall have to deal, for an indefinite period, with the King and with the existing state of things in the Congo. I shall say to Belgium that she need be in no hurry, and that anything we may do before she makes up her mind to take over the Congo will be provisional, and subject to revision directly the Congo passes out of the King's hands into hers.[2]

He would then demand from Leopold II that the commercial aspect of the Congo question be referred to arbitration. As regards the humanitarian aspect, the king-sovereign would be told that he had one year within which to change the system and if he failed Britain would 'cease to recognize the existence of the State'. Consular jurisdiction would be established, import duties on British goods forbidden and a gun-boat placed on the Lower Congo. Grey concluded:

> I know there may be some technical difficulties in the way of the course which I propose. But public opinion here will make light of technical difficulties, and I consider that the state of slavery disclosed by our last consular reports is such as to transcend technical difficulties and the letter of Treaties. I am convinced that, probably during the year which would intervene before we took action after making our announcement, some arrangement would be made with the consent of

---

[1] The whole text of this letter is quoted in G. M. Trevelyan: *Grey of Fallodon*, London 1937, pp. 198–200. Its gist is contained in the record of a conversation between Grey and the U.S. chargé d'affaires. Grey to Bryce, 28 February 1908, FO 367/115, no. 3, Africa.

[2] Ibid.

the other powers by which the Congo would be transferred
from the hands of the King . . .

My own feeling is that we are justified in any measures
which will result in taking the Congo out of the hands of the
King. He has forfeited every claim to it he ever had; and to
take the Congo away from him without compensation would
be less than justice, for it would leave him still with all the
gains he has made by his monstrous system.[1]

Grey had revealed enough of this attitude during the last
debate to make a substantial impact in Belgium. The
Congophile press tried to rouse Belgian patriotic fervour in
order to repulse British intrusion in the Congo question;
nevertheless, they could not dispel the apprehension that
failure to annex on satisfactory terms would invite foreign
intervention. But, as one historian has pointed out, this was
not the only consideration which the Schollaert government
had to take into account; there was also the over-riding fact
that to make annexation acceptable to Belgians as a whole
it had to be on better terms than the last government had
announced.[2] Indeed, the country, so far as popular opinion
could be ascertained, was still opposed to the colonial venture
and unless satisfactory modifications in the terms of annexation were made and the annexation quickly accomplished
the forthcoming summer elections might well be fought on
the colonial issue. In that event it was not unlikely that the
moderate Left which favoured annexation in principle might
ally with the anti-annexationists within the Catholic party
to defeat the government.[3] It is in the light of these considerations that the amendments of March to the Colonial Bill
have to be seen.

In the first place, the government accepted the proposals
of the parliamentary committee with regard to the approval
of loans by parliament, the granting of concessions and the
examination of decrees by the Colonial Council.[4] Next, it

---

[1] Ibid.
[2] Stengers: *Belgique et Congo*, p. 178.
[3] Hardinge to Grey, 7 March 1908, FO 367/115, no. 49, Africa.
[4] See Stengers: *Belgique et Congo*, pp. 174–5.

was agreed that instead of the king appointing all the members of the Colonial Council, he should only appoint eight of its fourteen members and the remainder should be appointed by parliament. Finally, and most important, the colonial budget was to be passed by parliament. Together these amendments established the principle of parliamentary sovereignty in the prospective colony. Nevertheless, on the question of spelling out the rights of the Congolese to which the British reformers attached great significance the king-sovereign was firmly resolved that no concession should be made and the government acquiesced.[1]

With the publication of the Additional Act, followed a few days later by the amended Colonial Bill, the Congo question took a new turn. Simultaneously with the publication of the amendments the Belgian government lodged a protest at the Foreign Office. Lalaing complained against the last debate in the British parliament in which the British government seemed to have departed from their former attitude of reserve. The negotiations over the Treaty of Cession and the subsequent elaboration of the Colonial Law were matters of internal sovereignty which no foreign power ought to criticize. Belgium, Lalaing continued, intended to annex the Congo State together with all its obligations under the Berlin and Brussels Act.

> The special régime which those Acts set up in the Conventional basin of the Congo would, in fact, be binding upon Belgium in the same manner as it was on all those Powers who had possessions in the interior of that basin. The Belgian Government did not, however, admit that they could be required to furnish further information on the decisions they might be led to adopt in this respect.[2]

It was anticipated in Belgium that this protest, coupled with the new terms of annexation, would compel silence from the Foreign Office. They might have known better, for

---

[1] Ibid. Quotes Leopold to Schollaert, 9 March 1908, Archives Générales du Royaume (Brussels), Papiers Schollaert–Helleputte, no. 1.

[2] Grey to Hardinge, 5 March 1908, *Accounts and Papers*, 1908 (Cd. 4153), lxxi, 71.

in fact it had the opposite effect. It marked the beginning of a protracted controversy, sometimes mild and friendly, at other times sharp and acrimonious, between Brussels and London. One reason for this has already been indicated: it was the natural revulsion against the Congo administration which Grey felt as a result of his knowledge of the Leopoldian system at work. But apart from this, there was the continued and intensified pressure exerted by the reform movement in England. The C.R.A., in a detailed analysis of the Additional Act, pointed out that it 'did not touch the fundamental issue at stake, that is, the economic rights of the natives'.[1] They claimed that the terms on which Belgium proposed to annex would perpetuate the existing system and consequently urged Grey to inform the Belgian government that the terms of transfer were still unacceptable to Britain. A parliamentary delegation consisting of Charles Trevelyan, Sir Gilbert Parker and Ramsay Macdonald called on Grey to drive the points home.[2] In addition the chambers of commerce made similar protests severally. This pattern of pressure, popular, parliamentary and mercantile, was one with which the Foreign Office always had to reckon.

There was, however, one immediate result of the Belgian protest. It provided the Foreign Office with the opportunity of opening formal discussions on the details of the reforms which they expected Belgium to institute after annexation. On the instruction of Grey, a memorandum was prepared for presentation to the Belgian government which reviewed at great length the currency and taxation policy of the Congo State in the light of the Berlin Act, the Congo commission of inquiry and the reports of British consular officers.[3] The reason for concentrating attention on currency was stated to be because there was

> probably no more potent means of putting a stop to the abuses in the Congo than the existence of a circulating medium

---

[1] C.R.A. to Grey, 20 March 1908, FO 403/399.

[2] Grey, 19 March 1908, FO 367/116, memorandum.

[3] 'Memorandum respecting Taxation and Currency in the Congo Free State', encl. in Grey to Hardinge, 27 March 1908, *Accounts and Papers*, 1908 (Cd. 4135), lxxi, 71.

in sufficient amount. It would, on the one hand, shield the native from the exorbitant exactions of the State, which the latter is only enabled to enforce in virtue of a system of taxation in labour, while on the other hand, it would, if not entirely destroy, at any rate seriously diminish the enormous profits of the trading companies and of the State, in its capacity of a trader.[1]

The memorandum then went on to point out the 'fixed determination' of the Congo government to dispense with a proper standard of value in spite of the recommendations of its commission of inquiry. It also maintained that the reform decree issued as a result of the inquiry had been nugatory in effect and the consular reports were quoted to show that the condition of the Congolese was still one of 'veiled slavery'.

In the despatch accompanying the memorandum Grey outlined in some detail the aspect of the administration where he thought reforms were necessary.[2] The British government felt that

in fairness they should leave the Belgian Government in no doubt that in their opinion the existing administration of the Congo State has not fulfilled the objects for which the State was originally recognized, or the conditions of Treaties, and that changes are therefore required, which should effect the following objects:

(1) Relief of the natives from excessive taxation.
(2) The grant to the natives of sufficient land to ensure their ability to obtain not only the food they require, but also sufficient produce of the soil to enable them to buy and sell as in other European Colonies.
(3) The possibility for traders whatever their nationality may be to acquire plots of land of reasonable dimensions in any part of the Congo for the erection of factories so as to enable them to establish direct trade relations with the natives.

---

[1] Ibid.
[2] Grey to Hardinge, 27 March 1908, ibid.

In order to remedy the situation, the despatch went on to make three suggestions for reform. In the first place, currency should be introduced throughout the Congo State at the earliest date. Secondly, the Congolese in the concessionary areas should not be compelled by direct or indirect means to render their labour to the companies without remuneration. Finally, a large increase, in accordance with prevailing farming methods, should be made in the land allotted to the Africans. The despatch closed by hinting that the British government had intended to refer to arbitration the land and trade system of the Congo State. They preferred, however, to defer the question of arbitration now that there was prospect of an early annexation by Belgium.

Grey had solicited the co-operation of the State Department and had also communicated to them a copy of his despatch.[1] The American ambassador was consequently instructed to make similar representations independently. In their memorandum, the American government claimed to have assumed 'certain well-defined obligations, which may not be lightly evaded'. It was pointed out that the policy pursued by the Congo government was 'enslaving, degrading and decimating the native population'. To the three demands already put forward by the British government the United States added two others: 'the inhibition of forced labour', and 'the procurement and guarantee of equal and exact justice to all inhabitants of the Congo through the establishment and maintenance of an independent judiciary'.[2]

A few days after Hardinge had read the Foreign Office despatch to Davignon, Grey seemed to have changed his mind. The British ambassador was summoned to London and told to suggest to the Belgian Foreign Minister a declaration from his government that they would abolish forced labour immediately after annexation and that they would agree to refer all purely commercial questions to arbitration

---

[1] Grey to Bryce, 18 March 1908, FO 367/116, no. 7, Africa.

[2] Encl. 2 in Wyndham to Grey, 2 April 1908, FO 403/399, no. 70, Africa, confidential.

at the Hague.[1] This was a considerable modification of the three points raised in the despatch of 27 March. It must not be forgotten, however, that forced labour formed the basis of the exploitation of the Congo. If forced labour was abolished a new form of taxation would have to be evolved and that could only be by the introduction of currency throughout the country. Nevertheless, the abolition of forced labour alone would hardly have relieved the burden of the Congolese and Grey was aware of this. An explanation for the change could only be that Grey saw in the abolition of forced labour a reform with sufficiently dramatic impact to satisfy the British reformers and relieve him of further pressure from them.

The State Department was once more prepared to back the new move.[2] A declaration of this kind, convenient as it might be for Grey, was in fact impossible for the Belgian Cabinet. As Davignon pointed out to Hardinge,[3] such an open declaration by the Belgian government also implied a public censure on the past administration of the Belgian king in the Congo. It would thus mean that a Catholic and Conservative government pledged to the support of the dynasty was condemning before the world the king who was at its head and whose position it was pledged to maintain. There was also another consideration. The Belgian government had always assured the people that the colonial venture would entail no expenditure from the Belgian treasury. If forced labour was declared abolished the government would have found it impossible to maintain this argument against the anti-annexationists.[4] Grey's new move, therefore, did not produce the desired result.

---

[1] Hardinge to Grey, 5 April 1908, FO 367/116, no. 76, Africa, confidential; Grey to Bryce, 6 April 1908, ibid., tel. no. 2, Africa.

[2] Bryce to Grey, 9 April 1908, ibid., tel. no. 1, Africa. There was, however, a divergence in procedure. While Hardinge conveyed his instructions verbally Wilson embodied his in a formal memorandum. Encl. in Hardinge to Grey, 18 April 1908, FO 367/116, no. 92, Africa, confidential.

[3] Hardinge to Grey, 18 April 1908, ibid.

[4] The favourite argument of those Belgians who opposed annexation was as follows: Reform would be necessary if and when Belgium annexed.

As far as declaration of general principles went, however, the Belgian government professed to be in agreement with the British government.[1] 'The question of improving the lot of the natives', they said, 'is not less a matter of solicitude in Belgium than it is in England. It is one of the loftiest pre-occupations of our country, which is fully sensible of the importance of the civilizing mission which falls to its lot in Africa.'[2] The statement met all the demands of the British government as regards currency and taxation. It hinted at fresh agreements being made with the concession companies and pointed out that even in these concessions the Congolese could still be given extended rights with regard to the free disposal of produce. They summarized their plans as follows:

> an immediate amelioration in the moral and material conditions of existence of the inhabitants of the Congo, and the extension, as rapidly as possible, of a system of economic freedom to the different regions of that vast country.[3]

But these reforms, according to the Belgian government, would be outlined after and not before the annexation.

Here, then, was the crux of the whole diplomatic *impasse*. The Congo reformers in Britain distrusted Leopold II and what they regarded as his servile cabinet. The Foreign Office was no less distrustful of the evasiveness of the Belgian government. Both the Congo reformers and the Foreign Office, therefore, saw in the annexation arrangements grave obstacles to reforms. The Belgian government, on the other hand, were undertaking annexation under the domination of a wilful monarch. They were bound by their promises to the Belgian tax-payer that annexation would impose no

---

These reforms, one of which should normally entail the abolition of forced labour, were bound to reduce the Congo budget to such an extent that Belgium would have to vote money for a considerable time to cover the deficit; the experience of other colonial powers had proved the contention; therefore Belgium should not annex.

[1] Memorandum communicated by Count Lalaing, 25 April 1908, FO 367/117.

[2] Ibid.

[3] Ibid.

financial burden. They might have believed in the need for reforms; but reforms, as they were well aware, would be a repudiation of their sovereign and would necessarily tax the Belgian treasury. Pressed to give guarantees and to outline reforms, their reply could only be an appeal to be trusted— which the British government could hardly be expected to do. Each side could claim a justification for its stand. The Foreign Office could argue: it is all right for you to ask us to trust you. But you are promising reforms after annexation and at the same time negotiating annexation on terms which would make reforms impossible. In any case why not now, as evidence of good faith, give a categorical assurance that forced labour would be abolished? On its side the Belgian government could simply reply: how can we give details of the reforms when we are not yet in possession of the colony and have not had an opportunity of studying the problem at first hand? The two positions were apparently irreconcilable. As a solution, Arthur Hardinge proposed that Britain should defer her recognition of the treaty of transfer, and reserve her full liberty of action in regard to it, until she was able to judge the effect of the new measures Belgium would adopt.[1]

This solution was accepted by Grey, for it left the future open and his hands free. In communicating it to Lalaing, Grey declared his sympathy for the inability of the Belgian government to decide on the reforms until after annexation. The British government, also, could not commit itself finally until they had discussed those measures.

> The Belgian Government would of course, in accordance with the provision of the Berlin Act which was binding upon all the Powers notify us of the annexation, and we must reserve our liberty to discuss the actual measures to be applied in the Congo by the Belgian Government before committing ourselves in reply to that notification.[2]

---

[1] Hardinge to Grey, 9 May 1908, FO 367/117, no. 108, Africa, confidential.

[2] Grey to Hardinge, 23 June 1908, ibid., no. 81, Africa.

This statement gave rise in Belgium to an examination whether they were bound to notify the annexation of the Congo to other powers and whether the powers could lay conditions on their recognition of the annexation. The basis of the claim by the Foreign Office was Article 34 of the Berlin Act. Even before Grey's despatch arrived Arendt had argued that 'the union of the Congo State to Belgium has been envisaged from the moment of its creation as the final end of its organic development', and consequently recognition by the powers was not essential.[1] It was accepted by the ministry, however, that the powers should be notified of the annexation if only on the ground that it was an act of diplomatic courtesy.[2]

Leopold II refused this. Ostensibly, his argument was that Britain had created a precedent by annexing the Transvaal in 1900 without notifying the powers; what he actually feared was that notification might open the door to a surrender to British demands and the reversal of his system in the Congo. He suggested that the Congo State rather than Belgium should notify the powers that it had ceased to exist and that Belgium had taken over.[3] When the ministry objected, he compelled Davignon to take legal opinion on the matter.[4] Van Heuvel, minister of state and a lawyer, reported that 'a communication [to the powers] would not only have the advantage of being a display of courtesy, it would constitute an indispensable act for the practical settlement of international relations',[5] but still the king-sovereign remained adamant.[6]

---

[1] Arendt, 1 June 1908, Ier sér., Congo, ix, 2933, memorandum.

[2] Davignon to Leopold II, 24 July 1908, Ier sér., Congo, x, 2677.

[3] Leopold II to Davignon, 24 July 1908, Ier sér., Congo, x, 2678 (copy).

[4] Davignon to Leopold II, 4 August 1908, Ier sér., Congo, x, 2717.

[5] M. Van Heuvel to Davignon, 2 August 1908, Ier sér., Congo, x, 2713.

[6] Carton de Wiart to Davignon, 11 August 1908, Ier sér., Congo, x, 2741, and 21 August 1908, Ier sér., Congo, x, 2782.

While the battle over the question of notification was being waged between the Foreign Office and the Belgian government, and between the latter and Leopold II, popular attention was focused on the debate in the Belgian Chamber with regard to the Treaty of Cession. The government, as has been said, wished to rush through the bills before the summer elections so that annexation would not feature in the campaigns. Since the Liberal and Socialist opposition parties desired to exploit at the election the natural apprehensions of the Belgian people towards the colonial question, they saw no need to hurry on the debate.

The debate on annexation opened on 15 April and was welcomed without enthusiasm by the British press. Their attitude was best summarized as follows by the *Daily News*:

> The Treaty is drafted, the constitution framed; King Leopold has fixed his price, the Ministry is in earnest, and Europe awaits the result. There will be some days or weeks of talk . . . and then one evening the Belgian people, the least adventurous, the least imperialistic in the world, may suddenly realise that an irreparable vote has made them the owners of a country with eighty times the area of her present territories. Never before was greatness forced by circumstances upon a more reluctant people.
>
> For our part we have seen enough of imperialism elsewhere to doubt whether Belgium would be wise, in her own interest, to take over the Congo on any terms. On the other hand, we are clear that on almost any terms the natives have something to gain by the change. Moreover, if Belgium should refuse to annex it would be difficult to devise any other alternative to King Leopold's misrule.[1]

But although the 'Belgian solution' seemed so obvious and inevitable it was not so readily accepted in Belgium itself for the discussion on the arrangements for annexation was not concluded in the Chamber until 20 August. One reason was the break from 6 May to 19 June for the election of the retiring half of the deputies. The main reason, however,

---

[1] *Daily News*, 16 April 1908.

was the diversity of opinion prevailing on the issue. According to *L'Etoile Belge*, there were convinced annexationists, resigned annexationists, annexationists who did not want to annex and anti-annexationists on principle. As the interminable and wearisome arguments proceeded the British ambassador reported that nearly the entire Belgian press had become unanimous in urging that the most important debate in Belgium since 1831 should not be allowed to degenerate into a meeting of parrots. In the end, however, the Additional Act, the Treaty of Cession and the Colonial Bill were passed without any substantial amendments.

The main provisions of the Treaty of Cession and the Additional Act have already been outlined. As regards the Colonial Law, in addition to the concessions already made, the government accepted the principle of the independence of the judiciary. Furthermore, every act of the king was to be countersigned by a minister who thereby became responsible. A provision in the Colonial Law also laid down that the granting of concessions was to be made the subject of a special law. Meanwhile, all decrees granting concessions exceeding 10,000 hectares would have to be presented to parliament. Beyond this, the executive could not, except in the case of the Katanga Company, delegate its powers to third parties. On the treatment of the Congolese, it was provided that laws should be enacted as soon as possible defining their rights to real property and personal liberty. Finally, there was a provision that no one in the Congo should be compelled to work for trading companies or individual concessionaires.

While some of the Belgian press hailed annexation of the Congo enthusiastically and others cautiously, the mass of the Belgian people remained coldly aloof. Across the channel, the reformers pondered over what annexation meant in terms of the Berlin Act. One obvious gain was the disappearance of the Congo State and the reversion of Leopold II, King of the Belgians and Sovereign of the Independent State of the Congo into Leopold II, King of the Belgians. It was evident also that given goodwill and good intentions on the part of the Belgian government the terms of annexation afforded sufficient opportunity for substantial reforms in the Congo administration. The question was: could the goodwill and the good intentions of the Belgian government be taken for granted?

For their answer the C.R.A. turned to the declarations made in the Belgian Chamber by the prime minister and the Minister of Justice which had endorsed the theories of the Congo State on 'vacant lands' and on the rights of the Concession companies.[1] They came to the conclusion that the 'tone and substances of both these declarations would seem to justify the gravest suspicion as to the value of the vague assurances of a general character given to His Majesty's Government'.[2] Therefore, even before annexation was voted the C.R.A. was urging that Britain should

> resolutely withhold recognition of a Belgian annexation . . . until the Belgian Government was in a position to give explicit guarantees that the Treaty responsibilities binding upon their successors towards this country and towards civilization, and embodied in the Acts of Berlin and Brussels and in the Anglo-Congolese Convention of 1884 were fulfilled.[3]

They asked for three fundamental changes in the administration of the Congo: abrogation of the Congo State interpretation of the principles of 'vacant lands' and the recognition of the Congolese communal rights in land; restoration to the Congolese of 'all exportable produce of commercial value' and of their rights to trade in them with all traders until after proper delimitation of inhabited and ownerless lands; and lastly, abolition of forced labour 'for purposes of acquiring public or private revenues'.[4]

The call by the C.R.A. for non-recognition of the annexation was, of course, not an initiative; it was a decision which

---

[1] E.g. The prime minister had said: 'It is certain that in the *terres vacantes* the native has not the actual right to collect the natural products, but the State has the right, if it so desires, to relinquish to them the collection of products the exploitation of which has not been conceded.' *Annales Parlementaires* (Chambre), 2 July 1908.

[2] C.R.A. to Grey, 7 July 1908, FO 367/118.

[3] Ibid.

[4] Ibid.

the Foreign Office had taken two months earlier.[1] However, its adoption by the reformers strengthened Grey's hand and established for the time being a measure of collaboration between the Foreign Office and the C.R.A. Thus in defining and explaining the British case for non-recognition Grey readily adopted the arguments of Morel. As has been seen, the Foreign Office, in its memorandum formulating the essential reforms which the Belgian government should inaugurate, had asked for the introduction of currency and the increase of land earmarked for the Congolese.[2] For Morel this was a gross misunderstanding or lack of understanding of fundamentals. 'The first recommendation', he told Holt, 'did not touch the main issue and the second left the door open for an illusory settlement of a most dishonest character.'[3] The fundamental question was one of 'restoring to the native those interchangeable commodities of which he has been deprived'.[4] He set out to impress this firmly on Grey[5] and his effort showed in the memorandum which the Foreign Office communicated to the Belgian government in November.

In an earlier memorandum[6] the Belgian government had stuck to giving general undertakings rather than specifying the reforms which they hoped to carry out. They had also tentatively put forward the suggestion that the best method for reaching a settlement on outstanding points of disagreement might be by 'a direct understanding between all the Powers having possessions in the conventional basin'. The appeal to what amounted to an international conference was ingenious: they were aware that it would be difficult, if not impossible, to persuade the powers, and especially France, to attend such a conference. The British reply of

---

[1] Supra, p. 231.

[2] Supra, pp. 226–7.

[3] Morel to Holt, 26 November 1908, J.H.P. 18/5.

[4] C.R.A. to Grey, 1 July 1908, FO 403/400.

[5] Altogether Morel prepared three memoranda which he sent to Grey on 7 July, 20 July and 8 August 1908, ibid.

[6] Belgian memorandum communicated by Count Lalaing to Grey, 13 July 1908, *Accounts and Papers*, 1908 (Cd. 4178), lxxi, 71.

November[1] recognized that it was not easy for the Belgian government to offer a definite date within which reforms were to be introduced. Nevertheless, it asked for assurances of a more definite character than those so far given by the Belgians. In particular, it called for 'some immediate amelioration' in the condition of the natives and proceeded to explain what that meant. Traditional landmarks existed in the Congo (and were still recognized by the Congolese) which defined the boundaries of communal land before the advent of the concession system. These landmarks afforded the means of demarcating the area within which the Congolese should be free to trade in all the natural produce of the soil and to cultivate for their own use. The memorandum went on:

> Such a return to native communal tenure in land produce, as it existed prior to 1891–2, would lead to a sensible and immediate alleviation of the unhappy condition in which at present the original inhabitants of the country find themselves, deprived, as they are, of all right to these same products of the soil, which are the only means by which they can earn more than a bare subsistence, and with no protection either from the concessionary companies or the State in the shape of a guaranteed fair minimum price for the rubber or other produce gathered. They would thus be enabled to await with some patience the results of the fuller investigation into their rights which the Belgian Government promise, and which . . . must take a considerable time.[2]

Passing on to the question of arbitration, it was pointed out to the Belgian government that this had been requested only as regards 'the purely *commercial* obligations of the Congo State'. The British government agreed on the need for a direct understanding between all the powers having possessions in the conventional basin. However, they reserved their full liberty to press for arbitration if the Belgian method did not prove feasible 'within a reasonable time'. The

---

[1] Encl. in Grey to Lalaing, 4 November 1908, *Accounts and Papers*, 1908 (Cd. 4396), lxxi, 71.
[2] Ibid.

memorandum emphasized that there could be no arbitration
as regards the rights of the Congolese; neither would Britain
recognize the annexation until assurances were received that
the matter 'would be settled in a manner satisfactory both
to them and to public opinion in this country'.[1]

The insistence by the British government on the Congolese
right to the natural produce and the refusal to accept arbitration on this point aligned the Foreign Office with the C.R.A.
In the United States the position was the same. The State
Department had continued at every turn to put forward
the same views as the Foreign Office and the American
C.R.A. had kept in close touch with the parent organization
in England. Thus when the date of Belgian annexation came,
it was certain that neither the British nor the American
government would recognize the change.

Belgium, however, did not call on the powers to recognize
her annexation. Confronted with the obstinate opposition of
the king to this line of procedure the Belgian cabinet arrived
at a clever formula which presented the powers with a
fait accompli. Each Belgian representative abroad was instructed simply to inform his host government that the law
approving the treaty of annexation of the Congo by Belgium
had been promulgated and published in the *Moniteur Belge*
of 20 October. As a result, the sovereign powers of the Congo
State were transferred to Belgium which would immediately
take over the administration of the colony and issue, on
request, a new exequatur to consuls in the Congo State.[2]
Whether or not this notification was in accord with the

---

[1] Ibid.

[2] The relevant section of the circular reads:

'I request you to bring to the knowledge of the government to
which you are accredited, that the law approving the treaty of
annexation of the Independent State of the Congo by Belgium, was
promulgated and published in the *Moniteur Belge* of 20th October.

'Consequently, the sovereign powers of the Congo State have been
transferred to Belgium, who will immediately assume the administration of the Colony of the Congo.

'The King's government will hasten to deliver a new exequatur to
consular agents of foreign states who so desire . . .'
Circular, 23 October 1908, Ier sér., xi, 2930.

provisions of Article 34 of the Berlin Act was really academic. None of the powers laid any claim to the Congo State and no one had any objection in principle to Belgian annexation. Nevertheless, Grey hoped that the powers might seize the opportunity to present a united front in obtaining specific reforms from Belgium. With this aim in view he despatched on 7 November a circular letter to British ambassadors which asked them to ascertain in what form their host governments would reply to the Belgian notification.

The reactions of France and Germany were crucial for it was almost certain that if either or both decided to act with Britain, Belgium could hardly resist and the other powers might likely join. Neither France nor Germany, however, could afford to offend Belgium because of the ever-present fear that in such an event Belgium might be driven into the arms of the other rival power. France, it had been said, would welcome an international conference called by other powers to discuss the right of neutral Belgium to acquire a colonial territory. The right of pre-emption which France had over the Congo State placed her at an advantage if Belgium was to be prevented by the conference from annexing the colony. In a briefing for the president on the eve of his visit to London the Quai d'Orsay thus again summarized their position:

> We are thus completely free, not to bring up ourselves the question of neutrality, but to participate in the discussions and decisions of which it might be the object . . .[1]

As it happened the Foreign Office had forgotten or, more probably, had conveniently dropped the question of Belgian neutrality. France therefore had no further use for a conference. Consequently, when the British ambassador came to ask how France would reply to the Belgian notification he was told that French recognition depended entirely on the settlement with Belgium of outstanding tariff and boundary disputes.[2] Since the Belgian government had agreed to

---

[1] Note du Department, 21 May 1908, *D.D.F.*, 2nd ser., xi, no. 363.
[2] M. Pichon to French Ambassadors in London and Berlin, 13 November 1908, ibid., no. 553 and M. Pichon to M. Milliès-Lacroix (Minister for Colonies), 23 December 1908, ibid., no. 591.

settle these disputes without any delay it became evident that French recognition was in fact assured.

As regards Germany, she hoped, like France, that British action might open the way for her aggrandizement in the Congo.[1] But the request by Britain for information on German reaction to the Belgian notification came at an unhappy moment. Following the interview given by William II to the *Daily Telegraph* a veritable crisis prevailed in the Wilhelmstrasse. The British ambassador was brusquely told by A. Kiderlen-Waechter, the acting Foreign Secretary, that Germany had taken note of the Belgian annexation. In fact, like the French, Germany also made reservations although she did not bother to communicate them to the Foreign Office. The Belgian government was informed that Germany welcomed annexation because she believed that certain defects which had long existed in the Congo administration would be remedied and that the frontier dispute and the Rabinek affair, which were outstanding between her and the Congo State, would be quickly settled.[2]

Both France and Germany, then, were prepared to sacrifice the main issue and to conclude agreements on outstanding matters which were relatively minor in character. Belgium, of course, was ready to satisfy both powers for she in turn feared that either power might otherwise join with Britain and precipitate a crisis.

As for the rest of the powers, they were probably relieved that Belgium had decided to annex. Slow to believe the stories of atrocities under Leopold's rule and always suspicious of the imperial designs of Britain, all of them had declined to heed British appeals for co-operation. They were satisfied that, with the Congo under a European government, a benevolent administration for the colony was assured. Their interest in the Congo had always been minimal and it would have been surprising indeed to expect a different reaction at this time.

Thus Grey's decision not to accept the Belgian solution unless it guaranteed a change of system in the Congo was

[1] See Willequet, op. cit., pp. 198 ff.
[2] Ibid.

rejected by all the powers except the United States.[1] This attitude which continued to keep the Congo question open also necessitated the continued existence of the C.R.A.

That decision was taken at a meeting of the executive committee which met on 9 October. 'Today', Morel told them, 'it is possible for us to close down on a definite though not a complete victory.'[2] They could point at the disappearance of the irresponsible autocracy of Leopold II and its substitution in the Congo by the government of Belgium, which could more easily be checked by public opinion. That alone was a basic and far-reaching step towards a better era in the administration of the territory. Morel remarked, however, that the Belgian government had given no 'satisfactory guarantees' that the Leopoldian system would be swept away. He drew attention to the fact that Grey needed to be backed up by organized public opinion in order to strengthen his hand in future negotiations with Belgium and that would be lacking if the C.R.A. was dissolved. It was therefore resolved that

> Having regard to the absence of any definite and tangible guarantees from the Belgian Government that the present system of administration will be changed for one based upon recognition of native tenure in land, freedom of commerce, and abolition of forced labour, the Association cannot regard its work at an end . . .; the Association assures His Majesty's Government of its warm support in declining to recognize a Belgian annexation of the Congo until satisfactory guarantees of a change of system have been given, and earnestly trusts that His Majesty's Government will countenance no arrangement which does not place the just rights of the natives and their relations with the outer world upon a footing of permanent security.[3]

---

[1] The United States was to adopt a similar policy during the Manchurian crisis of 1931–2. H. L. Stimson: *The Far Eastern Crisis*, New York 1936, p. 98.

[2] C.R.A. to Grey, 14 October 1908, FO 367/118.

[3] Ibid. Morel later revealed that 'Grey privately expressed himself very pleased that we have decided to go on. . . .' Morel to Harold Spender, 6 November 1908, M.P., F. 8.

Having thus justified their continued existence, the C.R.A. also thought it necessary to demonstrate that Grey had the support of the nation. A letter which appeared in *The Times* of 23 December expressed 'deep satisfaction' with Grey's despatch of 4 November. He was also assured that

> this firm stand on fundamental principles of justice and equity taken in the . . . Despatch will have incalculable result for good and will, under any circumstances, be strenuously supported by all sections of public opinion in Great Britain.[1]

The letter was signed by an impressive list: eleven peers including Cromer and Balfour, nineteen bishops, seventy-five members of parliament, presidents of several chambers of commerce, several newspaper editors and some other well-known names from different walks of life.

The autumn of 1908 was the high-water mark of co-operation and understanding between the Foreign Office and the C.R.A. Acting under the pressure of the latter since 1904 the Foreign Office had cajoled Belgium until she had annexed the Congo. But Belgian annexation, as will be seen in the next two chapters, was far from being the end of the Congo question. The Foreign Office and the C.R.A. were in agreement that it was not enough for Belgium to annex the Congo; she must also completely abandon King Leopold's colonial system which had wrought so much evil in that part of Africa. Until the latter was achieved British interest in the affairs of the Congo was to remain as keen as ever and this was to lead to important developments with regard to relations between the Foreign Office and the C.R.A. as well as between the British and Belgian governments.

---

[1] *The Times*, 23 December 1908.

VIII
Non-recognition

The problem which confronted Grey now was the definition of a policy of non-recognition in terms of Anglo-Belgian amity. He had to resolve the problem of how Britain could retain the long-standing friendship of Belgium while refusing, alone among European powers, to recognize the annexation of the Congo by Belgium. For a short while the solution seemed simple and easy. While withholding recognition he proposed gently and patiently to encourage and direct Belgian colonial policy towards the desired reforms. This policy could only succeed, however, if the Belgians were ready to respond promptly and satisfactorily to his pressure. It was by obtaining visible signs of reform that he hoped to be able to justify his attitude before the critical British public. As the Belgian government was reluctant to institute radical changes Grey's policy was soon frustrated and under the continued onslaught of the reformers Anglo-Belgian relations reached a state of tension which it had not attained before nor ever since.

The fundamental issue which precipitated the tension was the contradictory interpretation by the reformers and the Foreign Office of Grey's policy of non-recognition. On the one hand, the Foreign Office believed that non-recognition was the limit, at least for the meantime, of the pressure they could exert; on the other hand, the reformers understood it to be only the beginning. Morel believed that

236

governments moved 'just in proportion to the extent in which they are frightened'.[1] Thus if Grey was pressed hard enough he would be inclined to take stronger measures than mere non-recognition.

Morel began 'frightening' the Foreign Office gradually. In January he sent Grey a 'Memorial on Native Rights in the Land and its Fruits in the Congo Territories'.[2] The memorial was intended as ammunition for Grey and, acknowledged by him to be a very valuable document,[3] most of its arguments were worked into the next despatch to the Belgian government.[4] Apart from Morel's striking conclusion that the land policy of the now extinct Congo State constituted a violation alike of natural rights and of the laws of nations, the memorial was also notable for its complete distrust of the Belgian government. The essential features of the Congo system, he argued, had been well known to successive Belgian governments. The majority of the present government had defended them in principle and denied their effects in practice. Indeed, the Colonial Minister, Jules Renkin, had left the administrative board of the Congo *Compagnie des Grands Lacs* to enter the cabinet.[5] The Belgian government, therefore, could not plead ignorance as to the reforms required. On the contrary, there were several signs that they intended to perpetuate the old system. Thus, for example, they had assured the Belgian electorates that annexation would cost nothing while it was clear that grants-in-aid would be essential if reforms were introduced.

Although Morel did not press any particular line of action at this time on the Foreign Office, there could be no doubt that he expected a dynamic policy from Grey. In a second memorandum in which he analysed the colonial policy of

---

[1] Morel to Pierre Mille, 31 December 1908, M.P., F. 8.
[2] C.R.A. to Grey, 15 January 1909, FO 367/164.
[3] Grey, n.d., ibid., minute; *The Times*, 15 February 1909.
[4] *Accounts and Papers*, 1909 (Cd. 4396), lix, 565.
[5] Morel harboured special resentment for the Belgian Colonial Minister. He told Langley: 'I repeat again and again that M. Renkin is not to be trusted. You cannot make a silk purse out of a sow's ear.' Morel to Langley, 3 January 1909, FO 367/164.

the Belgian government he expressed a hope that the Foreign Secretary might find 'it both impossible and intolerable to permit an indefinite prolongation of the present situation'.[1] The idea implicit in the general attitude of the reformers, that further action on the part of Grey was essential, was given expression again a few days later. At the meeting of the executive committee of the C.R.A. a resolution was adopted expressing 'profound appreciation' of the stand taken by Grey in refusing recognition of the annexation.[2] They called for demonstrations throughout the country to show the British government that sentiments on the Congo question were not weakening and that they would be supported 'in any measures, however drastic', which they might adopt.

Grey envisaged no further action for he did not believe in antagonizing the Belgians more than was necessary. He was certain that he had taken all the diplomatic measures which the situation required. His non-recognition meant that the British government would not take out fresh exequaturs for their consuls in the Congo. Meanwhile more consular officers were to be sent to the Congo to scrutinize the administration. In addition, at the end of the negotiations then going on for the settlement of the Congo-Uganda boundary, Britain would not enter into any formal agreement with Belgium.

Grey was also encouraged to suspend further action because there was within Belgium itself a small but vocal group still devoted to the cause of reform. As early as 17 December when the first colonial budget was discussed in the Belgian Chamber, Vandervelde and his Socialist party had pressed the government for an explicit statement as to the reforms that would be instituted. Soon after, they had come out with a public declaration not to slacken their effort to secure reform in the Congo administration. This reforming spirit was, indeed, not confined to the socialists alone. As Hardinge noted, moderate Belgians of all parties

---

[1] Morel to Grey, 4 February 1909, ibid.
[2] C.R.A. to Grey, 13 February 1909, ibid.

expected a programme of reforms to be laid before the Chamber at an early date.[1] On the basis of this assurance Grey could well feel that the Congo question would soon solve itself without further intervention from Britain.

His future policy was briefly outlined to the American government which was still acting in concert with Britain. Both governments, he told the American ambassador, should merely maintain their present position on non-recognition until the expected Belgian reforms were announced.[2] For the benefit of the reformers, however, he played the tune a bit higher. On 25 February Sir Gilbert Parker, moving an amendment to the speech from the throne for the reformers, decried the irresolute attitude of the Foreign Office.[3] Grey assured the House that the time was not ripe for strong measures because the old system was not likely to continue under a Belgian administration. He defended the Belgian delay in replying to his despatch of 4 November as a good sign, for it showed that they were considering serious measures of reform. But in concluding, Grey promised that the government 'will not take any definite action with regard to recognition until the Belgian reply has been before Parliament and Parliament has had an opportunity of expressing its own view if it so desires.'[4]

The decision to allow parliament to express an opinion before recognition was accorded was a far-reaching one. Its implication when it was repeated by Grey in March 1910 will soon be discussed. Equally remarkable was the promise which Grey gave to the representatives of the Associated Chambers of Commerce who waited on him a few days later. He assured them of his 'diplomatic support' for any attempts which British traders might make to trade in the Congo.[5]

Why did Grey make these important pronouncements? The answer probably lies in the fact that he did not expect

---

[1] Hardinge to Grey, 18 December 1908, FO 367/76, no. 248, Africa.
[2] Grey to Bryce, 10 February 1909, FO 403/409, no. 4, Africa.
[3] Hansard, 25 February 1909, 5th ser., i, 943–47.
[4] Ibid., 960.
[5] *The Times*, 4 March 1909.

to be called upon to execute them. He was clearly confident that the next Belgian Note would contain the necessary assurances and enable him to persuade parliament to recognize the annexation. The announcement in Brussels that Prince Albert, the heir-apparent, and the Belgian Minister for the Colonies were going to the Congo in April seemed to have given the impression that radical changes were imminent. We now know that he underrated the influence of Leopold II under whose scrutiny the Belgian reply was prepared. The king was determined that no satisfaction should be given to the demands of the British government and the Belgian cabinet was too weary with the protracted struggle of the preceding months to drag out the matter with him. Neither were they prepared to jeopardize their position with the electorate by promising reforms which might strain the Belgian treasury. The reformers were evidently more alive to the Belgian situation at this time than the Foreign Office.

It is not surprising then that the Belgian reply which was communicated on 15 March[1] proved to be such a disappointment for the Foreign Office. It repeated the previous vague assurances as to Belgium's intention to fulfil the treaty obligations incurred by the Congo State and called for patience and confidence on the part of Britain. They could not be expected, the statement went on, to draw up 'in their final form weighty resolutions on colonial matters' scarcely four months after the annexation. They discussed the issues to which the British memorandum had specifically drawn attention, namely, the further extension of lands to be assigned to the inhabitants for the purposes of trade and cultivation; respect for the freedom of labour and the right to the free disposal of the produce of the land; and arbitration on the interpretation of the treaties which bound the Congo State in commercial matters. As regards the first, the Belgian government declined the Foreign Office suggestion that traditional landmarks be used for demarcation. It was argued that such marks scarcely existed, that in any case

---

[1] Lalaing to Grey, 15 March 1909, *Accounts and Papers*, 1909 (Cd. 4396), lix, 565.

their use would mean abandoning all land to the Congolese, and that the plan was opposed to 'every principle of law' as well as inconsistent with practices existing in other parts of equatorial Africa, notably in British possessions. They asserted that the plan being pursued by the Belgian government, that of applying the decrees of June 1906, would make the Congolese better provided for than those in most of the neighbouring colonies. The memorandum altogether ignored the issue of forced labour and went on to consider that of arbitration. Here the Belgians, while professing their sympathy with arbitration as a means of settling international disputes, still opposed it and reverted to their earlier proposal for 'a direct understanding between the Powers' which they knew to be diplomatically impossible.

Thus, except for the statement that religious missions would be accorded facilities for the acquisition of land necessary for the development of their work, a statement which was hedged about with restrictive clauses, the Belgian memorandum did not advance the position any farther than its predecessor. The Foreign Office realized that it was unprofitable to continue the controversy. The problem was to determine what next should be done. Clearly recognition of the annexation under the circumstance was unthinkable; but to do nothing beyond non-recognition was bound to alienate the reformers. Grey's solution was to press for arbitration on the commercial aspects of the question.[1]

The great advantage which this decision had was that it made possible the continued co-operation of Britain and the United States over the Congo question. It was soon to be discovered, however, that the administration of President Taft, who had been elected in December 1908, was not as interested in the Congo question as that of President Roosevelt.[2] For the meantime, the two governments had to find

---

[1] Langley, 24 March 1909, FO 367/164, minute.

[2] Although the United States did not give a formal recognition to Belgian annexation they took steps as soon as it was convenient to grant a *de facto* recognition. See Buisseret (Belgian minister in Washington) to Davignon, 28 July 1910, Ier sér., Congo, xvi, 4537; C. P. Bryan (U.S. minister in Brussels) to Davignon, 16 January 1911, Ier sér., Congo, xvii, 4751 (copy).

common grounds for action. The suggestion made by the Belgian government to the State Department for an understanding among all the powers having possessions in the Congo basin was particularly unacceptable because the United States did not occupy any territory within that region. But if the United States asked for arbitration under their bilateral agreement of 1891 with the Congo State both Britain and herself would be proceeding along similar lines.[1]

In the end, arbitration did not take place. The reasons are obscure. The Foreign Office asserted later that they could not after all go to arbitration with the Belgian government when Britain had not yet recognized the authority of the latter in the Congo.[2] Plausible and justifiable as this reason might seem, there could be no doubt that arbitration would still have been pressed if the Foreign Office had found it opportune. Perhaps it might be that arbitration was abandoned because it was found to be too troublesome and inconvenient. Furthermore, since British traders had not ventured into the Upper Congo and been turned away no evidence could be found to support the British case.

But apart from general reasons of this kind two can be further adduced. In the first place, despite the content of the Belgian memorandum an attitude of compromise was apparent in Belgium. The Belgian government had to contend with the fact that the Congo question was exploited by the Liberal and Socialist opposition for reasons of domestic politics. As long as the Leopoldian system persisted the opposition had a good weapon for scoring such points against the government as the adoption on 31 March of the motion calling for the immediate abolition of forced labour.[3] There was also the question of national *amour propre* which demanded that Belgium should be removed from the unfavourable limelight focused on her by the reform agitation abroad. As Count Lalaing was instructed to tell Grey, the attacks of the C.R.A. would mislead the English public about

---

[1] Grey to Whitelaw Reid, 31 March 1909, FO 367/165.

[2] *Aide-mémoire*, encl. in Grey to Lalaing, 11 June 1909; *Accounts and Papers*, 1909 (Cd. 4396), lix, 565.

[3] *Annales Parlementaires* (Chambre), 31 March 1909.

the intentions of the Belgian government and 'they would make people think that Belgium was unable to create civilization in the Congo'.[1] In order to retrieve the position some attempt had to be made to show the goodwill of the Belgian government.

Consequently, according to Article 6 of the Colonial Law, a commission of seven members was set up for the protection of the Congolese. A seat on this commission was offered to Reverend H. Ross Philips, the legal representative of the B.M.S. in the Congo.[2] Again, the Belgian government showed for the first time less reluctance towards the granting of sites to the protestant missions.[3] At the same time a plan was drawn up to induce British enterprise to enter the Congo trade. The Belgian Colonial Ministry would have liked to send an official Congo trade mission to the British chambers of commerce. Fearing, however, that France and Germany might ask for similar missions and that Belgian commercial circles might be offended, the plan was modified. Instead of an official mission, the *Fédération pour la défense des intérêts belges à l'étranger* was to undertake the task.[4] Subsequently, Max Horn, a member of this organization, was entrusted with it.

The Max Horn mission, although it won the sympathy of the Foreign Office, was not successful in attracting British enterprise to the Congo. Indeed, the one factor which had emerged during the agitation in England was that while the mercantile classes were agitating to ensure free trade in the Congo they were not anxious to rush in there. As early as July 1908 Morel had tried to launch a company to operate in the Congo with the object of inducing British enterprise to follow the example. By this means he had hoped to force into the open the question of freedom of trade and, if the

---

[1] Grey to Granville, 24 March 1909, FO 367/165, no. 35, Africa.
[2] Thesiger to Grey, 8 April 1909, ibid., no. 36, Africa.
[3] F.O. to Baptist Missionary Society, 18 May 1909; Congo Balolo Mission to F.O., 19 May 1909, FO 403/409. It took further pressure from the Foreign Office before the Belgian government actually came to grant the missionary sites but the gesture at this time was important.
[4] Morel to Grey, 1 July 1908, FO 367/118.

Congo administration interfered with the company, to provide the British government with the concrete evidence, which they lacked, of a breach of international agreement. Even Morel, however, had failed to generate sufficient interest in the project. Some months later a similar scheme was formulated by John H. Harris and Messrs Irvine and Dundas of Liverpool.[1] Again it collapsed for lack of support. There was never, as was supposed to exist, a body of English merchants ready to plunge into the Congo trade and who were hindered from doing so by the policies of the Congo State or the Belgian government. The support which the reform movement received from the mercantile elements arose from an established tradition of upholding the principle of the Open Door in overseas markets, a support which was strengthened by the argument of the reformers linking free trade with humanitarianism.

The second reason for dropping the question of arbitration probably lay in the determined opposition to it of the C.R.A. Morel, who paid a special visit to the Foreign Office on the issue, made the position of his organization quite clear.[2] He warned that if the government accepted arbitration in their next reply the C.R.A. would regard it as a surrender to Belgium. The fear of the C.R.A. was that arbitration might go against the British case and therefore permit the Belgian government to perpetuate King Leopold's system.

It is significant that it was four days after this interview that Grey decided against arbitration for the present. Although he was anxious to refer all commercial questions to arbitration, he told the American government,[3] recent reports from the Congo showed that under the guise of forced labour, the whole time of many Congolese was occupied in furnishing supplies to the State compulsorily. That was a position 'indistinguishable from slavery' and Britain could not go to arbitration on the question whether slavery was legitimate.[4]

---

[1] J. A. C. Tilley, 14 May 1909, FO 367/165, memorandum.
[2] G. R. Clerk, 21 May 1909, ibid., memorandum.
[3] Grey to Bryce, 25 May 1909, FO 403/409, no. 13, Africa.
[4] Ibid.

The attitude of the C.R.A. was symptomatic of the gap which had been widening between them and the Foreign Office. Although their objectives were the same both were now concentrating attention on different means for attaining them. How wide the breach was could be seen in the comments made by the Foreign Office on the interview, already mentioned, between Morel and G. R. Clerk.[1] As a solution to the Anglo-Belgian deadlock Morel had gone on to suggest that Congo trade should be considered as the produce of slavery and treated as such. Exits for Congo produce through the Sudan should be blocked and every Belgian boat leaving the Congo with rubber and ivory stopped and the cargo confiscated. British representatives in every major European capital should make it clear that Britain was absolutely resolved to go through with 'the business regardless of the cost', and should try to secure the support of the government. According to Morel, if a British or an Anglo-American squadron was stationed in Congo waters, it would set the Congo ablaze and not a Belgian official would be left alive. In addition, the Congo State should be proclaimed a barbarous country and British consular jurisdiction established. Morel believed that the mere threat of such active measures would scare Belgium into submission. If France and Germany intervened then Britain, trusting in her right, ought to face the situation. Concluding, he warned that unless energetic action was taken he would 'kick over the traces and raise a storm the like of which had never yet been seen . . . [for] whereas Gladstone at the time of the Bulgarian atrocities had been supported by 11 important towns, he, Morel, had 69 behind him'.

The response of the Foreign Office was sarcastic. 'When asked for remedies', Langley said, 'Morel fails lamentably.' Charles Hardinge noted that 'Morel, though an honest fanatic must be suffering from a swollen head' and Grey, that Morel was 'prepared for universal war'. A year later the Foreign Office was to adopt Morel's programme of action.[2]

---

[1] G. R. Clerk, 21 May 1909, FO 367/165, memorandum.
[2] Infra, p. 252.

Meanwhile, whatever the Foreign Office thought of Morel, there could be no doubt that his views represented the general opinion of the reformers. A resolution adopted unanimously by the executive committee of the C.R.A. on the same day as the above interview emphasized that the 'mere refusal' to recognize the annexation was inadequate to meet 'the requirements of national duty and national honour'.[1] A week later, Dilke raised the Congo question during his speech on the motion of adjournment for Whitsun. He charged the government with over-caution in handling the Congo question which had been responsible for the lack of progress towards a final settlement.[2] Developing the subject further, E. N. Bennett argued that the annexation had increased British difficulties on the Congo question. Non-recognition, he went on, was 'simply a counsel of despair' which the Belgians scoffed at. His remedy was a 'peaceful blockade' of the Congo. 'A single British cruiser sent to the mouth of the Congo and the occupation of the Boma Custom House would probably end the vile system of Congo misrule once and for all.'[3]

Grey resisted the pressure to embark on forcible measures and tried to frighten the opposition by claiming that 'if this [Congo] question were rashly managed it might make a European question, compared with which those we had to deal with in the last few months might be child's play.'[4] He promised to publish the last Belgian memorandum with his own reply and afford the House an opportunity for discussing the matter further.

In order to strengthen his position Grey now laid the whole subject before the cabinet. His belief, he said,[5] was that though their progress would be slow, the Belgian government would in time change the old system. Their Colonial Minister was at that moment touring the Congo and

---

[1] Encl. in C.R.A. to Grey, 25 May 1909, FO 367/165.

[2] Hansard, 27 May 1909, 5th ser., v, 1384–6.

[3] Ibid., 1386–90.

[4] Ibid., 1395. Grey was referring to the recent settlement of the Near-Eastern question.

[5] Grey, 29 May 1909, FO 367/165, memorandum.

it would be 'premature, if not outrageous' to prejudge the measures which he would propose on his return. The possibility of strong measures in the last resort was not to be discarded and these would be supported by the government if the United States or any other power decided on taking the initiative. It was doubtful, however, if that would ever happen and if Britain acted she would be doing so alone. Grey assured the cabinet that he had drafted for Belgium

> a reply which does not commit us to any positive step, and which does not compromise our view as regards the existing state of things in the Congo and the need for reform, but which gives the Belgian Government more time to put an end to the abuses.[1]

The cabinet rallied to his support and the reply was approved.

Grey's attitude inevitably brought the relations between him and the reformers to breaking-point. In a letter to the *Morning Post* soon after the last debate Morel asked 'Is England Turning Craven?'[2] and strongly indicted Grey's vacillation. He urged a more decisive policy and 'if necessary, to go to war'. The religious leaders of the country held a private meeting at Lambeth Palace under the chairmanship of the Archbishop of Canterbury. The delegates included the Bishops of London, Southwark and Stepney representing the Anglican Church; Rev. Dr Clifford, president of the Baptist World Alliance; Rev. Dr Scott Lidgett, president of the Wesleyan Methodist Conference; and Rev. J. H. Shakespeare, secretary of the Baptist Union. It was resolved that the Archbishop should write to warn Grey about his unsatisfactory attitude on the Congo question.[3] When the terms of the Foreign Office memorandum were known[4] the

---

[1] Ibid. Grey had assured the American government of his support if they resorted to force on the Congo question. Grey to Bryce, 25 May 1909, FO 403/409, no. 13, Africa. There is no record of the American response to this invitation.

[2] *Morning Post*, 3 June 1909.

[3] Archbishop of Canterbury to Grey, 12 June 1909, FO 403/409.

[4] *Accounts and Papers*, 1909 (Cd. 4466, Cd. 4701), lix, 511.

executive committee of the C.R.A. was summoned immediately. The meeting was also attended by representatives of auxiliaries in various towns and cities throughout the country, representatives of missionary bodies and interested members of parliament from both sides of the House. They adopted a resolution which considered Grey's reply as 'profoundly disappointing' and called upon him to take some 'definite action' in co-operation with the United States.[1] Within a few weeks the Foreign Office received over thirty such resolutions from various organizations in the country.

On 22 July yet another debate on the Congo question took place in the Commons. Dilke again attacked what he regarded as the 'weakening attitude' of Grey.[2] Sir George White called for 'some more forcible measure' and drew Grey's attention to the intensity of feeling on the subject throughout the country and the need to avoid further delay. Grey vigorously defended himself against the charge that there had been a weakening in his position. At the same time he adopted a tougher attitude aimed, no doubt, at generating a better response from the Belgian government. As long as annexation was deferred, he said, the situation remained explosive. A time might come when some question would arise in connexion with British subjects in the Congo and Britain would refuse the right of Belgium to deal with it. That would cause Belgium a special embarrassment. He concluded on an even more menacing note:

> We wait . . . until their Colonial Minister has returned and until we have heard from them, subsequent on his return, what they propose to do. But undoubtedly as time elapses and we come to the end of this year and are still in the same position as now, the British government will have to consider what steps it is going to take to uphold its undoubted treaty rights.[3]

---

[1] C.R.A. to Grey, 19 July 1909, FO 367/166.
[2] Hansard, 22 July 1909, 5th ser., viii, 632.
[3] Ibid., col. 656.

Grey's speech was acceptable to most of the reformers. For the extremists among them, however, nothing could convince them to trust him again. Morel was the leader of this group. 'I have definitely given up Sir Edward Grey', Morel informed Grey's friend, Thomas Hodgkin, 'he will do nothing on his own initiative unless the public compel him.'[1] Consequently, Morel abandoned for the time being direct pressure on the Foreign Office and reverted to the earlier tactic of stirring up public opinion. Under his banner now marched Sir Arthur Conan Doyle, who placed his popular pen and enormous influence at the disposal of the campaign. Conan Doyle went into communication on the Congo with such influential friends as Rudyard Kipling, Whitelaw Reid (the American Ambassador), President Taft, Prince Henry of Prussia, the Prince of Wales, and so on. His letters on the Congo also appeared in *The Times*. In September he published *The Crime of the Congo*, a sixpenny booklet which served as a handbook on the Congo question for the man in the street. It was translated into French and, with £500 from Cadbury,[2] into German also. In the autumn both Conan Doyle and Morel undertook a successful lecture tour of the country stirring up considerable enthusiasm for Congo reform.[3]

With the Archbishop of Canterbury Morel organized a great public demonstration, which filled the Royal Albert Hall, in order to express 'the protest of Christian England' against cruelties in the Congo. It was unanimously adopted, following the motion of Dr Clifford, supported by the Bishop of Oxford,

> That this meeting, remembering the special responsibility assumed by the people and Government of this country in the events which led to the creation of the Congo Free State, and recalling the participation of Great Britain in the Berlin Conference of 1885; and believing that no greater

---

[1] Morel to Hodgkin, 11 August 1909, M.P., F. 8.
[2] Cadbury to Morel, 10 July 1909, M.P., F. 8.
[3] See E. D. Morel: *The House of Commons, the Foreign Office and the Congo*, London 1910, p. 15.

danger can threaten a Christian nation than failure to abide by the moral obligations it has deliberately contracted; declares that so long as the cruel oppression which, in violation alike of the principles of humanity and of definite Treaty obligations, the natives of the Congo have long been suffering, is maintained, the people of Great Britain are bound to press forward unflinchingly their demand for a complete reform of the whole system of administration in the Congo territory.[1]

It was at this time also that Morel published his best work on the Congo. Entitled *Great Britain and the Congo*, this book was primarily, in the words of Morel himself, 'a very fierce criticism of the Foreign Office attitude'.[2] Indeed, it marked the final break between Morel and Grey. It was also the beginning of Morel's open hostility towards the Anglo-French entente and of his flirtation with Germanophilism. He did not condemn the entente for what it stood for; he castigated it because of the influence which he imagined the entente exercised over Grey in his handling of the Congo question. From this standpoint he readily moved on later to a general condemnation of Grey's foreign policy as a whole by accusing him of seeking to preserve the entente at all costs even if it meant perpetuating Anglo-German tension. Morel eventually came to the conclusion that there was more to the entente than Grey had revealed, apparently a secret treaty which committed Britain to France more than the public suspected. Thus Morel's campaign for 'open diplomacy' was born and so was the role which he was subsequently to play in the organization of the Union of Democratic Control.[3] Morel, the professional humanitarian, perhaps embodied, more than any other Englishman, the transition from the great nineteenth-century crusade against slavery to the twentieth-century crusade for peace.

Meanwhile the object of Morel's latest book was different. In the autumn of 1909 he merely wanted to attack France

---

[1] *The Times*, 20 November 1909.
[2] Morel to Dilke, 1 September 1909, M.P., F. 8.
[3] See H. Hanak: 'The Union of Democratic Control during the First World War', *Bulletin of the Institute of Historical Research*, vol. xxxvi, no. 94, 1963, pp. 168–80.

and the entente as an indirect means of exerting pressure
on Grey. 'If there is one thing the Government does dread',
he explained to T. L. Gilmour of the *Morning Post*, 'it is a
campaign against the Entente Cordiale, and they have been
told that such a campaign will be waged from Land's End
to John O'Groats if they abandon the Congo natives to their
fate.' Since Grey would not adopt the forcible measures
advocated by Morel, the criticism against the entente
persisted until, for Morel, it became an obsession.

Grey, however, was not indifferent to the public agitation
which the Congo question evoked. He had become convinced
after the last Commons debate that a change of policy was
justifiable. As a result he instructed consul Thesiger, who
had recently returned from his post in Boma, to draw up a
memorandum on a new attitude towards the Congo question. First, he was to determine the reforms which Britain
should demand from the Belgian government as the minimum conditions necessary for the recognition of the annexation. Secondly, he was to advise on the question of establishing consular jurisdiction over British subjects, in the event
of the British demands not being met, on the basis that
there was no recognized authority in the former Congo
State. Lastly, he was to suggest further measures involving the
use of force which Britain could adopt if she was driven to it.[1]

Thesiger suggested the avoidance of such debatable subjects as the concession companies, which would lead to
discussion and dilatoriness. The British government should
rather concentrate on the question of freedom of trade, the
solution of which would also greatly benefit the Congolese.
Britain should insist that those territories directly controlled
by the State be immediately thrown open to free trade 'in
the fullest sense of the word'.[2] Furthermore, traders should

---

[1] Thesiger, 2 September 1909, FO 367/117, memorandum.

[2] Ibid. The area which this proposal would have affected included the
Cataracts district, the *Fondation de la Couronne*, the concessions of the
Abir and Anversoise companies, the Ubangi, Uele and Aruwimi
districts, all the districts between Stanleyville and the eastern frontier
and between Lado and the northern boundary of Katanga (excluding
the rights granted to the *Société des chemins de fer des Grands Lacs*), and the
Lomami concession.

251

be free to establish factories on the Upper Congo and the Congolese should be permitted to trade in the produce of the forests. The State monopoly of the ivory and rubber trade in the Upper Congo must be abandoned. Payment of taxes in produce and labour should be abolished and a tax in money substituted in their place. Finally, missions of all denominations should receive equal treatment in the allocation of facilities for the expansion of their work.

Having thus answered the first question on the minimum reforms to be demanded, Thesiger went on to suggest, as regards the second, that an ultimatum be given to the Belgian government. Should Belgium fail to introduce the reforms within the time specified in the ultimatum the British government could first of all introduce consular jurisdiction. The moral effect of that action, Thesiger believed, would be very great and the prestige of the authorities in the eyes of the inhabitants would be diminished. It would also bring matters soon to a head either through the refusal of the Belgian government to recognize the consular jurisdiction or through its refusal to indemnify British subjects for some injustice they had suffered. That would then provide Britain with the necessary excuse to adopt stronger measures. The towns of Boma and Matadi would be occupied and a naval blockade placed at the mouth of the river. Thesiger believed that the resistance of Belgium would be weak since the resultant unrest by the inhabitants was likely to keep their hands full.

These proposals were no more than a repetition of what the C.R.A. had long outlined for the government and dismissed by the Foreign Office as unfeasible.[1] Now Charles Hardinge regarded Thesiger's memorandum as 'excellent'. Grey, too, commended it to the cabinet.[2] In his covering memorandum, the Foreign Secretary warned that

> Towards the end of the year, if nothing satisfactory is forthcoming from the Belgian Government, I should propose to formulate to them that if, within a reasonable time, these

[1] Supra, p. 245.
[2] Grey, 19 October 1909, FO 367/117, memorandum.

reforms had not been carried out, we should no longer be able to recognise, even unofficially and provisionally, the existing Government of the Congo; and to inform them of the assumption of British consular jurisdiction.[1]

Grey expected, however, that Belgium would thereupon appeal to the powers and an international conference would be summoned to resolve the dispute. Such a conference would 'put things on a better footing than they are now'. On the other hand, if Belgium proved obstinate and persisted in interfering with British subjects in the Congo by force, Grey intimated that the government would have 'to be prepared to resort to such measures as Mr. Thesiger has stated to be possible'.[2] It is known from a memorandum of 1 January 1910 that the cabinet approved Grey's line of procedure.[3]

In Brussels there was some awareness that relations with Britain on the Congo question were moving towards a climax and might soon get out of hand.[4] There were some important outstanding questions with Britain which, on account of the non-recognition, could easily lead to a crisis. In particular, two boundary disputes remained to be settled. The first was the Lado enclave which the British government was claiming. The second, and more explosive, was the eastern frontier of the Congo which touched Uganda and Northern Rhodesia (Zambia) as well as German East Africa (Tanzania).[5] On 19 May 1909 Britain and Germany had concluded an agreement partitioning the disputed region

---

[1] Ibid.
[2] Ibid.
[3] E. Barrington, 1 January 1910, FO 367/211, memorandum.
[4] Grey seemed to have given a warning of this kind to the Belgian ambassador. Grey, n.d., minute on Hardinge to Grey, 1 October 1909, FO 367/129, no. 119, Africa, confidential. It is probably on account of this that Lalaing's despatches assumed a distinctly alarmist note. E.g. Lalaing to Davignon, 14 October 1909, Ier sér., Congo, xiv, 3882 and 3883.
[5] For details of negotiations relating to the Eastern boundary of the Belgian Congo see W. R. Louis: *Ruanda-Urundi*, Oxford 1963, pp. 54 ff.

of Mfumbiro between themselves.[1] The British government had then decided to send a British force to occupy a post within their sector. Since Belgium still considered the Mfumbiro to be a part of their Congo colony the British action was regarded as 'an act of aggression'.[2] The British government, on the other hand, refused to negotiate a settlement because they had not recognized the authority of Belgium in the Congo. Meanwhile, Belgian soldiers were sent into the disputed territory to confront the British contingent. For a small neutral country like Belgium the position was critical and undesirable.

Another unsatisfactory situation existed in Katanga. For some time the potentialities of Katanga as an area very rich in mineral resources had begun to be realized. There was also the mild climate of the territory which made European settlement possible. As was to be expected under such circumstances prospectors and traders were eager to get there and most of these people were British subjects from Rhodesia and South Africa. This immigration raised the question of a definition of the rights of the State to land and the produce of the soil. The Belgian government had inherited both from the Congo State and since its annexation was not recognized by Britain there was a possibility that the rights of a British immigrant might lead to a clash between Britain and Belgium. It was indeed in the hope of this that Morel had written to South Africa urging British subjects to rush to Katanga.[3]

Even more alarming was the rumour of an approaching raid to seize Katanga by British subjects from South Africa. This rumour which lasted from 1909 to 1910 could be briefly summarized. In January 1909 a Lieutenant J. Joubert-Pienaar asked Count Lalaing if it would be possible to concede land in Katanga for 400 to 500 Boer families who wished to emigrate. The request was refused. From this time

---

[1] The agreement was not communicated to the Belgian government until 1 July. Grey to Hardinge, 1 July 1909, FO 367/128, no. 70, Africa.

[2] Hardinge to Grey, 10 July 1909, ibid., no. 86, Africa.

[3] *Rand Daily Mail*, 20 May 1909; and *Africanus, South Africa and the Congo* (anonymous, but presumably Morel).

onwards, however, the idea began to spread that certain Boers wished to raid Katanga. Thus by November the *Sunday News* of Johannesburg reported that at least two expeditions manned and financed by Johannesburg men were scouring the borders of the Congo,[1] a rumour which Joubert-Pienaar himself seemed to have helped in spreading. In April 1910 the impression that a plan existed for the raid against Katanga increased as a result of a report from Forthomme, the Belgian consul in Johannesburg.[2] He had met an Irishman, J. Jeffreys, in a club and this man had told him that he was recruited by a certain Prince as part of a band of 2,000 men to raid a territory north-west of Rhodesia —which could mean Katanga. Prince, Forthomme said, was an impoverished adventurer who seemed lately to have come into some money, which he spent freely, and who spoke to his intimates of an armed expedition which he was organizing against a northern target.

Almost simultaneously with Forthomme's report, the Belgian legation in London received a letter from one Douglas Blackburn who claimed to be a handwriting expert in the Criminal Investigation Department of Natal.[3] He promised on the payment of twenty pounds for his expenses, to procure a document

—fifty copies of which are being printed with extra precautions as to secrecy—gives full particulars of a huge and daring scheme for taking advantage of certain flaws and omissions in the Congo treaty, to take possession of a portion of the Congo for trading purposes.[4]

Blackburn said that the coup was being planned by certain British and American financiers and had influential backing. A secret agent was despatched by the Belgian Foreign

---

[1] *Sunday News*, 21 November 1909.
[2] Forthomme to Davignon, 4 April 1910, Iᵉʳ sér., Congo, xv, 4264, urgent and confidential.
[3] Encl. in Melot to Davignon, 5 April 1910, Iᵉʳ sér., Congo, xv, 4269.
[4] Ibid.

Ministry to meet Blackburn.[1] Renkin, dismissing Forthomme's disbelief in the rumours of invasion, asserted that 'the Government must henceforth consider as possible the eventuality in which it would have to defend Katanga against a surprise attack'.[2]

Blackburn obtained fifteen pounds from the Belgian agent at their first interview and vanished, though he continued to write and to promise the documents. The whole affair, however, came to an abrupt end after the receipt of a further report on Blackburn from Forthomme.[3] Evidently, Blackburn was never a member of the Natal Criminal Investigation Department, but had worked on the *Times of Natal*. He was known to possess some flair for forging handwritings. Forthomme concluded: 'Chronic alcoholic, head over ears in debt, he left in the colony a reputation for trouble-making.'[4] This was also the end of the raids and rumours of raids against Katanga.

Nevertheless, it is clear that by the autumn of 1909, the possibility of a crisis in Anglo-Belgian relations over the Congo question was realized in Belgium. Reviewing the position in October Arendt was compelled to wonder how much longer the British government would be able to resist the pressure for intervention which was being exerted on them.[5] It seemed that only a prompt elaboration of reforms could avert the threatening crisis. Consequently, between 26 September and 5 October Belgian Congo policy was apparently reversed. On the former date the Colonial Minister who had recently returned from the Congo tour had been full of enthusiasm for the splendid work of civilization achieved in the Congo. He had also flatly denied the existence of the alleged atrocities and rejected the accusation

---

[1] Davignon to Melot, 7 April 1910, Ier sér., Congo, xv, 4278, very confidential.

[2] Renkin to Minister for Foreign Affairs, 23 May 1910, Ier sér., Congo, xvi, 4381.

[3] Forthomme to Davignon, 25 June 1910, Ier sér., Congo, xvi, 4467.

[4] Ibid.

[5] Arendt, 9 October 1909, Ier sér., Congo, xiv, 3879, memorandum.

that freedom of trade did not exist in the Congo.[1] But on the latter date Davignon was assuring Hardinge that 'a thorough and far-reaching programme of colonial reforms' was under preparation.[2]

On 28 October the long-awaited reforms were published as *exposé des motifs* to the colonial budget for 1910.[3] The *exposé* maintained the principle that vacant lands belonged to the State. However, the government proposed that the whole country should be thrown open to complete and unrestricted freedom of trade. They believed it was prudent and desirable that this should be done gradually and three stages were laid down. On 1 July 1910 one half of the Congo would be thus opened; of the remaining half, one third would be opened on 1 July 1911 and another one third on 1 July 1912. With regard to the remaining one third no time limit was indicated. 'The government', it was declared, 'will examine later on the advisability of coming to fresh arrangements with the interested parties.' Finally certain small portions were reserved for exploitation by the State.

As the zones were successively thrown open, the *exposé* continued, the Congolese would be entirely free to collect the produce of the forests and to sell them to private traders. Land up to a maximum of ten hectares was to be sold, on application, to these private traders for the erection of trading factories and the existing rate of 5,000 fr. on trading licences was to be abolished and replaced by a moderate tax calculated on the weight of the rubber collected. Taxes on the Congolese would be collected in money and in order to ensure the availability of coins the government would henceforth pay cash for the food and labour provided by the inhabitants. Thus the system of *ravitaillement*, that is, providing State agents with food, was to be abandoned and the agents would be given money with which to pay for the food. The *exposé* also announced that many labourers on government works were now free labourers and that the term of service of the rest would be reduced to three years.

[1] *L'Etoile Belge*, 26 September 1909.
[2] Hardinge to Grey, 5 October 1909, FO 367/167, no. 121, Africa.
[3] Encl. in Granville to Grey, 29 October 1909, ibid., no. 140, Africa.

The provisions of the *exposé* were subsequently embodied in a royal decree of 22 March 1910.[1] They afforded great satisfaction to the Foreign Office, for Grey thought them 'much better' than he had 'expected would be forthcoming at once'.[2] Thus it became unlikely that the cabinet decision on the punitive steps which were to be adopted in the Congo would be executed. This was confirmed by the prime minister during a speech at Guildhall on 9 November.[3] But it did not mean that the British government was so satisfied as to be willing to recognize the annexation because, although the Belgian reform proposals had ameliorated the situation, there were still vital points to be cleared up before recognition was possible.[4] The *exposé* only prepared the ground for reopening the Anglo-Belgian dialogue which had ceased since the previous June.

There were four questions on which Grey sought to be reassured: first, would the new system apply to the Kasai and Katanga companies; secondly, what steps were to be taken to compensate the concessionary companies affected by the reforms; thirdly, would the service of the loan necessary to balance the deficit in the colonial budget fall on the Belgian government or on the colony; finally, what was the reason for postponing the introduction of the reforms into some parts of the Congo territories until 1 July 1912.[5] These four questions arose partly from doubts within the Foreign Office as to Belgian intentions and partly as a result of reactions from the C.R.A. It was the Foreign Office that wished to ascertain whether the Kasai and Katanga concessions, the largest two in the Congo, would be affected by the reforms. The Foreign Office was also dissatisfied with the delay in opening up the entire Congo region until 1912. On the other hand, the C.R.A. raised the question not only

---

[1] *Accounts and Papers,* 1911 (Cd. 5559), ciii, 177.

[2] Grey, n.d., FO 367/167, minute.

[3] *The Times,* 10 November 1909.

[4] See Lalaing to Davignon, 11 November 1909, Ier sér., Congo, xiv, 3952; Grey to Hardinge, 17 November 1909, FO 367/211, no. 120, Africa.

[5] Grey to Hardinge, 29 November 1909, ibid., no. 122, Africa.

of the delay but also of the financial arrangements. They observed that

> the Belgian Government, alone among Governments of Christendom, claims the right to govern a tropical dependency in Africa by means of enormous taxes wrung from its inhabitants, and by the issue of loans, the interest upon which it expects African subjects to pay, and caps this claim by demanding of these same African subjects that they shall provide subsidies for the Belgian heir-apparent and his sister, for ex-officials, for missionary societies, medical and philanthropic institutions in Belgium, that they shall provide for the upkeep of museums, institutes, and tropical greenhouses in Belgium and that they shall even pay the salaries of the governing body of the Congo in Brussels and the cost of newspapers and periodicals, presumably intended for the edification of the members of that body.[1]

The C.R.A. attached the greatest importance to this question of finance, which they regarded as the test by which the intentions of the Belgian government as a whole must be judged.

We might conclude then from the tone of Grey's despatch to the Belgian government that while he was ready to renew the correspondence with the Belgian government he considered the time for forcible action as past. His policy, as he told the American government, was once again that of 'benevolent expectancy'.[2]

Curiously enough, it was at this time that the German government decided to intervene in the Congo question in support of Britain. Theobold von Bethmann-Hollweg, who had recently become Chancellor, abandoning the attitude of reserve which his predecessor had observed, saw in the Congo question a basis for reaching an Anglo-German rapprochement.[3] He anticipated that the spectacle of Britain and Germany acting together in this humanitarian cause would inspire a more friendly opinion in both countries.

---

[1] C.R.A. to F.O., 17 November 1909, FO 403/409.
[2] Grey to Bryce, 1 December 1909, FO 367/211, no. 23, Africa.
[3] Willequet, op. cit., pp. 235 ff.

Count Metternich was instructed, therefore, to propose to Grey that the question of freedom of trade should be joined to the outstanding frontier dispute on which both Britain and Germany were already collaborating against Belgium. In other words, the broad issue of the Congo question should be settled by an exclusively tripartite agreement between Germany, Britain and Belgium or by Anglo-German pressure on Belgium.

The proposal put Grey in a difficult position. Britain had been acting for nearly two years with the United States in the matter and it seemed improper to reach a settlement without their participation. Again France had been assured by Grey that the Anglo-German conversations with Belgium were limited to the frontier dispute. To have widened the basis on the lines suggested by Germany without including France, a limitrophe power of the Congo State, was also objectionable. Grey suggested to the Germans that all the powers with special treaty rights in the Congo should consult together.[1] Grey never received the German reply to this proposal. As a matter of fact, the idea of an international conference did not appeal to the Wilhelmstrasse. In the eyes of Bethmann-Hollweg it could not further the cause of Anglo-German *rapprochement* which had been his motive for proposing the tripartite agreement. Consequently, the German representatives at the negotiations for the settlement of the frontier dispute were instructed to confine themselves solely to that subject.

But even if the chancellor had persisted by yielding to the idea of an international conference it is doubtful whether it could really have taken place. Apart from French objections, which had not relaxed,[2] Belgium was showing at this

---

[1] Grey to Bertie, 29 November 1909, FO 367/129, no. 34, Africa.

[2] France was ready to exploit the diplomatic position. When they heard through British sources of the German move, the French ambassador in Brussels (M. Beau) was instructed to make the following declaration to Belgium: 'If Belgium had difficulties of another nature [that is, other than frontier questions], M. Pichon, whose spokesman here I represent, places his services at her disposal.' Davignon to d'Arschot (Paris), 10 December 1909, Ier séc., Congo, xv, 4042.

time every intention of effecting the necessary reforms. Thus, in reply to the four questions posed by the Foreign Office Hardinge had reported, after an interview with the Colonial Minister, in very optimistic terms.[1] Renkin had promised that free trade would apply to the territories of the Kasai and Katanga companies. As regards the compensation to the concession companies, that would not be necessary. Already the Abir and Mongala companies had surrendered their rights of monopoly to the old Congo State and as for the rest of the concession companies, although their monopolies of certain specified products could not be removed by direct legislation, private traders would be allowed to settle and open shops or factories in those districts. They would be allowed to sell European or other products to the Congolese and to hire them as labourers. As the concession companies no longer possessed powers of compulsion, it was hoped that they might find it in their interest to part for cash with some and perhaps ultimately with all their former rights.

With regard to the third question about the service of the colonial loans, Renkin revealed that it would fall technically on the colony but that sooner or later it must be covered by a Belgian grant-in-aid. Meanwhile, too much publicity could not be given to this fact for reasons pertaining to domestic politics. Belgian elections would take place the following May, it was pointed out, and the government could not announce a Belgian loan for the Congo without giving the opposition a very valuable weapon for attacking them. Renkin defended the decision to introduce the reforms gradually. He argued that if free trade were immediately proclaimed all over the country, the companies on the spot could secure a position which would increase the difficulties of future commercial rivals.

On the whole, the assurances from the Colonial Minister were of such a character as to remove the basis for a serious question like the convocation of an international conference. Moreover, it was obvious that strong support for the Belgian

---

[1] Hardinge to Grey, 8 December 1909, FO 367/211, no. 167, Africa, confidential.

reforms was building up both in Britain and in Belgium. On 29 November *The Times* came out in favour of British sympathy for, and patience with, Belgium.[1] On 5 December a rare exhibition of Belgian unity was seen when a memorial calling for international sympathy was issued above the signatures of nine ministers of state, the presidents of the senate and the chamber, the president of the court of cassation, the Archbishop of Malines, the president of the synod, the Chief Rabbi and the burgomasters of the large towns.[2] They were joined by Vandervelde in an article for the *Contemporary Review* of December. Hardinge, in reporting his interview with the Colonial Minister, assured Grey that

> M. Renkin is quite serious in his determination thoroughly to reform the Congo Colony. He may, and probably will, make mistakes; but I think, with Belgian Liberals and Socialists like M. Speyer and Vandervelde, that he is moving in the right direction . . .[3]

It is reasonable to assume that the crisis in Britain over the Finance Bill which led to the dissolution of parliament on 3 December would have neutralized any serious attempt to convoke an international conference. In the subsequent electioneering campaign the Congo question was swamped. Morel attempted to rouse interest by circulating a questionnaire in which parliamentary candidates were asked whether they would support a British ultimatum giving Belgium until 1 August 1910 to abolish the Leopoldian system. He met with either impatience or diffidence.

But perhaps the most important factor in the Congo question at this time was the death of Leopold II on 17 December. It was seen by most people as the removal of the last major obstacle to Congo reform. His successor, Albert I, had visited the Congo earlier in the year and there was a strong rumour that he favoured a complete change. In particular, the disappearance of the old king meant that

---

[1] *The Times*, 29 November and 6 December 1909.

[2] *The Times*, 6 December 1909.

[3] Hardinge to Grey, 8 December 1909, 367/211, no. 167, Africa, confidential.

cordial relations between the British and Belgian royal families could be re-established.[1] Since his accession, Edward VII, disgusted by the reports of atrocities committed in the Congo under the autocratic rule of his Belgian cousin, had cut off all relations with him and would not even permit Leopold II to pay a royal visit to England. Ten days after the latter's death, however, the king was instructing Hardinge to arrange for the resumption of relations and for the exchange of royal visits.

Signs that a new régime had been inaugurated were soon evident. In his speech during the taking of the oath of succession, Albert emphatically proclaimed:

> In the Congo the nation wishes a policy of humanity and progress. The colonizing mission can but be a mission of high civilization. . . . When she [Belgium] engages to apply in the Congo a policy worthy of her none has the right to doubt her word.[2]

This was seen, not as the empty declaration that his predecessor had been fond of, but as a serious gesture of good intentions. Albert also dismissed the Congo camarilla in the royal household which included the former governor-general of the Congo, Baron Wahis, and it was soon announced that the Belgian sovereign had renounced part of the sum due to him from the Congo funds under the 'tribute of gratitude' arrangement.[3]

But not even the death of Leopold II and the accession of Albert I was enough to satisfy the C.R.A. According to Morel the

> whole point at issue today is whether we should act as though our hopes had been transformed by a magic wand into realities, or whether we should face the existing facts as they are placed before us in the Belgian Government's reform scheme.[4]

---

[1] Sir Sidney Lee: *King Edward VII*, London 1927, ii, 274–7. P. Magnus: *King Edward the Seventh*, London 1964, pp. 320–1.

[2] *The Times*, 24 December 1909.

[3] Hardinge to Grey, 21 January 1910, FO 367/211, no. 7, Africa.

[4] *The Times*, 27 December 1909.

The C.R.A. were of course not aware of the assurances which Renkin had given to Hardinge, for these assurances could not be published owing to the Belgian government's desire to keep them from the electorate until the May elections. Thus, on the one hand, the C.R.A. continued to base its case on the published version of the reform proposals and to try to rouse the Foreign Office into action. On the other hand, the Foreign Office had in their possession assurances which modified the proposals but which they were precluded from communicating to the C.R.A.

From now on, indeed, it seemed that a closer relationship began to develop between the Belgian government and the Foreign Office. The policy of the former was to give Grey every possible help in restraining the excesses of the C.R.A. Max Horn at last succeeded in attracting an important British investor to the Congo. Messrs Lever Brothers, the soap merchants of Port Sunlight, agreed 'to study the possibility of establishing an extensive trade' in the Upper Congo.[1] At the same time, the Foreign Office was informed that others wishing to follow Lever's example would be welcomed.[2] It was soon made known from Brussels that following the introduction of reforms a diminution in colonial revenue amounting to over one and a half million francs was anticipated. This dealt with one of the most effective arguments of the C.R.A. for they believed that unless there was a fall in revenue the Leopoldian system must still be in operation. The Belgians went further and also announced the end of the use of forced labour for public works.[3] On the eve of the Congo debate in the House of Commons scheduled for 10 March, King Albert I revealed that he was devoting £40,000 to combat sleeping-sickness and another £20,000 for building hospitals in the Congo. Then the Belgian Foreign Ministry communicated to Grey for his use during the debate a memorandum giving details of 'the interim measures taken . . . for the execution of the reforms which

---

[1] Horn to Langley, 16 February 1910, FO 367/211. See also infra, p. 276.

[2] Ibid.

[3] Arendt, 3 March 1910, memorandum, Ier sér., Congo, xv, 4198.

it had decided to introduce in the administration of the Congo Colony'.[1]

The first debate on the Congo question in the new parliament was opened by George White from the government bench. In a moderately worded speech he reviewed the protracted interest which the country had taken in the question and, after condemning as usual the vacillation in British policy, called for an explanation from Grey. He was supported by Gilbert Parker who spoke for the opposition. Parker analysed the reform proposals of the Belgian government as well as their colonial budget for 1910, and suggested that the time had come when strong action was really necessary. Reading from the Belgian memorandum, Grey informed the House of the reforms already proposed by Belgium. He reminded them of the progressive opening up of the country to free trade and the right of the inhabitants freely to harvest and sell the products of the soil. He announced the Belgian proposal to facilitate commerce by a reduction of fiscal charges on commercial establishments and by simplifying the procedure for the sale of land. The House also learnt that new internal lines of navigation were to be opened up; that more coins were to be introduced for circulation within the colony; and that the inhabitants were to pay their taxes in money while the tax in labour was to be progressively abolished. Finally, Grey pointed out that the new budget had taken into consideration a decline in revenue from the Congo.

But Grey also admitted that there were flaws in the Belgian reform proposals which necessitated his continued refusal to recognize the annexation. He was still not satisfied that the introduction of reforms throughout the whole territory should be drawn out till 1912. Secondly, he wanted to see that officials habituated in the old régime were not entrusted with the job of applying the new reforms. Thirdly, the reforms did not yet apply to the concessionary companies although the Belgian government had promised to reach

[1] Encl. in Hardinge to Grey, 8 March 1910, FO 367/211, no. 38, Africa, confidential; Davignon to Melot, 8 March 1910, Ier sér., Congo, xv, 4211.

an agreement with them. Concluding a well-balanced speech which was designed to please everyone, Grey promised the House that

> [We] will not recognise the annexation and that we will not ask the House to do so until we are in a position to lay before Parliament reports from our own Consuls . . . showing that in effect a change of system has taken place . . .[1]

The significance of this debate was two-fold. First, it outlined obviously for the Belgian government the steps along which their reforms must proceed before Britain recognized the annexation.[2] Moreover, the rather benevolent tone of Grey's speech was taken in Belgian government circles as a triumph for the idea of preparing the memorandum used in the debate by the Foreign Secretary. Arendt recommended that in future such memoranda on the progress of the colonial enterprise should be issued for the benefit of foreign governments.[3]

The second significance of the debate, something which was not immediately grasped by the reformers, was that Grey had made British recognition of the annexation dependent not merely on the decision of the government but also on the concurrence of parliament and after specific conditions had been fulfilled. The British consuls in the Congo must first of all report that the old régime had disappeared beyond recall before parliament would be called upon to decide on recognition. Thus, in fact, recognition of the annexation was deferred as long as the Belgian government wished to maintain the instalmental character of their reforms.

Meanwhile, the C.R.A. were still dissatisfied with Grey's declaration. According to Parker,

> it means that nothing is going to be done; it also means that Grey's back was never really in the thing, though perhaps sentimentally he was all right.[4]

---

[1] Hansard, 10 March 1910, 5th ser., xiv, 1765–6.
[2] Melot to Davignon, 11 March 1910, Ier sér., Congo, xv, 4221.
[3] Arendt, 16 March 1910, Ier sér., Congo, xv, 4230, memorandum.
[4] Parker to Morel, 12 March 1910, M.P., F. 8.

Morel appealed for support from the Archbishop of Canterbury, who replied:

> I am certain that I can speak for those who took part in the great Albert Hall demonstration of November last when I say that we are not merely disappointed but are rendered profoundly uneasy by Sir Edward Grey's speech in the House of Commons . . .[1]

Morel circulated this to the press. But although Dilke pressed the Foreign Secretary for more action in another Congo debate of 21 March, the result was the same: Grey was determined not to do more than delay the recognition of the annexation.[2] The final major attempt to force Grey into taking extreme measures was made on 28 April in a memorial signed by 162 members of parliament but again it produced no better result than the debates. Henceforth, the C.R.A. had to be content with ensuring that Grey did not recognize the annexation contrary to the undertaking he had previously given in the Commons.

While on the surface Grey appeared to be doing nothing, he in fact kept close watch on Congo affairs. His expectation was that the reports of the consuls would be progressively satisfactory; but this did not prove to be the case. All the consular reports were unanimous in doubting the sincerity of the Belgian government as regards their intention to introduce reforms. In a memorandum prepared in London, vice-consul Campbell pointed out[3] that while the areas to be thrown open to free trade in July 1910 and 1911 were exhausted by ruthless exploitation, it was the territory reserved until 1912 (the territory described by Renkin as 'les régions actuellement les moins preparées') that offered the best facilities for trade. He controverted the Belgian claim that 'la contrainte n'est plus guère appliquée à l'heure actuelle'. Forced labour was still applied in the territories he had visited and it would be more correct to claim that

---

[1] Archbishop of Canterbury to Morel, 19 March 1910, ibid.; *The Times*, 21 March 1910.
[2] Hansard, 21 March 1910, 5th ser., xv, 839–54.
[3] Encl. in Campbell to Grey, 12 March 1910, FO 367/211.

the Congolese were no longer imprisoned for failing to provide the required rubber quota. On the other hand, the chief or capita was liable to imprisonment if the supply fell short and these agents could be trusted to bully those under them into greater exertions. Campbell emphasized that 'no scheme of real reform can be honestly applied by the present staff of officials'. This example which he gave is worth quoting:

> On 27th February, 1909, the Vice Governor-General signed an ordinance forbidding the natives to work rubber in the Maringa-Lopori Zone and the Mongalla district during the last six months of the year. The ordinance was hidden away from all but State officials till the 8th of July, 1909, and, in the meantime, a dozen or more sites were offered to traders and put up for auction in the very districts where trade in the only commercial product was forbidden during half the year. In the month of October, 1909, I met 3 officers and 80 soldiers compelling some of the natives in the Maringa-Lopori Zone to break this law. . . . The Vice-Governor-General knew of this as his approval of all rôle d'imposition is necessary.[1]

Finally Campbell noted that the hereditary chiefs were being suppressed under the application of the 1906 decree on the establishment of native *cheffries*. Upstarts, who lacked the prop of tradition, were being substituted and to these people were entrusted the responsibility for the collection of rubber and other taxes.

Most of the foregoing criticisms were furnished almost simultaneously by vice-consul Armstrong although he was writing independently from the Congo. He strongly recommended withholding the recognition of the annexation.[2]

On the basis of these reports Grey instructed Hardinge to make a very stiff representation in Brussels. The British government, he said, had been waiting with the hope that conditions in the Congo would be such as to enable them

---

[1] Ibid.
[2] Armstrong to Grey, 16 March; 17 March; 25 March 1910, FO 367/212.

268

to recognize the annexation but the period of waiting could not be indefinitely postponed. He mentioned recent consular reports which gave cause for anxiety and which made the prospect of early recognition very bleak. He drew attention to the conduct of subordinate officials, the powers of the concessionary companies, and the treatment of foreign traders. Grey asked that if the Belgian reply did not merely show 'an attitude to refute or an indignant denial' of the consular reports, 'but an expression of gratitude' for the help which the British government was lending in the reform of the administration, then it would be possible to reassure British public opinion that the policy of 'friendly expectation' would be eventually justified.[1]

Hardinge, however, was apprehensive of the resentment which might be provoked by asking the Belgian government in writing to express gratitude for the criticisms levied on their colonial administration.[2] As a result, he was allowed to express the meaning verbally.[3] Nevertheless, Renkin, whom Hardinge tackled on the subject, was not prepared to show anything like gratitude for the criticism. He denied outright the charges of the consular officers and suggested that they were 'perhaps unconsciously biassed'.[4] Later he and his staff formulated an indignant and detailed refutation of the charges.[5]

Although Hardinge was inclined to regard the Belgian reply as 'very friendly and courteous', the Foreign Office thought it most unsatisfactory.[6] In spite of the assurances of the Belgian government, there was evidence that most of the officers who had operated the pernicious system of

---

[1] Grey to Hardinge, 15 April 1910, FO 403/409.

[2] A. Hardinge to C. Hardinge, 19 April 1910, FO 367/212, private.

[3] F.O. to Hardinge, 20 April 1910, ibid., tel. no. 5, Africa.

[4] Hardinge to Grey, 30 May 1910, ibid., no. 96, Africa, confidential. Cf. Hardinge to Grey, 10 June 1910, FO 367/213, no. 101, Africa, confidential.

[5] Renkin to Davignon, 1 June 1910, Ier sér., Congo, xvi, 4393 and 4396.

[6] See minutes by J. A. C. Tilley, 13 June 1910; W. Langley, n.d.; and Grey, n.d., ibid.

Leopold II were being reassigned to their posts.[1] It seemed to suggest a return to the past. Consequently, it was decided to administer a very sharp rebuke to the Belgian government. They were told, therefore, that their reply had given no assurances 'of any value' in regard to the criticisms of the consular officers and that they seemed totally unable to appreciate the attitude of the British government. The Belgian government ought to have shown a determination to sweep away the old order by the withdrawal of agents associated with it; on the contrary, they had demonstrated that they were content to retain these agents. In the circumstances, the British government have 'but little confidence' in any early improvement of the colonial administration and the time was passing within which it would be possible to maintain friendly relations between the two countries.[2]

It might have seemed then that after a preliminary reluctance on the part of Grey he was now ready to act on the lines which the reformers expected. In fact this was to be the harshest communication between the Foreign Office and the Belgian government on the Congo question. The Belgians, who were beginning to take Grey's benevolence for granted, were heavily jolted into a flurry of action aimed at avoiding further deterioration in Anglo-Belgian relations. Meanwhile, the first reforms had been inaugurated on 1 July and the way was opened for the recognition of the annexation.

---

[1] Mackie to Grey, 11 May 1910, FO 367/213, no. 43, Africa. The most notorious of these was one commandant Sarrazyn whose appointment provoked a strong protest from the humanitarians. Anti-Slavery and Aborigines Protection Society to Grey, 10 June 1910, FO 403/409.

[2] Grey to Hardinge, 6 July 1910, FO 367/213, no. 106, Africa.

IX
Recognition

The opening of one half of the Congo to free trade and the abolition of forced labour for revenue purposes within it paved the way for the dissolution of the Congo reform movement, for everyone soon realized that in time the whole Congo would be brought under the new system. Nevertheless, as Grey would not accord recognition until the reforms had actually been applied throughout the Congo and the British consuls had sent in favourable reports, the Congo question was overtaken by the Agadir crisis, in which the Belgian colony nearly became a pawn. It was not until 1913 that the Congo administration seemed sufficiently transformed to present a satisfactory picture to the reformers and British recognition came at last.

There were two factors which Grey took into consideration in refusing it earlier. The first was the determination of the reformers to oppose such a step before they were certain that the promises of the Belgian government had been fulfilled. They believed it was the least they could do in view of the reluctance of 'that weak-kneed invertebrate politician whose name is Grey'[1] to act more forcibly. On 14 July the executive committee of the C.R.A. met under Lord Mayo to consider their future policy and Grey was informed later that, while they welcomed the reforms introduced since 1 July, he ought not to have acquiesced in the preceding

---

[1] Morel to Holt, 21 September 1910, J.H.P. 18/7.

delays. The association pledged itself to continue pressing its demands until the entire Congo was affected and hoped that Grey would continue to withhold the recognition.[1]

What was significant in the C.R.A. resolution, however, was not its insistence on non-recognition but the absence of the usual programme for exerting pressure on the Belgian government which had been a feature of earlier resolutions of this kind. The reason soon became evident. For the first time the C.R.A., much to the gratification of the Belgian government,[2] issued a publication in which it was actually admitted that the situation in the Congo had considerably improved and that the era of atrocities had gone.[3] They no longer assumed that the Belgian reforms would be as superficial as those of Leopold II. On the other hand, a strong suspicion existed that Belgium would swiftly slip back to the practices of the régime which she had replaced unless Britain maintained her vigilance. Hence the desire that recognition should be withheld. So confident had Morel become of the future of the Congo, however, that he left on a protracted tour of West Africa from which he did not return till March 1911.

The second factor which Grey had to consider was the reports of his consular officers in the Congo, which he had promised to present to parliament before granting recognition. These reports, with a few exceptions had continued to show insufficient improvement in the administration. From the Kasai region, vice-consul Thurstan announced that the Kasai company had decided once more to start collecting rubber by forced labour.[4] In Katanga, vice-consul Beak, who seemed to have been convinced that Katanga was properly a British sphere of influence, saw nothing good in the Belgian administration.[5] He goaded the leading traders

---

[1] C.R.A. to Grey, 22 July 1910, FO 367/213.

[2] Lalaing to Davignon, 25 August 1910, Ier sér., xvi, 4584.

[3] *The Present State of the Congo Question*, August 1910; *Morning Post*, 30 September 1910; *O.O.C.R.A.*, 7 October 1910.

[4] Thurstan to Campbell, 25 July 1910, encl. in Campbell to Grey, 25 August 1910, FO 367/214, no. 74, Africa, confidential.

[5] Beak to F.O., 1 August 1910, FO 403/418, no. K.3, Africa; Beak to F.O., 11 November 1910, FO 367/216, no. K.45, Africa.

in Katanga into forming a chamber of commerce in order to exert more pressure on the administration and he encouraged Rhodesian merchants to flock in.[1]

The most serious of these reports came from vice-consul Armstrong and acting-consul Campbell. The former, after a tour of the Uele district, concluded 'that a direct system of slavery has been created, and is being maintained by the Government.'[2] His evidence was based on the fact that the government had deprived the chiefs of the Mamvu clan of their position because they refused to force their people to collect rubber. In their places had been substituted the chiefs of a neighbouring clan who coerced the Mamvu by the use of military expeditions, imprisonment and flogging. Confirmed by the report of Campbell, the charge amounted to that of bad faith on the part of the Belgian government which had persistently denied that such practices existed any longer. According to Campbell, a lieutenant Arnold who had been convicted for murder was then at large in the Congo, his expenses being defrayed by the Belgian government.[3]

At the same time, there were also reports from other areas which showed that the new measures were being seriously applied. Reverend John Whitehead of the Baptist Mission at Lukolela, who had been one of the bitterest critics of the Congo State, claimed that the Congolese were at last able to pay their taxes in money and were generally more fairly treated.[4] Vice-consul Thurstan had earlier reported on the reintroduction of forced labour in the Kasai district. He affirmed, at the conclusion of the tour, that 'the situation has changed, and changed in a very radical manner'.[5] On the whole, he had

---

[1] Beak to F.O., 30 August 1910, FO 367/214, no. K. 13, Africa.

[2] Armstrong to Grey, 3 November 1910, FO 403/425.

[3] Campbell to Grey, 1 December 1910, FO 367/259, no. 109, Africa. The officer who had been responsible for Arnold's free trip in the Congo was subsequently punished after the British protest. Hardinge to Grey, 8 February 1911, FO 367/260, no. 27, Africa.

[4] Campbell to Grey, 18 August 1910, FO 367/214.

[5] Encls. I and II in Campbell to Grey, 31 December 1910, FO 367/259, no. 121, Africa.

heard of no complaint of any sort against a white agent of the Compagnie du Kasai, and of no serious charge against a capita [armed sentry]. Forcible measures are no longer used to compel the natives to make rubber; they are no longer beaten, imprisoned, or overawed by the guns of soldiers or capitas. Instead of the work being incessant, as formerly, it is a fact that the majority of the Bakuba are now making no rubber at all.[1]

These reports are not as contradictory as they might seem at first sight and certainly did not appear so to the Foreign Office; they rather led to the conclusion that the abuses were inseparable from the collection of taxes in rubber. Where that practice had been abandoned, as in the areas thrown open on 1 July, the condition of the area seemed to improve fairly rapidly. Where, on the other hand, the collection of taxes in rubber continued it seemed almost impossible for the Belgians to prevent cruelty and abuses. Under these conditions, Grey decided that Britain could not recognize the annexation.[2] While acknowledging the improvements made in the areas already affected by the reforms, Grey laid it as a condition for recognition that the reforms be accelerated to cover the whole Belgian Congo at once.

This was, of course, a condition which the Belgian government could still not accept. Renkin, with whom Hardinge conferred, pleaded that the new system must be worked by new officials whose recruitment and training required time. Furthermore, he pointed out that three years was really not too long to uproot the fiscal system which had grown up in the Congo over two decades. Renkin's main reason, however, lay in Belgian domestic politics and the determination to spread over a number of years the deficits expected to result from the new system.[3]

Nevertheless, from the autumn of 1910 the attitude of

---

[1] Ibid.

[2] Grey to Hardinge, 3 March 1911, FO 367/259, no. 29, Africa.

[3] Hardinge to Grey, 8 March 1911, FO 403/425, no. 53, Africa, confidential.

both the British reformers and the Foreign Office show an awareness that a new era had dawned in the administration of the Congo. This change was undoubtedly the culmination of the zeal for reform manifest in Brussels. The removal of Leopold II from the scene and the substitution in his place of the liberal Albert I, coupled with an ardent desire to win world respect by obtaining the long-delayed British recognition of the annexation, had generated a new spirit into the colonial administration. The stubborn and indifferent attitude which had characterized the rule of Leopold II and had influenced Renkin was dropped. This sign which we had noticed at the beginning of 1910 had become pronounced after the Foreign Office despatch of June.

One of the main features in this change of policy is evident from the colonial budget of 1911 which showed an even larger deficit than that of 1910. Furthermore, the anticipated fall in rubber output from 1,165 tons in 1910 to 715 tons in 1911 implied that force was no longer being applied on a substantial scale in the collection of rubber. Next, it was officially reported that in future the State would not buy rubber or ivory, thus indicating that State trading, a practice which had been persistently attacked by the reformers, was going to cease.

Another feature of the new era was the willingness of the Belgian Ministry of Colonies to avoid acrimonious discussions with the Foreign Office. The report of vice-consul Campbell had elicited, as has been said, a long refutation from Renkin contrary to the more cautious attitude of the Belgian Ministry of Foreign Affairs. When Campbell not only reasserted his former indictment but added fresh ones, the folly of such correspondence was recognized and abandoned. Henceforth, attention was concentrated not towards a detailed analysis aimed at rebutting the consular reports but to the safer course of making a general statement about their exaggerated character.[1] In order still more to reduce

---

[1] Bassompierre, 9 November 1910, Ier sér., Congo, xvii, 4619, memorandum; Davignon to Ministry of Colonies, 14 November 1910, Ier sér., Congo, xvii, 4685.

the chances of friction arising from these consular reports, a more sensible formula was devised whereby the missionaries and consular officers brought complaints against the administration before the local officials rather than refer them to the Foreign Office for formal diplomatic action.[1]

An interesting aspect of these attempts to reach an Anglo-Belgian *rapprochement* on the Congo question was the outcome of the efforts which had been going on to attract British capital into the Congo.[2] The efforts were largely fruitless because of the unwillingness of the British merchants to be identified with the Congo system. A 'Congo Rubber Plantations Syndicate' floated in Mincing Lane collapsed for lack of support.[3] The Belgian government was only able to secure an agreement with Lever by which he was to form a new company called *Société anonyme des Huileries* with a capital of 25,000,000 fr. in order to exploit oil palm resources within a concession comprising five circular areas each having a radius of sixty kilometres and totalling 1,100,000 hectares. Within each of these areas the company had the option of eventually leasing palm-bearing lands not exceeding 750,000 hectares.

The concession was attacked in Belgium by the socialists led by Vandervelde, for they considered it so vast as to create a monopoly which would be contrary to the free trade clause of the Berlin Act. They also complained that it would harm the interests of the inhabitants who had always traded in palm produce and urged that rather than grant such concessions, it was only necessary to expand indigenous enterprise by improving transport facilities.[4] As a result of

---

[1] Renkin to Ministry for Foreign Affairs, 28 September 1910, Iᵉʳ sér., Congo, xvi, 4618; Hardinge to Langley, 29 September 1910, FO 367/214, private.

[2] Supra, p. 243.

[3] The prospectus of the company appeared on 15 July. Its object was said to be to establish trading stations and acquire valuable rubber concessions 'in the vast treasure lands of the famous Congo' and it was claimed that the company had Morel's support. The Belgian Colonial Ministry welcomed the company. Hardinge to Grey, 4 August 1910, FO 367/213, no. 139, Africa.

[4] Hardinge to Grey, 25 March 1911, FO 367/260.

this agitation the agreement was apparently modified to secure to the Congolese in the area the right to gather and trade in all the produce within the concession without detriment to the interests of the company in the development of the palm oil industry. No one cared to define exactly what this modification meant in practice.[1]

Surprisingly, no public protest was immediately made in Britain against the new Congo concession.[2] The Foreign Office, dismissing the uneasiness expressed by their consul at Boma, supported the concession as a success for British enterprise.[3] Morel was uncertain as to the course his organization should pursue. Privately, he made known his apprehensions of the harmful effects which the concession might have on the Congolese.[4] But he seemed to have been anxious not to antagonize so powerful a personage as Lever, hence he avoided any public pronouncements on the issue. When Ernst Vohsen, secretary of the newly formed German Congo League, voiced his astonishment that Morel had not fought more vigorously against the concession, Morel could only prevaricate. The Lever concession was a *fait accompli*, he replied, and it would have been quixotic for the C.R.A. to have taken an open stand against it. He doubted 'whether the concession technically violates the Berlin Act' for, since no trade in palm produce previously existed between Europe and the Upper Congo, Lever was not interfering with any existing trade.[5] In any case, Lever was a manufacturer rather than a merchant. Morel argued that any enterprise going into the Upper Congo and providing earning capacities for

---

[1] But see Lord Hailey: *An African Survey*, London 1957, pp. 751–3, which discusses further developments after the period covered by the present work.

[2] It was not until May 1912 that the concession was attacked during question time in the Commons. Hansard, 9 May 1912, 5th ser., xxxviii, 551–3.

[3] Langley, n.d., minute on Mackie to Grey, 6 October 1911, FO 367/225, no. 59, Africa.

[4] E.g. Morel to Lever, 25 April and 1 May 1911, J.H.P., 18/8 (copies).

[5] Morel was of course exaggerating. Official statistics show that palm products averaged over 4 per cent of the exports. It did not exceed this figure because the administration was more interested in rubber.

the Congolese, under almost any conditions, was better than the situation then existing. However, he accepted

> that the scheme, which I think ought to be very beneficial has been started on lines which I consider, and have always considered, unsound . . . I have told him [Lever], as I would tell anyone else, that all he wanted could have been secured without any concessions of land at all, simply on an ordinary trade basis. However, I cannot force other people to share my views.[1]

What Morel did not reveal was that a few months earlier he had received from Lever a much-needed cheque for £100 to help in the reform campaign.[2]

Although Belgian attempts to attract British enterprise into the Congo continued, there was no other significant response during our period.[3] But there were still other signs which showed the readiness of the Belgian government to make themselves agreeable to the Foreign Office and to British public opinion. When Rev. John Harris and his wife were sent by the Anti-Slavery Society to revisit the Congo and report on the effects of the Belgian reforms, the Belgian government promised every assistance to them.[4] Again, since 1907 the B.M.S. had been trying without success to acquire land for the expansion of their work in the Upper Congo. In 1909 the Belgian government had seemed ready to grant land to the mission but they had found some excuse to defer actually doing so. On 23 May 1911 Grey instructed Hardinge to make a formal representation on behalf of the mission and four days later Hardinge was able to report a definite

[1] Morel to Vohsen, 11 November 1911, M.P., F. 8; quoted also in Wuliger, op. cit., pp. 270–1.

[2] Lever to Morel, 24 July 1911, M.P., F. 8.

[3] Max Horn wrote: 'I am sorry to confess that, although I repeatedly have draw [sic] the attention of the principal Chambers of Commerce and African traders to the openings afforded by the Congo to British enterprise, Messrs Lever Brothers example has not been followed hitherto by other British firms.' Max Horn to Langley, 13 October 1911, FO 367/261.

[4] Davignon to Hardinge, 23 March 1911, encl. in Hardinge to Grey, 24 March 1911, FO 367/260, no. 65, Africa.

willingness by the Belgian government to grant the sites required.[1]

In addition to the foregoing actions, the Belgian government also published an ordinance which took account of the criticisms levied by the reformers on the position of traditional chiefs in the Congo. By this ordinance local authorities were to mark out for the approval of the district commissioners the boundaries of the chieftaincies on the basis of the customs and traditions of the inhabitants. The chiefs and sub-chiefs were to be given medals as the outward sign of their office and were forbidden to inflict any corporal punishment exceeding twelve strokes. Women, old men and children were totally exempted.[2]

Perhaps the most striking sign of the reforming spirit was shown in the arrangements reached between the colonial government and the concession companies of Kasai, Abir and Anversoise. When the decree of 1910 threw the whole Congo open to free trade in stages, the government had rejected a plea for compensation by the Kasai company on the ground that the company did not hold a monopoly. The company had then threatened legal action. In January 1911 the government reached a compromise with it.[3] Shares in the company valued at more than eleven million francs which the government had inherited from Leopold II were returned to the company and in exchange the company relinquished the monopoly which it enjoyed. In the case of the Abir and the Anversoise a different arrangement was made. By a convention dated 28 July 1911 the Abir and its subsidiary, the Isangi company, received 70,000 hectares for exclusive exploitation in exchange for the surrender of the rest of the vast territory previously conceded to them. As regards the Anversoise a convention of the same date gave them 60,000 hectares on similar terms.[4] Thus although the

---

[1] Hardinge to Grey, 27 May 1911, FO 367/225, no. 92, Africa.

[2] *B.O.*, May 1911.

[3] *B.O.*, January 1911.

[4] The conventions are enclosed in Watson (chargé d'affaires) to Grey, 12 August 1911, FO 367/261, no. 127, Africa. Soon afterwards the Abir and Anversoise companies merged together to form the *Compagnie du Congo Belge*.

government still maintained the principle of concessions which it had inherited from the Congo State it made available, by these arrangements, an area of nearly fifteen million hectares for the application of the reform decrees.

By the middle of 1911, then, Anglo-Belgian relations on the Congo question could be described as friendly and hopeful. So close indeed had they become that Grey could tell the Belgian ambassador that he was instructing his consular officers to prepare their future reports not with an eye to an ideal régime but to compare the present position with the one that had existed prior to the reforms.[1] This relaxation in the inquisitorial character of the consular investigations was received with great relief in Brussels and generated great expectations about an early recognition.

Meanwhile the reformers, influenced also by the evident change of attitude which had taken place and its result in the Congo, were envisaging the end of their campaign. Since July 1910 a committee presided over by Lord Cromer had been set up to sponsor a public tribute to Morel for his Congo reform work. The presentation took place on 29 May 1911 when a sum of three thousand guineas, increased to four thousand guineas by John Holt just before the ceremony began, was presented to Morel.[2] He was showered with praise by Vandervelde of Belgium, Anatole France and Pierre Mille of France, Ludwig Deuss of Germany, and René Claparade of Switzerland, all of whom had collaborated with him in their respective countries. His courage, honesty, integrity and heroism were also extolled by several of his English colleagues who had worked for the C.R.A. Although Morel warned in his acceptance speech that it was not yet time to lay down arms, he spoke, not about the Congo, but about humanitarian causes generally. Indeed, he acknowledged that a radical change had taken place in the Belgian

---

[1] Lalaing to Davignon, 11 May 1911, Ier sér., Congo, xviii, 430.

[2] In addition Morel received the statuette of a Congo chief made by Herbert Ward while his wife was given a portrait of Morel painted by William Rothenstein as well as a jewel ornament. *The Times*, 30 May 1911.

colony and relegated the role of the organization to that of
watching vigilantly.

The uneventful progress towards British recognition of the
annexation which might now have been expected was
suddenly disturbed by the Agadir crisis and its repercussions.
The question which then arose was whether the Congo
could not be used for satisfying German colonial ambitions
in order to preserve the peace of Europe. In fact, this was
not new. In 1905 the French had made an unofficial offer
to Germany of her right of pre-emption over the Congo
State in return for a free hand in Morocco but Germany had
not risen to the bait.[1] Two years later, when it seemed that
Germany might make common cause with Britain in
exerting pressure on the Congo State, Joseph Caillaux had
accused the Germans through the French press of having
proposed a partition of the Congo between Britain, France
and herself.[2] The accusation had the desired effect by
deterring further initiative from Germany until 1910. In the
meantime, although the German attitude indicated a lack of
interest, there was a growing awareness of the possibilities of
the Congo for Germany. Thus during the negotiations over
the eastern boundary of the Congo the German government
had again proposed a joint Anglo-German action on the
Congo question with results which we have already seen.[3]

Hitherto, Germany had not shown any desire for a territorial arrangement at the expense of the Congo. By July
1911, however, a change of policy took place. In a memorandum dated 17 July 1911, the Foreign Secretary, Kiderlen-
Waechter, outlined for the chancellor the aim which
Germany was pursuing towards the settlement of the
Agadir crisis.[4] Germany, according to him, must try to
obtain the whole French Congo:

[1] For details of this offer see Willequet, op. cit., pp. 189–190 and
377–9.
[2] Supra, p. 203.
[3] Supra, pp. 259–60.
[4] Kiderlen-Waechter had demanded the French Congo on 16 July as
compensation for letting France have a free hand in Morocco. J. Cambon
to de Selves, 16 July 1911, *D.D.F.*, 2nd ser., xiv, no. 71.

. . . it is the last occasion which we have of obtaining something worthwhile in Africa without going to war. Portions of the Congo, however rich they may be in rubber and ivory, will be useless to us. It is essential for us to push as far as the Belgian Congo in order to be in the running the day the latter will come to be shared, and in order to be able, for as long as it exists, to link up with our East Africa by crossing through it.[1]

Kiderlen-Waechter thus envisaged a band of German territory stretching across the whole of Central Africa from East to West.

The key to the fulfilment of this idea obviously lay in the French right of pre-emption. In asking for the French Congo, however, the Germans were studiously careful not to mention this subject. This was a tactical manoeuvre to prevent Belgium from suspecting German motives.

Nevertheless, the implication of the German demand was obvious to the French ambassador in Berlin and he quickly pointed it out to Bertie during his visit to Paris.[2] If the French had expected that this information would alienate Grey and stiffen his attitude towards the Germans they were to be disappointed. The mention of the right of pre-emption seemed to have indicated to the Foreign Secretary the line along which Franco-German negotiations should proceed. Three days later he sent a telegram to Bertie in which he suggested 'that the admission of Germany to a share in French pre-emption rights of Belgian Congo might be a possible element of bargain.'[3] The next day Grey told Count Metternich that it would be impossible for France to cede the whole French Congo but that both powers could negotiate on a rectification of 'the frontier of the French

---

[1] Quoted in E. Jaeckh: *Kiderlen-Waechter intime*, Paris 1926, pp. 292–3. See also Willequet: op. cit., p. 280; and I. C. Barlow: *The Agadir Crisis*, Raleigh, N. Carolina 1940, pp. 264–5.

[2] 'Germany as the Congo riverain Power in the place of France would claim to stand in her shoes and have the right of pre-emption when the Congo Free State is for disposal which it will most probably be before long.' Bertie to Grey, 17 July 1911, *B.D.*, vii, no. 391.

[3] Grey to Bertie, 20 July 1911, ibid., no. 402.

Congo'.[1] He also referred the ambassador to central Africa, where he promised that Britain would not stand in the way of Germany. If the Belgian Congo were to change hands, Grey pointedly remarked, Germany could have a free hand and Britain would content herself with Katanga and a narrow strip in the East to complete her Cape to Cairo railway.[2] Grey was clearly trying to bring France and Germany to concentrate on a settlement in the Congo basin.

Two events, however, seemed to have made such a settlement unlikely. On the same day that Grey suggested admitting Germany to the pre-emptive rights of France, *The Times* carried a long report and a leading article accusing Germany not only of demanding the cession of the

---

[1] Grey to Goschen, 21 July 1911, ibid., no. 411.

[2] Grey omitted this portion of his conversation with Metternich in his despatch to Goschen while Metternich made a full report of it. Metternich to Bethmann-Hollweg, 21 July 1911, *G.P.*, xxix, 202. It was not until 1 August that Grey wrote a memorandum recording his suggestion on the Belgian Congo. The memorandum is not published in the *B.D.* and because of this the portion referring to the Congo is quoted here in full:

'In the course of a conversation with Count Metternich on 21st ultimo in which I assured him that as regards Africa generally we were not jealous of German expansion, I took the occasion to observe that we really did not desire to extend our own territories in Africa.

'As an example, I gave the case of the Belgian Congo. If ever this territory came into the market, my personal view was that we should not be a competitor for the purchase of any large parts of it. There was a part which went right into Rhodesia, and which obviously we should like to buy in order to round off our possessions there; further north we might wish to make some small acquisitions, which would be more in the nature of a rectification of the frontier, and of course, we should like to have a means of through communication between British East Africa and British territories in the South. But, if Germany desired expansion in Africa, and such things as the Portuguese colonies and the Belgian Congo came into the market, Germany would find that there would be no territorial ambitions on our part that would be a serious impediment to her expansion.

'Of course the French right of pre-emption would have to be taken into account, and unless Belgium and Portugal were prepared to sell their colonies there could be no changes . . .'
Grey, 1 August 1911, FO 367/225, memorandum.

whole French Congo but also of France's pre-emptive rights over the Belgian Congo.[1] Although these were the ultimate objectives of the German Foreign Minister, he had never said as much publicly and therefore could not actually be accused of having made such demands. It has been suggested, and with good reason, that someone in the Foreign Office who did not like Grey's attitude on the question might have inspired the article published by *The Times*.[2] The clamour in the British, French and Belgian press which resulted from the news made further negotiation on the basis of the French right of pre-emption for the meantime impossible. The second event was the famous jingoistic speech made by Lloyd George at Mansion House on 21 July[3] which roused German public opinion and stiffened the attitude of the German government.

Meanwhile publicity had been given to the idea that the pre-emptive right of France was negotiable and the Belgian government naturally took alarm. Flotow, the German ambassador in Brussels, was tackled and informed that the French right of pre-emption could not be given up by France. A few days later Davignon informed Hardinge of the allegation that Germany desired the French right of pre-emption as compensation and warned that France could not barter the right without consulting Belgium. He pointed out that the right had no more *raison d'être* since the Belgian annexation and that the prospect for its sale had 'passed out of the region of practical politics'.[4]

A curious situation now arose in the Franco-German negotiations. On 27 July Caillaux offered Germany the

---

[1] *The Times*, 20 July 1911.

[2] See, Willequet: op. cit., p. 283, note 1. He suggests that it could have been either Crowe, Nicolson or Bertie. There is a note in *The History of the Times*, p. 700, as follows: 'von Schoen (German ambassador in Paris) reported the Matin as saying that the information came to the *Times* from the Foreign Office. No papers on the point exist in the archives of P[rinting] H[ouse] S[quare]. It is not improbable that van Schoen was correct.'

[3] *The Times*, 22 July 1911; Barlow: op. cit., pp. 298–9.

[4] Hardinge to Grey, 28 July 1911, *B.D.*, vii, no. 436.

Frenchpre-emptive rights[1] but foundthat Kiderlen-Waechter
had become more cautious. Perhaps he feared that he was
being lured into a trap which might damage German
relations with Belgium; perhaps also he had begun to doubt
whether it was really possible to obtain the pre-emptive
rights. Anyway the French Ambassador reported Kiderlen-
Waechter as only saying that 'Germany wanted to have
territorial access to the river, and that this was the essential
point of the transaction'.[2] In Brussels, Flotow told Davignon
that Kiderlen-Waechter begged the Belgian government to
discount the malicious rumours which were being spread
about German intentions.[3]

For the moment, therefore, the pre-emptive right of
France dropped out of the negotiations. But it had by no
means been forgotten by the German Foreign Minister who
was merely biding his time. On 26 October he bounded
back into the attack when he suddenly demanded that the
French government should address him a 'secret letter
declaring that if in certain eventualities the question of
taking over the Belgian Congo were to arise, the French
government would take no steps without first consulting the
German Government'.[4] The German Foreign Minister thus
for the first time showed his hand. The French government,
with the settlement well in sight, was inclined to refuse the
request but by the end of the month their attitude was
modified and they were willing to insert a general statement
that:

In the event of the territorial status of the conventional basin
of the Congo coming to be modified by the act of one or
other of the contracting Powers, they must confer between

---

[1] 'Notes de M. Fondère: Conversations Lancken et Caillaux', *D.D.F.*,
2nd ser., xiv, no. 105.
[2] J. Cambon to de Selves, 1 August 1911, *D.D.F.*, ibid., no. 134.
[3] Flotow to van der Elst, 4 August 1911, A.E.B., AF. 1, 20A; Willequet: op. cit., p. 288.
[4] Grey to Carnegie (chargé d'affaires, Paris), 28 October 1911, *B.D.*,
vii, no. 610; J. Cambon to de Selves, 26 October 1911, *D.D.F.*, 2nd ser.,
xiv, 480.

themselves as well as with the other signatory Powers of the Act of Berlin of 25 February 1885.[1]

This was satisfactory to Kiderlen-Waechter and the Franco-German agreement of 4 November, by which Germany obtained a large slice of the French Congo, brought the crisis to an end.

The Agadir crisis, however, had only served to heighten the need for an improvement in Anglo-German relations. That improvement, it was thought, could be effected by territorial arrangements in Africa. Speaking in the House of Commons on the Moroccan agreement, Grey once more threw out a hint for Germany to look more to Africa for colonial expansion. Since it was only the Portuguese colonies and the Belgian Congo that had a doubtful future, we might conclude that it was to these territories that Grey was pointing.[2]

Anyway this was the interpretation which Metternich put on the statement in his report to Bethmann-Hollweg.[3] On 9 December Metternich returned to the subject in a realistic appraisal of Anglo-German relations. The great mass of the British people, he told the chancellor, were alarmed by the catastrophe which had nearly resulted from the Agadir crisis and were showing themselves anxious to enter into friendly relations with Germany. They were as eager to know the desires of Germany as to meet them and agreements could easily be reached on the question of the Belgian Congo or the Portuguese colonies. As regards the former, Britain

---

[1] De Selves to P. Cambon, 30 October 1911, ibid., no. 496.

[2] Grey actually said: 'They say in Germany . . . that it is part of our policy always to stand in Germany's way and object to Germany's expansion. It is unfortunate that the Morocco question has come up so often. But that is a special case by itself . . . [The] wise policy for this country is to expand as little as possible, and certainly no further the African possessions. . . . If there are to be changes brought about by the goodwill and negotiation with other Powers, then we are not an ambitious competing party . . . [If] Germany has friendly arrangements to negotiate with other foreign countries, we are not anxious to stand in their way.' Hansard, 27 November 1911, 5th ser., xxxii, 61–62.

[3] Metternich to Bethmann-Hollweg, 28 November 1911, *G.P.*, xxix, 272–5.

would be prepared to give Germany diplomatic support in acquiring it. Britain had not yet recognized the annexation and if Morel continued the agitation the recognition would be deferred for a long time. For the moment, Belgian suspicions were roused because of the German possessions near their colony and it was necessary not to drive them prematurely into the arms of France. Nevertheless, a secret agreement with Britain was possible by which, in certain circumstances, Germany could acquire the Belgian colony in the future. Metternich then went on to suggest a more immediate agreement on the Portuguese colonies and to advocate a pause in the German naval programme.[1]

Before proceeding to discuss the reaction of the German government to this proposal the impact of the Agadir crisis on the reform movement might now be considered. It will be remembered that Morel had come out in 1909 against the general foreign policy of Grey because of the latter's attitude of benevolent expectancy on the Congo question. Morel had also become hostile towards France partly because of the obstacles which she had placed in the way of summoning an international conference for the settlement of the Congo question and partly because of restrictions on trade in the French Congo which Morel detested. Consequently, when the Agadir crisis came Morel placed himself squarely behind the claims of Germany.[2]

It was this pro-German attitude of Morel which made him see in Germany's bid for the Congo a new way of settling the Congo question. In his address to the executive committee of the C.R.A. on 7 November Morel opposed a premature recognition of the annexation by Britain. Like Metternich he saw that as long as the agitation continued and the recognition was not accorded the Congo question

---

[1] Metternich to Bethmann-Hollweg, 9 December 1911, quoted in full in Willequet; op. cit., annexe no. vi, pp. 436–42.

[2] Morel's views are set out in the following: 'The National Interest in the Franco-German Dispute', *The Nineteenth Century*, November 1911, pp. 834–47; 'The True Story of the Morocco Negotiations', *The Nineteenth Century*, February 1912, pp. 233–51; *Morocco in Diplomacy*, London 1912.

remained open and Britain could with good conscience support a German take-over of the Congo. Germany's main object in central Africa, Morel said, was the Open Door which coincided with the just rights of the Congolese and the national interests of Britain.[1]

Morel's appeal was helped by the consular reports which were published at this time.[2] He was able to point out that the Belgian reforms did not offer any guarantee of permanence and that the concessions made to the Congolese could be revoked whenever the government wished. In those zones where reforms had been introduced trade was still restricted; in the other areas, the government was trafficking in arms. Finally, the rubber plantations planned by the government meant that they would resort again to forced labour. Morel therefore urged Grey that Britain should initiate an international conference on the Congo question and that a Franco-German Congo-Morocco agreement should be sought.[3] When he received no reply he reiterated in another letter that

> To the Association it would not seem beyond the bounds of possibility for one of the great African Powers sincerely desirous of vindicating the obligations contracted by Europe towards the Native Races of the Congo to suggest a Conference which should affect all the territories comprised within the conventional area as defined at Berlin in 1885. The recent exchange of territory which has taken place between France and Germany . . . would seem in the Association's view to provide an excellent opportunity for a final settlement of the entire Congo question on the basis of the Berlin Act.[4]

Morel's arguments were published in the press and, like rumours which had been floating around the previous autumn about German intentions, raised fresh alarm in Brussels where it was feared that his ideas might gain

[1] *Daily Telegraph*, 8 November 1911.
[2] *Accounts and Papers*, 1911 (Cd. 5860), lii, 601. The contents of this White Book have already been described. Supra, pp. 267 ff.
[3] C.R.A. to Grey, 5 December 1911, FO 367/262.
[4] C.R.A. to Grey, 2 January 1912, FO 367/314.

currency and lead to more serious consequences for the Belgian colony. Davignon urgently asked the Colonial Minister for permission to assure the British government that 'the legal reservations formulated at the time of the signature of the decree of 22 March 1910 are theoretical reservations which do not constitute any indications of an intention on our part to return to the former system of the Congo State.'[1] Renkin agreed and on 3 January Lalaing informed the Foreign Office of the position.[2]

Events showed the anxieties of the Belgian government to have been justified. The *Kreuz-Zeitung* of 20 December carried an article by Theodore Schiemann on Anglo-German relations which declared that these relations could be improved if both countries acted together in the Congo question on the line suggested by the C.R.A. Schiemann, as the Belgian ambassador in Berlin pointed out, was a journalist who occupied a very high position in the German press, frequented the court, was in close and constant communication with the German Foreign Office, and was not likely to have written anything on foreign policy contrary to the views of the government.[3] These apprehensions were also shared by Lalaing who noted that 'the idea of improving Anglo-German relations, at the expense of a weak State, could be presented in an attractive manner to the British.'[4]

It is interesting to note that on the same day the Schiemann article appeared Metternich went to see Grey and the Belgian Congo was one of the subjects discussed. According to Grey it was Metternich who raised it at this interview.[5] Metternich, however, ascribed the initiative to Grey.[6] The discrepancy has no relevance here; what ought to be noted

---

[1] Davignon to Ministry of Colonies, 11 December 1911, Ier sér., Congo, xvii, 5098.

[2] Langley, 3 January 1912, FO 367/314, memorandum.

[3] Greindl to Davignon, 20 December 1912, Ier sér., Congo, xviii, 5103.

[4] Lalaing to Davignon, 2 January 1912, Ier sér., Congo, xviii, 5119. See also Lalaing to Davignon, 3 January 1912, Ier sér., Congo, xviii, 5122.

[5] Grey to Goschen, 20 December 1911, *B.D.*, vi, no. 480.

[6] Metternich to Bethmann-Hollweg, 20 December 1911, *G.P.*, vol. xxxi, 81–86.

is the mutual recognition by both that since Belgium showed no disposition towards parting with her colony an agreement on the subject was premature. But this was not the last time that the idea of an Anglo-German *rapprochement* based on some understanding concerning the Belgian colony was to be toyed with at the diplomatic level. It featured some weeks later in the Haldane Mission[1] and the result was the same as on the earlier occasions. One thing was clear: mindful of the strategic implications of alienating Belgium neither the British nor the German government was willing to take the responsibility of formally proposing an understanding based on the expropriation of Belgium. The result was that the Congo survived as a Belgian colony.

Now followed the slow process towards the British recognition of the annexation. Hardinge, who had become disgusted with its tardiness and Grey's unwillingness to despatch him on a fact-finding tour of the Congo, asked to be withdrawn from Brussels.[2] He was replaced by Francis Villiers who, on account of his previous experience in the African Department, was familiar with the Congo question.

On the side of the reformers, Morel soon became disillusioned about this latest prospect for an international

---

[1] E. L. Woodward: *Great Britain and the German Navy*, Oxford 1964, pp. 335 ff.

[2] Hardinge was said to have given the following reasons for his departure from Brussels: 'Since last year I have felt that I no longer rendered real services in Brussels to my Government and that the question of recognition was making no progress. I spent my time supporting the demands of the British Consuls, which did not even appear always very reasonable to me, and I requested Sir Edward Grey to send me to the Congo, convinced that with my African experience, and with the knowledge of Belgian methods I had acquired in Brussels, it would be possible for me to provide my Government a more faithful report on the true situation than the young consuls, sometimes steeped in prejudices, afford. . . . But my Minister refused. He probably feared that the anti-Congolese party would suspect me of partiality because of my long stay with you, an absurd idea! Therefore I have asked to be relieved of my post. . . .' Lalaing to Davignon, 8 July 1911, Ier sér., Congo, xviii, 4986. This reason for Hardinge's departure from Brussels is confirmed by himself. A. Hardinge: *A Diplomatist in Europe*, p. 222. But there is no evidence in support of it in the F.O. archives.

conference. He began to concentrate his attention once again on ensuring that Grey did not go back on his word and recognize the annexation without giving them an opportunity to express their opinion. In the Congo White Book of the previous November, there was the record of a conversation between Hardinge and Renkin in which the British ambassador had expressed the hope that Grey would accord recognition with the opening of the third and last zone in July 1912.[1] The *Indépendance Belge* of 8 February 1912 had also previewed British recognition in July. Morel regarded the position with grave apprehension and he set in motion a counter-manoeuvre to thwart what he conceived to be a conspiracy in the Foreign Office to grant the recognition by July 1912.

He sent to Grey the copy of a recent letter from John H. Harris who was touring the Congo. According to this letter, Harris claimed to have received information that the annexation would be recognized by July and posed three questions which he regarded as fundamental and which must be answered before recognition was granted: first, was it certain that the old system had disappeared beyond recall; secondly, were there any safeguards which precluded the creation of another system of oppression with little difference from the previous one; and thirdly, would recognition carry with it, in practice, the lapse of those responsibilities and limitations which were imposed in the Congo by the Berlin Act and Brussels Convention. Harris doubted the possibility of obtaining satisfactory answers to all or any of these questions and urged that until it was possible to answer all three recognition would be premature. 'There is', he concluded, 'a feature of the old system to which the Belgian Government appears to be firmly wedded, and which, for want of a better term, I must call "Government commercialism".'[2]

Morel also tackled Lord Cromer, whom he informed that

---

[1] Hardinge to Grey, 8 March 1911, *Accounts and Papers*, 1911 (Cd. 5860), lii, 601.

[2] Harris to Morel, 30 December 1911 (copy), encl. in Morel to Grey 19 February 1912, FO 367/315.

the Foreign Office was planning to recognize the annexation by July and without any indication whether this recognition would be subject to the Belgian government making the reforms permanent.[1] Britain, Morel complained, was thus intending to give Belgium a free hand to revive not 'all the horrors of the old system, but the evil principles of that system which strike at the root of all civilised conceptions of government in the African Tropics'.[2] He hoped that Cromer would use his influence with the Foreign Office and also support a debate which would soon be raised in the Lords. On 6 March Morel again protested to Grey against a premature recognition 'until the safeguards of law have taken the place of unfulfilled promises'.[3] He got the Newcastle-upon-Tyne Chamber of Commerce, whose secretary was under his influence, to make a similar protest to the Foreign Office.[4] A week later Morel forwarded yet another protest against recognition signed this time by the twenty-eight members of the executive committee of the C.R.A. and by the secretaries of its fourteen branches.[5]

The Foreign Office ignored Morel's feverish activities. The abuse he had been showering on Grey and his hostility towards the entente had made him *persona non grata*. The Foreign Office could tell Cromer that there was 'no reason whatsoever to suppose that the Belgian government have any intention of returning to the ancient order of things'[6] or that they still stuck to their pledge of obtaining parliament's consent before the recognition. But they would make no reply to Morel. The debate which Morel initiated in the House of Lords through the Bishop of Winchester forced a public statement from them. Under the onslaught of the

---

[1] Morel to Cromer, 2 March 1912, encl. in Cromer to Tyrrell, 4 March 1912, FO 367/315.

[2] Ibid.

[3] C.R.A. to Grey, 7 March 1912, FO 367/315.

[4] Newcastle Chamber of Commerce to Grey, 7 March 1912, ibid.

[5] C.R.A. to Grey, 13 March 1912, ibid. Similar protests by the non-conformist bodies came later: Baptist Missionary Society to Grey, 22 March; Baptist Union to Grey, 1 May; Wesleyan Methodist Church to Grey, 10 May 1912, FO 367/315.

[6] Montgomery to Cromer, 8 March 1912, ibid.

bishop, supported by the Archbishop of Canterbury and Cromer, Morley left a distinct impression that the Foreign Office was still pledged to giving an opportunity for a debate on the Congo before the recognition. He also let it be understood that more consular reports would be published soon.[1]

Although Morley made a valiant, and to some extent, satisfactory defence of the Foreign Office and their policy towards the Belgian government, there was a vital issue which remained open. This was, in fact, the subject which Morel had been pressing for some time, namely, the permanence of the Belgian reforms. After the debate, Morel took it up directly with Morley.[2] At last the Foreign Office did the only sensible thing. Langley wrote to Lalaing to inquire whether they could publish the conversation in which the latter had given assurances that there would be no return to the old system—the very purpose which had led the Belgian government to send the communication. Lalaing, of course, agreed and the record of the conversation featured prominently in the next Congo White Book published the following month.[3] Morel responded:

I am delighted to hear it, for this is one of the two fundamental reforms which the C.R.A. has laboured to secure for eight years. Had I known that this pledge had been given as far back as January, the knowledge would have spared His

[1] Hansard (Lords), 21 March 1912, 5th ser., xi, 586–96.

[2] Morel wanted the Foreign Office to tell the Belgian government: 'We contend that the native population of the Congo is entitled to dispose freely in trade of the produce of the soil, first because that right is the basis of all human freedom, secondly because the exercise of it is essential to free commercial intercourse between that native population and British subjects. But, under your legislation, this principle, which we regard as vital, is explicitly made subject to your will and pleasure, and is, moreover, accompanied by the reassertion of a principle in regard to land which recognises no right in land to the native whatsoever. We are, therefore, entitled to ask either that by way of legislation or satisfactory assurances, you place your good intentions for the future beyond doubt.' Morel to Morley, 1 April 1912, FO 367/315.

[3] Grey to Villiers, 18 January 1912, *Accounts and Papers*, 1912–1913 (Cd. 6145), lix, 343.

Majesty's Government the trouble of perusing and myself the trouble of writing many folios.[1]

Morel went on to ask that in order to fulfil the second fundamental reform the Belgian government should enact 'a simple measure of land legislation recognizing tribal and communal land tenure'.[2]

Despite Morel's reservation this was the turning point of the Congo agitation since the Belgian annexation. A few weeks earlier Morel had still been urging a means of depriving Belgium of the Congo by an arrangement between Britain, France and Germany.[3] But after May he became more interested in keeping alive the agitation until the last zone had been opened than in any change in the imperial authority in the Congo. For the first time, Morel and the C.R.A., were permanently reconciled to the Belgian annexation of the Congo.

On 7 June the reformers made their final views on the Congo known in a lengthy memorial to Grey[4] which was signed by members of the executive committee of the C.R.A., representatives of its thirteen branches, representatives of the Anti-Slavery and Aborigines Protection Society, the Baptist Union, the B.M.S., the Wesleyan Methodist Missionary Society and the Newcastle and Birmingham Chambers of Commerce. There were also eighty-eight other names including the bishops of London, Hull and Stepney, four peers and thirty-three members of parliament.

---

[1] *The Times*, 9 May 1912.

[2] Ibid.

[3] This new scheme arose from Belgium itself. Jules Gernaert, a Belgian statesman, evolved a plan by which France, Britain and Germany would buy out Belgium in the Congo and save the latter from international complications while satisfying the colonial appetite of Germany. Having been repulsed by the Belgian government he approached Morel in March 1912. Morel took up the plan. In a letter of 11 April to Sir Walter Runciman he urged Britain to take the initiative in sponsoring the plan; and in a second letter of 17 April he made the same suggestion to Morley. These letters received no response and the whole scheme fizzled out. See Morel to Runciman (president of the Board of Agriculture), 11 April; Morel to Morley, 17 April 1912, FO 367/315.

[4] C.R.A. to Grey, 7 June 1912, FO 367/316.

The main purpose of the memorial, according to the signatories, was to concentrate attention on the vital subject of traditional land tenure. They argued that it was indisputable that 'ultimate control' of the land must be vested in the colonial authority. But it was also necessary, they said, that that authority should take cognizance of the indigenous system of land ownership. Drawing attention to the existing law instituted by Leopold II which gave the Congolese 'no rights in the land outside the purely arbitrary and circumscribed boundaries assigned to their villages', the memorial urged that the inhabitants should be entirely free to harvest forest produce according to their customs and traditions. It ended with what were described as subsidiary matters which needed the attention of the Belgian government. These included the high incidence of taxation exacted from the Congolese; the retention of many of the officials and agents who had operated the Leopoldian system as well as the promotion of old soldiers to village chiefs; the uncertainty caused by the government scheme for large rubber plantations which led to the use of forced labour; and, finally, 'the interference of a mercantile Administration with trade'.[1]

It was thus implied by the reformers that if the Foreign Office could secure satisfactory assurances on the subjects outlined in the memorial recognition might be accorded. The main issue of traditional land tenure could be interpreted as a plea that Belgian colonial legislation on this subject should be brought into harmony with that of Britain, for while in the Congo the land was held to belong to the State and not to the Congolese, in British colonies the land belonged to the inhabitants subject to the control of the State. The practical results, it was realized, would be the same if the Belgian system was fairly and honestly administered.[2] The only real solution, therefore, was to trust the Belgian government and to see how their professions for reform were translated into practice. Already the published reports had claimed, and the reformers had admitted, a

---

[1] Ibid.

[2] See minutes by J. A. C. Tilley, 11 June, and W. Langley, 13 July 1912, FO 367/316.

radical change in the areas opened for reform; it was left to be seen what would be the reports from the area to be opened in July 1912.

Meanwhile, the Belgian government, still agitated by the prospect of an Anglo-German settlement at the expense of the Congo, an agitation which in fact by now had no foundation, were offering profuse assurances to the Foreign Office as regards their future colonial policy.[1] These assurances, however, served some useful purpose for they made excellent reading in a White Book. They were, therefore, conveniently summarized for this purpose by the British ambassador.[2]

Taken as a whole, these assurances amounted to a complete answer to the demands of the reformers. On the all-important question of land tenure, the Belgian government pleaded that they did not wish to be tied down by abstract or juridical principles. At the moment the Congolese, according to the system which the Belgian administration had introduced, were free to dispose freely of the products of vacant lands. Although the State alone could dispose of the lands themselves, they would do so for the benefit of the inhabitants, the revenue so derived being devoted to administrative purposes and to the development of the country. On the ancillary issue whether the Congolese might cultivate vacant lands beyond the limits laid down by the decree of 1906 which was still being applied, the Belgian government admitted that the permission of the State was required. They affirmed, however, that they were extremely desirous that the inhabitants should expand their agricultural productivity and that instructions would immediately be given so that requests for land from groups of Congolese would be granted.

For the rest, according to these Belgian assurances, it had already been found that the rates of taxation in money at first imposed were excessive and exemptions or remissions

---

[1] Villiers to Grey, 16 May 1912, FO 367/315, no. 37, Africa; Langley, 22 June 1912, FO 367/316, memorandum; Davignon to Villiers, 2 July 1912, ibid.

[2] Villiers to Grey, 12 July 1912, *Accounts and Papers*, 1912–13 (Cd. 6606), lix, 359.

were being granted and would continue to be granted wherever the burden was proved to be too heavy. The government confessed that they were under an obligation to retain the services of the officers who had served the former Congo State; in any case, it would have been unjust and imprudent to have removed other than those against whom charges of cruelty could be proved. The Belgian government promised not to use forced labour in the new plantations which they planned to establish. It was pointed out that these plantations were established in order to open up a new source of prosperity for the colony and to serve as experimental centres: it was uncertain whether they would even continue to be run by the State since a recent investigation had advised that the system was unsound and that the number of the plantations should be reduced to a minimum.

Having received these assurances Grey felt it was time to set the final stage for recognition of the annexation. On 17 July, he told the Belgian ambassador that consul Lamont was making a tour of the last zone and when his report was received it would be laid with other papers before the end of the year. Grey hoped then to be able to tell parliament that improved conditions in the Congo had made recognition possible and thus to recognize with 'the general goodwill of parliament'.[1]

While he waited for the consular reports, Grey seized the opportunity offered by the parliamentary questions of Sir Gilbert Parker to reassure the C.R.A.[2] The C.R.A. hailed this information as fulfilling the conditions they had asked for. Furthermore, in a speech to the International Colonial Institute, which was given great prominence in the Belgian press, the Belgian Colonial Minister restated at length all the pledges which they had given to the Foreign Office.[3] As far as principles were concerned, then, the C.R.A. were satisfied. They now waited with the Foreign Office to see how these

[1] Grey to Villiers, 17 July 1912, FO 367/316, no. 67, Africa.
[2] Hansard (Commons), 23 July 1912, 5th ser., xii, 961; and 25 July 1912, ibid., 1324.
[3] 'Speech by M. Renkin', encl. in Macleay (chargé d'affaires) to Grey, 31 July 1912, FO 367/316, no. 62, Africa.

were observed in practice as reported by the British consular officers.

The White Book which was published in February 1913 covered the period from November 1911 to January 1913.[1] It embodied the representations received from the reformers as well as the assurances and pledges given by the Belgian government—the object being no doubt to show how the former had been adequately met by the latter. A second important feature was the consular reports. In a despatch of 29 April 1912 consul Lamont described what he called a 'sweeping change' in the administration. Instead of the former twelve districts, the Congo had been divided into twenty-two districts and again further sub-divided into smaller units. 'This system', said the consul 'was similar to that now in operation in the British and French West African colonies.'[2] He also pointed out that a reorganization in salaries, functions and discipline of the officials had been instituted similar to those of the British territories.

On the operation of the new system in specific areas, vice-consul Campbell, who toured the Katanga area, reported that

> To anyone who has seen various districts of the Congo under the old régime it is abundantly clear that conditions have improved considerably both as regards trade and the treatment of the natives.[3]

Lamont himself had undertaken a protracted tour of the Upper Congo and especially the third zone which had been opened to free trade on 1 July 1912. He recalled a visit he paid to the head of a British mission around Leopoldville who had complained to him of the leniency being then shown to the Congolese.[4] Like Casement, Lamont noted the sparseness of the population on the Lower Congo but while Casement had attributed this directly to the administrative system, Lamont found that

---

[1] *Accounts and Papers*, 1912–13 (Cd. 6606), lix, 359, op. cit.
[2] Lamont to Grey, 29 May 1912, ibid.
[3] Encl. 2 in Campbell to F.O., 30 August 1912, ibid.
[2] Encl. 1 in Lamont to Grey, 20 November 1912, ibid.

Sleeping sickness has wrought, and even now continues to work, sad havoc with the natives; other causes are refusal of women to bear children; abortion is extremely common . . . native husbands do not excuse pregnant wives from the daily drudgery of domestic duties, and finding it easier to accomplish these without the burden of motherhood, they avoid that responsibility by every means in their power. Over and above, a high rate of infant mortality prevails.[1]

At the mission stations of Leopoldville, Kinchassa, Bolobo, Bolengi, Lulonga, Upoto and Yalemba, where complaints against the Congo system had been rife, Lamont reported that he did not 'receive complaints as to the ill-treatment of natives, but was assured on the other hand, that a very different state of affairs prevailed compared with that of former years'.[2] He found the government stations neatly laid out and the Congolese labourers to be 'a fat, well-treated body of men, if anything, very much better off than thousands of the poor labouring classes at our own doors in Europe'.[3] The tax was not oppressive and the jail-houses were clean and sanitary.

In the second section of his report, Lamont made a more detailed examination of his tour of the third zone. This zone consisted of the Uele and Aruwimi districts, the northern part of the Stanleyville district and most of the region lying between the Lualaba and Lomami rivers. He had divided the zone so that he could investigate the Lower Aruwimi and Uele districts while vice-consul Purdon visited the rest.

Lamont claimed that his route had been unknown to anyone and that it was off the beaten tracks. His investigation, however, did not reveal any difference from his experience in the Lower Congo. He had not come across a single instance of cruelty towards the inhabitants nor of overtaxation nor of forced labour. The Congolese inhabitants of the regions suffered 'no restriction of any kind' as regards the amount of land they could cultivate and Lamont

---

[1] Ibid.
[2] Ibid.
[3] Ibid.

blamed their indolence for not taking full advantage of that fact. Trading companies were springing up in many districts and no barriers were placed against them. He also observed that the higher officials of the administration he met were men who were quite equal to the work they had in hand, and capable of giving due expression to the altered requirements of administration under the new régime. In a revealing passage he said:

A good deal of stress has been laid on the question of the removal of officials who under the old régime had acquired a reputation for ultra-severity in their dealings with the natives. It should not be overlooked, however, that the harshness of officials was, in many cases no doubt, born of the system under which they were obliged to produce certain quantities of rubber every month; now that this forced collection is finished, the relations of the official to the native are quite materially altered . . . The Government is quite determined to punish any outrages committed by its officials or any other Europeans on the natives, and that it does so I am fully cognisant.[1]

The conclusions reached by Purdon, although hopeful, were more critical. In the territory exploited by the Lomami company he observed that the inhabitants in the neighbourhood of Obenge Benge were 'practically slaves' and heavily overtaxed.[2] With regard to the Belgian administration itself he said that there was still a wide difference between British and Belgian methods. The Congolese were taxed four times as heavily as the South African Bantu and in the greater proportion of the district he had visited they were 'purely and simply a machine for the convenience and enrichment of the State, and trading companies'.[3] He concluded:

There is no possible evasion of the fact that the white man in the past (and occasionally in the present) has incurred and

---

[1] Ibid.
[2] Encl. 2 in Lamont to Grey, 16 December 1912, ibid.
[3] Ibid.

justly so, much odium at the hands of the Congo native. The white man everywhere, whether he be State official or trader, openly takes the black woman as his mate, and ignores the effect of such action on the native mind. The prestige and status of the future white inhabitants of the Congo are already formed and prejudged in the native mind, and are entirely based on the actions of the present white personnel.

The only native policy that I have heard expressed is that the native should be taught to work, that he should have no opinion in fixing a price on the goods that he is practically compelled to sell, and that he should be treated with severity and justice, and taught to respect the white man.[1]

Morel, who subjected the White Book to his usual microscopic examination, was suspicious of Lamont. The consul's comments, he said, were 'hardly convincing' and did not convey an 'overwhelming confidence in his judgment'.[2] Nevertheless, he admitted that the reports strengthened the universally accepted view that the administration had undergone an immense change for the better. It was only necessary to look back five or six years, he pointed out, to realize how great was the general change which had resulted from the abolition of the Congo State; otherwise, judgement of the present situation could easily get out of perspective when the abuses even then existing were read.

On 25 April Morel summoned what came to be the last meeting of the executive committee of the C.R.A. In reviewing for them the trend of the Congo question during the past nine years Morel accepted that the association had achieved its main objectives. He recalled, however, that their demand for a Belgian legislation to secure the land to the Congolese had not been realized but he thought that there was no need to press further for this because the assurances which the Belgian government had given were adequate. On the main achievements of the association he recounted that

[1] Ibid.
[2] 'Memorandum on The Congo White Book', ? March 1913, M.P., F. 4.

First and foremost the entire Leopoldian policy, so long and so persistently defended, not only by the Congo State Government but by successive Belgian Governments, has been completely abandoned. The false economics, the vicious principles and attitude of mind which we denounced remorselessly, and which we were derided for denouncing, have been recognised as false and vicious. The atrocities have disappeared or have been reduced to impotence, and with their disappearance swarms of irregular levies which terrorised the countryside have also disappeared. The revenues are no longer supplied by forced or slave labour. The rubber tax has gone. The native is free to gather the produce of his soil and dispose of it in trade. He can buy and sell—the primal essential of human liberty. A responsible Government has replaced an irresponsible despotism. Money is no longer flowing from the Congo into a Brussels exchequer. Belgium is sinking money in the Congo. She is running the Congo at a loss.[1]

At the end of the meeting a resolution proposed by Morel and supported by Lord Channing was unanimously carried recommending that British recognition of the annexation need no longer be withheld.[2] In a second resolution it was agreed that the life of the C.R.A. should end when the recognition had been officially accorded.[3]

The last White Book on the Congo question was published in May 1913.[4] It contained a despatch from Brussels which showed that the Belgian government had instituted an official inquiry on the situation in the Lomami region which vice-consul Purdon had criticized.[5] There were also two reports on the Kasai region which, except for the fact that the trade in the region was dominated by the Kasai company, was of a generally favourable character.

The time thus came for Grey to redeem his promise not to

---

[1] *O.O.C.R.A.*, July 1913.

[2] Ibid.

[3] Ibid.

[4] *Accounts and Papers*, 1913 (Cd. 6802), xlv, 717.

[5] Lamont to Grey, 22 January 1913; Villiers to Grey, 25 March 1913, ibid.

recognize the annexation until parliament had had the opportunity of discussing the consular reports. Opening the debate on 29 May, Grey declared that the condition of affairs in the Congo had completely changed since it came under Belgian control. He pointed out that every other country had either explicitly or practically recognized the annexation and Britain should now do the same because further postponement of recognition would give Belgium 'a justifiable sense of complaint, and would impair those cordial relations' which Britain desired with Belgium. He concluded that it was 'neither justifiable nor politically expedient that we should refuse to give the Government of Belgium that recognition of their annexation of the Congo Colony which has practically been given by all the other Powers'.[1]

It has been suggested by one writer that 'so important had Belgian non-hostility become that, despite some strong domestic opposition, the British government finally abandoned the policy adopted in 1908 and accorded long-delayed recognition to Belgian annexation of the Congo'.[2] In fact, as has been shown, the C.R.A. had declared itself in support of the recognition. Moreover, in the Congo debate initiated by Grey the subsequent three speakers, Gilbert Parker, Silvester Horne and J. Ramsay MacDonald, who were the parliamentary spokesmen of the C.R.A., had all supported the Foreign Secretary. It was soon after this debate that the obsequies of the C.R.A. was performed.[3] Gilbert Parker was in the chair and was flanked by the Archbishop of Canterbury, the Bishop of Winchester, Cromer and other prominent names in the church, in parliament and in the literary and mercantile world. Morel, naturally, was the centre of attraction as praises were showered on him from all sides. Looking back on the movement for Congo reform, he

[1] Hansard, 29 May 1913, 5th ser., liii, 346–7.
[2] E. Thomas: 'Anglo-Belgian Military Relations and the Congo Question, 1911–13', *Journal of Modern History*. (1953), xxv, 157–65. See also Slade: *King Leopold's Congo*, p. 212.
[3] The ceremony was held at the Westminster Palace Hotel on 16 July. *O.O.C.R.A.*, July 1913.

assured them that 'under the Providence of God, we have struck a blow for human justice that cannot and will not pass away'.[1] It was the last echo of the great humanitarian agitations which had punctuated British history throughout the nineteenth century and so strongly influenced British foreign policy.

If then there was no 'strong domestic opposition' to the British recognition of the annexation, was the timing dictated by military considerations? During the first Moroccan crisis Britain had held informal military conversations with Belgium for the defence of its neutrality should this be infringed. It was an initiative consistent with the guarantee afforded by Britain and the other four great powers since 1839 and also with the traditional British policy of keeping away every great European power from the Low Countries. With the end of the Algéçiras conference, the 'little plans', as Major-General J. M. Grierson, Director of Military Operations, called them,[2] which had been hatched among the Anglo-Belgian military chiefs, were called off. Nevertheless, it is necessary to note the main points of the plans since their alteration later is relevant to the subsequent discussion.

The underlying consideration in British strategical thinking was that intervention on the Continent in defence of Belgian neutrality would depend on naval power. Consequently, the role of the army would be relegated to that of a raiding party conveyed to the scene of its operations by the navy, whose superiority would keep the channel clear of enemy shipping. In addition, the British attacking force would confine itself to Belgium, deploying its strength according to the line of the German advance. Thus if the Germans moved on Antwerp the British force was to head for the triangle Brussels-Aerschot-Louvain; on the other hand, if the Germans marched through the Ardennes the British concentration was to take place in the triangle Namur-Ciney-Dinant.[3]

---

[1] Ibid.

[2] Grierson to Barnadiston, 17 April 1906, *B.D.*, iii, no. 13.

[3] Barnadiston to Grierson, 30 March 1906, ibid., no. 10.

The plan for despatching a British force to Belgium was by no means the only one. Another mooted at the time, chiefly by the army, envisaged relegating the navy to the secondary role of ferrying a British force across to France to fight side by side with the French at the main theatre of the war. This plan, which lay dormant until the crisis had blown over, was more energetically canvassed following the army reforms connected with Lord Haldane's tenure at the War Office. Thus commenting on the position of British strategy at the beginning of 1908 Lord Hankey, secretary of the Committee of Imperial Defence has said:

> From the point of view of the study of the Supreme Command the significant feature is that the naval and military plans were as yet being worked out almost in complete isolation. The War Office knew nothing of the naval plan. The Admiralty knew next to nothing of the War Office plan.[1]

Although these two divergent plans were slightly modified by their exponents they persisted until the outbreak of war.

It was the imminence of a rupture between France and Germany in the summer of 1911 which high-lighted the divergence in the military plans of the Admiralty and the War Office. Winston Churchill has given the classic account of a special meeting of the Committee on Imperial Defence which was summoned on 23 August 1911 to consider British strategy in the event of intervention on the Continent, but which showed the Cabinet that no common plan in fact existed.[2] There is no record of any decision on strategy reached at this meeting. Nevertheless, there was a consensus of opinion that the eloquence and lucidity of the army

---

[1] Lord Hankey: *The Supreme Command*, London 1961, Vol. I, p. 64.

[2] W. S. Churchill: *World Crisis*, London 1923, pp. 55–59. A. J. Marder: *From the Dreadnought to Scapa Flow*, London 1961, Vol. I, pp. 244–5; Viscount Esher Oliver: *Journals and Letters of Reginald Viscount Esher*, London 1938, Vol. III, p. 58; Major-General Sir C. E. Callwell: *Field-Marshal Sir Henry Wilson: His Life and Diaries*, London 1927, Vol. I, pp. 99–101.

spokesman, Sir Henry Wilson, had won the day.[1] The Cabinet reshuffle which followed this meeting of the committee brought Churchill to the Admiralty and ensured effective collaboration with the plans of the army.[2]

Sir Henry Wilson was the key figure in the development of the strategy which was to ensure that when war came the British expeditionary force would be bound for French rather than Belgian destinations. 'For years', according to Churchill, 'he had been labouring with one object, that if war came . . . [Britain] should act immediately on the side of France.'[3] From 1907 to 1910 when he was commandant of the Staff College at Camberley he had established close relations with his French counterpart, General Foch. His appointment as Director of Military Operations in 1910 gave him the opportunity to finalize his plans and by March 1911 it had been agreed with the French that in the event of British intervention six divisions would be sent to the Continent.[4] More significant, from the point of view of our discussion, was the Wilson-Dubail agreement of 20 July 1911.[5] By this agreement, the British Expeditionary Force was to land at Rouen, Le Havre and Boulogne and proceed along two independent lines: from Le Havre and Rouen through Amiens to St Quentin and from Boulogne to

---

[1] Hankey writes: 'So far as I was concerned, if General Wilson had failed to convince me, Admiral Wilson had filled me with dismay, and I was reluctantly driven to admit . . . that the Senior Service on this occasion had sustained a severe defeat. No formal conclusions were recorded as the result of this meeting and, shortly after, the crisis passed off. But there is no doubt that, if war had broken out, the Expeditionary Force would have been sent to France as in 1914 . . .' Hankey: op. cit., pp. 81–82.

[2] Callwell: op. cit., pp. 109–10; F. A. Johnson: *Defence by Committee: The British Committee of Imperial Defence*, London 1960, p. 119.

[3] Churchill, op. cit., p. 53.

[4] J. E. Tyler: *The British Army and the Continent, 1904–1914*, London 1938, p. 102, quoting *Les Armées Françaises*, I, i, 48.

[5] *B.D.*, vii, no. 640, p. 629; memorandum of meeting held on 20 July 1911, between General Dubail (French Chief of Staff) and General Wilson.

Douai. The zone of concentration was fixed in the region between Arras, St Quentin and Cambrai.[1]

The divergence between these arrangements and those of 1906 is obvious. As Tyler points out, 'The Grierson plan for a controllable force operating independently in Belgium for primarily British objects has given place to one subordinated to French directives and strategy.'[2] Even more important, perhaps, was the fact that the acceptance of the Wilson-Dubail agreement minimized, though it did not dispose of, the need for a friendly Belgium. As will soon be shown, the attitude which Belgium would adopt in the event of German infringement of her neutrality was becoming uncertain. It was obvious that if the small British force landed in Belgium they would make little headway if she were indifferent or hostile. On the other hand, acting side by side with the French forces, it would not only bolster the morale of the French army but also be more effective in the fighting.

What, it might be asked, had made the Belgian attitude so uncertain to British observers? One reason which affected Belgian policy may be noted. The Anglo-Belgian military conversations initiated in 1906 had shown that Britain was prepared to intervene in Belgium in fulfilment of her international obligations. Britain, however, had not continued the conversations. The Belgians, in the meantime, seem to have recovered from the near-panic created by the first Moroccan crisis and discovered that the Barnadiston-Ducarne arrangements were hardly reconcilable with their neutrality.[3] Baron Greindl, Belgian ambassador in Berlin, confident of successive Belgian governments, and like most of his colleagues staunchly Germanophil, was expressing their attitude when he wrote on 5 April 1906 of 'the singular proposals which

---

[1] This was the plan outlined by Wilson to the Committee of Imperial Defence meeting of 23 August 1911. It was later modified by the famous French Plan XVII.

[2] Tyler: op. cit., p. 125.

[3] Cf. Jonathan E. Helmreich: 'Belgian Concern over Neutrality and British Intentions, 1906–14', *J.M.H.*, xxxvi, (1964), 418.

Colonel Barnadiston has made to General Ducarne'.[1] A few weeks later, he clearly attacked British 'intrigue' aimed at protecting 'us against a German attack which the German Government has never contemplated'.[2] This view was strengthened by the Hague Peace Conference of 1907 which had reaffirmed that Belgian neutrality would be respected. It seemed to most Belgians that their security was not threatened.

Nevertheless, the need for an effective Belgian army capable of offering resistance to any invader was acutely felt by Leopold II, for it was not easy to forget the hint dropped by William II in 1904.[3] To his appeals for strengthening the Antwerp fortifications and substituting personal service for the inefficient system of *remplacements* the Belgian parliament and public opinion remained either indifferent or hostile. At the end of 1908 the king, who had a year to live, was able to goad Franz Schollaert, leader of the Catholic majority, into introducing a law to abolish the *remplacements*. Schollaert had to convince the chamber, however, that such reforms were necessary, for it was argued that the powers, especially Britain, were guarantors of the safety of the country. It was here that the deterioration in Anglo-Belgian relations over the Congo question helped. In order to counter the argument of the *Ligue Antimilitariste* it was pointed out that Belgium could no longer rely on her guarantors; certainly not on the English, who had refused to recognize Belgian annexation of the Congo. Belgium, so the plea continued, must fall back on her own resources in order to maintain her independence. Underlining the altered

[1] Greindl to Favereau, 5 April 1906, *Auswärtiges Amt, European politics during the decade before the War as described by Belgian diplomatists*, Berlin 1915, no. 17, pp. 26–7.

[2] L. Albertini: *The Origins of the War of* 1914, London 1957, Vol. III, p. 422, quoting J. Wullus-Rudiger: *La Belgique et l'équilibre européen*, Paris 1935, p. 25.

[3] The German Emperor had warned that 'he would "allow himself to be guided by strategic considerations alone" if Belgium did not join him in the event of war.' Neal Ascherson: op. cit. Cf. Daye: op. cit., pp. 466–7, quoting *Memoirs du chancelier prince de Bullow*, Paris 1930, pp. 110–11.

situation further, the Belgian Chief of Staff was asked to
furnish plans for repelling an invasion not only from the
direction of Germany but also from the West.[1]

Thus allusion to Britain as a potential aggressor was made
to serve as a weapon against opponents of military reform.
There was also another purpose behind it. It was meant to
act as a pressure on the British government to recognize the
annexation of the Congo. The need for an early recognition
had become more urgent following the Franco-German
settlement of the Agadir crisis which hinted at a future
partition of the Congo as well as the Haldane Mission.[2]

If indeed it was military strategy solely which influenced
Grey in his Congo policy it is difficult to see why he should
not have modified his attitude considerably, for it was about
this time that he was receiving reports that Belgium was
becoming anti-British. Since October 1911 the French
General Staff had been actively canvassing the idea of an
offensive in Belgium which would anticipate German
violation of her neutrality.[3] The French government raised
the issue in March 1912 with the Foreign Office but Arthur
Nicolson, the Permanent Under-Secretary, was non-committal. The army took up the idea. Sir John Ffrench, who
had succeeded Lord Nicholson as Chief of the Imperial
General Staff, seemed to have had reservations on the
Wilson-Dubail agreement which made no provision for
landing in Belgium and he sought an alternative plan that
would be purely Belgian.[4] Consequently, Bridges, the military
attaché in Brussels, was instructed to 'try out the ground' in
an interview with Jungbluth, the Belgian Chief of Staff. Thus
on 23 April Bridges informed Jungbluth that if war had
broken out at the time of the Agadir crisis England, without awaiting Belgian invitation, would have landed troops
in Belgium. This was certainly not the view of the British
government and indeed contradicted the Wilson-Dubail
agreement. As Professor Emile Cammaerts has said, however,

[1] Wullus-Rudiger: op. cit., p. 66.
[2] Supra, pp. 281–90.
[3] Albertini: op. cit., iii, pp. 428 ff.
[4] Cf. Tyler: op. cit., pp. 130 ff.

the incident 'left a painful impression in Brussels'.[1] Commenting on a plan drawn up by General Ceulemans to counter a German invasion Greindl could not resist pointing out that 'the idea of an enveloping movement from the north has certainly entered into the arrangements of the *Entente Cordiale*'. Jungbluth, in fact, had warned that Belgian arms would in the circumstance have been turned against the English forces and his stand was confirmed in writing on the authority of the Foreign Minister. Belgian apprehension was impressed on Captain Kelly, British naval attaché, by the Belgian War Minister when he said that 'a breach of Belgian neutrality lay more from England than anywhere else';[2] and also on Bridges a few weeks later.[3] The British minister, Sir Francis Villiers, was in turn told by Baron van der Elst, secretary general at the Belgian Foreign Ministry, that if Belgian neutrality was violated 'it would *not* be from the German side';[4] a view which was re-echoed by Count Buisseret, Belgian minister at St Petersburg.[5] Finally the *XX*e *Siècle*, which was regarded as the organ of the premier, reported on 7 November 1912, that the Entente Cordiale was 'as dangerous for Belgium in case of war as Germany could be'.[6]

It was easy for the British representatives in Brussels to interpret Belgian equivocation as the result of the failure by Britain to recognize the annexation. Nevertheless, there were more fundamental reasons which they seem to have overlooked. Cultural and political ties bound the majority of Belgians to Germany. Secondly, German investments in Belgium had given her by 1912 a dominant influence in that country. There was also the immediate significant factor that

---

[1] Emile Cammaerts: 'The Belgian Military Conversations of 1912', *The Contemporary Review*, cxiiv (1933), pp. 50–1.

[2] Capt. Kelly to Villiers, 12 September 1912, encl. in no. 324, B.D., viii.

[3] Villiers to Grey, 9 October 1912, ibid., no. 326.

[4] Villiers to Langley, 5 October 1912, ibid., no. 325.

[5] Minute by Onslow on Villiers to Onslow, 2 November 1912, ibid., no. 327.

[6] Klobukowski to Poincaré, 7 November 1912, *D.D.F.*, 3rd ser., iv, no. 385.

'the Belgian Government was unwilling to look the danger in the face however menacingly it loomed up ahead'.[1] Above all:

> as a result of England's entry into the Dual Entente, the declarations of Colonels Barnadiston and Bridges, and the emotion provoked in England by the plan to fortify Flushing, a complete reversal of opinion occurred in official Belgian circles concerning the opportuneness and efficacy of British assistance.[2]

Grey, on his part, did not apparently share the anxiety in the Brussels embassy for in the autumn of 1912 he saw nothing which endangered peace in Europe.[3] The issue as far as he was concerned was whether the initiative for violating Belgian neutrality would eventually come from the western allies or from Germany. His view was that if 'Germany does not violate the neutrality of Belgium no one else will do so'.[4] Later he squashed French plans to anticipate Germany in invading Belgium.[5]

Then, as the work of the Committee of Imperial Defence proceeded, it was inevitable that the position of the Low Countries would be examined. At the meeting held on 6 December 1912, which was presided over by the prime minister and was attended by Lloyd George, Winston Churchill, Haldane, Desart, Ffrench and Nicolson, the subject of 'Trading with the Enemy' was discussed.[6] The conclusion was reached that

> in order to bring the greatest possible economic pressure upon Germany, it was essential that the Netherlands and Belgium

---

[1] Albertini: op. cit., Vol. III, p. 446.

[2] Helmreich: op. cit., p. 426, quoting Gaiffier (general director of policy), 9 October 1913, Belgian Foreign Ministry Archives, Classement Neutralité, Indépendance, Défense Militaire de la Belgique, XIII, note for Davignon.

[3] Esher: op. cit., Vol. III, p. 88.

[4] Minute by Grey on Villiers to Grey, 9 October 1912, B.D., viii, no. 326, minute.

[5] Joffre, op. cit., Vol. I, p. 54.

[6] 'Trading with the Enemy', 6 December 1912, Cab. 2/3/1.

should either be entirely friendly to this country, in which case we should limit their oversea trade, or that they should be definitely hostile, in which case we should extend the blockade to their ports.[1]

It was at this meeting, and as a result of it, that Nicolson was asked to ascertain 'whether, in the event of a European war, Belgium would be likely to be on our side or against us'.[2]

As Nicolson himself had anticipated, Villiers, to whom the inquiry was directed, was unable to give a clear answer although he pointed out that if Britain and France entered Belgium before the Germans actually did, and without the prior agreement with or invitation from the Belgian government, they would be unwelcome. In spite of this exchange and Villiers' hint at 'some distrust of us due to the impatience, rapidly growing, at our delay in recognizing the annexation of the Congo' British official policy as represented by Grey did not alter. He merely reaffirmed to Count Lalaing that Britain would not be the *first* to violate Belgian neutrality.[3]

Although, as we have seen, the annexation of the Congo by Belgium was recognized by Britain a month later, there is no justification to draw the conclusion that a connexion existed between the recognition and the anxiety over Belgian attitude. In fact, the date of the recognition is sufficiently explained by the progress of reform in the Congo. As should by now be clear, the problem of recognition and the problem of military co-operation were two quite separate aspects of British policy which had been developing largely in independence of each other for many years. If the British government had really been worried by an overwhelming urge to secure Belgium's military collaboration they would probably have been tempted to give in on the Congo question much earlier. The actions of the Foreign Secretary do not show he was in any haste. It would be recalled that he had promised in July 1912 to lay the necessary documents

---

[1] Ibid.

[2] Nicolson: op. cit., p. 398.

[3] Grey to Villiers, 7 April 1913, B.D., viii, no. 330.

before the end of the year which would enable him to recognize with the consent of parliament.[1] It was in fact not until February 1913 that the White Book was published. One could well understand the impatience of the Belgians which Villiers had observed.

Finally, although the Congo question dominated Anglo-Belgian relations between 1907 and 1911 its significance as a corrosive factor was diminishing. This was especially the case as far as Grey was concerned. Hence, in spite of the Agadir crisis, he maintained until May 1913 his adherence to the procedure for recognition which he had outlined in March 1910. In any case, in the spring of 1913 few were aware of the catastrophe which would overwhelm Europe the following year and there was, in the circumstance, no conceivable reason then for Grey hastily to appease the Belgian government for the purpose of tidying up British military strategy. Britain recognized Belgian annexation of the Congo when she did merely because there was no further justification for a contrary action.

It would be interesting to examine to what extent subsequent Belgian policy in the Congo justified the expectations and optimism of the C.R.A. but this subject does not belong to the present work.[2] It must be observed, however, that under the pressure of Britain Belgium had reluctantly assumed responsibility for a task which was not, and could not, be easy. The mass of the Belgians were not interested in an imperial venture; they wanted their resources to be ploughed back into the country and not exported to balance colonial budgets. Therefore, the policy of the Belgian government with regard to administrative changes in the Congo which would entail expenditure of Belgian revenue had to be cautious. Nevertheless, in the short term between the annexation of the Congo and British recognition the Belgians had succeeded in uprooting the worst evils of the Leopoldian system. With the prospects of the mineral

---

[1] Supra, p. 297.
[2] See Roger Anstey: *King Leopold's Legacy*, London 1966.

riches of Katanga becoming brighter and with the palm oil
enterprise of Lever indicating other channels for offsetting
the decline in rubber production, the future looked more
promising for the Congo under its new paternalistic régime
than under the irresponsible autocracy of Leopold II.

Appendix I

W. H. Bentley to A. H. Baynes, 29 November 1888, *B.M.S.*
Papers

We have made an arrangement with Mr. Roger Casement
to come & help us for some 3 or 4 months; & expect him
here at the end of December. This will free Mr. Slade to
take Mr. Harrison's place at Lokolele; that he may free
Mr. Grenfell from the "Peace". Mr. Casement was first
known as a Purser on one of the Coast line of Steamers.
Then he entered the service of the State, for transport work.
Then the Belgians cleared all the English out of their
service by handing them over to the Sanford exploring
Expedn. Mr. C[asement] transported their St[eamer] the
"Florida". When she was ready he was appointed to their
Station up the Kasai. The day they started he had a difference
of opinion with the manager & left them. He was at once
engaged by the State to manage the transport & shiftings
of camp of the Railway Surveyors; & had just finished that
business & was adrift again when I made the arrangement
with him. It was no sudden move however; for you know
how much talk and writing there [h]as been about the
collateral work & the advisability of employing a "lay
helper" or two. Mr. Grenfell & I both felt the difficulty of
that, & nothing was done. When going down country with
my wife I learned from Mr. Hoste of Lukunga (A.B.M.U.)
that Mr. Casement had been recently led to Christ. I was
specially glad to hear it for Casement is very highly esteemed
by every one out here; a perfect gentleman & very good &
patient with the natives. At Mbanza Manteke I saw him but
Mr. Richards & the news of the work there took all my
attention. On my return Richards & I were talking about
him, & he said that he had an idea that Casement would
like to enter our service if it were possible. I had neither

thought or hinted of anything of the kind but made a mental note of it. At Wathen Slade told me of the letter he had written to you & of correspondence which had passed between himself & Mr. Grenfell, on the subject of lay helpers. Casement was felt to be the fittest man we could find anywhere to help us. I wrote to Mr. Grenfell & obtained his opinion about the matter. He thought that under the circumstances we might very well take him for a short time provided that I could make sure of certain points, if so by all means make a purely temporary arrangement, he was in full accord. At this point Mr. Slade, who was very friendly with Casement, & very anxious for the matter; wrote of his own accord & privately to C[asement] while I was away on the S.S. road. It was a rather unconstitutional step; but as no harm has come of it never mind. On my return he had received his answer; I wrote to Mr. Grenfell telling him what had been done & sent him the reply. He answered that as far as C[asement] was concerned we might go further. He knew what we were talking about & was evidently ready to look at the proposal very favourably; he was quite ready to support me in anything I might do. Then came the telegram which only accentuated what we felt. It seemed that we might well make such a temporary arrangement as would help until at least Mr. Cameron was here. The Railway Engineers came here a fortnight ago & we invited Mr. Casement to stay with us for the day or two. A favourable opportunity offered to talk the matter over.

The railway survey was over & he was therefore seeking another appointment. No further railway operations would be attempted until after the rains were over (May). Any how he would like to have some employment for a few months. At the same time it was a great pleasure & gratification to him that we should think of asking him to come to our assistance. He would like to be doing something really useful in the country. He did not know whether he would be able to render us satisfactory service; & all things considered such a temporary engagement as we suggested would be most agreeable to him & most convenient to both parties. I feared that we would scarcely be able to offer him anything worth his while in the way of salary; our single missionaries received an allowance of £120 per ann[um] & boarded themselves out of that. He said that would be sufficient for him; so all such details were arranged; & he agreed to join us as lay helper or whatever the position may be called, for 3 or 4 months at a remuneration identical in every way with the allowance to single men in our mission. At the end of the period there is no further responsibility on either side. So far I am sure that we could not have done better either in terms or type of man. He is an Irish man I believe & well connected. Mr. Bannister the vice consul at Loanda married his aunt. Jefferson who bought a position in Stanley's expedition & is with him now if they are alive, is his cousin. His general bearing & all that I have learned mark him as a gentleman. His treatment of the natives is all that could be desired so far as I can learn; I managed very delicately to get an assurance also that there had been nothing in his manner of life out here which would cast reflection on us did he become identified with us. I do not think that we have any grounds of apprehension on those lines. Then as to his religious convictions & experience. He speaks very definitely of his conversion & faith in Christ, which he dates from the early part of this year & attributing much to the influence & conversation of Mr. Hoste . . . . Mr. Casement will free Mr. Slade at once or at least as soon as he returns from the coast & Mboma [Boma]. He will manage the transport, building, planting, accounts & correspondence, & the general work of the station.

Appendix II

NOTE GIVEN BY KING LEOPOLD II TO JONES

F.O. 10/807 (unsigned, undated)

Monsieur le Ministre,

Par ma lettre du 14 Mars dernier, j'ai eu l'honneur de demander à Votre Excellence de bien vouloir nous communiquer les faits d'abus dans l'Etat du Congo auxquels se référaient les rapports des agents consulaires mentionnés dans une déclaration de Lord Cranborne à la Chambre des Communes, en ajoutant que l'intention du Gouvernement du Congo était de soumettre ces faits à un examen des plus attentifs et d'ordonner éventuellement les recherches qui pourraient être utiles à l'établissement des responsabilités— Votre Excellence sait d'ailleurs que le Gouvernement de l'Etat ne tolère pas que les actes délicteux notamment à l'égard des indigènes, restent impunis sur ses territoires.

La presse anglaise vient d'annoncer que M. le Consul Britannique qui est rentré récemment en Angleterre, après avoir effectué un voyage dans l'Etat Indépendant du Congo, est occupé à préparer son rapport pour le Foreign Office.

Je viens prier Votre Excellence de bien vouloir demander à Son Gouvernement de nous communiquer, lorsqu'il se trouvera rédigé, le rapport que M. Casement remettra prochainement, d'après les journaux, à son Gouvernement.

L'intérêt de la vérité et le souci de ne pas laisser s'accréditer d'inexactes opinions demandent que nos deux Etats s'entendent pour donner au rapport du Consul et aux observations qu'il appellerait de notre part une même et simultanée publicité.

Bibliography

I. IN THE PUBLIC RECORDS OFFICE, LONDON.

Much of the Foreign Office correspondence which constitutes the major source of the present work has not before been used. This is especially so in the case of the series after 1902. A detailed description is given below.

For the Casement Inquiry, I have consulted his original diary which was one of those impounded by the prosecution after Casement's arrest in 1916. They can now be seen with the special permission of the Home Secretary. Although there are still people who doubt the authenticity of the diaries (and, indeed, they have never been subjected to expert examination) there is no doubt in the mind of a layman like myself, after reading several letters written by Casement, that he was the author of at least the greater part of the diaries.

FO 84, Slave Trade:
  23 volumes listed under Belgium and containing diplomatic correspondence with Brussels, and, under Portugal containing consular correspondence with Loanda. Another 15 volumes listed under Belgium relate to the Slave Trade Conference in Brussels.
FO 63, Portugal, 1888–1900:
  21 volumes of correspondence with consuls at Loanda under whom was the Congo consulate. In 1900 a consul was appointed for the Congo and Loanda ceased to have any supervision over Congo State affairs.
FO 10, Belgium, 1893–9:
  62 volumes of diplomatic correspondence listed under Africa. These also include consular correspondence relating to the Congo State. Other volumes marked Various (Treaty and Africa) contain interesting information on the Congo.
FO 2, Belgium, 1899–1902:

20 volumes listed under Africa and containing diplomatic and consular correspondence relating to the Congo State.

FO 27, France, 1898–1905:
9 volumes listed under Trade in French Congo. The correspondence relates to the seizure of the trade goods of British merchants by French concession companies.

FO 10, Belgium, 1903–5:
23 volumes listed under Africa and containing diplomatic and consular correspondence.

FO 2, Africa, 1903–5:
6 volumes listed under Belgium relating to Congo State affairs.

FO 367, Africa, 1905–13:
32 volumes listed under Belgium and the Congo. There are 31 other very important volumes marked Congo Administration, Case 616.

FO 403, Africa, Confidential Prints:
41 volumes relating to the Congo State.

FO 800, General:
These contain the private papers of Lansdowne, Grey and the Foreign Office officials. For the present study FO 800/116 (Lansdowne), FO 800/41 (Grey) and FO 800/2 (Sanderson) are the most useful. The most important documents in the Grey Papers relating to the Congo are copies of documents in the FO files above. I have preferred to use the originals.

HO 161, The Casement Diaries:
The diaries consist of an Army Field Note Book, HO 161/1; a Letts's Pocket Diary for 1903, HO 161/2; a Letts's Diary for 1910, HO 161/3; a Letts's Desk Diary for 1911, HO 161/4; and an Accounts Book for 1911 with some entries for 1910, HO 161/5.

II. IN THE ARCHIVES OF THE MINISTÈRE DES AFFAIRES ETRANGÈRES, BRUSSELS

The archives of the Belgian Ministry for Foreign Affairs have been very useful for most of the Belgian diplomatists took a great interest in the Congo question. The destruction of the archives of the Congo State, on the orders of Leopold II, is an irreparable loss although Belgian historians such as Professor J. Stengers and A. Roeykens have helped considerably in piecing together the missing information.

Congo; Politique et Administration Générale, Ier série, 1876–1913:

21 volumes containing diplomatic and consular correspondence on the Congo question. These volumes are of first-class importance.

Congo; Politique et Administration Générale, 2e série, 1880–1919:

5 dossiers similar to the above but not as useful.

Série noire reliée, E.I.C.:

The majority of these volumes are devoted to correspondence on specific topics. Volumes 1, 10, 11, 12 and 13 are relevant.

The following separate dossiers are self-explanatory:

AF. 1, 9, Congo—Portugal, 1884–1921.

AF. 1, 11, Congo—Missions religieuses.

AF. 1, 17, Congo—U.S.A.

AF. 1, 26, Congo—Grande Bretagne.

AF. 1, 38, Delimitations.

AF. 1, 40, Congo—Nil.

The following private papers were available to me:

Papiers Lambermont.

Papiers Strauch.

III. IN THE MINISTÈRE DES AFFAIRES AFRICAINES, BRUSSELS.

The archives of the Belgian Ministry of Colonies (now Ministry of African Affairs) are jealously guarded and the documents which were made available to me were very disappointing. The relevant documents have been described in Mme. Van Grieken-Taverniers, *Inventaire des archives des Affaires étrangères de l'Etat Indépendant du Congo et du ministère des Colonies, (1885–1914)*.

The most useful dossiers are the following:

I.R.C.B. 506—Lettres et rapports, Van Eetvelde-Leopold II, 1891–1906.

I.R.C.B. 508—L'opinion publique et le Congo, 1909–1912.
I.R.C.B. 717—Campagne anticongolaise.
I.R.C.B. 721—L'opinion publique et l'E.I.C.

IV. PRIVATE PAPERS

Two sets of private papers have proved indispensable. The first set is of course the Morel papers, which are a mine of information. Less known but equally important for the study of the Congo question are the John Holt papers. The papers of the Aborigines Protection Society and the Baptist Missionary Society are also useful.

On the official side, the Salisbury papers are meagre, but taken together with those printed in the Letters of Queen Victoria are essential for understanding British Congo policy until 1900.

Morel Papers (in The London School of Economics and Political Science):

> F. 4—Papers relating to the Congo Reform Association in Britain as well as the United States, Germany, and Switzerland.
> F. 5—Congo Documents, 1887–1913.
> F. 8—Letters received by Morel from several correspondents. The most important are those from John Holt, Fox Bourne, Dilke, Cadbury, Casement, Grattan Guinness, Harris, Archbishop of Canterbury, and the Foreign Office.
> F. 9—Miscellaneous correspondents.
> Box H—History of the C.R.A. (unpublished manuscript written by Morel).

John Holt Papers (in the possession of John Holt and Company, Liverpool):

> Box 12, File 4—Fox Bourne.
> File 5—Roger Casement.
> File 7—W. A. Cadbury.
> Box 13, File 2—Dilke, Emmott, Everett.
> File 3—Gosselin.
> File 4—Grattan Guinness, J. Harris.
> File 7—J. F. Hutton.

Box 15, File 3—H. H. Johnston.

Box 17, File 2—Lord and Lady Monkswell.

Box 18, Files 1–14—E. D. Morel.

Box 22, File 4—W. Redmund, Samuel, W. T. Stead.

Box 23,   —Various pamphlets on the Congo.

Dilke Papers (in the British Museum, London):
This is a disappointing collection as far as the Congo question is concerned.

Salisbury Papers (in Christ Church College Library, Oxford):

Box A/49—Letters from Lord Vivian and Francis Plunkett.

Aborigines Protection Society Papers (in Rhodes House, Oxford):

Fox Bourne's correspondence:

C 150/1—247.
C 151/1—235.
C 152/1—256.
C 153/1—124.
C 165/1—175.

John Harris's correspondence:

D 3/1—12.
D 4/1— 6.
D 5/1— 2.
D 6/1.

Territorial Section, Congo:

G 261—General correspondence, 1900–6.
G 262—General correspondence, 1908–9.
G 263—General correspondence, 1909.
G 264—General correspondence, 1910–14.
G 485—Congo question, miscellaneous.

Baptist Missionary Society Papers (at the headquarters of the Society in London):
These have not yet been catalogued. The most important correspondences are those of A. H. Baynes, G. Grenfell,

H. Bentley, and H. Stapleton. The minute books of the Western Sub-Committee are also useful.

Congo Balolo Mission Papers (at the headquarters of the Regions Beyond Missionary Union in London):
Various pamphlets by Grattan Guinness.

Académie Royale des Sciences Coloniales, Brussels:
Correspondance Leopold II—Van Eetvelde.

V. PUBLISHED DOCUMENTARY SOURCES

Accounts and Papers:

Correspondence relative to the Execution of Mr. C. Stokes in the Congo State, and the Trial of Captain Lothaire; 1896 (C.8276) lix, 163.

Correspondence and Report from His Majesty's Consul at Boma respecting the Administration of the Independent State of the Congo; 1904 (Cd. 1933), lxii, 357.

Further Correspondence; 1904 (Cd. 2097), lxii, 445.
Further Correspondence; 1905 (Cd. 2333) lvii, 437.
Further Correspondence; 1907 (Cd. 3450), lvii, 799.
Further Correspondence; 1908 (Cd. 3880), (Cd. 4097), (Cd. 4135), (Cd. 4396), lxxi, 1.

Further Correspondence; 1909 (Cd. 4466), (Cd. 4701), lix, 511.

Further Correspondence; 1911 (Cd. 5860), lii, 601.

Report from His Majesty's Commissioner for British Central Africa respecting the Anglo-Congolese Frontier in the neighbourhood of Lake Mweru, and the circumstances attending the arrest of the late M. Rabinek; 1903 (Cd. 1536), xlv, 631.

Despatch from His Majesty's Minister at Brussels respecting the Commission for the Protection of the Natives instituted by the Government of the Independent Congo State under the decree of 18 September, 1896; 1903 (Cd. 1754), xlv, 665.

Despatch to certain of His Majesty's Representatives Abroad in regard to alleged cases of ill-treatment of Natives and to the existence of Trade Monopolies in the Independent State of the Congo; 1904 (Cd. 1809), lxii, 517.

Correspondence respecting the Report of the Commission of Inquiry into the Administration of the Independent State of the Congo; 1906 (Cd. 3002), lxxix, 1.

Belgian Decree of 22nd March, 1910, relative to the collection of the natural products of the soil in the Domain Lands of the Congo; 1911 (Cd. 559), cii, 177.

Correspondence respecting the Administration and Finances of the Congo; 1912–13 (Cd. 6145), lix, 343.

Hansard.

Annales Parlementaires.

British Documents on the Origins of the War 1898–1914, especially Vols. VI, VII and VIII.

Documents Diplomatiques Français 1871–1914, 2ᵉ série, especially Vols. IV, XII and XIV.

Die Grosse Politik der europäischen Kabinette 1871–1914, especially Vols. XXIX and XXXI.

Letters of Queen Victoria, 3rd series, Vols. I, II and III.

Bulletin Officiel du Congo, 1886–1913.

VI. NEWSPAPERS AND PERIODICALS

I have relied a great deal on newspaper cuttings in the British and Belgian diplomatic archives as well as in the Morel and John Holt collections.

Britain:

Aborigines Friend
Daily News
Morning Post
The Times
West Africa
West African Mail

Belgium:

Indépendance Belge
Journal de Bruxelles
Mouvement Géographique
La Réforme
Le Patriote

Bibliography

Other newspapers and periodicals have also been cited in the footnotes where relevant but the above are the most useful.

VII. PUBLISHED WORKS.

ANSTEY, R. T. *Britain and the Congo in the Nineteenth Century*, Oxford 1962.

ANSTEY, ROGER *King Leopold's Legacy*, London 1966.

ASCHERSON, N. *The King Incorporated*, London 1963.

BANNING, E. *Mémoires Politiques et Diplomatiques*, Brussels 1927.

BARLOW, I. C. *The Agadir Crisis*, Raleigh, N. C. 1940.

Biographie Coloniale Belge, 5 vols., Brussels 1948–56.

BOULGER, D. C. *The Reign of Leopold II*, 2 vols., London 1925.

BUELL, R. L. *The Native Problem in Africa*, 2 vols., New York 1926.

Cambridge History of British Foreign Policy, Vol. III, Cambridge 1923.

CARTON DE WIART, BARON, *Léopold II, Souvenirs des dernières années, 1901–9*, Brussels 1944.

CATTIER, F. *Droit et administration de l'Etat Indépendant du Congo*, Brussels 1898.

CATTIER, F. *Etude sur la situation de l'Etat Indépendant du Congo*, Brussels 1906.

CEULEMANS, P. *La Question arabe et le Congo*, Brussels 1959.

COCKS, F. S. *E. D. Morel: the Man and his Work*, London 1920.

COLLINS, R. O. 'The Anglo-Congolese Negotiations, 1900–6', *Zaire*, 1958, xii, 479–91.

COOKEY, S. J. S. 'West African Immigrants in the Congo, 1885–96', *Journal of the Historical Society of Nigeria*, Vol. 3, no. 2, December 1965, pp. 261–70.

COOKEY, S. J. S. 'The Concession Policy in French Congo and British Reaction, 1898–1906', *J.A.H.*, no. 2, Vol. VII June 1966, pp. 263–78.

CROWE, S. E. *The Berlin West Africa Conference*, London 1942.

DAYE, P. P. *Léopold II*, Paris 1934.

DE LICHTERVELDE, L. *Léopold II*, Brussels 1926.

DESCAMPS, E. *New Africa: An Essay on Government and Civilization in New Countries and on the Foundation, Organization and Administration of the Congo Free State*, London 1903.

326

Dictionary of National Biography

ENSOR, R. C. K. *England, 1870–1914*, Oxford 1960.

FOX BOURNE, H. R. *The Other Side of the Emin Pasha Relief Expedition*, London 1891.

FOX BOURNE, H. R. *Civilization in Congoland*, London 1903.

GRENVILLE, J. A. S. *Lord Salisbury and Foreign Policy*, London 1964.

GREY, E. *Twenty-Five Years 1892–1916*, 2 vols., London 1925.

GWYNN, S. AND TUCKWELL, G. *Life of Sir Charles Dilke*, 2 vols., London 1917.

HARDINGE, A. *A Diplomatist in Europe*, London 1927.

HERTSLET, E. *The Map of Africa by Treaty*, 3 vols., London 1909.

HINDE, S. L. *The Fall of the Congo Arabs*, London 1897.

HIRD, F. *H. M. Stanley*, London 1935.

JOHNSTON, H. H. *George Grenfell and the Congo*, 2 vols., London 1908.

JULIEN, CH. A., etc. *Les Politiques d'Expansion Imperialiste*, Paris 1949.

KEITH, A. B. *The Belgian Congo and the Berlin Act*, Oxford 1919.

LANGER, W. L. *The Diplomacy of Imperialism*, New York 1956.

LEE, S. *King Edward VII*, Vol. II, London 1927.

LE FEBVE DE VIVY, L. *Documents d'histoire précoloniale belge, 1861–1865*, Brussels 1955.

LINDLEY, M. F. *The Acquisition and Government of Backward Territory in International Law*, London 1926.

LOUIS, W. R. *Ruanda-Urundi*, Oxford 1963.

MACALPINE, G. W. *Abstract of the Report of the Commission of Enquiry into the Administration of the Congo Free State*, London 1906.

MAGNUS, A. *King Edward VII*, London 1964.

MASOIN, F. *Histoire de l'Etat Indépendant du Congo*, 2 vols., Namur 1912.

MAURICE, A. *H. M. Stanley: Unpublished Letters*, London 1955.

MONGER, G. W. *The End of Isolation: British Foreign Policy 1900–1907*, London 1963.

MOON, P. T. *Imperialism and World Politics*, New York 1926.

MOREL, E. D. *King Leopold's Rule in Africa*, London 1904.

MOREL, E. D. *Red Rubber*, London 1906.

MOREL, E. D. *Great Britain and the Congo*, London 1909.

MOREL, E. D. *Ten Years of Secret Diplomacy*, London 1915.

OLIVER, R. *Sir Harry Johnston and the Scramble for Africa*, London 1959.

RANIERI, L. *Les relations entre l'Etat Indépendant du Congo et l'Italie*, Brussels 1959.

RENOUVIN, P. *La Crise Européene et la Première Guerre Mondiale*, Paris 1962.

ROEYKENS, A. *Les débuts de l'œuvre africaine de Léopold II*, Brussels 1955.

ROEYKENS, A. *Léopold II et l'Afrique*, Brussels 1958.

SAINTOYANT, J. *L'Affaire du Congo 1905*, Paris 1960.

SANDERSON, G. N. *England, Europe and the Upper Nile*, Edinburgh 1965.

SINGLETON-GATES, P. AND GIRODIAS, M. *The Black Diaries*, Paris 1959.

SLADE, R. *English-Speaking Missions in the Congo Independent State*, Brussels 1959.

SLADE, R. *King Leopold's Congo*, London 1962.

STANLEY, H. M. *The Congo and the Founding of its Free State*, 2 vols., London 1885.

STANLEY, H. M. *In Darkest Africa*, 2 vols., London 1890.

STENGERS, J. *La première tentative de reprise du Congo par la Belgique*, Bulletin Société Royale belge de Géographie, 1949.

STENGERS, J. *Rapports sur les dossiers Léopold II—Cuvelier et Léopold II—Liebrechts*, Bulletin I.R.C.B. 1953.

STENGERS, J. *Quand Léopold II s'est-il rallié à l'annexion du Congo par la Belgique*, Bulletin I.R.C.B. 1952.

STENGERS, J. *Textes Inédits d'Emile Banning*, Brussels 1955.

STENGERS, J. *Combien le Congo a-t-il coûté là a Belgique?* Brussels 1957.

STENGERS, J. *Belgique et Congo: l'élaboration de la charte coloniale*, Brussels 1963.

STENMANS, A. *La reprise du Congo par la Belgique*, Brussels 1949.

STINGLHAMBER, G. AND DRESSE, P. *Léopold au travail*, Brussels 1949.

TAYLOR, A. J. P. 'Prelude to Fashoda', *English Historical Review*, 1950, lxv, 52–80.

THOMSON, R. S. *Fondation de l'Etat Indépendant du Congo*, Brussels 1933.

TREVELYAN, G. M. *Grey of Fallodon*, London 1937.

TWAIN, M. *King Leopold's Soliloquy*, London 1907.

VAN DER SMISSEN, E. *Léopold II et Beernaert*, 2 vols., Brussels 1950.

VERBEKEN, A. *La Révolte des Batetela en 1895*, Brussels 1958.

VAN ZYULEN, P. *L'échiquier congolais*, Brussels 1959.

WAUTERS, A. J. *Histoire politique du Congo belge*, Brussels 1911.

WILLEQUET, J. *Le Congo belge et la Weltpolitik*, Brussels 1963.

WOODWARD, E. L. *Great Britain and the German Navy*, Oxford 1935.

WOOLF, L. *Empire and Commerce in Africa*, London 1919.

WULLUS-RUDIGER, J. *La Belgique et l'équilibre éuropéene*, Brussels 1935.

VIII. UNPUBLISHED THESES

MCSTALLWORTH, P. *The United States and the Congo Question, 1884–1914*, Ph.D. Ohio State University, 1954.

WULLIGER, R. *The Idea of Economic Imperialism with Special Reference to the Life and Work of E. D. Morel*, University of London, 1955.

Index

Index

332

Index

Ubangi, 12, 251 n.; River, 50 n.
Ubangi-Bomu expedition, 12
Uele basin, 12, 15, 251 n., 273, 299
Uganda, 253
Union Minière du Haut Katanga, 175
United States of America, 86 ff.,
 117, 120, 130, 170 ff., 180, 188–
 189, 191, 202, 203, 206, 209, 221,
 241–2, 247, 260, 261
Upoto, 299
Union of Democratic Control, 250

Van Calcken, 136
Van der Elst, Baron, 310
Van Eetvelde, Baron, 30, 33, 41,
 113, 120, 212, 157
Van Heuvel, 225
Van Ronslé, 114
Vandervelde, Émile, 84, 156, 205,
 238, 262, 276, 280
Van Gèle, Captain, 12
Verité sur le Congo, Le, 85
Vermeersch, Father, 154, 167 n
Villiers, Sir F. H., 19, 93, 95, 96,
 98, 125, 141, 290, 310, 312,
 313
XXᵉ Siècle, Le, 154, 205, 310
Vohsen, Ernst, 277

Wack, Henry Wellington, 172
Wahis, Baron, 85 n., 263
Wales, Prince of, 249

Walford, George, 30, 31
Wallwitz, Count, 89, 186
Wamba basin, 15
Ward, Herbert, 107, 108
Wathen, 65
Wauters, A. J., 13, 123, 154
Wesleyan Methodist Church, 247,
 292 n.; Missionary Society, 294
West Africa, 73
West African Mail, The, 107, 108,
 128, 138
West African Missionary Associa-
 tion, 145
White, George, 265
Whitehead, Rev. John, 103, 273
Whiteley, James, 172
Wiener, Sam, 89
William II, Kaiser of Germany,
 308
Williams, George Washington, 35–
 36, 171
Wilson, Sir Henry, 306
Wilson, H. L., 188–9, 207, 209
Wilson-Dubail agreement (1911),
 306–7, 309
Woeste, Catholic leader in Belgian
 Parliament, 71

Yakoma, 50 n.
Yalemba, 299
Yambata, 215
Yellala Falls, 8

The Ibadan History Series

General Editor K. D. DIKE PH.D.

CHRISTIAN MISSIONS IN NIGERIA 1841–1891

The Making of a New Élite

by J. F. A. AJAYI, Professor of History, University of Ibadan

The first major study of Christian missionary activity in Nigeria, which also touches on Sierra Leone, Ghana and Dahomey. In discussing every aspect of the missions' work and its effects, the author stresses the emergence of a new élite as their most crucial contribution to Nigerian history.

Contents: Christianity and Civilization; The Return of the Exiles; Missionaries, Traders, and Consuls; The Mission and the State; Civilization around the Mission House; Towards Selfgovernment in Church and State; Bishop Crowther, 1864–77; The Turning of the Tide. Appendix. Bibliography. Index.

Demy 8vo   xvi + 317 pages   Maps, Plates.

THE ZULU AFTERMATH

A Nineteenth-Century Revolution in Bantu Africa

by J. D. OMER-COOPER, Professor of History, University of Zambia

A detailed study of the factors involved in the emergence of the militaristic Zulu Kingdom and its far-reaching consequences in early nineteenth-century central and southern Africa.

Contents: Bantu South Africa before the Mfecane; The Zulu Kingdom; The Birth of the Swazi nation; Soshangane and the Empire of Gaza; The Ngoni Invasion of East Central Africa; The Invasion of the Highveld by Mpangazita and Matiwane; Moshesh and the Basuto Nation; The Career of Sebetwane and the History of the Kololo; Mzilikazi and the Ndebele; The Devastation of Natal and the Flight to the South; The History of the Fingo People; The Mfecane in the History of South and East Central Africa. Bibliography. Index.

Demy 8vo   xiv + 208 pages   Map, Plates.

THE MISSIONARY IMPACT ON MODERN NIGERIA 1842–1914

A Political and Social Analysis

by E. A. AYANDELE, Department of History, University of Ibadan

The emphasis in this work is on the reactions of various sections of the African community—chiefs, educated Africans, ordinary people and slaves—to missionary activity and also to other agencies linked with it, in particular the colonial administration.

Contents: The Beginnings, 1842–1875; Missionary Enterprise and the Pacification of Yoruba-land, 1875–1900; The Missions and 'Southern' Nigerian Politics and Society, 1875–1900; The Triumph of Gin; The Missionary Impact on Society. Bibliography. Index.

Demy 8vo   xx + 393 pages   Maps, Plates.

THE SOKOTO CALIPHATE

by MURRAY LAST, Northern History Research Scheme, Ahmadu Bello University, Zaria

An account, based largely on nineteenth-century Arabic documents from Sokoto, of the origins and history of the caliphate until the coming of the British in 1903. It includes, in particular, a study of the rôle of the vizierate in maintaining the administrative and the spiritual position of the caliphate.

Contents: The Establishment of Dār al Islām in Sokoto 1754–1817: 1168–1232 (The Community; The Jihad; The Early Caliphate); The Maintenance of Dār al Islām in Sokoto 1817–1903: 1232–1320 (The Consolidation of the Caliphate 1817–1859: 1232–1276; The Composition of the Caliphate; The Period of Security and Settlement 1859–1903: 1276–1320); The Vizierate in Sokoto 1804–1903:

1218–1320 (The Viziers, The work of the Viziers); Concluding Remarks.

Demy 8vo   lxxxii + 272 pages   Glossary. Sources, Maps, Genealogies, Bibliography. Indexed, Cased.

In Preparation

THE INTERNATIONAL BOUNDARIES OF
NIGERIA 1885–1960

The Framework of an Emergent African Nation

by J. C. ANENE, Professor of History in the University, Nsukka

A pioneer work in its field. The author has studied, from field-work, oral tradition and primary documentary sources the types of indigenous frontiers—not necessarily stable—which existed before European boundary intervention, and objectively assesses the results of that intervention and its consequences for modern Nigeria.

Contents: Introduction; The Atlantic Littoral and the Problems of the Hinterland; The Eastern Boundary—I; The Eastern Boundary—II; The Western Boundary—I; The Western Boundary—II; The Northern Boundary; Conclusion. Bibliography. Index.

Demy 8vo   xi + 300 pages   Maps, Cased.

NIGER DELTA RIVALRY

Itsekiri Urhobo Relations and European Enterprise 1884–1936

by OBARE IKIME, Department of History, University of Ibadan

A detailed study of the ways in which European, particularly British, trade, administration and development increased the tensions between a trading coastal people, the Itsekiri, and their agricultural neighbours in the hinterland—tension which remain a political factor in Nigeria today.

Contents: Indigenous Antecedents; Early European Activities and Itsekiri Urhobo Relations, 1485–1883; The Regime of Chief Nana, 1884–1894; The British Penetration of Urhoboland, 1892–1912; The Native Court System and

the Career of Chief Dogho, 1900–1925; The Reorganisation
of the 1930's. Appendices. Bibliography. Index.

Ready autumn 1968

Demy 8vo   ix + 380 pages   Maps, Plates.

Other titles will follow.

HUMANITIES PRESS